third edition

THE RESEARCH ACT
A Theoretical Introduction to Sociological Methods

NORMAN K. DENZIN

University of Illinois, Urbana-Champaign

PRENTICE HALL, ENGLEWOOD CLIFFS, NEW JERSEY 07632

Library of Congress Cataloging-in-Publication Data

Denzin, Norman K.
    The research act.

    Bibliography.
    Includes indexes.
        1. Sociology — Methodology.   2. Sociology — Research.
I. Title.
HM24.D44 1989   301'.01'8   88-12522
ISBN 0-13-774381-5

Editorial/production supervision and interior design: *Marjorie Shustak*
Cover design: *Wanda Lubelska Design*
Manufacturing buyer: *Peter Havens*

10 9 8 7 6 5 4 3 2 1

ISBN 0-13-774381-5

Prentice-Hall International (UK) Limited, *London*
Prentice-Hall of Australia Pty. Limited, *Sydney*
Prentice-Hall Canada Inc., *Toronto*
Prentice-Hall Hispanoamericana, S.A., *Mexico*
Prentice-Hall of India Private Limited, *New Delhi*
Prentice-Hall of Japan, Inc., *Tokyo*
Simon & Schuster Asia Pte. Ltd., *Singapore*
Editora Prentice-Hall do Brasil, Ltda., *Rio de Janeiro*

Contents

PART II INTERPRETATION TO METHOD: STRATEGIES FOR OBSERVING, SAMPLING, RECORDING, AND INTERVIEWING

three   Naturalistic Inquiry   69

four   The Sociological Interview   102

PART III THEORY TO METHOD: INTERPRETIVE STRATEGIES

five   The Social Experiment and Its Variations   121

PART IV   TRIANGULATION AND THE DOING OF
SOCIOLOGY

Preface

In this book I offer an interpretive, symbolic interactionist view of sociological theory and research methodology. I call the approach I present "interpretive interactionism." I argue that if sociologists are to bridge the gap that exists between their methods, their theories, and their areas of substantive expertise, they must adopt a *common* interpretive framework that judges these activities from the same perspective. Interpretive interactionism, with its roots in hermeneutics, critical theory, feminist theory, pragmatism, and symbolic interactionism, stresses the self-reflective, political nature of everyday and scientific conduct. It provides such a frame, for it proposes that the research act, itself, is an instance of interpretive, symbolic interaction. Sociologists, like ordinary interactants, organize their conduct on the basis of negotiated, unpredicted events. The research act revolves around such interactions. They constitute a continual focus of this third edition of *The Research Act*.

This edition carries forth the themes of the first and second editions. Again I stress the logic of triangulated, naturalistic inquiry, and the methods of interpretation that involve the use of interactional, ethnographic, life history, and biographical and historical materials. I analyze seven key sociological methods: interviews, experiments, surveys, participant observation, life histories, unobtrusive methods, and film and photography. I have added a new chapter on "Film, Photography, and Sociology," in which I take the position that there are at least three different ways that visual recordings may be used: (1) to reveal something about society; (2) as tools to enhance ethnographic or field studies; and (3) as recordings of social action produced in a laboratory context. I argue for a greater use of film and photography in contemporary sociology. As a result of this new chapter, I have considerably shortened the treatment of unobtrusive methods, and refer the reader to the second edition of this book and to Webb et al., 1981, for a fuller discussion of this method. I have also taken up, especially in Chapters 10 and 11, criticisms of my approach.

Over the last decade the human disciplines have witnessed an explosion in qualitative, interpretive approaches to the study of human group life. These approaches go by various names, including semiotics, structuralism, poststructuralism, deconstructionism, critical theory, structural Marxism, existentialism, interpretive theory, the "new" social history and the sociology of science, hermeneutics, feminism, cultural studies, film theory, and psychoanalysis. In some cases these are new names for old methods. There has been a blurring of boundaries and genres between the human disciplines (Geertz, 1983). Anthropologists use life stories, write poetry, and conduct interactional analyses. Literary scholars use the methods of semiotics, and some sociologists produce hermeneutic readings of social and cultural texts.

The third edition of *The Research Act* is written against the backdrop of these new developments. While it is not possible to treat each of these new approaches in detail, they will be drawn upon as the need arises.

It is hoped that the perspective and problems treated in this book will shed new light on old issues. It will perhaps lead sociologists and other practitioners in the human disciplines to better link their vague images of social reality with those research activities that bring theory and method back together again. The "new," interpretive sociology, if there is to be one, will weave these elements of the research act into a single fabric, and that fabric will join the sociological community with the diverse worlds of human experience and interaction.

ACKNOWLEDGMENTS

I wish to thank the following individuals for their assistance, comments and suggestions: Martha Bauman Power, Peter K. Manning, David R. Maines, Carl J. Couch, Howard S. Becker, Lonnie Athens, Norbert Wiley, and Katherine E. Ryan. Thanks to the following individuals who graciously reviewed the manuscript: Michael G. Flaherty, Eckerd College; Larry M. Lance, University of North Carolina at Charlotte; and Don McTavish, University of Minnesota. I also want to thank Ed Stanford, Bill Webber, and Nancy Robertsfor giving me the opportunity to keep this book alive.

Norman K. Denzin
Champaign, Illinois

1

An Interpretive Point of View

Not being wrong is not the same thing as being right. But since, despite the social science talk of "crucial tests of theories," we don't prove things right or wrong, the real test has always been how useful or interesting that way of looking at things is to an audience. If you look at things from a sociological perspective, what can you see what used to be invisible? [Becker, 1986, p. 2]

Nor is it enough to say that research and theory must be married if sociology is to bear legitimate fruit. They must not only exchange solemn vows — they must know how to carry on from there. Their reciprocal roles must be clearly defined. [Merton, 1967, p. 171]

We can, and I think must, look upon human life as chiefly a vast interpretative process in which people, singly and collectively, guide themselves by defining the objects, events, and situations which they encounter. . . . Any scheme designed to analyze human group life in its general character has to fit this process of interpretation. [Blumer, 1956, p. 686]

The sociological enterprise rests on three interrelated activities: theory, research, and substantive interest. The current state of the discipline reflects this three-part division. Texts, monographs, and readers respectively display concern for theory, research methods, and substantive specialty, whether that speciality be deviance, family sociology, medical sociology, social psychology, education, or race and ethnic relations. This division has created unfortunate consequences for the discipline of sociology. It has produced a breach between these inseparable components of the sociological act. Theory cannot be judged independently of research activity. Research methods are of little use until they are seen in the light of theoretical perspectives. Substantive specialty is of little use or interest until it is firmly embedded within a theoretical framework and grounded upon sound research strategies.

The separation of theories, methods, and substantive specialities now characterizes sociology, which has specialists in each area. Seldom are the three combined into a common individual mind, let alone within a common theoretical perspective. (See Becker, 1986, p. 218; Hill, 1969; Mills, 1959.) This present state of contemporary sociology sets the tone for my discussion in this book. The separate elements of the sociological act must be reunited. Such a synthesis appears in the research act — that is, in those endeavors that take the sociologist from the vague realm of theory to substantive issues in the empirical social world. One strategy by which theory, research, and substantive interest can be combined is the application of a single theoretical perspective to all phases of the research, or observational act. What is needed is a common theoretical framework that can be consistently applied to all phases of the sociological act. In this book the theoretical perspective of symbolic interactionism will be systematically applied to these issues. (See Blumer, 1969b; Lindesmith, Strauss, and Denzin, 1988; Mead, 1934; Stone and Farberman, 1970.)

DIFFERENT VIEWS OF THEORY AND METHOD

To better develop the argument that theory and methods stand at some distance from one another, it is necessary to consider the view of methodology taken by several prominent sociologists. The term *methodology* has historically occupied an ambiguous role in the sociological enterprise. There are scholars who see little connection between methods, research activities, and the process of theorizing. In a perplexing passage, which contradicts the quotation at the beginning of this chapter, Merton (1967, pp. 140–41) states:

> At the outset we should distinguish clearly between sociological theory, which has for its subject matter certain aspects and results of the interaction of men and therefore is substantive, and methodology, or the logic of scientific procedure. There is, in short, a clear and decisive difference between *knowing how to test* a battery of hypotheses and *knowing the theory* from which to derive hypotheses to be tested. It is my impression that current sociological training is more largely designed to make students understand the first than the second.

Merton suggests that theory is of greater value than methodology. He further suggests that methods as such have little, if any, substantive-theoretical content. From Merton's perspective, methods are "atheoretical" tools suitable for any knowledgeable and skilled user.

This position, which potentially leads to a wide gap between theory and methodology, contrasts with Blumer's (1931, 1940, 1954, 1956, 1969b), for as the quotation from Blumer beginning this chapter implies, he calls for research and theoretical designs that accurately reflect and capture what he regards as the special features of human interaction. From his perspective, the study of methodology demands a consistent theoretical perspective; theory and method must go hand in hand. Becker (1970) and Garfinkel (1967) have also called for a blending of theory and method.

Becker (1986) goes even further than Blumer. In the statement quoted at the outset of this chapter, he suggests that theories are never proven right or wrong; they are only more or less persuasive to one or another audience of readers. Theories, in this view, are interpretations of the social world. These interpretations may be imposed by the sociologist, as in Merton's case, or they may flow from the experiences and interpretations of those studied. Blumer and Becker advocate the latter approach, as do I. This perspective is closely aligned with what is called "interpretive" theory in anthropology (Bruner, 1984; Geertz, 1983; Clifford and Marcus, 1986; Turner and Bruner, 1986); in sociology (Becker, 1986; Denzin, 1984b, 1988b; Rabinow and Sullivan, 1979); phenomenological philosophy (Heidegger, 1962; Merleau-Ponty, 1973), hermeneutics (Gadamer, 1975), ordinary language philosophy (Winch, 1958), cultural studies (Hall, 1980) "structuration" theory (Giddens, 1984), and in Habermas's work "critical" theory (1981/1984).

Other sociologists have tended to use methods with little thought for either their theoretical implications or their differing ability to shed light on theory. Many sociologists now use only one method in their studies — thereby eschewing the potential value of other methodologies. Small-group theorists rely nearly entirely upon the experiment, while family sociologists primarily use the survey technique, and students of organizations overemphasize field strategies such as participant observation. This tendency has given rise to a rather parochial, specialty-bound use of research methods.

Closely related to this position is the tendency to develop within limited boundaries theories resting on special methodologies — what Merton (1967) terms "middle-range sociology" — and while it brings theory and method closer together, a specific commitment to special areas of inquiry seriously limits the far-ranging value of general theory. To read of a tightly integrated theory of small-group interaction is pleasing because it is theory but disappointing because it is not developed from a more abstract set of formulations. Small-group theory exists hand in hand with theories of the family, of political sociology, of delinquency, and so on, but seldom do these specialized theories with their localized methods come together in one large and more general theory.

Some social psychologists, such as Couch (1987a), contend that one key research site, the laboratory, where the technology of audiovisual recordings can be employed, offers the greatest promise for the merger of theory and method, and the discovery of generic sociological principles. This position goes beyond the narrow, specialty-bound use of methods just discussed. It offers the foundations of a genuine theory of social structure (see Couch, 1984b; Couch, Saxton, and Katovich, 1986).

A POINT OF VIEW

Methods are of high theoretical relevance. In this book seven sociological methods will be analyzed from the perspective of symbolic interactionism. The interview, the experiment, the survey, participant observation, historical and life history analysis, unobtrusive methods, and the use of film will each be shown to have different theoretical relevance for symbolic interactionism. It will be argued that significant advances in substantive sociological theory will occur only after sociologists develop a consistent and viable framework for the dual analysis of theory and method. While I have chosen to employ symbolic interactionism as my theoretical perspective, it would have been possible to employ any of a number of other theoretical stances. Structural functionalism, social behaviorism, conflict theory, feminist theory, critical theory, cultural studies, or ethnomethodology could have been used. Any of these approaches would lead to significantly different conclusions. It is important for practitioners within these other schools of thought to develop their own synthesis of theory, method, and specialty. Such statements would undoubtedly support the thesis that methods can no longer be viewed as "atheoretical" tools. Each theory demands and produces a special view of the research act. (See Cicourel, 1964, 1974a, 1974b, for an ethnomethodological account of methodology; also Garfinkel, Lynch, and Livingston, 1981, for a view of science; and Couch, 1984a, on the laboratory.)

   While it is possible to apply a set of methodological principles in the evaluation of research strategies, this application often produces an even wider gap between theory and method. (See Campell and Stanley, 1963, for an illustration of this approach. Most sociological textbooks on research methodology use this strategy. See Black and Champion, 1976; Phillips, 1976. Major exceptions are Bogdan and Taylor, 1975; Cicourel, 1964; Derek Phillips, 1971; Johnson, 1975; Lofland, 1971; Schatzman and Strauss, 1973.)

THE INTERRELATIONSHIP OF THEORY AND METHOD

The sociological discipline rests on these elements; theory, methodology, research activity, and the sociological imagination. *Theory* is interpretation. It gives order and insight to what is, or can be observed. *Methodology* represents the principal ways in which sociologists act on their environment; their methods, be they experiments, surveys, or life histories, lead to different features of this reality, and it is through their methods that they make their research public and reproducible by others. As the sociologist moves from theories to the selection of methods, the emergence of that vague process called *research activity* can be seen. In this process, the personal preferences of a scientist for one theory or method emerge. Furthermore, selection of a given problem area (delinquency, alcoholism, or the family) often represents a highly personal decision.

   Order is given to theory, methodology, and research activity through the use of what Mills (1959, pp. 211–12) termed the "sociological imagination":

> The sociological imagination, I remind you, in considerable part consists of the capacity to shift from one perspective to another, and in the process to build up an adequate view of a total society and its components. The sociological imagination can also be cultivated; certainly it seldom occurs without a great deal of routine work. Yet there is an unexpected quality about it. . . . there is a playfulness of mind back of such combining as well as a truly fierce drive to

make sense of the world, which the technician as such usually lacks. Perhaps he is too well trained, too precisely trained. Since one can be *trained* only in what is already known, training sometimes incapacitates one from learning new ways; it makes one rebel against what is bound to be at first loose and even sloppy. But you cling to such vague images and notions, if they are yours, and you must work them out. For it is in such forms that original ideas, if any, almost always first appear.

The sociological imagination demands variability in the research process. The processes by which sociology is done should not be made inflexible; an open mind is required. What some regard as doctrinaire will be challenged by others; therefore, methodological and theoretical principles must always be evaluated in terms of the sociological imagination.

THE SYMBOLIC-INTERACTIONIST PERSPECTIVE

Symbolic interactionism rests on three basic assumptions. First, social reality as it is sensed, known, and understood is a social production. Interacting individuals produce and define their own definitions of situations. Second, humans are assumed to be capable of engaging in "minded," self-reflexive behavior. They are capable of shaping and guiding their own behavior and that of others. Third, in the course of taking their own standpoint and fitting that standpoint to the behaviors of others, humans interact with one another. Interaction is seen as an emergent, negotiated, often unpredictable concern. Interaction is symbolic because it involves the manipulation of symbols, words, meanings, and languages.

Integral to this perspective is the view that the social world of human beings is not made up of objects that have intrinsic meaning. The meaning of objects lies in the actions that human beings take toward them. Human experience is such that the process of defining objects is ever-changing, subject to redefinitions, relocations, and realignments. The interactionist assumes that humans learn their basic symbols, their conceptions of self, and the definitions they attach to social objects through interaction with others. Each person simultaneously carries on conversations with himself or herself and with significant others. Behavior is observable at the symbolic and the interactional levels.

Interactionists regard human interaction as their basic source of data. Their fundamental theoretical concerns involve a greater understanding of how it is that humans are able to take one another's perspective in concrete instances of interaction. Interactionists assume that face-to-face interaction occurs in social situations. Some, such as Goffman (1971, 1974), have attempted to untangle the various elements that make up the joint actions of interacting individuals. From Goffman's analysis and other analyses, it is possible to assemble the following seven features of focused interaction. First, focused interaction involves two or more individuals *taking one another's point of view*. Second, interaction occurs in *social settings* which can be physically located and described. Third, *social objects* fill social settings and will be acted on by the individuals under study. Fourth, when taking one another's perspective, individuals use a set of *rules* that tacitly guide and shape their ongoing interactions. These rules may be civil or legal in nature, as when a member of a police department arrests a juvenile for committing a delinquent act. They may be polite or ceremonial in nature and may be displayed in the formalities that persons proffer one another at cocktail parties. The rules will be relationally specific to the individuals in question. Husbands and wives and close friends typically act in terms of rules and understandings unique to their relationship. Fifth, all interaction involves persons *differentially related to one another*. They may be strangers, intimates, friends, colleagues, enemies, or politely civil acquaintances (Davis, 1973). The total amount of time two or more individuals spend in one another's presence is termed the *occasion* of interaction. Sixth, every focused exchange between these individuals is termed an *encounter*. Social situations furnish the occasions for interaction, which in turn produce the conditions for encounters (see Goffman, 1961b). Seventh, the interaction process is filtered through *gendered* social identities.

Any interactional episode will display unique configurations of these seven elements of focused interaction. Each element can assume different forms over time, within the same encounter or across encounters. In these senses interaction is regarded as a temporal, situated, and gendered production. Any sociological investigation can focus on any or all of these features. The relationships that bind individuals together will be of shifting equality. The setting may be rigid or flexible. It may be known or foreign. It may be private or public. It may be rented or owned. The objects acted on may be owned, rented, or borrowed, and relevant or irrelevant to the interaction. The individuals will be differentially self-reflexive as they interact (see Denzin, 1975). Their gender will shape the interaction.

These features can be briefly illustrated by considering the sociological interview. It typically involves two strangers confronting each other in the interviewee's home territory. Rules of polite civilty will govern conduct, and the main object which is acted upon will be the interview schedule. The interviewer may consider himself or herself a status inferior and act accordingly. While the interviewer is highly reflexive concerning the interview, the respondent may approach the task nonchalantly, taking only a casual interest in the questions asked. It appears that the production of an interview involves gendered, symbolic interaction. In this sense, all research activity can be regarded as an interactional production. Such productions can be analyzed and studied in terms of the features of face-to-face interaction just discussed. (See Katovich, 1984, on interaction in the laboratory experiment.)

METHODOLOGICAL CONSIDERATIONS FROM INTERACTION THEORY: NATURALISTIC INTERACTIONISM

Given these basic assumptions of symbolic interactionism, it is now possible to propose a set of principles that this perspective demands of its methodologies. Central to the interactionist's view of research activity is the method of *naturalistic interactionism* (see Mead, 1934). This involves the studied commitment to actively enter the worlds of interacting individuals. It involves an attempt to develop theories about interaction that rest on the behaviors, languages, definitions, and attitudes of those studied. Naturalistic interactionism attempts to blend the symbolic conversations persons have with themselves with their observable behaviors and utterances (Denzin, 1971). The basic unit of analysis for naturalistic behaviorism is the joint act, or the occasions of interaction. (See Chapters 3 and 4 for an elaboration of this perspective.)

If human behavior is observable at two levels—the symbolic and the interactional—then central to understanding such behavior is the range and variety of symbols and symbolic meanings shared, communicated, and manipulated by interacting selves in social situations. Society contributes two essential elements that reflect directly on concrete interactions: (1) the symbols, or various languages provided and communicated through the socialization process, and (2) the concrete behavioral settings in which interaction occurs.

An interactionist assumes that a complete analysis of human conduct will capture the symbolic meanings that emerge over time in interaction. But the sociologist must also capture variations in ongoing patterns of behavior that reflect these symbols, images, and conceptions of self. These symbols are manifold and complex, verbal and nonverbal, intended and unintended. Verbal utterance, nonverbal gesture, mode and style of dress, and manner of speech all provide clues to the symbolic meanings that become translated into interaction and emerge from it.

The *first methodological principle* is that symbols and interaction must be brought together before an investigation is complete. Focusing only on symbols, as an attitude questionnaire might, fails to record the emergent and novel relationships these symbols have with observable behavior. If I am studying the relationship between the use of marijuana and the strategies of concealing the drug in the presence of nonusers, I will want to show that a marijuana user's attitude toward outsiders is reflected in her behavior in their presence. It would be insufficient to document only the fact that users do not like to get "high" when an outsider is present. Committed to the interactionist position, I must go further and demonstrate how this attitude is influenced by contact with nonusers.

Becker (1953, 1955, 1962) has provided such an analysis that, although dated, is instructive. In his interviews (1962, p. 597) it was discovered that among sporadic smokers, fear of discovery took two forms: that nonusers would discover marijuana in their possession; and that they would "be unable to hide the effects of the drug when . . . 'high' with nonusers." This type of user adopts strategies to conceal the effects and presence of marijuana and may even smoke infrequently because it is not possible to find a "safe" setting. Among regular users, such fears are not present, although Becker indicated that as their interactional contacts change regular users may find it necessary to revert to only occasional use. One regular user who had married a nonuser eventually turned to irregular use. The following excerpt from

Becker (1962, p. 598) describes this pattern and demonstrates how the meanings attached to the social object (marijuana) actually emerged in patterns of interaction:

> (This man had used marijuana quite intensively but his wife objected to it.) Of course, largely the reason I cut off was my wife. There were a few times when I'd feel like . . . didn't actually crave for it but would just like to have had some. (He was unable to continue using the drug except irregularly on those occasions when he was away from his wife's presence and control.)

A *second methodological principle* suggests that because symbols, meanings, and definitions are forged into self-definitions and attitudes, the reflective nature of selfhood must be captured. That is, the investigator must indicate how shifting definitions of self are reflected in ongoing patterns of behavior. Investigators must, therefore, view human conduct from the point of view of those they are studying—"take the view of the acting other in concrete situations." This may range from learning the other's language to capturing his or her salient views of self. Returning to the example of the marijuana user, it would be necessary to learn the language of marijuana subcultures, which, as Becker shows, includes special words for getting "high" and has various categorizations for "outsiders," as well as terms for classes of dealers and special terms for smoking equipment.

Taking the role of the acting other permits sociologists to escape the *fallacy of objectivism*—that is, the substitution of their own perspective for that of the people under study. Too often sociologists enter the field with preconceptions that prevent them from allowing those studied to "tell it as they see it." Someone studying the use of marijuana, for example, may incorrectly generalize from her own experiences with it to the group of users who are being examined. Often investigators will find that the meanings they have learned to attach to an object have no relevance for the people they are observing. This error occurs frequently in areas of conduct undergoing rapid change; studies of racial interaction, political activity, fads and fashions, and even analyses of stratification hierarchies in bureaucracies may provide cases where the definitions of the sociologist bear only slight resemblances to the actual situation.

Everyday and Scientific Conceptions of Reality

It is necessary to maintain a distinction between the sociologist's conceptions of a subject's behavior and the motives and definitions that subjects ascribe to their own conduct. The way a subject explains his behavior is likely to differ from the way a sociologist would. Marijuana users, for example, do not employ such terms as *morality, rationalization, collusion, social control, subculture, socialization, and role behavior.* Commenting on this fact, Becker notes that the sociological view of the world is "abstract, relativistic and generalizing" (1964, p. 273). On the other hand, the everyday conception of reality that guides our subject's conduct is specific, tends not to be generalizing, and is based on special concepts that often lack any scientific validity.

These everyday concepts are the "product of people doing things together" (Becker, 1986, p. 1). They are also called *shared, cultural understandings.* They have the common-sense qualities of seeming to be natural, practical, simple and literal, ad hoc, and accessible (see Geertz, 1983, pp. 85–91; Garfinkel, 1967, pp. 262–83); that is, ordinary interactants use these terms as a matter of course in their dealings with one another. They assume that they are mutually understandable. They are "experience-near" understandings; that is, they derive from common experiences (Geertz, 1983).

An ordering of concepts can be proposed. *First-order concepts* are those of the language of everyday life. *Second-order concepts* are abstract and sociological in nature. It is important that these two levels not be confused. (See Schutz, 1962, pp. 27–48.) Rock (1973, p. 22) commenting on recent developments in deviance theory, discusses the concept "deviant":

> The problem is that people rarely call one another "deviant" in everyday life. They may resort to such typifications as "homosexual," "thief," "eccentric," "boor," or "freak." *Deviant* is preeminently a second-order construct which renders problematic what underpins "boorishness," "thieving," "homosexuality" and the like.

First-order concepts may serve as second-order concepts for everyday interactants, however. In that case, the observer must probe to uncover their underlying meanings. The term *homosexual,* for example, is not necessarily a primary, or first-order, concept for homosexuals. Warren (1974, pp. 101–22) offers an extensive analysis of the language and vocabulary of a homosexual community. The word *gay* replaces *homosexual* as a label, and within the gay world there are a variety of identities—each a variation on the "gay," or lesbian identity—that one can assume. Radical drag, Nelly queen, Mother, Auntie, Sister, size queen, and shrimp queen are just a few of the variations embedded in the concept "homosexual," at least as noted by Warren.

These points suggest that it is insufficient merely to state that sociologists must take the role of the acting other in their investigations. A distinction must be made between everyday conceptions of reality and scientific conceptions of that reality. An adherence to my second principle suggests that the sociologists both learns the everyday conceptions of this reality and interprets that reality from the stance of sociological theory. This is the strategy Becker employed in his analysis of the marijuana user, as Warren did in her study. Becker began with a symbolic-interactionist conception of human conduct and applied it to behavior in the marijuana subculture. His concepts were shaped by the meanings given them by the user, but he retained their sociological meaning. The sociologist must operate between multiple worlds when engaging in research—the everyday worlds of the subjects and the world of his own sociological perspective. Sociological explanations ultimately given for a set of behaviors are not likely to be completely understood by those studied; even if they prove understandable, subjects may not agree with or accept them, perhaps because they have been placed in a category they do not like or because elements of their behavior they prefer to keep hidden have been made public. An irreducible conflict will always exist between the sociological perspective and the perspective of everyday life (Becker, 1964). This is a fact that the sociologists must recognize. I raise this problem at this point to indicate that a commitment to my second principle goes further than merely taking the role of the other; sociologists must also place their analyses within an interpretive-sociological framework. This interpretive framework must be grounded in the worlds of lived experience. In one sense, our theories have already been written for us. They are alive in the social worlds we study. We need to learn how to listen to and hear these theories.

Taking the role of the acting other leads to the *third methodological principle:* The investigator must simultaneously link human symbols and gendered conceptions of self and the social circles and relationships that furnish those symbols and conceptions. Too frequently, failure to achieve this link leaves studies of human conduct at an individual level; as a consequence, the impact of broader social structures on subjects' conduct can be only indirectly inferred. This principle is not unique to the interactionist perspective but derives ultimately from a conception of sociology which holds that the impact of social structure on groups and individuals must be explained.

Here is an example of how this principle works. In my studies of the American alcoholic and Alcoholics Anonymous (AA) (Denzin, 1987a, 1987b), I examined the stories alcoholics tell one another at AA meetings. I learned that the printed literature of AA constituted an important framework for any given alcoholic's recovery experiences. Alcoholics would find a story in AA's *Big Book* and apply that story to their own lives. They would see their recovery through the eyes of this printed cultural text. Consider the following AA speaker. He had over 30 years of sobriety in AA. He states:

> Bill Wilson could have told my story. Same circumstances. Bright prospects for a prominent career in business. Good schools. . . . Heavy social drinking in the early days. The best drinks, best bars. . . . But the drinking got heavier. . . . I started hitting the bottle more and more. . . . Went into a sanitarium to dry out. . . . That was in the early 40's. People were talking about this AA thing. . . . A friend got me a copy of the *Big Book*. . . . I threw it away. (Denzin, 1987b, p. 169)

Later in his story, this alcoholic tells how he came to surrender to his alcoholism and to recover in AA. By connecting his experiences to those of Bill Wilson, one of AA's co-founders, he joins his personal history to the history of the AA social movement. His story becomes part of AA's story. He links his experiences to a social group. He has fulfilled the third methodological principle.

This story offers an excellent instance of how a person's attitude toward a social experience represents a combination of her own attitudes and those of her social groups. My third principle is satisfied when personal and social perspectives are blended in a fashion similar to the one just described. In Chapters 5 through 10, I show that the major methods of the sociologist meet this requirement in different ways.

The *fourth methodological principle* derives from the statement that any society provides its members with a variety of behavior settings within which interaction can occur. Research methods must therefore consider the "situated aspects" of human conduct—that is, whenever sociologists engage in observation, they must record the dynamics of their specific observational situations. Situations vary widely in terms of the norms governing conduct within them, and participants in any behavioral setting both create and interpret the rules that influence normal conduct within that situation. Recording the situationality of human interaction would be less important if it were not that symbols, meanings, conceptions of self, and actions toward social objects all vary because of the situation. As shown by Becker's study of marijuana users, in "safe" situations among regular users, marijuana smokers are likely to get "high" and feel no restraints in discussing the effects of the object on their conduct; in "unsafe" situations, they will go to extremes of secrecy and concealment.

"Situating" an observation or a respondent may require no more than asking the respondent to answer questions in terms of the situations in which she normally engages in the behavior under study. Stone (1954) achieved this goal in his study of female shoppers in a large urban locale; he explicitly situated his respondents by symbolically placing them within their favored shopping locale, thus permitting a designation and description of relevant activities on that basis.

Social selves, I am suggesting, are situated objects that reflect ongoing definitions of social situations. For this reason, both the meanings attached to these situations and the types of selves and interactions that emerge within them must be examined. Stone's investigation treats the meanings attached to shopping situations and indirectly implies the types of selves that flow from them. Becker's study achieves both goals: the meaning or definitions of the situation and the self-attitudes of marijuana users in varying situations.

Implicit thus far has been the assumption that the forms and processes of interaction must be reflected in sociological methodologies. Since the emergent relationship between self-conceptions, definitions of social objects, and on-going patterns of interaction must be recorded, analyzed, and explained, the *fifth methodological principle* is that research methods must be capable of reflecting both stable and processual interactional forms. Speaking of models of causation, Becker (1963, p. 23) makes the following argument for processual analyses of human behavior:

> All causes do not operate at the same time, and we need a model which takes into account the fact that patterns of behavior *develop* in orderly sequence. Each step requires explanation, and what may operate as a cause at one step in the sequence may be of negligible importance at another step. The explanation of each step is thus part of the explanation of the resulting behavior.

The symbolic interactionist demands that process or sequence be given primary emphasis in any scientific investigation. Social processes, whether they involve becoming a marijuana user, a recovering alcoholic, a student of sociology, an advocate of a political position, or an intimate confidant of another, involve time and its passage. The sequences or phases that persons go through as they move from one stage to another must be uncovered and causally analyzed before an investigation is regarded as complete.

A discussion of the individual methods of the sociologist will reveal that some are better suited than others for the foregoing kinds of analyses.

The Place of Methods

The *sixth methodological principle* necessarily becomes more abstract and reflects directly on the place of methods in the entire sociological enterprise. It states that the very act of engaging in social research must be seen as a process of symbolic interaction, that being a scientist reflects a continual attempt to lift one's own idiosyncratic experiences to the level of the consensual and the shared meaning. It is in this context that the research method becomes the major means of acting on the symbolic environment and making those actions consensual in the broader community of sociologists.

Sociologists who adopt the survey as a method of research do so with the belief that when they report their results, other investigators will understand how they proceeded to gather observations. The word *survey* designates a social object that has some degree of consensus among other sociologists. But more than this, the word implies a vast variety of actions in which one will engage after one has adopted the method. Persons will be sampled, questionnaires will be constructed, responses will be coded, computers will be employed, and some form of statistical analysis will be presented. If, on the other hand, participant observation is chosen as a method, smaller samples will be selected, documents will be collected, informants will be selected, and unstructured interviewing will be done.

If a situation can be imagined in which two sociologists adopt different methods of study, the impact of symbolic interaction on their conduct can be vividly seen. Suppose that the same empirical situation is selected—for example, a mental hospital. The first investigator adopts the survey as the method of study; the second, participant observation. Each might make different kinds of observations, engage in different analyses, ask different questions, and—as a result—reach different conclusions. (Of course, the fact that they adopted different methods is not the only reason they will reach different conclusions. Their personalities, their values, and their choices of different theories will also contribute to this result.)

Ultimately, sociologists' actions on the empirical world are achieved by the adoption of specific methodologies. Their actions are translated into specific methods through lines of action that reflect their definitions of those methods. At the heart of this interaction is the *concept*, or a set of concepts. Concepts, in conjunction with the research method, enable sociologists to carry on an interaction with their environment. Observers indicate to themselves what a *concept* and a *method* mean and symbolically act toward the designation of those meanings. Sociologists are continually reassessing their imputed object meanings — assessing them against their relationships to theories, their ability to be observed by others, and their ability to generate understanding and explanation of empirical reality. Sociologists act through their methods.

This point can be illustrated by again turning to my study of the American alcoholic. Beginning with an interactionist conception of human conduct, I applied the generic principles from that perspective to the problem of how occupancy of a position in a subculture shapes a person's perceptions and activities. My theory suggested that an intimate knowledge of the subject's perspective must be learned, and to this end I adopted the open-ended interview and participant observation as methodological strategies. Beginning with this conception, my main line of action was to approach alcoholics and to have them present their experiences as they saw them. The final result of my analysis was a series of research findings that modified current understandings of alcoholism. In formulating my research observations and conclusions, I continually assessed my findings against my conceptual framework; my methods and concepts continuously interacted with observations and theory—that is, symbolic interaction guided the process of research and interpretation.

The scientist, then, designates units of reality to act upon, formulates definitions of those objects, adopts research methods to implement these lines of action, and assesses the fruitfulness of any activity by the ability to develop, test, or modify existing social theory. Thus, both concepts and research methodology act as empirical *sensitizers* of scientific observation. Concepts and methods open new realms of observation, but concomitantly close others. Two important consequences follow: If each method leads to different features of empirical reality, then no single method can ever completely capture all the relevant features of that reality; consequently, sociologists must learn to employ multiple methods in the analysis of the same empirical events. This is termed *triangulation.*

It can be argued, of course, that all research methods stand in an instrumental relationship to the scientific process. Methods become plans of action employed as sociologists move from theory to reality. They are the major means of organizing creative energy and operational activities toward concepts and theories and, as such, they at once release and direct activity, the success of which is assessed by the ability to satisfy the normal criteria of validity while establishing fruitful ties with theory.

Research methods serve to provide the scientist with materials that may later be placed in interpretive schemes of thought. By observing several discrete instances of a concept or a set of concepts, scientists are able to move above the single instance to the more common problems that transcend immediate perceptions and observations. A failure to move beyond particularistic observations leaves the sociologist at a level of descriptive empiricism. Articulations between observations and some variety of theory must be established. To the extent that Becker's investigation was related to a theoretical framework, he satisfied this demand. I can now claim another important role for methods in the scientific process: Methods are one of the major ways by which sociologists gather observations to test, modify, and develop theory and interpretation.

In this sense, methods go hand in hand with the following less rigorous techniques of theory work. It is reasonable to argue, I believe, that methods do not do all the relevant work for the sociologist. As I stated earlier, underlying the use of methods must be a sociological imagination. It is necessary to recognize that such techniques as introspection, the use of imagined experiments, and the playful combination of contradictory concepts also serve as aids in the development of theory. Methods, because of their more public nature, are too frequently given greater attention than these other techniques that are of equal relevance. (In Chapter 2, I will develop further the use of introspection and imagined experiments in the construction of social theory.)

The *seventh methodological principle* indicates that from the interactionist's perspective, the proper use of concepts is at first sensitizing and only later operational; further, the proper theory becomes interpretive and formal; and last, the proper causal proposition becomes universal. By *sensitizing concepts* I refer to concepts that are not transformed immediately into *operational definitions* through an attitude scale of checklist. An operational definition defines a concept by stating how it will be observed. Thus if I offer an *operational definition* for "intelligence," I might state that intelligence is the score received on an IQ test. But if I choose a *sensitizing approach* to measuring intelligence, I will leave it nonoperationalized until I enter the field and learn the processes representing it and the specific meanings attached to it by the persons observed. It might be found, for example, that in some settings intelligence is measured not by scores on a test but rather by knowledge and skills pertaining to important processes in the group under analysis. Among marijuana users, intelligence might well be represented by an ability to conceal the effects of the drug in the presence of nonusers. Once I have established the meanings of a concept, I can then employ multiple research methods to measure its characteristics. Thus, closed-ended questions, direct participation in the group being studied, and analysis of written documents might be the main strategies of operationalizing a concept. Ultimately, all concepts must be operationalized — must be measured and observed. The sensitizing approach merely delays the point at which operationalization occurs.

Goffman's treatment (1936b, pp. 146–47) of stigma provides an excellent example of what I mean by "sensitizing a concept." He began with a rather vague and loose definition of "stigma," which he held was "an attribute that is deeply discrediting." Three types of this attribute were designated: abominations of the body or physical deformities, blemishes of character (mental disorder, homosexuality, addiction, alcoholism), and tribal stigma of race, nation, and religion. Moving beyond classification, he analyzed data collected in such traditional sociological specialties as social problems, ethnic relations, social disorganization, criminology, and deviance. From these areas, relevant commonalities were organized around the theme of the stigma. In summarizing this analysis, he states:

> I have argued that stigmatized persons have enough of their situations in life in common to warrant classifying all these persons together for purposes of analysis. An extraction has thus been made from the traditional fields of social

problems. . . . These commonalities can be organized on the basis of a very few assumptions regarding human nature. What remains in each one of the traditional fields could then be reexamined for whatever is really special to it, thereby bringing analytical coherence to what is now purely historic and fortuitous unity. Knowing what fields like race relations, aging and mental health share, one could then go on to see, analytically, how they differ. Perhaps in each case the choice would be to retain the old substantive areas, but at least it would be clear that each is merely an area to which one should apply several perspectives, and that the development of any one of these coherent analytic perspectives is not likely to come from those who restrict their interest exclusively to one substantive area.

Sensitizing a concept permits the sociologist to discover what is unique about each empirical instance of the concept while uncovering what it displays in common across many different settings. Such a conception allows, indeed forces, the sociologist to pursue the interactionist view of reality to an empirical extreme.

The notion of formal theory as opposed to other types of theory will be further developed in Chapter 2. At this point it is necessary to indicate only that such a stance relates directly to the assumption that universal explanations of human behavior can be developed. With Simmel (1950, pp. 3–25), I argue that human conduct represents itself in interactional forms that differ only in content. The job of sociology is to discover the forms that universally display themselves in slightly different contexts. Simmel termed this the strategy of "formal sociology," an attempt to abstract different commonalities or similarities from generically different phenomena. The synthesis of these common threads into a coherent theoretical framework represents the development of "formal theory."

Society, for Simmel (1950, pp. 9–10), existed only in forms of interaction:

> More specifically, the interactions we have in mind when we talk of "society" are crystallized as definable, consistent structures such as the state and the family, the guild and the church, social classes and organizations based on common interests.
>
> But in addition to these, there exists an immeasurable number of less conscious forms of relationship and kinds of interaction. Taken singly, they may appear negligible. But since in actuality they are inserted into the comprehensive and, as it were, official social formations, they alone produce society as we know it. . . . Without the interspersed effects of countless minor syntheses, society would break up into a multitude of discontinuous systems. Sociation continuously emerges and ceases, emerges again. . . .

The sociological task, for Simmel, (1950, p. 14), became the isolation of these forms of interaction.

> In its very generality, this method is apt to form a common basis for problem areas that previously, in the absence of their mutual contact, lacked a certain clarity. The universality of sociation, which makes for the reciprocal shaping of the individuals, has its correspondence in the singleness of the sociological way

of cognition. The sociological approach yields possibilities of solution or of deeper study which may be derived from fields of knowledge continually quite different (perhaps) from the field of particular problem under investigation.

As examples of this strategy, Simmel suggests that the student of mass crimes might profitably investigate the psychology of theater audiences. Similarly, the student of religion might examine labor unions for what they reveal about religious devotion; the student of political history might examine the history of art. The argument, I believe, is clear: A series of concepts and propositions from the interactionist perspective are thought to be sufficient to explain the wide range of human behavior—whatever the social or cultural context.

More contemporary advocates of this position include Goffman and Homans. Goffman (1967, pp. 44–45) proposes a "formal sociological" stance for the analysis of face-to-face interaction:

> Throughout this paper it has been implied that underneath their differences in culture, people everywhere are the same. If persons have a universal human nature, they themselves are not to be looked to for an explanation of it. One must look rather to the fact that societies everywhere, if they are to be societies, must mobilize their members as self-regulating participants in social encounters. One way of mobilizing the individual for this purpose is through ritual; he is taught to be perceptive, to have feelings attached to self and a self expressed through face, to have pride, honor and dignity, to have considerateness, to have tact and a certain amount of poise. . . . If a particular person or group of society seems to have a unique character of its own, it is because its standard set of human-nature elements is pitched and combined in a particular way.

While the reader need not accept Goffman's theoretical perspective, its thrust is apparent: A small set of very abstract and general principles can explain all human behavior. In the statements of Simmel and Goffman, there is an explicit commitment to formal sociological theory. Goffman's theory would be based on functional theory and certain portions of symbolic interaction. In this context I can now *define* formal theory as any set of interrelated interpretations which are ordered in such a way that some are more specific than others and hence capable of being derived from higher-order statements. A last feature of the formal theory, which distinguishes it from other types of theory, is the fact that it explicitly rests on empirical referents. Goffman's formulations are based on the observation that whatever face-to-face interaction occurs, participants will be observed employing strategies of tact, pride, defense, honor, and dignity. His highest-order proposition holds that all societies train their member-participants in the rituals of face-work because to do otherwise would leave a society without members who could routinely engage in interaction. His lower-order propositions then include predictions concerning the balance between various types of rituals and their enactment in daily encounters.

The work of Goffman illustrates the use of formal theory as I have defined it. Contrast this perspective with that of Merton (1967, pp. 39–72), who believes that sociologists should develop middle-range theories of specific problem areas. Merton's formulation is too restrictive. It leads to the endless proliferation of small-scope theories. "Grand theory" represents the other alternative; it suggests that one very abstract and general theory can be developed to explain all human behavior. Unfortunately, as it is currently practiced, grand theory has few empirical referents. Formal theory, empirically grounded at all points, is preferable to a grand theory with a few empirical referents or to a series of middle-range theories, each of which have their own methods and specific domains.

Basic to formal theory will be universal interactive propositions that are assumed to apply to all instances of the phenomenon studied — at least until a negative case is discovered. By stating that these propositions will be interactive, I suggest that they will describe interrelationships between processes that influence one another. In Becker's analysis (Rose, 1962, p. 592) of the marijuana user, an explicit reliance on interactive propositions of universal relevance can be seen:

> Generalizations stating necessary conditions for the maintenance of use at each level were developed in initial interviews, and tested and revised in the light of each succeeding one. The stated conclusions hold true for all the cases collected and may tentatively be considered as true of all marijuana users in this society, at least until further evidence forces their revisions.

Becker's generalizations rest on the assumption that they apply to all persons who have ever used marijuana. More abstractly, his formulations bear a relationship to a formal theory concerning symbolic interaction and the development of self-attitudes in a group setting. The passage quoted earlier, describing the marijuana user who altered his using patterns after marrying a nonuser, represents a description of an instance of interaction. The user's attitudes toward the object shifted and changed as he was forced to interact daily with a person who did not hold his definitions.

If the fact of human behavior is interaction, then sociological interpretations must take an interactional form. In this sense, Becker's analysis fits the criterion. The *seventh principle*, to summarize, is that methods must be constructed so that they contribute to formal, interpretive theory while at the same time permitting sensitizing concept analysis and the discovery of universal interactive interpretations.

A Reservation on Theory

I must express a serious reservation concerning the foregoing recommendations involving formal theory. Theory should not be pursued for its own sake; nor will theory alone provide interpretations of the phenomenon in question (see Molseed and Maines, 1988). Theory is always incomplete and provisional, to be taken up anew when the researcher returns to the field. The endless proliferation of propositions (see Collins, 1975) does not make for interpretation. Theory and propositions are of use *only* when they yield meaningful interpretations of the processes under study. Formal theory is a means to a goal, not a goal in its own right.

The Interactionist Principles in Review:
The Naturalistic Method

I have shown that interaction theory suggests seven principles against which methods and sociological activity may be evaluated. These principles are as follows:

1. Symbols and interactions must be combined before an investigation is complete.
2. The investigator must take the perspective or role of the "acting other" and view the world from the subjects' point of view; but in so doing the investigator must maintain the distinction between everyday and scientific conceptions of reality.
3. The investigator must link the subjects' symbols and definitions with the social relationships and groups that provide those conceptions. Gender must be studied.
4. The behavior settings of interaction and scientific observations must be recorded.
5. Research methods must be capable of reflecting process or change as well as static behavioral forms.
6. Conducting research and being a sociologist is best viewed as an act of symbolic interaction. The personal preferences of sociologists (definitions of methods, values and ideologies, and so on) serve to shape fundamentally their activities as investigators, and the major way in which they act on their environment is through their research methods.
7. The proper use of concepts is first sensitizing and then operational; the proper theory becomes formal and not grand or middle-range; and the causal proposition more properly becomes interactional and universal in application

These principles, which constitute the essence of the naturalistic method will reappear in my subsequent analysis of theory and method. They are somewhat peculiar to the interactionist perspective, but their use gives sociologists one consistent theoretically grounded point of evaluation. They demand that observations be lodged in the natural worlds of everyday life. I now turn to salient features from the scientific method which must be combined with the interactionist point of view. By wedding the two, a degree of rigor and precision may be added to the final set of evaluative principles. I assume, then, that any theory and research methodology must meet the following additional preconditions.

CONSIDERATION FROM SCIENTIFIC METHOD:
THE CAUSAL PROPOSITION, RIVAL CAUSAL FACTORS,
AND THE INTERACTIVE CONTEXT OF OBSERVATION

The Causal Proposition

All research methods must provide answers to the problem of causal inference. A method must permit its user to gather data concerning time order and covariance between processes, while allowing rival causal factors, to be discarded. When it is claimed that one variable or process caused another, it must be shown that the causal variable occurs before that it is assumed to cause; that is, as the causal variable changes value, so too must the variable being caused. When investigators formulate causal statements, they must recognize that other variables — rival causal factors — not directly measured or considered may be causing the variations observed. Before discussing the nature of rival causal factors, it is necessary to describe the causal proposition itself. Becker's analysis (1962, p. 606) of marijuana use provides an illustration. Central to his theory is the point that

> The extent of an individual's use of marijuana is at least partly dependent on the degree to which conventional social controls fail to prevent his engaging in the activity. Apart from other possible necessary conditions, it may be said that marijuana use can occur at the various levels described only when the necessary events and shifts in conception of the activity have removed the individual from the influence of these controls and substituted for them the controls of the subcultural group.

This and previous excerpts from Becker's study provide the basis for the following propositions.

> *Proposition 1:* A potential marijuana user must have regular access to the drug.
>
> *Proposition 2:* A potential user must learn the proper means of acting toward it before he will become a regular user.
>
> *Proposition 3:* An individual will engage in marijuana use to the extent that he symbolically removes the effects of conventional social control mechanisms upon behavior.
>
> *Proposition 4:* A regular user who systematically comes in contact with non-users will alter his drug-using patterns (using the drug only among members of the subculture) or will adopt strategies of secrecy when in the presence of nonusers.
>
> *Proposition 5:* The extent of use among nonusers will vary by the strength of the nonusers' negative attitudes. If these negative attitudes are strong and if the situation does not permit concealment, then nonregular use will occur.

Additional propositions could be developed from Becker's argument, but the foregoing are sufficient to illustrate the essential features of the causal proposition. Becker's primary causal variable is the reduction in effect of normal mechanisms of social control. His basic dependent, or caused, variables are the degree and nature of drug use. Given these dependent variables, he proceeds to establish time order between the variables by showing that the degree of use varies by the attitudes of nonusers with whom the user is in contact; the degree of access to the drug; the attitudes the person develops toward the drug; and the situations available for its use. Regular and systematic use thus occurs when marijuana is available on a routine basis, when the user's interactional partners sanction and reinforce its use, and when the user has learned how to act toward the effects of the drug.

It is important to note that Becker has introduced additional causal factors into his final explanatory network. No single variable is assumed to cause marijuana use. The five factors outlined are his additional causal factors, and he carefully points to the situations under which they will have the greatest impact. These propositions meet the normal criteria of the causal proposition: time order, covariance, and the partial consideration of rival or additional causative factors.

Rival Causal Factors

While Becker's study treats additional causal factors that influence the extent of marijuana use, it does not give careful consideration to rival factors that may have distorted or, in fact, caused his observed causal relationship. Rival causal factors may emerge from the following: time and its passage, the situations of observation, characteristics of those observed, characteristics of the observer, and interaction among any of the preceding four elements. These are properties intrinsic to the interaction process outlined earlier. In short, the generic question asked when an observer focuses upon rival causal factors is whether or not the causal propositions that have been formulated accurately represent the events under study, or whether aspects of the process of making those observations caused the differences. An investigator who concludes that rival factors have caused observed differences will be unable to generalize the findings to other situations, and the research will have failed to reach the goal of developing sound causal propositions.

Traditionally, rival causal factors have been treated as falling into two broad classes: either factors external to the observations themselves, or factors that arise from or during the observational process. External factors are termed conditions of *external validity*; internal factors are termed conditions of *internal validity*. Questions of external validity ask to what populations, settings, treatment variables, and measurement variables the causal propositions may be generalized (Campbell, 1963a, p. 214). Questions of internal validity ask whether the assumed causal variables made a difference, or whether the observational process caused the difference. Under *internal validity* Campbell (1963a, p. 215) presents the following eight factors:

1. *History:* The other specific events occurring between the first and second measurement in addition to the experimental variable.
2. *Maturation:* Processes within the respondent operating as a function of the passage of time per se (not specific to the particular events), including growing older, growing hungrier, growing tired, and the like.
3. *Testing:* The effects of taking a test upon the scores of a second testing.
4. *Instrumentation:* Changes in the calibration of a measuring instrument or changes in the observers or scores that may produce changes in the obtained measurements.
5. *Statistical regression:* Regression operating when groups have been selected on the basis of their extreme scores.
6. *Selection:* Biases resulting in differential recruitment of respondents from the comparison groups.
7. *Experimental mortality:* The differential loss of respondents from the comparison groups.

8. *Selection-maturation interaction, and so on:* In certain of the multiple-group quasiexperimental designs, such as the nonequivalent control-group design, such interaction is confounded with (that is, might be mistaken for) the effect of the experimental variable.

A brief discussion of each of these dimensions of internal validity is required. By *history* is meant the passage of time that occurs between the beginning and the end of a study. In my AA study (Denzin, 1987b), which involved participant observation in a local community of recovering alcoholics, history played an important part. Over the course of 5 years, two new treatment centers opened. These centers brought in alcoholics from other regions of the United States. These alcoholics brought new perspectives to the AA experience that had to be accounted for. I had to include history in my study. *Maturation processes* were also critical, for over the duration of my study many alcoholics became sober and changed their outlooks on themselves, their work, and their alcoholism. I had to include this process in my interpretations. *Testing* was less critical in my research, for I did not employ formal testing, or measurement instruments, as might be the case in a long-term social survey where subjects are given the same instrument to answer several times. Because of this factor, *instrumentation* changes did not occur in my study. Since I did not select my subjects on the basis of test scores, *statistical regression* problems did not occur. I did have *selection* problems, however, for each of the treatment centers in the community selected different types of alcoholics (middle class, lower class, only women). *Experimental, or research, mortality* was also a problem, for many alcoholics who come to AA stop coming after a period of time. My research spoke only to those alcoholics who stayed. There was thus an interaction effect created by the *selection-maturation* factors.

External validity is seen by Campbell (1963b, p. 215) as involving the following factors:

1. *The reactive or interaction effect of testing,* in which a pretest might increase or decrease the respondent's sensitivity or responsiveness to the experimental variable and thus make the results obtained for a pretested population unrepresentative of the effects of the experimental variable for the unpretested universe from which the experimental respondents were selected.
2. *Interaction effects* between *selection* bias and the *experimental variable.*
3. *Reactive effects of experimental arrangements,* which would preclude generalization about the effect of the experimental variable for persons being exposed to it in nonexperimental settings.
4. *Mulitple-treatment interference,* a problem wherever multiple treatments are applied to the same respondents, and a particular problem for one-group designs involving equivalent time-samples or equivalent materials samples.

Campbell's concern is clear. Changes in observers, measuring instruments, and subjects during the course of a study can distort the events investigated as well as the research findings. The passage of time as seen by subjects' maturation, or as evidenced in historical shifts and events, can introduce distorting influences, as can unique characteristics of respondents.

The Interactive Context of Observation

As far as it goes, this system is fine, but it lacks a theoretically grounded set of criteria for the evaluation of research methods. I turn to interaction theory for such a grounding. My earlier treatment of this theory suggests that for human interaction to occur, the following elements must be present: two or more persons able to take the role of the other, a situation in which interaction can occur, and time to carry out that interaction. When these factors are present, an interactional sequence is observed. Persons dining, making love, listening to a record, or negotiating a purchase are in such sequences.

Placed within this context, it is evident that social research becomes a type of symbolic interaction. Role-taking must occur, meaningful symbols must be present, situations must be available, and time must be allocated for the research (filling out a questionnaire, taking part in an experimental task). Any encounter between an investigator and a subject shall be termed an *observational encounter*. The interactants shall be called *observer* and *observed*. The situations will range from laboratories, offices, classrooms, living rooms — even automobiles. The time sequence may be brief, lasting no longer than a few minutes, or extend into months and years, as it does in long-term field studies.

Every research method represents a special combination of these interactive elements. Some, like the experiment, are relatively short-term, include persons who remain unacquainted, and occur in structured situations. Others, like the life history and participant observation, take the investigator to diversely structured situations, rest on multiple identities, lead to the development of close relationships between observer and observed, and extend over long periods of time.

Each of the interactive elements (time, rules, relationships, objects, characteristics of observers and observed) introduces into any study a special set of potentially distorting factors. An observer who is not aware of her own characteristics, who fails to attend to unique features of time and its passage, or does not record the nature of the situations where the observations occur, cannot develop completely valid causal propositions.

The observer   Observers vary in interactive style, self-concepts, interpretations of the research project, and ability to relate to those observed. I assume that any observer who gathers an observation brings into the observational sequence a series of attributes that make his observations different from those of any other observer. Some experimenters, for example, are overattentive to the emotions of subjects; others are underattentive. Some survey interviewers insist on using first names; other are more formal. The list of possible variations is endless, yet every stylistic difference can distort the processes under study. It may be confidently asserted that every observer is unique (see Gadamer, 1975).

The observed   No respondent is perfectly duplicated by another, and the unique characteristics of respondents and subjects may also introduce distortion into an observation. When it is realized that observers interact with those observed, it can be seen that the interaction between an interviewer and a respondent, an experimenter and a subject, an observer and an informant, may itself create differences across observational encounters.

The situation   Because all interaction occurs in social situations, the settings of observation may become sources of invalidity. One interview may take place in a living room, another in an office, and still another in an automobile. Each of these settings is different from the other, and each has different rules governing permissible, comfortable, and serious interaction. To the extent that there is variation, the behavior that occurs will also vary. Thus, situations of observation must be treated as a class of rival interpretive factors.

Time and its passage   Interaction involves an orderly sequence of events that unfold over a temporal period. Every observational encounter must be seen as having its own unique temporal career. Some are long; others, short. Some are difficult; others flow smoothly. During the passage of time, events extraneous to an observation may occur (this is what Campbell means by historical factors' jeopardizing internal validity). Yet the passage of time also signals changes in observers and those observed. Self-concepts change, intents of the investigation may shift, and symbols may take on new meanings. The following statement by Geer (1964, pp. 328–29) illustrates the type of change that may occur in the first week of a field study:

> Throughout the time the undergraduate study was being planned, I was bored by the thought of studying undergraduates. They looked painfully young to me. I considered their concerns childish and uninformed. I could not imagine becoming interested in their daily affairs — in classes, study, dating, and bull sessions. I had memories of my own college days in which I had appeared as a child: overemotional, limited in understanding, with an incomprehensible taste for milk shakes and convertibles.
>
> Remembering my attitudes as I began to sort out the thirty-four comments in the field notes on the prefreshmen, I expected to find evidence of this unfavorable adult bias toward adolescents. But on the third day in the field I am already taking the students' side. . . . Perhaps the rapid development of empathy for a disliked group does not surprise old hands at field work, since it seems to happen again and again. But it surprised me; I comment on it seven times in eight days.

Campbell's dimension of mortality, maturation, testing effects, and instrumentation also relate to time. In studies that require repeated observations, the mortality factor becomes crucial. Persons observed at time two may differ from those observed at time one. Loss of subjects, or even observers, can create distortion, and this can also happen with testing effects in which the subject takes on a special attitude because of the interpretation given the first test, interview, or experimental session. Similarly, shifts in measuring instruments over time may occur.

Observers, situations, subjects, and measuring instruments, then, become social objects within the research design. They are objects whose meaning shifts because their meaning is created through the process of interaction. The sociologist must be aware of these changes, and record his interpretations of them.

Treatment of the Rival Factor: Three Strategies

In subsequent chapters, I will show how each research method addresses the potential distortion created by the rival factors of time, situations, observers, and observed. Here I want only to indicate the possible strategies for their treatment. In formulating causal, interpretive propositions, sociologists have three basic strategies of control and design.

Experimental method   Under conditions of great rigor, as in experiments, the sociologist can explicitly design situations of observation where time order, covariance, and rival causal factors are manipulated or controlled. The use of the *experimental model* of interference is the strongest strategy for formulating the causal proposition and, by implication, is the strongest method of controlling rival causal factors. (See Lieberson, 1986.)

Multivariate analysis   Under conditions of less rigor, such as the social survey, the sociologist loses the control given by the experimental model and must resort to a method of analysis termed the *multivariate method*. Events remain uncontrolled, but the investigator constructs comparisons within the sample that parallel, as nearly as possible, the experimental model. The investigator may compare college-educated persons with high-school-educated persons on attitudes toward sexual permissiveness, constructing two comparison groups that vary on the independent variable (education) and measuring the relationship of education to the dependent variable (sexual permissiveness). In the analysis, the sociologist will attempt to treat rival causal factors by classifying them as events that were either antecedent to the main variables or intervening between them. The same classification will be maintained in the attempt to establish covariance and time order for the principle variables. An important consequence follows from this strategy. The investigator, who lacks control over the temporal occurrence or variables, must infer their relationship and is therefore one step below the experimenter, who can control or manipulate variables. (See Lieberson, 1985; Blalock, 1985.)

Analytic induction   The last model of inference the sociologist may use is *analytic induction*. Experimental control is again absent, but now the investigator follows the events she is studying through time. This is best represented in studies employing participant observation and life histories. Rather than snap-shooting the relationship between variables as the survey method so often does, the user of analytic induction engages in long-term studies that permit the direct identification of time order, convariance, and rival causal factors. Here too, experimental control is lacking. But while experimental and survey models lead to causal propositions that treat proportions of events subsumed under a proposition (for example, 90 percent of those college-educated favor permissive sexual attitudes, while only 35 percent of those high-school-educated favor such permissiveness), analytic induction generates propositions that attempt to cover every case analyzed; it leads to universal-interactive propositions. Another important feature of analytic induction is its emphasis on negative cases that refute the investigator's propositions. In the search for universal propositions, the user of this method seeks cases that most severely test a theory, and until the propositions cover every case examined, the theory remains incomplete. (See Manning, 1977.)

These three strategies (experimental method, multivariate analysis, and analytic induction) represent the major means the sociologist has for examining and generating causal, interpretive propositions. They also represent the principal strategies of handling rival causal factors. The experimental model controls them, the survey methods infers them, and analytic induction follows their occurrence over time.

Each research method employs one or more of these strategies, and each in its own way treats rival causal factors. Consequently, each method can be evaluated in terms of its ability to construct sound interpretations. To the extent that one method permits greater control of situations, time, observers, and subjects than another, it is superior to the other.

The Logic of Triangulation

Unfortunately, no single method ever adequately solves the problem of rival interpretive, causal factors. For example, while experiments can establish valid causal propositions, the problem of observer reactivity (presence in a laboratory) potentially creates a situation where subjects act as they think the experimenter wants them to. Following Webb et al. (1966, 1981), I conclude that no single method will ever permit an investigator to develop causal propositions free of rival interpretations. Similarly, I conclude that no *single* method will ever meet the requirements of interaction theory. While participant observation permits the careful recording of situations and selves, it does not offer direct data on the wider spheres of influence acting on those observed. Because each method reveals different aspects of empirical reality, multiple methods of observations must be employed. This is termed *triangulation*. I now offer as a final methodological rule the principle that multiple methods should be used in every investigation, since no method is ever free of rival causal factors (and thus leads to completely sound causal propositions), can ever completely satisfy the demands of interaction theory, or can ever completely reveal all the relevant features of empirical reality necessary for testing or developing a theory. A similar conclusion is reached by Webb and colleagues (1966, pp. 173–74):

> It is too much to ask of any single class that it eliminate all the rival hypotheses subsumed under the population-, content-, and reactive-effects groupings. As long as the research strategy is based on a single measurement class, some flanks will be exposed. . . . If no single measurement class is perfect, neither is any scientifically useless . . . for the most fertile search for validity comes from a combined series of different measures, each with its idiosyncratic weaknesses, each pointed to a single hypothesis. When a hypothesis can survive the confrontation of a series of complementary methods of testing, it contains a degree of validity unattainable by one tested within the more constricted framework of a single method. . . .

I will offer a definition of each method that rests on several discrete but interrelated strategies and techniques. For example, I will show that participant observation is best seen as a method that combines survey data, descriptive statistical analysis, quasiexperimental variations, document analysis, and direct observation.

My last criterion under the category of validity, then, is the triangulation of methodologies. This proposes a new line of action for the sociologist as well as a new set of symbolic meanings for the research process generally. I concur with Webb and colleagues (1981, p. 315), who argue that in the present stage of social research, single-method investigations are no longer appropriate. The combination of multiple methods in a single investigation will better enable the sociologist to forge valid propositions that carefully consider relevant rival causal factors.

A Caveat on Cause

Elsewhere (Denzin, 1983, 1984) I have argued that sociologists should not blindly pursue the goal of formulating causal propositions; nor should they be preoccupied with causal issues. I repeat this caveat in the present context for several reasons. First, students should not be given the impression that sociologists only ask causal questions. Many sociologists seek to describe and interpret social experiences; they do not make causal analysis one of their goals (see Denzin, 1983). Second, a focus *only* on causal questions leads to a tendency to ignore *how* social interaction and social processes unfold in social situations. Causal analysis asks *why*. Interpretive analysis asks *how*. In my AA study, for example, I did not ask why individuals became alcoholics; I asked, instead, how they came to see themselves as alcoholics. This way of asking the question led to a focus on social process, and not to a preoccupation with antecedent causal variables. Researchers differ on asking how questions versus why questions. My preference is to always focus on how an event or process is produced and created, and not to ask only why it happened, or what caused it (see also Lofland, 1976).

In the present context, it is useful to distinguish two versions of the causal question (see Garfinkel, 1967; Schutz, 1962). Sociologists as scientists ask scientific, causal questions, of the order just discussed. Everyday, ordinary individuals also ask causal questions, to which they seek causal answers. They may ask, for example, why the unemployment rate is so high in their local community. A husband may ask his wife why dinner isn't ready at 6:00 P.M. In each of these contexts, a person, or collectivity of persons, seeks a causal understanding of a set of social events.

Both Schutz and Garfinkel have argued that in everyday life individuals answer causal questions by using standards of cause and effect that are not "scientific." A wife may say that supper is late because she had to get the children at a baseball game that went extra innings. Or she may state that supper is late because, in order to get ready for a concert at 8:00, she did not have time to make the necessary meal preparations. In these two situations, the wife refers to the past (the game went extra innings) and to the future (the concert at 8:00). Garfinkel and Schutz argue that in everyday life individuals give these "because" and "in order to" answers to causal questions. This is the case because causality in everyday life resides in social experience and in social interaction. Cause is not outside time in a causal variable. Cause, at this level, is subjectively interpreted. It is part of social experience. Cause, conceptualized in this manner, speaks to the how, and not the why, question.

Given the foregoing considerations, it is suggested that sociologists give equal time in their research to both forms of the causal question—that is, to both the why and the how problems of everyday life.

A BRIEF COMPARISON OF METHODS

Tables 1-1 and 1-2 provide a comparison of the seven major research methods to be analyzed in subsequent chapters. Table 1-1 compares the methods in terms of the ability of each to meet the requirements of symbolic interactionism as developed in this chapter. It raises 6 questions: How well does each method permit the observer to (1) combine symbols with interaction, (2) take the perspective of the observed, (3) enter the subject's world and link the subject's meanings to that world, (4) record the behavior settings of observation, (5) reflect change and process, and (6) sensitize concepts. Each method is rated on a scale of "high" to "low," and the frequency with which users of the method meet the criteria, if relevant, is noted. Taking each method in turn, we can see that the *experiment* is strongest in its ability to record behavior settings and to reflect change and process. This method seldom permits an entry into the world of the subject; symbols are seldom combined with interaction; the role of the subject is seldom taken; concepts are seldom sensitized. Users of the *survey* seldom combine symbols with interaction and they seldom take the role or attitude of the subject except in the case of open-ended questions. Behavior settings can be recorded but seldom are. Change is difficult to establish, and concepts are sensitized only when open-ended questions are used. *Participant observation* ranks high on all dimensions, and this fact reflects the commitment of most users of this approach to some version of symbolic interactionism. (See Wax, 1971, pp. 38–41.) *Unobtrusive methods* rank low on everything but the ability to record behavior settings and to sensitize concepts. (The reasons for this will be

TABLE 1-1 Comparison of Major Sociological Methods in Terms of the Principles of Symbolic Interactionism

	Experiment	Survey	Participant Observation	Unobtrusive Methods	Life History and Historical Method	Interview	Film
Combines symbols and interaction	Possible but moderate	Seldom	High	Low	High	High	High
Takes role of the observed	Seldom	Seldom	High	Low	High	High	High
Enters subject's social worlds and links symbols to them	Seldom	Possible but seldom	High	Low, difficult	High	High	High
Records behavior settings	High, with rigor	Possible, but seldom	High	Moderate	High	High	High
Reflects change and process	High but probabilistic	Moderate	High	Low	High, but retrospective	High	High
Sensitizes concepts	Seldom	Seldom, except in index construction and open-ended questions	High	Moderate	High	High	High

developed in Chapter 9.) Like participant observation, the *life history and historical method* ranks high on all dimensions. The fact that this method is evaluated favorably in Table 1-1 must be regarded with guarded enthusiasm, however; for, as Table 1-2 shows, it has mixed results when assessed in terms of the principles of causal analysis. *Interviews* and *film* also rank high on each dimension. This is the case because each allows the researcher to actively enter the situation being studied. (See Douglas, 1985, on interviewing; Collier and Collier, 1986, on visual anthropology and film; Becker, 1986, pp. 221–317, on photography and sociology; and Denzin, 1985, on video cameras.)

Table 1-2 selectively applies Campbell's treatment of external and internal validity with the properties of causal analysis. It raises 12 questions: How well can any method (1) control rival factors; (2) measure time order; (3) record covariance between variables; (4) respond to time and historical factors; (5) handle maturation; (6) control testing effects and (7) instrumentation; (8) permit triangulation; (9) reduce subject bias, (10) subject mortality, and (11) reactive effects. Last, it asks (12) to what universe the findings of the method can be generalized. The *experiment* emerges as one of the strongest methods when these factors are considered, although its universe of generalization is typically only that of the college sophomore. The reactive effects of observation are often high, and selection bias is often unknown. The *survey* handles time order poorly, except in panel designs. It is subject to the problems of testing effects, and instrumentation changes may make it highly susceptible to the particularities of interviewer–interviewee encounters. *Participant observation* is rated "medium to good" on most dimensions, a fact which suggests that its ability to meet the criteria of proper causal analysis is only as strong as its user's commitment to these criteria. A similar conclusion can be drawn for the *life history and historical method*. However, this method handles the control of rival causal factors poorly. Mortality is low if a single subject or a pool of subjects is followed over a long period of time. The loss of a subject can virtually destroy the life history method, particularly if the lost subject is the primary source of data. Subject mortality is less severe for the other approaches. The *unobtrusive method* produces few reactive effects, but because the investigator seldom establishes a relationship with the subjects, this method has difficulty meeting the criteria of the sound causal proposition.

The *interview* is rated good to high on nearly every dimension. This method or research technique is typically used in conjunction with the survey, participant observation, and life history approaches. Hence, to the extent that these methods rank high in each of the criteria in Table 1-2, so too does the interview. *Film*, which here includes the use of video and nonvideo cameras, as well as movies made by the researcher, or Hollywood, also scores high. Film and photography have traditionally been used as "tool(s) for the exploration of society, and photographers have taken that as one of their tasks" (Becker, 1986, p. 1224). Film methods offer a means of penetrating and revealing unfolding interaction in social situations. They permit the capturing of the relevant contextual elements that shape action. They address history and maturation when they seek to explore a particular

TABLE 1-2 Comparison of Major Sociological Methods in Terms of the Principles of Causal Analysis

	Experiment	Survey	Participant Observation	Unobtrusive Methods	Life History and Historical Method	Interview	Film
Control of rival factors	Excellent	Good (multivariate analysis)	Fair	Fair	Low	Good	Fair
Time order	Excellent	Poor (except panels)	Excellent	Fair	Fair (with documents)	Good	High
Covariance of variables	Excellent	Very good (probabilistic)	Good (analytic induction)	Fair	Good	Good	High
History	Fair	Fair	Excellent	Low	Excellent	High	High
Maturation	Fair	Fair to poor	Excellent	Low to poor	Excellent	High	High
Testing effects	Fair	Fair to poor	Good	Low	Good	Fair	Low
Instrumentation	Good	Fair to poor	Good	Fair	Good (if reported)	Good	High
Possibility of triangulation	Good	Fair to low	Excellent	High	Good (if reported)	High	High
Selection bias	Fair	Good	Fair to medium	Fair	Fair to low	Good	Fair
Mortality	Medium	Medium	Medium	Unknown	Low	Good	High
Reactive effect	Moderate	High (social desirability)	Low	Nil	Diminished by familiarity	Medium	Medium
Universe of generalization	College sophomores	Adults, communities	Case studies of institutions	Behavior in public places	Single individuals, communities	Members of group	Public culture

Source: Suggested by Professor David Knoke of Indiana University.

event and its effects on persons. Fictional films are especially strong in this regard. Photographic methods also tend to be low on reactive effects and mortality, although they may be subject to the problems of selection bias (that is, who is chosen to be filmed or photographed). Tables 1-1 and 1-2 are intended to underscore the last criterion under *validity*—namely, the triangulation of methodologies. No method perfectly answers all the questions raised in this discussion.

THE IMPLEMENTATION OF TRIANGULATION: PHASES OF THE RESEARCH ACT

The researcher committed to the logic and method of triangulation will necessarily view the research act processually. Therefore, different methods will have different relevance for each phase of the research. At least 8 phases make up the research act:

1. *Asking the question:* The researcher puzzles over some empirical regularity. She asks *how* a particular event or set of experiences is interpreted by interacting individuals. As noted earlier, in my AA study, I asked how individuals came to define themselves as alcoholics. Ideally the researcher can ask the question that is to be answered in a single sentence.

2. *Deconstruction:* Once the question is asked, the researcher must examine the traditional theories, concepts, and understandings that surround the phenomenon being studied. This literature must be critically read and deconstructed— taken apart and traced back to its original sources and meanings (Denzin, 1984b, p. 10). This can also be called a critical review of the research literature on the subject under study.

3. *Exploration and capture:* Multiple instances of the phenomenon must be sought out and explored in their natural, interactional settings. Systematic, regular observations and interviews will be undertaken. An attempt will be made to formulate a triangulated research strategy that will permit the collection of multiple instances of the phenomenon.

4. *Intense involvement and bracketing:* The researcher becomes lodged within the research act and completely enters the worlds of those under investigation. He begins to live the research. Bracketing involves a reduction of the phenomenon into its essential elements. I found, for example, that the essential elements of the alcoholic self involved time, emotionality, relations with others, drinking and non-drinking, bad faith, or denial, and surrender to alcoholism as a disease. I isolated these elements in my interviews and observations of alcoholics as they talked at AA meetings. Bracketing allows the researcher to come to grips with the basic features of the phenomenon being studied.

5. *Tentative interpretations:* The researcher begins to formulate interpretations about how the processes and interactions that have been observed interrelate and influence one another.

6. *Contextualization:* In this step, the researcher advances more developed interpretations that are contextualized in interaction. Thus she has to locate what is being studied in the lives and biographies of interacting individuals. Contextualization isolates and illuminates the meaning of the phenomenon for the persons studied (Denzin, 1984b, p. 10). In this phase the researcher returns that which was previously bracketed to the world of interaction.

7. *Examination of deviant cases:* Exceptions to patterned regularities are now examined in order to make more sharply focus the interpretive analysis. Negative or deviant cases highlight unique experiences and reveal the different ways in which the phenomenon being studied operate in the social world.

8. *Advancement of alternative interpretations:* On the basis of negative and deviant cases, the researcher sets forth alternative interpretations of the phenomenon in question. In my AA study, I was led to develop an interpretation of two types of alcoholics: situational and committed. Situational alcoholics develop alcoholic identities for only a limited period of time in order to solve a problem in their lives. When the problem is solved, they cease to think of themselves as alcoholics. Committed alcoholics see themselves as being alcoholics for the rest of their lives. They have surrendered to their alcoholism, while situational alcoholics have not.

9. *Presentation of final interpretive analysis:* Deviant cases are now incorporated into a coherent, interpretive framework that attempts to deal with every instance of the phenomenon investigated. This interpretation will always be provisional and somewhat incomplete, to be taken up anew when the researcher returns to the field (Denzin, 1984b, p. 9).

The seven sociological methods—the experiment, the survey, participant observation, unobtrusive methods, the life history and historical method, the interview, and the use of film—enter at different points in the research act. In my research on AA and the American alcoholic, I have employed all of these methods. In phases 1 and 2, I read extensively in the research literature. I spent a great deal of time reviewing experimental and survey studies of alcoholism and alcoholics. I then critically deconstructed this body of work, so as to develop my own point of view. In phases 3 and 4 I employed interviewing, participant observation, unobtrusive methods, and collected life stories and viewed films about alcoholics. (See Denzin, 1988b, for a review of this research.) In phases 5, 6, and 7, I focused my interviewing on negative cases. I examined films produced by Hollywood that presented different types (male, female, young, old) of alcoholics. I also attempted to fit my interpretations into the biographies of those I was studying. I kept asking myself if my interpretations seemed to make sense for these lives. Phases 8 and 9 of my research are still in process. I am currently studying films and the American alcoholic, attempting a historical analysis of how media images of the alcoholic and his family have changed over the past 40 years. I am also studying alcoholic families. This requires that I modify my understandings of the recovering alcoholic to fit alcoholic family life. In so doing, I am attempting to follow the principles outlined in this chapter.

DISCOVERY VERSUS VERIFICATION VERSUS INTERPRETATION

Should sociologists give more attention to verifying or to modifying existing theory? Or should they be concerned with discovering new theory? Or should they not be concerned with theory at all, and give their attention instead to describing and interpreting the social world? Many sociologists have abandoned theory development for a concern with refining their methods and skills of verification (see the chapters in Blalock, 1985). Methods, however, are of value only to the extent that they lead to better social theory (see Lieberson, 1985). Other sociologists discover new theory by rewriting existing, classical sociological theory (see Collins, 1985). This strategy keeps theory removed from the empirical world, and contributes little to our understanding of life in contemporary society (see Mills, 1959). Some social scientists turn away from the use of the term *theory* and focus their attention primarily on interpretation of the social and cultural worlds (see Geertz, 1983).

Sociology should make the invisible more visible (see Becker, 1986). Theory should contribute to better understandings of the social. Theory as interpretation should be grounded in the worlds of lived experience. Paraphrasing Karl Marx, we can argue that the purpose of sociology is not just to understand the world, but to change it to the better. Theory should yield interpretations that illuminate those areas of social life that requiring change.

My own concern with combining principles from interaction theory and causal-interpretive analysis represents a dual interest in discovery and interpretation. Interactionism tells sociologists how to approach the empirical world; the principles of causal, interpretive analysis tell them how to identify warrantable, repeatable, reproducible interpretation of that world. The two problems are inseparable. Until sociology has a set of criteria that permits discovery and interpretation, the separation between theory and method will persist.

CONCLUSIONS

In this chapter I offered an extensive discussion of theory, methods, and the research act. I offered a set of principles from symbolic interactionism and the scientific method. I have termed my approach *naturalistic interactionism*. I then compared seven research methods in terms of their ability to meet the principles that should organize the research act.

SUGGESTED READINGS

BECKER, HOWARD S., *Doing Things Together*. (Evanston, Ill.: Northwestern University Press, 1986). A valuable collection of Becker's writings over the past 15 years on the topics of theory, method, research, photography, social organization, and sociology.

BLUMER, HERBERT, *Symbolic Interactionism*. (Englewood Cliffs, N.J.: Prentice-Hall, 1969). A key source, especially Chapter 1, for understanding the symbolic interactionist perspective in sociology.

CLIFFORD, JAMES AND GEORGE J. MARCUS (eds.), *Writing Culture: The Poetics and Politics of Ethnography*. (Berkeley: University of California Press, 1986). This book contains a number of highly controversial papers on interpretive theory in anthropology.

Sociological Inquiry, vol. 56, no. 1 (Winter 1986), special issue on "Gender Roles and Women's Issues." Several of the articles in this issue address feminist theory and sociological research.

2

Sociological Theory

Which brings us, finally, to theory . . . the essential task of theory building is not to codify abstract regularities but to make thick description possible, not to generalize across cases but to generalize within them . . . cultural theory . . . is not . . . predictive. [Geertz, 1973, pp. 24, 26]

Contemporary sociologists have been preoccupied with "theory," yet have seldom tried to make clear what a theory is. [Homans, 1964, p. 951]

Theory has not often been designed with research operations in mind. Theory as we have it in social science serves indispensably as a very broad frame of reference or general orientation. Thus modern theories of culture tell us that it is usually more profitable to focus on the learning process and the control of what is learned rather than on the innate or hereditary traits. But they do not provide us with sets of interrelated propositions which can be put in the form: If x_1, given x_2 and x_3, then there is a strong probability that we get x_4. Most of our propositions of that form, sometimes called "theory," are likely to be *ad hoc* common-sense observations which are not deducible from more general considerations and which are of the same quality as the observation, "If you stick your hand in a fire and hold it there, you will get burned." [Stouffer, 1950, p. 359]

One of the most valuable functions of the research method is its ability to contribute to the growth and refinement of social theory, but to state only this much sidesteps the central question of why sociologists want theory in the first place. To answer this question, I must briefly treat sociology as a social institution.

As I noted at the end of Chapter 1, considerable controversy surrounds the place of theory in the social sciences. The three authors just quoted offer differing views on this topic. Geertz sees theory as creating the conditions for thick description and interpretation. Homans (as we shall see soon) and

Stouffer take a natural science view, arguing that theory should permit predictions, and it should take the form of propositions. In this chapter these views will be discussed and contrasted.

I must briefly treat sociology as a social institution. I will then discuss what theory is not, and what theory is. I will then discuss new varieties of social theory, including feminist theory.

THE SOCIOLOGICAL COMMUNITY

It is instructive to view any science from three perspectives: as a social institution, as a method, and as a body of accumulated knowledge (see Smelser, 1968, pp. 3–44). (A synthesis of these perspectives provides a central theme of subsequent chapters.) Viewing science as a method demands a treatment of current sociological research strategies; viewing it as a body of accumulated knowledge requires discussion of theory construction and verification. But science as an institution is best expressed once it is understood that any scientific community is a human community composed of differing personalities, values, and political pressures. (These human elements are given fuller treatment in Chapter 12.)

The sociological community, like all scientific communities, is a social and political production (see T. Kuhn, 1962). It contains individuals, singly and collectively, attempting to produce new and differentially valid images and theories of the empirical social world (see Latour and Woolgar, 1979). Often the canons of scientific rigor are set aside and replaced by the more commonplace standards of deceit, pride, enthusiasm, bewilderment, and hero worship (see Gouldner, 1970). Sociologists, like any other interacting individuals, are caught up in the struggle of making sense out of whatever it is they are doing at the moment (see Garfinkel, Lynch, and Livingston, 1981). They are often led to advance accounts or explanations of their actions, and frequently they cloak these explanations in "scientific" terms and statements. They argue that they are being scientific, when in fact their actions may be motivated by other concerns, such as personal advancement, economic security, or simply a good grade in a course (see Churchill, 1971, pp. 182–91; and Garfinkel, 1967).

The Politics of Sociology

As Becker and Horowitz (1972, pp. 48–66) and Merton (1972, pp. 9–47) have observed, American sociology emerged from the decade of the 1960s somewhat battered and bruised. Attacked by radicals and conservatives, by outsiders and insiders, by politicians and blacks, by women and college students, sociology came under bitter inspection. Guidelines that had held for generations were judged worthless. Radicals demanded that old academic structures be overturned. The old sociology was no longer relevant to a new age in which *relevance* was the key word. A racist, capitalist society was on the verge of collapse. The new sociology (Gouldner, 1970) would return sociology to the people, and it would be self-reflexive. Conservative paradigms such as structural functionalism and qualitative paradigms such as symbolic interactionism were viewed critically. Interactionists were not sufficiently critical, had no theory of social structure, and besides had been co-opted by Washington bureaucrats. Structural functionalism perpetuated the racist-sexist status quo. In the 1960s, sociologists took to the picket line, often becoming activists, critics, or radicals.

The claims, challenges, and issues of the 1960s have not been resolved. No new leaders and no new answers have come forth. The 1970s witnessed a decline in political controversy; sociological practitioners argued over deduction versus induction, qualitative methods versus quantitative methods. New, challenging images of society and new theoretical formulations were set aside for procedures that would "professionalize" the sociological community. (But see Collins, 1975, for a major exception, and Wiley, 1976, pp. 235–39.)

The decade of the 1980s has repeated, in certain respects, the preoccupations of the 1970s. Sociology has become even more fragmented (Becker, 1986); no general theory organizes the discipline. Neofunctionalists are attempting a comeback (see Alexander, 1982). Giddens (1984), like Habermas (1981/1984), continues to attempt to build a totalizing theory of society, while postmodern theorists like Lyotard (1979/1984) and Baudrillard (1983), after Foucault (1980), argue that no such theory is possible (see Denzin, 1986, for a review). Methodological theorists (Blalock, 1984) promote greater rigor in causal model building. Others, like Collins (1985), contend that sociology's current problems stem (in part) from a failure to theorize the knowledge that has been accumulated over the past decade. Current sociology is in the doldrums, or rather in an interregnum (Wiley, 1985, 1986). In some senses, sociologists appear to want theory because having one allows them to ignore the discord and fragmentation that exists in their discipline. Becker cynically observes that the "mysterious concentration on Marx-Weber-Durkheim, the Holy Trinity," by contemporary sociologists comes from the desire to "provide the final word on the integration of the field" (1986, p. 220). It probably also comes because of habit and training. Sociologists have been taught to be theoretical.

Some claim that the social sciences are witnessing the demise of old paradigms and that in the future a new theory and paradigm will come forth (Couch, 1987). This seems unlikely; it is highly probable that in the next decade of sociological work, the issues and problems of the 1960s will reappear. Sociological debate is endless; issues seldom find full and complete resolution; paradigms are necessarily open-ended. Each generation of sociologists must rediscover the errors and debates of previous generations. Factionization, fragmentation, disagreement, and discord are constant features of all scientific communities. Sociology, like anthropology, was founded on discord. To the extent that it remains alive and lively, discord and debate will be core values in the sociological community.

Sociology as Social Organization

From the interactionist perspective, social organization consists of patterned and intertwined lines of action. Common symbolic meanings are attached to social objects, and regular styles of acting toward those objects may be observed. A completely formed social organization takes on a life of its own. Patterns of entry and exit become fixed, salient values are agreed upon, and various functions and role positions crystallize. Just so, contemporary sociology has a special form of organization. In other words, it is a viable, changing, shifting unit of social organization that has as its center a small cluster of values and goals.

The common thread in this social structure is the belief that certain goals should be pursued. First, sociologists should be able to describe the phenomena they are studying so that others can repeat their descriptions with a high degree of agreement. Such descriptions may take various forms; Becker, for example, stated how a marijuana user learns the values of a deviant subculture.

Description is essential for the second goal—explanation, probably the most elusive of the sociologist's goals. It involves essentially, as Homans (1964) states, the construction of a system of interrelated propositions that permits the scientist to "make sense" out of the events observed. To say that a set of events has been explained is to argue that their occurrence in the future can be predicted. Thus, prediction is the third goal. It follows and provides a test of the explanation. A sociologist who claims to have explained why a given set of variables occurs together must be able to predict their future relationships.

A fourth scientific goal of the sociologist, which follows from symbolic interactionism, is attaining an intimate familiarity with the social processes under investigation. The researcher who has not yet penetrated the world of the individuals being studied is in no firm position to begin developing predictions, explanations, and theories about that world. Intimate familiarity follows directly from the goal of sound descriptions. To be intimately familiar with those under study, a scholar should be able to understand their language or languages, what social objects they value, how they define one another, what social situations they typically interact in, when they are likely to be in those settings, and what kinds of relationships exist between them.

The fifth scientific goal of the sociologist is theory construction. Until theory is developed, fully adequate descriptions, explanations, and predictions cannot be forthcoming, since it is theory that provides their framework. If it is the job of a scientist to discover and systematize knowledge, then theories become the expression of what is known, what is predicted, and what is assumed. In the construction of theoretical frameworks, the full-fledged nature of sociology as a science emerges, for in theory, methods take on meaning, observations become organized, and the goals of prediction and explanation are reached.

Another goal that has concerned the sociologist is control. It is often assumed that once explanation and prediction have been achieved, the analyst is in a position to control the processes she has explained. But control is elusive. To some, the term *control* may imply that under ideal experimental conditions the effect of one variable upon another can be controlled; to others, *control* means manipulation. Thus, in Becker's analysis of marijuana use, it might be argued that members of society could use his information to control the spread and use of the drug. Perhaps they might, but the pursuit of control as a goal takes the sociologist out of scientific enterprise and into politics. To recommend how marijuana use may be controlled involves a value decision that the use of marijuana is undesirable. I am not suggesting that sociologists avoid making value decisions, since they cannot. (Indeed, setting theory construction as a goal is a value decision itself.) I do not want to make control one of the central goals of sociology, however, or discuss it as such. Instead, I assume that the sociologist is a member of a human community which stresses certain values over others, and that the sociologist is committed, at least in part, to the pursuit of knowledge for its own sake.

I must insert the following point. Knowledge and truth are political constructions (Foucault, 1980). Sociologists who receive grants from the federal government study what the government wants studied — and often controlled (criminologists who study crime are an example). Some sociologists want changes the government does not want. The sociologist's personal and research values are often in conflict with the government's wishes. If, as an interpretive sociologist, the researcher is committed not only to understanding but also to changing social situations, he will often have to work for change outside normal or formal channels. Such research may also not be funded because it does not conform to the positivist methodological paradigm. Many feminist, Marxist, and interpretive scholars have found this to be the case for their research.

A Disclaimer on the Goals of Theory

Thus far I have suggested that theory, in its various forms, organizes the research act. Theory, which builds on descriptions of the empirical world, leads to explanation, prediction, and control of the phenomenon in question. Hence four of the major goals of the sociological enterprise can be seen as deriving from theory. These goals are understandable only if a particular view of theory is allowed. This is the view that sees theory from a natural science, or logical positivist, perspective (see Smith, 1986). *Under this view, theory is a body of theorems and propositions, deductively interrelated, such that some can be deduced from others.* Theory, in this sense, offers explanation, prediction, and control.

Consider the following definitions of theory, as given in a standard dictionary:

1. Contemplation or speculation
2. The analysis of a set of facts in their ideal relations to one another, as essays in *theory*
3. A more or less plausible or scientifically acceptable general principle offered to explain phenomena
4. A guess

Each of these definitions stresses the nondeductive, nonpropositional form of theory. The words *guessing, contemplation,* and *essays* are used. These meanings suggest that theory's use lies in the realm of understanding, making sense of, writing about, or interpreting a phenomenon.

Now reconsider the quote from Geertz at the beginning of this chapter.

He argues that theory's task is to make thick description possible. He also argues that theory is not predictive. Elsewhere in the same text (1973, p. 26), he suggests that "the essential task of theory is not to generalize across cases, but to generalize within them." He argues that the interpretive anthropologist does not begin with a set of observations that are subsumed under a governing law. Instead, generalizing *within* cases means locating a set of behaviors or experiences within an interpretive framework that makes sense. The aim is the analysis of social discourse (Geertz, 1973, p. 26).

This means that "cultural" theory is not predictive in the sense that future occurrences are predicted on the basis of general laws or theorems. By making interpretive sense out of a cultural or social phenomenon, the researcher does, however, formulate interpretations that hold for (make sense of) past and future occurrences. This means that the researcher begins with "thick descriptions" of a set of experiences and then diagnoses, or interprets, those events within an evolving theoretical framework. A *thick description* is one that goes beyond the mere or bare reporting on an act (that is, that individual A did B). This is a *thin description* (Ryle, 1968, pp. 8–9). A thick description describes and probes the intentions, motives, meanings, context, situations, and circumstances of action (see Denzin, 1983, p. 143).

Perhaps an example will help. In my AA studies, I spent considerable time recording and describing the stories alcoholics tell around the AA tables (see discussion in Chapter 1). I presented these stories in the words of the speakers. I gave a brief biographical history of each individual. I described the meeting where the discourse occurred, and located that meeting within the local culture of AA meetings. I then offered an interpretation of the stories and the speakers, based on the speaker's location in the AA social structure. I compared the stories of speakers who frequently relapsed (drank again) with those told by old timers and those told by alcoholics still in treatment. My goal was to offer an interpretation that would hold for the experiences of any alcoholic who would come (or had come) to AA.

Geertz (1973, p. 27) describes this process in the following words:

> Such a view of how theory functions in an interpretive science suggests that the distinction . . . that appears in the experimental or observational sciences between "descriptive" and "explanation" appears here as one, even more relative, between "inscription" (thick description) and "specification" (diagnosis) . . . Our double task is to uncover the conceptual structures that inform our subject's acts, the "said" of social discourse, and to construct a system of analysis in whose terms what is generic to these structures . . . will stand out against the other determinants of human behavior.

Under this formulation, theory operates as interpretation. The scientific goals of description, prediction, explanation, and control are redefined, if not made irrelevant, under this view. Indeed, the attempt is to make sense of something in terms of the language, meanings, and intentions of those studied. Thick description replaces thin description. Prediction becomes interpretation. Explanation in terms of general laws is not sought. This interpretive view of theory and goals of science is at odds with much of what is practiced today in the social sciences. It is the view taken in this book.

Dysfunctions of the Sociological Reward Structure

The reward structure of contemporary sociology favors the foregoing goals in varying degrees. The valued sociologists are those who can either contribute novel refinements to existing methods or construct new social theories (Hill, 1969)—both worthy pursuits. Becker's (1970, pp. 6–7) now dated analysis of the winners of major sociological awards for the years 1958 through 1968 revealed that the awards were given to sociologists who used the methods of participant observation and historical analysis. He noted a paradox. During this same time period, the chairs of the methodology section of the American Sociological Association (ASA) were individuals identified with the methods of survey research, statistical analysis, sampling, and the use of mathematical models. Becker concluded that the major ASA methodologists had failed the discipline; they had ignored those important methods and procedures that the larger discipline had judged to be associated with outstanding sociological work. If a student were to update Becker's analysis through 1988, I suspect the same conclusions would be reached. This would simply require a listing of the winners of the C. Wright Mills, MacIver, Sorokin, Bernard, DuBois-Johnson-Frazier, Common Wealth, and Career of Distinguished Scholarship awards. This list would be compared to the names of the chairs of the ASA Methodology and Theory Sections for this time period.

There is another paradox. Rewards are not given for the more mundane and time-consuming features of doing sociology. Replications of existing studies, for example, are seldom rewarded, and this means, in effect, that sociology remains a noncumulative science. Bonjean, Hill, and McLemore (1967, p. 9) have observed that between 1954 and 1965, some 2,080 scales and indices appeared in the *American Journal of Sociology*, the *American Sociological Review*, *Social Forces*, and *Sociometry*. Of these scales, only 47 or 2.26 percent, were used more than 5 times. This points to an important feature of current sociology: Apparently many sociologists feel more compelled to construct their own scales and indices than to use those that already exist, almost as if they felt that each new scale developed could build a reputation for its constructor and user.

Neither is the reporting of negative results rewarded. Unless sociologists can show positive relationships between their variables, their research typically remains unpublished. Yet the obvious value of reporting studies that have failed—another way of stating that negative cases should be examined—is clear. Sociologists could certainly benefit by learning what causal propositions, what designs, and what strategies failed for others; at the very least, past mistakes might not be repeated.

Nor are studies that take long periods of time usually rewarded. There exist in the literature only a few studies that took longer than one or two years to complete—studies such as Lipset, Trow, and Coleman's of the International Typographical Union (1962), which ranks as a sociological classic in the area of organizational analysis (from inception to publication, some 13 years elapsed); or Becker, Geer, Hughes, and Strauss's study of socialization in medical school (1961), which took nearly 5 years from inception to publication, and which also ranks as an outstanding investigation. These two studies are cited as representative of the small number of investigations that exceed the normal length of sociological research—yet they are classics, and the research reported in them significantly influenced the subsequent careers of the investigators. A paradox must be noted. Sociologists shun long-term studies, yet reward those members of the discipline who carry out such research. There is a great need for long-term field studies, especially if the interactionist perspective is adopted, because events must be followed over time in their natural settings and investigations that have a natural history, a long-term focus, must be designed and carried out. Unless studies of this nature are rewarded, sociology will remain at the one-shot, short-term study level.

My discussion in subsequent chapters represents an attempt to shift the current reward and goal structure of sociology, with theory becoming a major goal and research methods seen as lines of actions taken toward the empirical world. With such a shift, studies that replicate and extend over long periods of time will take on special value.

METASOCIOLOGICAL CONSIDERATIONS: THE PROBLEM OF METAPHORS, ROLE MODELS, VALUES, AND IDEOLOGIES

A treatment of sociological values and of reward structures within the discipline leads to a consideration of metasociology.

Broadly speaking, metasociology concerns itself with "the methodological considerations necessary for carrying out sociological research, constructing sociological systems and criticizing such research and systems after they have been completed" (Furfey, 1959, p. 510). The domain of metasociology extends beyond methodological considerations or standards for appropriate theory. The use of one set of methodological or theoretical directives ultimately represents an involvement in value decisions, and metasociology directs attention to the study of value decisions as they become embedded in the sociological enterprise. A value decision refers to a declaration of preference, such as "Sociology is a science," or "Sociologists should concern themselves with problems of theory," or "A goal of sociology should be better theory." Each of these statements declares an intent, a desired condition, an "ought." Value decisions cannot be analyzed and empirically proven or disproven, but they can be studied for their logical nature, and the study of values becomes axiology. Scientific declarations are statements of "what is," such as this declaration: "The rate of suicide in Spain is low." All sociological statements ultimately rest on a series of values taken on faith. Their acceptance rests on the belief that they are correct lines of action for the sociologist.

Sociologists have long debated the relevance of models of science taken from physics and chemistry. The proponents of the physical science model claim that if it has worked for physics, it should work for sociology (Lundberg, 1955, 1956). Opponents of this model claim that the subject matter of sociology is no different from that of the physical sciences that physical models are inappropriate for sociological analysis. This position is well stated by MacIver (1931, pp. 25–27, 35):

> Sociology has been plagued all through its history by its tendency to seek for models in the fields of other sciences. At one time the fashion was to think of a society as a kind of organism, to make sociology a pale reflection of biology. Now the attitude changes and the first article of the creed has become the formula that sociology is a "natural science." . . .
>
> The trouble is that the social sciences suffer from certain embarrassments from which the "natural sciences" are more or less free. They have to deal with phenomena which involve a kind of causation unknown in the purely physical world, since they are "motivated," in fact brought into being, by that elusive complex, but undeniable, reality, the mentality of man. . . . Our aim is to understand and to convey to others the understanding of the intricate and often baffling web of social relationships, which, being created by man, must be understood by a similar creative capacity in ourselves.

MacIver's statement reflects the central problem of metasociology: What assumptions, beliefs, metaphors, and role models must sociologists adopt if their quest is to be scientific? His answer is to reject models and metaphors taken from the physical sciences, but he fails to offer a satisfactory alternative. It is insufficient to say that one model does not work. If it does not, then what should be adopted in its place? (Part III of this book attempts to provide a solution to MacIver's unanswered question.)

Alternative Metasociological Positions

Several alternative metasociological stances have been offered. Of these, the natural science model, the social science model (never systematically articulated), and a model taken from the humanities seem to be most important. Each model has its own bundle of metaphors and values, and each represents differing self-identity models for the sociologist.

The natural science model   If the natural science model is followed, logical-deductive theories and rigorous quantified measurement strategies are likely to be employed. Methods such as surveys and experiments will be used to a greater extent than life histories and participant observation. When findings are presented, the model will be the scientific article. Methods, hypotheses, and findings will be clearly spelled out. Terms will be precisely defined, and prose style will be free of ambiguous and evocative images (see Merton, 1967, pp. 1–37).

The positivist model   The positivist model will stress a language that is *analytic* ($3 + 5 = 8$) and *verifiable* by empirical, behavioral observation (person A drank a bottle of whiskey in a 1-hour period). It will not discuss phenomena that cannot be contained within an analytic and verifiable framework (see Smith, 1986, p. 3). This means it tends to gloss over or ignore subjective, inner phenomenological processes, including motives and intentions. The goal will be to predict and control behavior, not to investigate the realm of subjective experience (Smith, 1986, p. 4). Emphasis will be given to observations of behavior that are assumed to be reliable, valid, and intersubjectively verifiable (in other words, two or more observers will agree on what has occurred). This means that positivism makes claims about behavior that are empirically testable. The principle of verifiability organizes the positivist research model.

An additional consequence of adopting the natural science model will be a selective use of metaphors in the process of theorizing. Every sociological theory, Stone and Farberman (1967, pp. 149–64) suggest, "implies some image of man, communication, society and their interrelations." In the presentation of these interrelationships, as noted by Bruyn (1966, p. 133), the theorist is likely to employ some form of the metaphor, which is

> an implied comparison between things essentially unlike one another. . . . One image is superimposed upon another in order to provide a better perspective and understanding of the subject at hand.

Thus, Lundberg, an advocate of the natural science model, frequently used terms such as *force, vector,* and *velocity.*

The social science model   If the social science model is adopted, the metaphors of the physical sciences are dropped. The theorist uses words such as *drift, rebellion, anomie, strain, love,* and *hate* (see Matza, 1969), evocative words that stand in marked contrast to the more precise *vector* or *velocity.* The social science model, which has been heavily influenced by the perspective of the humanities, directs the analyst's attention to what is unique about human conduct. The ideal is "holding human beings up and seeing them for what they are," which immediately turns attention to the arts, literature, and drama, where human emotional experiences are vividly portrayed (Redfield, 1948; Homans, 1950).

An important consequence of the social science–humanities position is the mode of scientific presentation. Commenting on this, Merton (1967, p. 14) states:

> Through the generations, most sociological writing . . . has been in the style of the scientific essay. Unlike the long-established format of papers in the physical and biological sciences, it has only recently become established practice for papers in sociology to set out a compact statement of the problem, the procedures and the instruments of investigation, the empirical findings, a discussion of these, and the theoretical implications of what was found. Past sociological papers and particularly books were written in a style in which the basic concepts were seldom strictly defined, while the logic of procedure and the relationships between variables and the specific theory being developed remained largely implicit, in keeping with the long-established humanist tradition.

This style has had two important consequences for the sociologist. First, underlying concepts, propositions, and definitions are vaguely stated;

consequently, their role in cumulative sociological knowledge remains under-developed. Second, sociologists are continually rediscovering theories and insights in older works. Since so many theorists have adopted the essay form, sociologists must reread their work to discover exactly what was said. Merton (1967, p. 23) states:

> The predilection in the nineteenth century and, in some quarters, today for sociologists to develop their own "systems of sociology" means that these are typically laid out as competing systems of thought rather than into a cumulative product.

Not only do many sociologists attempt to develop their own systems of thought, which works against a cumulative nature for the discipline, but the essay form makes the goal of cumulative growth even more difficult. Contemporary sociologists are caught in a struggle between role models. In one sense, they bow in the direction of the physical sciences and attempt to be precise in their style of presentation, but, as Merton (1967, p. 29) notes:

> In another way, sociology retains its kinship with the humanities. It is reluctant to abandon a firsthand acquaintance with the classical works of sociology and pre-sociology as an integral part of the experience of the sociologist *qua* sociologist. Every contemporary sociologist with a claim to sociological literacy has had direct and repeated encounters with the works of the founding fathers: Comte, Marx and Spencer, Durkheim, Weber, Simmel and Pareto, Sumner, Cooley and Veblen, and the rest of the short list of talented men who have left their indelible stamp on sociology today.

The humanities model   It is important to distinguish between the humanities and social science models. Homans (1950, p. 17) has offered the following analysis:

> The men of letters, novelists and poets, may be, as some tokens suggest, resentful of the social scientists. They see the latter moving into their territory. But they have no reason to be afraid. If the social scientists are to do their job, they must follow a rigorous code, and it could not be better calculated to make their books and articles hard reading. The rules of theory-building contradict the rules of art at every point. Thus the obvious, or what looks like it, is the thing the writer is most careful to avoid. Since most efforts at serious conversation show that it hurts people to think about one thing at a time, a writer uses words that refer to several things at once. He also uses different words for the same thing, or he will be told he lacks variety. For the same reason, he must not repeat himself, whereas systematic discussion is notoriously repetitious, because the same things must be considered in several different connections. Finally, a writer, in a novel or poem, is always concerned with evoking a vivid and integrated sense of concrete reality, either physical or psychological, and his success in doing so is the measure of his charm. A theory begins by breaking up concrete reality and ends by leaving out most of it. The social scientists are not competing, and cannot compete, with the literary artists. They are doing a different job.

In my judgment, Homans has reversed the source of resentment. Sociologists have long been resentful of physical scientists, and this accounts for their continuing attempt to emulate those sciences. Perhaps the discipline would have advanced more rapidly had sociologists emulated novelists and artists. At the very least, the concern for a subject matter that reflected human events would have been cultivated; a sensitivity to human emotions and relationships, most evident in literature, is quite lacking in current sociological theory. If sociologists set for themselves the goal of understanding patterned forms of human behavior, then a valuable source of data for secondary analysis is the poems, novels, paintings, and musical compositions of artists in various historical periods (see Coser, 1963). I am proposing a dual interest in the humanities perspective—as a source of data and as a stimulation for the sociological imagination (see Aries, 1962).

These models—humanities, biological, social, and physical science—represent different ways of going about the job of theory construction. Each poses a different set of metaphors, lays out a different mode of scientific presentation, and stakes out only certain problems for analysis. It would seem apparent that social theory should combine these perspectives. If sociology is to remain close to its subject matter, metaphors must be adopted that reflect this subject. But if sociologists are to move closer to the goal of rigorous theory, some variant of the natural science model is needed. It should be remembered that an interest in the form of theory (for example, logical-deductive theory) must not replace a concern for the content (that is, what it is about—social systems, interaction). The metaphorical thrust of the humanities perspective furnishes the needed emphasis on content. This is not to say that the necessary substantive leads will invariably come from the humanities; they certainly will not, although the "art of social science," as Redfield (1948, p. 189) termed it, is broadened by an exposure to the humanities:

> If the social scientist is to apprehend, deeply and widely and correctly, persons and societies and cultures, then he needs experience, direct or vicarious, with persons, societies and cultures. This experience is partly had through acquaintances with history, literature, biography and ethnography.

Social scientists can employ a humanistic perspective in at least three ways. *First,* they may, as Redfield suggests, use it so as to gain a greater appreciation of the lives of persons in different times and places.

Second, methodologically they may adopt the "narrative" approach of novelists or playwrights. In this case, they attempt to present a moving depiction of the lives and actions of those they have studied. Some have even gone so far as to present data in the form of a play, complete with a cast of characters, acts, and scenes within acts (Bluebond-Langer, 1975). Investigators who adopt the "narrative" approach are often criticized for failing to give an analytic synthesis of their findings. It is sometimes charged that they distort their data to achieve a "dramatic" effect. The late anthropologist Oscar Lewis was often criticized on such counts. While Lewis produced moving accounts of life in cultures of poverty, he seldom gave the reader any systematic clues as to how his data should be understood and analyzed. Some degree of caution must be present when one adopts a "humanistic" perspective.

Third, as humanists, sociologists may make a commitment to ground their work more firmly in the worlds of "real" people. M. Brewster Smith (1974, pp. 1–8) has made efforts to infuse physiological social psychology with a deeper sense of humanism. He remarks:

> When I call for humanizing social psychology . . . I want rather to nudge our faltering social science toward close attention to human experience and human problems. Since, after all, our subject matter is Man, our science may be even better for it.

Humanistic sociology is ethnographic, journalistic, and historical in nature and focuses on the interactions of persons in their natural social worlds. (See Cowie and Roebuck, 1975; Lee, 1972; and Manning, 1973, pp. 200–225.) The researcher who employs the humanistic perspective does not cease to be a social scientist.

Blurred Genres

Geertz (1983, pp. 19–35) argues that a refiguration in current social theory has occurred. The golden age of empiricism in the social science is, if not over, waning. It is being replaced by a plethora of theories, images, models, and metaphors that see society and culture through different lenses, whether these be as (1) a text, (2) a drama, (3) a narrative production, (4) a game, (5) a series of speech acts, (6) a carnival (see Bruner, 1984), or (7) praxis, pragmatics, performance, and experience (Bruner, 1986, p. 22). Older biological models and metaphors, structural-functional models, and positivist paradigms are being replaced by these new images. With these images have come a host of new theories from philosophy and literary criticism, including poststructuralism, neo-Marxism, hermeneutics, feminist theory, semiotics, postpositivist and naturalistic philosophies of science, and deconstructionism. The names of such persons as Derrida, Foucault, Lacan, Barthes, Bakhtin, Benjamin, Althusser, Habermas, Lyotard, Baudrillard, Sartre, Merleau-Ponty, Ricoeur, Heidegger, Gadamer, Burke, and Taylor are associated with these new streams of thought. These authors, and others like them, now read societies as social texts and study cultural productions with the methods of literary, interpretive analysis. They question the relevance of the older natural science models and often work to refute these paradigms (see the essays in Geertz, 1983; Giddens, 1979; Rabinow and Sullivan, 1979; Turner and Bruner, 1986).

The phrase "blurred genres" means that the boundaries between the humanities and the human sciences have become less clear. It means that a growing number of scholars in the social sciences are attempting to understand a wide variety of phenomena, from revolutions to mental hospitals, carnivals, joke telling, tourism, popular music, discourse in AA meetings, and art and theatre worlds from the points of view and methods of aesthetics, linguistics, semiotics, cultural history, and literary criticism. All of this activity is making the social sciences less scientific and more "humanistic" or interpretive. It is altering the way in which science is viewed (Geertz, 1983, p. 8). It is also changing how society and culture are viewed. At the same time, social science writing is changing. It is becoming more essay-like and more self-consciously reflective (see for example Becker, 1985). The social, or human, sciences and the humanities have become truly interdisciplinary.

The Choice of Metaphors, Models, and Values

The career of a sociologist reflects a wide variety of personal choices and decisions. For example, an undergraduate major in the humanities who enters sociology in graduate school is more likely to adopt the stance I have just proposed than one who was an undergraduate in mathematics. The very choice of sociology, as opposed to another discipline, reflects a value-laden line of action, as does the choice of a particular field of specialization (for example, functionalist, interactionist, family specialist). Every sociologist approaches the profession from a spatial and temporal perspective that will never be fully replicated in the experiences of another sociologist. Only in an abstract sense is the common identity of sociologists shared. It is this fact that leads each researcher to take a peculiar line of action as she enters the field of research, selects thesis topics, or prepares lectures. In the final analysis, the selection of metaphors and models of scientific-theoretical conduct is personal. Yet, within the sociological community this selection must be consensual—if only in degree. The position I advocate calls for a movement away from metaphors and models that are alien to the subject matter of sociology.

The Use of Metaphor and Metonymy

As sociologists write, they employ metaphor and metonymy. When something is treated linguistically as if it were or might be something else, metaphor is being used. A novelist "might describe a helicopter hovering over an airfield as if it were an insect" (Lindesmith, Strauss, and Denzin, 1988, p. 90). A writer's work may be described, metaphorically, as "being on the cutting edge," or as "covering a wide terrain," or as "being a massive enterprise." Metaphorical language is poetic. It suggests concrete associations that might not be created if other words were used. Often a writer will use metonymy—the name of one thing is used for that of another related to it— "for example, the bottle for the drink" (Lindesmith, Strauss, and Denzin, 1988, p. 91). The discipline of sociology can be referred to, metonymically, as the ASA. In fact, not all sociologists belong to the ASA; and many do not accept all that the ASA stands for. Metaphor relates things that are similar; it exploits a proposed analogy between a literal object and its metaphorical substitute. Metonymy is "based on the sequential association between the literal object (the president) and its adjacent replacement (the White House, where the president lives)" (Lindesmith, Strauss, and Denzin, 1988, p. 91). The sociologist for the ASA is another example.

There are problems with metaphor and metonymy (see Becker, 1985, pp. 85–89, on metaphor; Lindesmith, Strauss, and Denzin, 1988, pp. 91–92, on metonymy). They can clutter a text. They can imply incorrect meanings. They can be overused and carry no concrete meaning (for example, what does "on the cutting edge" mean?). If they are not taken seriously and if their full implications are not developed, then they don't do the work the writer intends, and should be deleted from the text.

The Language and Rhetoric of Science

It is important to note that the language of science is never neutral. Such terms as *goals, prediction, explanation, control,* or *description* are value-laden. The words that scientists use "create the very reality they seek to describe and analyze" (Gusfield, 1981, p. 84). The social sciences are talking, writing, and reading disciplines. Social science practitioners achieve through their texts "the observability and practical objectivity of their phenomena" (Garfinkel, Lynch, and Livingston, 1981, p. 133). This rather awkward phrase means that sociologists, as Gusfield notes, create the realities they analyze through the texts that they write. Scientific writing is always rhetorical. It involves the use of language in specific ways that are intended to create scientific effects and meanings. Terms like *theory, hypothesis, deduction, induction, falsification,* and *validity* are part of the rhetorical apparatus of science. Science, in these senses, never analyzes an "objective" reality. It studies, instead, the realities that are created through the words that are used.

Writing Social Science

Writing social science involves learning how to think, talk, and write in a new language (see Becker, 1985). This language rests on sociological terms (*role, status, system, function, process, self,* and so on) whose meanings must be learned. Writing this language positions the writer in a particular passive, impersonal relation to the text. Social scientists typically hide behind the words they write; they act as if the text writes itself. In this way, they give an authority to what they write. Such a strategy distances the reader from the text, for it is hard to identify with what the author is saying. Consider the following piece of social science writing (Alexander, 1982, p. 105):

> If, however, an hypostasized conception of free will is accepted, then supra-individual determination will indeed be seen as eliminating voluntarism. When this reified notion is faithfully adhered to, no collective order can be acknowledged by a social theory which is committed also to encompass individual freedom.

What does this text mean? Who is writing it? Where is the author in the text? What do the terms *hypostasized, supra-individual, voluntarism,* and *collective order* mean? The author has created a reality with his text that does not speak to the world of lived experience. This is a text that speaks only to itself. No social scientist should write like this (see Mills, 1959).

THE SUBSTANCE OF SOCIOLOGICAL THEORY

In his indictment of modern sociological theory in 1954, Herbert Blumer traced sociologists' inability to develop sound theory to a misunderstanding of concepts. This charge is still valid and is compounded by a number of other difficulties. Perhaps most basic is a misunderstanding of what theory is and what it consists of. Theory, for the purposes of this book, is interpretation.

Social Theory Defined: The Positivist Position

Surely the most often voiced term in modern sociology, *theory* has had attached to it multiple levels of meaning and interpretation. Models are called "theories," classical sociological criticism passes for theory, as do exercises in metatheory, the history of theory, formal theory construction, syntheses of existing bodies of theory, conceptual frameworks, and interconnected sets of propositions. In the following section I will develop the positivist view of theory, and then contrast that view to several other forms of theory-work. It is important to keep in mind the definition of theory just given (that is, as a body of propositions), and to compare that view to the theory-as-interpretation position, which I take.

It is useful to begin with Homans (1964), whose work embodies the logical positivist position on theory (but also see Wallace, 1983, pp. 399, 402–6, for a recent statement of the logical positivist position). To paraphrase Homans, *theory* refers to a set of propositions that are interrelated in an ordered fashion such that some may be deducible from others, thus permitting an explanation to be developed for the phenomenon under consideration (1964, p. 951). A theory is a set of propositions that furnish an explanation by means of a deductive system. Theory is explanation. Durkheim's theory of suicide in Spain conforms to the foregoing specifications. It states the following: (1) In any social grouping, the suicide rate varies directly with the degree of individualism (egoism); (2) the degree of individualism varies with the incidence of Protestantism; (3) therefore, the suicide rate varies with the incidence of Protestantism; (4) the incidence of Protestantism in Spain is low; (5) therefore, the suicide rate in Spain is low.

General Characteristics of Social Theory

From this example I can now describe the central features of social theory. It consists first of a set of concepts that forms a conceptual scheme. Some of these concepts, as Homans notes, are descriptive and serve to show what the theory is about (individualism, suicide, and Protestantism). Others are operative, or relational, and specify empirical relationships between other elements in the theory (rate and incidence, when combined with suicide and Protestantism, specify such relationships; Durkheim's theory predicts conditions under which suicide rates would be high and low by specifying the relationship between individualism and religion). But taken alone, "a conceptual scheme is insufficient to constitute a theory" (Homans, 1964, p. 952). A theory must contain a set of propositions or hypotheses that combine descriptive and relational concepts. Propositions state a relationship, such as "Suicide rates vary directly with the degree of egoism in a society." Propositions must describe a relationship between two or more elements in a conceptual scheme.

Unfortunately, a set of propositions taken alone does not constitute a theory. The set must be placed in a deductive scheme. Durkheim achieved this feature by deducing his proposition 3 from propositions 1 and 2. Proposition 5, in turn, is derived from 3 and 4. "When propositions are so derived they are said to be explained and a theory is nothing if it is not explanation" (Homans, 1964, p. 952).

When a deductive system provides explanation, it also permits prediction. That is, while Durkheim explained the low rate of suicide in Spain by his theory, he could also have predicted suicide rates elsewhere. If, for instance, one did not know what the suicide rate in Eire was, but did know that the incidence of Protestantism was low, this proposition, together with proposition 3, would allow one to predict that the suicide rate there was low too (Homans, 1964, p. 952).

Theory, as the postivists define it, meets the goals of sociology. It permits the organization of descriptions, leads to explanations, and furnishes the basis for the prediction of events as yet unobserved. Only when all these features are present will social theory be said to exist; the absence of any element renders the final product something less than theory. Given this position, it is clear that contemporary sociology has few, if any, theories (but see Berger, Zelditch, and Anderson, 1966, for exceptions to this conclusion). There exist, instead, small attempts at theory, many conceptual frameworks, a few propositional systems without deductive schemes, and, more often than not, vague explanations that bear little formal relationship to theory (Maines and Molseed, 1986).

What often passes for theory in sociology, moreover, is not theory. Instead there are various types of theory-work, ranging from ad hoc classificatory systems to categorical systems, taxonomies, and vaguely interrelated conceptual schemes. In the following section, the most common designations of theory-work will be discussed.

What Theory Is Not: Levels of Theory-Work

There are at least five levels of theory-work: (1) ad hoc classificatory systems, (2) categorical systems or taxonomies, (3) conceptual frameworks, (4) theoretical systems, and (5) empirical-theoretical systems (Parsons and Shils, 1959, pp. 47–52).

Ad hoc classificatory systems   The ad hoc classificatory system consists of more or less arbitrary classes constructed for the sake of summarizing data. No attempt is made to fit classes to data so that relations between variables and dimensions can be summarized; the classes are independent of one another. This is basically a method of organizing observations so that more sophisticated theory development can follow. Examples include such schemes of analysis as Gordon's proposal for the treatment of responses to the "Who am I?" test, which proposes 30 categories for answers (1968, pp. 115–36). These answers range from an uncodable category to statements reflecting interpersonal style, situational references, material references, and statements describing ascriptive characteristics (such as age, sex, and name). Gordon's scheme is ad hoc in nature because a large proportion of his categories are not theoretically derived; they have been constructed to fit the data. To the extent that they are later placed within a theoretical scheme, they serve their function as theory-work, but ad hoc classificatory schemes are not theory.

Categorical systems or taxonomies   The *categorical system*, or taxonomy, is a movement beyond the ad hoc classification. It consists of a system of classes constructed to fit the subject matter so that relationships among classes can be described. There is often an interdependence between classes, so that classification into one category demands treatment in another. The system should bear a close relationship to empirical reality, and in this sense the categories mirror the reality described.

Taxonomies perform several functions for the sociologist. First, they specify a unit of reality to be analyzed (in Parsons' use, social systems) and indicate how that unit may be described (Zetterberg, 1965, pp. 24–28). Such definitions tell the sociologist what to look for, but they are primarily descriptions, not analytical explanations. Thus, the second function of the taxonomy is to "summarize and inspire *descriptive studies*" (Zetterberg, 1965, p. 26). Commenting on Parsons' framework, Zetterberg notes that his taxonomy of the pattern variables guided Stouffer and Toby "to a descriptive study which presented the distribution of some college students on the variable 'particularism-universalism'" (1965, p. 26). The taxonomy does not offer explanations; it only describes behavior by fitting it into a series of classes or categories. One of the basic goals of the positivist sociologist is the development of viable descriptive schemes that anticipate explanatory and predictive theories; this is the chief contribution of the taxonomy.

Erving Goffman's work, especially *Frame Analysis* (1974), reflects the powerful attraction of the ad hoc classificatory scheme and the taxonomy in contemporary sociological theory. *Frame Analysis* was widely acclaimed as Goffman's magnum opus (see Collins, 1985, pp. 215–20), yet the text turned primarily on an ad hoc classificatory scheme that organized everyday social experience into a series of oppositional categories (natural versus social frameworks, and so on). It did not offer a theory, in the propositional, formal, or conceptual senses of the word (see Denzin and Keller, 1981); at best it was a complex taxonomy that fitted social experiences into its conceptual, taxonomic structure.

Conceptual frameworks   The conceptual framework stands above the taxonomy. Here descriptive categories are placed within a broad structure of both explicit and assumed propositions. The theory of symbolic interaction is best termed a conceptual framework. Concepts such as "self," "object," "act," "interaction," and "socialization" are used to analyze the data, and a systematic image of the empirical world is assumed.

Much of what now passes as theory in sociology is really conceptual frameworks that systematically direct empirical and theoretical activity around a core set of problems (such as interaction, mental illness, or stigma). Because of this directive function, the conceptual framework offers the best hope for development of systematic theory.

Theoretical systems   The theoretical system moves closer to ideal theory. It represents a combination of taxonomies and conceptual schemes, but now descriptions and predictions are combined in a deductive fashion. Zetterberg's axiomatic presentation of Durkheim's theory of the division of labor

(1955, pp. 533–40) is an instance of a theoretical system. Theoretical systems are distinguished, somewhat arbitrarily, from *empirical-theoretical systems* by their lack of a precise empirical base.

Empirical-theoretical systems   The empirical-theoretical system represents the highest level of theory development. With it sociologists can move easily directly from theory to empirical propositions and observations. This level of theory-work contains all the elements theory should have — but there are few clear representations of this type of theory in contemporary sociology.

Postmodern Social Theory

The foregoing classifications of levels of theory-work does not speak to what a theory theorizes about. While the internal content of theory will be discussed, in a moment, it is necessary to make brief reference to what has recently been termed "postmodern" social theory (see Denzin, 1986a, for a review). Postmodern theory is both a form of theorizing about societies and a period in social thought (Denzin, 1986a, p. 194). As a form of theorizing it is characterized by a departure from attempts to develop grand theories or grand schemes about societies as totalities. It reflects a profound distrust of empirical-theoretical or purely theoretical, axiomatic, deductive schemes of thought. It reflects an attempt to make sense out of the post–World War II period of life in the world economy today. It examines how the mass media and computerized forms of knowledge shape everyday life. It studies how modern experience has become commodified and bought and sold in the marketplace (much as tourism, higher education, and religion have been).

Postmodern theory has emerged within the last decade, although C. Wright Mills used the term in 1959 (see Mills, 1959, p. 166). The names Foucault (1973, 1980), Derrida (1981), Lyotard (1979/1984), and Baudrillard (1983) are associated with this movement of social thought. Postmodern social theory reflects a break with the structural-functional, conflict, dramaturgical, symbolic interactionist, ethnomethodological, and structuration theories that have held sociologists' attention for the last several decades. It challenges positivist versions of theory construction. Empirically, it rests on detailed, close-up, documentary, ethnographic, and historical readings of specific social situations and institutions.

Tyler (1986, pp. 122–40), an anthropologist, has attributed the following characteristics to postmodern ethnography: (1) it is the discourse of the postmodern world — it is about the world that science made; (2) it is poetic, and its texts consist of fragments of discourse that are intended to evoke in the minds of the reader and writer "an emergent fantasy of a possible world of commonsense reality" (Tyler, 1986, p. 125); (3) it attempts to create texts that "evoke" the sense of fragmentary postmodern experience; (4) it does not make the observer an "objective" recorder of experience; rather, it locates the researcher in the center of the research act and makes no claim to objectivity; (5) it "goes against the grain of induction, deduction (and) synthesis (Tyler, 1986, p. 133); and (6) it works from the basic premise that all cultures are fragmentary, conflictual, processual, and always in motion (Bruner, 1986). Postmodern theory and ethnography work together; indeed, they are indistinguishable.

THE CONTENT OF THEORIES: POSITIVIST
AND POSTPOSITIVIST FORMULATIONS

Concepts

As an image of reality, concepts are perhaps the most critical element in any theory. Yet while one function of theory is to identify concepts for examination, the concept itself may turn back on a theory and become the major flaw in an otherwise excellent system. This is often the case in theoretical systems with vague, ill-defined, or inappropriately measured concepts.

A concept carries with it what all definitions of social objects contain: It designates and suggests a plan of action toward some social object. For example, the concept of self, which occupies a central position in the interactionist framework, is seen as a series of definitions persons hold toward themselves as social objects. Sociologists interested in observing this object have typically assumed that one strategy is to ask persons who they are. This simple question elicits self-definitions and can be seen as following from the definition given that object in the interactionist perspective.

When placed within a theoretical system, concepts become its major designating units. Concepts *define* the shape and content of theories. In the example from Durkheim, his major descriptive concepts were suicide, individualism, and Protestantism.

In addition to their designating function, concepts perform at least three other functions (Blumer, 1931). First, they introduce a new *orientation* or *point of view* into the scientific process. Second, they serve as tools or as means of translating perceptions of the environment into meaningful scientific dialogue and operations. Third, they make possible deductive reasoning and, thus, the anticipation of new experience and perceptions.

Ideally, the sociological concept permits new perceptions of reality by opening previously unexplored avenues of thought. Once this occurs, the concept will specify lines of empirical activity. If this happens, the sociologist will place observations into propositional schemes of reasoning—in short, into theory. At each of these steps, theory and methodological activity take on increasing importance. Research methods serve to operationalize the concept; theory both stimulates new concepts and provides a framework within which emergent propositions are placed.

Scientific Concepts versus Everyday Concepts

While all concepts propose lines of action toward social objects, scientific concepts must meet certain criteria. They must be consensually defined within the community of scientists. When Durkheim states that suicide rates vary by the degree of egoism, it is assumed that other sociologists know what he means. Everyday concepts seldom possess this quality; often they are not consensually defined, and most frequently they refer to what is sensed, not what is analyzed. Furthermore, the everyday concept lacks the development toward systematization that the scientific concept must have. In short, the scientific concept is continually evaluated by the canons of science; the everyday concept is evaluated by its ability to give order to the life of its users — everyday people. (See the earlier discussion in Chapter 1.)

These points can be illustrated by examining the concept "self." For the symbolic interactionist, *self* refers to a very special set of events. Within the theoretical system it is accorded high priority, and a number of tests and strategies have been developed for its measurement. The "Who am I?" test is but one of many. Kuhn and McPartland (1954, p. 68) have described the uneven scientific career of this concept as follows:

> Although the self has long been the central concept in the symbolic interaction approach to social psychology, little if anything has been done to employ it directly in empirical research. There are several reasons for this, one of the most important of which is that there has been no consensus regarding the class of phenomena to which the self ought to be operationally ordered. The self has been called an image, a conception, a concept, a feeling, an internalization, a self looking at oneself, and most commonly simply the self (with perhaps the most ambiguous implications of all).

The self as a concept has had a career, if an uneven one. Often the uneven careers of scientific concepts can work to the detriment of sound empirical and theoretical reasoning. When theorists fail to adequately formulate the meanings they give their critical concepts, they perpetuate myths and stereotypes about the phenomena in question. One concept that fits this situation is the concept "culture of poverty" and its related counterpart "cultural deprivation." (See Valentine, 1968.) Sociological and anthropological theorists from Frazier to Miller, Matza, and Lewis have repeatedly invoked the concept of a culture of poverty to explain why it is that the poor remain poor. They remain poor, culturally deprived, and educationally disadvantaged because their culture stresses values antithetical to work, savings, and sound economy. These scholars typically assume that everyone knows what a culture is, although they seldom bother to define the concept. Persons who live in the culture of poverty are there because they are deprived, and their culture keeps them deprived. It is difficult to know whether these theorists believe that deprivation precedes or follows location in a deprived culture of poverty. The causal links are neither empirically nor logically analyzed. The typical conclusion reached by most users of this concept is that the culture of poverty will remain as long as its users believe in it. In this sense the concept perpetuates that which it purports to illuminate and eventually eradicate.

If scientific concepts have careers of varying evenness, however, everyday concepts seldom do. Blumer (1931, pp. 522-23) notes:

> To my mind, the chief difference is that the abstraction embodied in the common-sense concept is just accepted and is not made the subject of special

analysis and study. Consequently abstraction is soon arrested and not pushed to the length that is true in the case of scientific concepts. . . . The common-sense concepts are sufficient for the crude demands of ordinary experience. Minor elements of inconsistency within experiences and a fringe of uncertainty can be ignored and are ignored. Hence experiences that might be productive of more refined abstractions do not arise as problems.

With such a background it is to be expected that "common sense," as the term strongly suggests, refers to what is sensed, instead of what is acutely analyzed.

That Blumer's position is correct is documented when a sociologist proposes to ask an ordinary individual what he means by a common-sense term. The individual takes its meaning for granted, and if pressed for an explanation, is likely to point to the reference of the designation. The person is not likely to show how that term relates to several others in a deductive scheme, as a scientist properly would. While persons daily make references to themselves and in so doing employ the concept "self," they do so without the heightened criticalness of the scientist.

Everyday interaction, based as it is on "assumed" understandings, lacks the critical nature of scientific dialogue. Individuals often "act as if" they understand one another, when in fact each has only a rough understanding of what the other is thinking or has just said. Garfinkel (1967, pp. 40–43), in an essay on ethnomethodology, which is a scientific attempt to understand how persons construct their own definitions of a situation, offers the following transcript of a conversation between a husband and wife. Garfinkel (1967, p. 43) has instructed the wife (*E*, "experimenter") to engage an acquaintance in a conversation and to insist that the person talked to (*S*, "subject") clarify the meaning of his remarks.

On Friday night my husband and I were watching television. My husband remarked that he was tired. I asked, "How are you tired? Physically, mentally, or just bored?"
  (S) I don't know; I guess physically, mainly.
  (E) You mean that your muscles ache, or your bones?
  (S) I guess so. Don't be so technical.
    (*After more watching*)
  (S) All these old movies have the same kind of iron bedstead in them.
  (E) What do you mean? Do you mean all old movies, or some of them, or just the ones you have seen?
  (S) What's the matter with you? You know what I mean.
  (E) I wish you would be more specific.
  (S) You know what I mean! Drop dead!

While sociological concepts have careers, they still have a great deal in common with everyday concepts. This is so because ultimately the subject matter of sociology is "precisely the matter about which people have convictions, prejudices, hates, the things about which they praise or blame one another." Hence, "it would be rather too much to expect our concepts to be as free of popular feeling and distortion as are most names in chemistry or physics" (Hughes and Hughes, 1952, p. 131). Hughes's observations point to one of the major problems of all sociological concepts. With few exceptions they have been derived from the modern English language. Words like *role, self, interaction, deviance, system, illness, observe, analyze,* and *record* have histories of usage that may extend back several hundred years. Rose (1960) estimates that the majority of sociological concepts now in use appeared with some regularity in the English language by about 1600. On the one hand, sociological concepts must have an everyday relevance. This is so because they should be derived from close-up studies of interacting individuals. On the other hand, they must have a meaning that is strictly sociological. If they do not, they become subject to the same ambiguities as everyday terms.

The Definition

Behind most concepts is a definition that permits the sociologist to move from the concept to a single case or instance of it. Definitions intervene between the perception of an instance of a concept and the operational process of acting on that instance. Thus, definitions attached to concepts become critical links in the theory process; they assist in the movement toward the second function of the concept — to facilitate observation. Returning to the example of the self, it can be seen that by defining the self as answers to the "Who am I?" test, the sociologist has moved from a conception of the object to its observation.

Because definitions occupy such an important role in the total structure of a theory, a series of ideal standards or norms are associated with their use. Definitions must be exact and state what they do and do not apply to. To state that the self is measured by answers to the "Who am I?" test precisely designates an empirical referent of that concept. Negative definitions ("The self is not the sum total of the attitudes a person holds") do not provide direct specifications for observation; they only tell what not to look for.

In addition to being exact and positive, definitions should be phrased in precise scientific terminology, not in everyday, common-sense terms. (The scientific definition is subject to the norms of consistency, precision, and criticalness.) Finally, definitions should not contain the term they propose to define. A tautological definition defines by naming and serves no designating function. If, for example, *self* is defined as "self-attitudes held toward the self," no external referent for its observation is given.

The sociologist may employ four types of definitions — nominal, real, operational, and sensitizing — in moving from concepts to observations.

Nominal definitions   First are nominal definitions, which "are declarations of intention to use a certain word or phrase as a substitute for another word or phrase" (Bierstedt, 1959, p. 126). One might, for example, define the concept "self" by the symbol S and use only that symbol when referring to the self.

Real definitions   The second major type of definition is the real defini-tion. It differs from the nominal definition because it "operates not only on the symbolic or linguistic level but also on the referential level" (Bierstedt, 1959, p. 126). A real definition gives meaning to a concept by resolving it into its constituent elements. For example, a social group might be defined as a number of persons called "members" who interact with one another. In this case, the concept is broken into elements (person, member, interaction). By combining these elements, symbolic meaning is given to the term. In addi-tion, specifications for its observation are offered. Real definitions take the form of propositions because they place a number of elements together in a relational system.

Operational definitions   The third major type of definition is opera-tional. This type relates a concept to the process by which it will be mea-sured. An operational definition of the self could be responses to the "Who am I?" test.

Sensitizing definitions   The fourth type of definition is sensitizing. A sensitizing definition of the self might state that an individual's self-concep-tion is conveyed in his hairstyle or style of dress. A sensitizing definition contains a prediction. It links a concept to social behavior. It sensitizes, or directs, the observer's activities to a class of events. Once the investigator has entered the field, more rigorous operational and relational definitions of the critical concepts may be employed.

The Hypothesis or Proposition

The next element of positivist theory that must be considered is the hypothesis. A hypothesis, or proposition (I view them as identical), is defined as a statement of relationship between two or more concepts. Durkheim's statement "In any social grouping, the suicide rate varies with the degree of egoism" is a proposition. It expresses an interrelationship between more than one concept. They combine concepts in an explanatory and predictive man-ner. A proposition can be no better than the elements that it comprises (concepts and definitions). In turn, concepts can be of no greater utility than the plans of action derived from them. And, last, definitions are of little value unless the concepts they define are ordered in a propositional system. There is a complex interdependence between all the elements of theory thus far discussed. A weak concept, definition, or proposition flaws any theory.

Because concepts represent tentative ways of looking at reality, proposi-tions become tentative statements concerning the occurrence and interrela-tionship of events in the empirical world. Propositions occupy the same tentative and processual position in theory as concepts and definitions do. Durkheim's propositions regarding suicide represent the cardinal feature of all propositions: They state relationships between two or more concepts where one element in the proposition is assumed to be the cause of another. In Durkheim's first proposition, egoism is assumed to be the cause of suicide.

That concept seen as causal is termed a *causal, determinant,* or *independent factor*; that concept which is caused is the *resultant, caused,* or *dependent variable*. When a proposition states an empirically observable event, the concepts it combines are variables. In some cases these variables have two values (for example, "present" or "not present"); in other cases they take values of degree ("greater" or "less"); in still other cases, differences in degree is expressed in terms of a unit of measurement ("income in dollars").

Any set of propositions must meet the following criteria. First, the status of the related concepts must be so clearly defined that it is apparent which is caused and which is causal. Unless readers can unequivocally determine this, it is difficult for them to work with the proposition. Zetterberg illustrated this rule in his discussion of Max Weber's book, *The Protestant Ethic and the Spirit of Capitalism*. He noted that Weber's work has been misunderstood because it fails to precisely state its key proposition (1965, p. 67). Its proposition is hinted in its very title: The Protestant ethic is the determinant, and the spirit of capitalism is the result. There are, however, at least four different ways of specifying the determinant and the result in this proposition. If the terms in italics stand for the variates that may be related, we have these possibilities:

1. The *Protestant* Ethic and the Spirit of *Capitalism*
2. The Protestant *Ethic* and the Spirit of *Capitalism*
3. The *Protestant* Ethic and the *Spirit* of Capitalism
4. The Protestant *Ethic* and the *Spirit* of Capitalism

There are four possible propositions stated in Weber's title. The first suggests a comparison of persons who are Protestants and become capitalists with non-Protestants who become capitalists. The fourth assumes "that some ethical precepts in Protestantism lead to a particular spirit which is manifested in a concern for one's material wealth and prestige" (Zetterberg, 1965, p. 68). Zetterberg suggests that

> All four ways of interpreting the thesis are in varying degrees present in Weber. Also, Weber's critics often touch upon some of these ways of interpreting the thesis in a haphazard way. Thus, claims by his critics that Weber has been proved right or wrong are usually restricted to one or two of these possibilities. Much confusion could have been avoided if the determinant and the result of the proposition had been more clearly specified.

Second, propositions must be so stated that they can be tested. In general, the more varied the tests of a proposition, the greater its power.

The third positivist rule states that propositions should be combined with other propositions so that a deductive theoretical system can be developed. Unless this combination is achieved, the explanatory power of any proposition is greatly reduced.

Fourth, propositions should be stated so that they predict and explain the domain specified by the concepts. If they do not, they remain at the level of description and do little to move the sociologist closer toward theory.

Fifth, some theoretical propositions must contain higher-order concepts. It is quite easy to formulate propositions of an ordinary nature. These are likely to contain few, if any, higher-order concepts and therefore contribute little to theory development. In Durkheim's theory, the proposition "Spain has a low suicide rate because the incidence of Protestantism is low" is relatively low-level, although it does permit a large body of data to be organized. Durkheim's higher-order proposition concerning rates of suicide and degree of egoism is much more powerful and more adequately meets this test. (See Stinchcombe, 1968, pp. 18–22.)

Sixth, propositions must be stated in terms of the normal rules of concepts and definitions. They must be positive and not negative; must be precise and stated in scientific terms; must not be tautological; and must be capable of being tested—logically, empirically, or operationally.

Seventh, propositions must be capable of reflecting both process and stability. The most common propositions in sociology take the form of direct relationships which assume that one variable simply causes variations in another (see Homans, 1964, p. 956–59). Durkheim's proposition concerning variations in suicide rates represents this kind of proposition. It is argued that as rates of egoism change, so too does the rate of suicide. There is nothing inherently wrong with these propositions—the problem is that virtually all propositions in contemporary sociology are stated in this form—ignoring the fact that a large proportion of human behavior involves situations in which variables interact in such a way that as one changes value, so too does the other. But this is not a one-way change, as Durkheim assumed in his analysis of suicide. In cases of interaction, variables mutually influence one another. (This rule was discussed in Chapter 1.) Becker's analysis of the marijuana user illustrates this type of proposition.

Eighth, some propositions should be stated so that they express the temporal and situational context under explanation. To understand any relationship, it is necessary to understand the context in which it exists. The necessity of expressing these references in the proposition derives from the fundamental fact that the social events sociologists analyze are embedded in ongoing units of social organization. Unless statements concerning the social nexus of these events can be made, propositions are reduced in explanatory power.

I have stated eight rules for the proposition:

1. The causal status of all elements in the proposition must be established unequivocally.
2. The proposition must be stated so that it is testable in more than one way. Common tests include logical consistency and operational and empirical adequacy.
3. Propositions should be placed within a deductive system.
4. Propositions must predict and explain the domain under analysis.

5. Some propositions must contain at least some concepts of high theoretical value.
6. Propositions must be stated in terms of the normal rules of concepts and definitions.
7. Propositions must be capable of reflecting both process and stability.
8. Some propositions should be expressed in a manner that permits temporal and spatial specifications.

Properties and Types of Propositions

Propositions give theory its quality of explanation. They represent an advance beyond concept development and permit the construction of deductive schemes. Sociologists have at their disposal a number of different types of propositions. Propositions can be categorized in terms of the number of concepts combined; their causal breadth (for example, the number of cases explained); the relationship between concepts (interactive, direct, and so on); and the causal status assigned to the independent variable (interchangeability with other independent variables).

THE ORDERING OF THEORIES

Ordering propositions into a theoretical scheme is conventionally seen as the logical outcome of concept formulation, construction of definitions, and the collection of data. In this conventional view, the axiomatic method of ordering propositions has become a major strategy. With it, certain propositions are treated as axioms, and from them theorems, or lower-order predictions, are derived. Concepts are viewed as either basic or derived. Basic concepts are introduced without definition, and derived concepts are constructed from them. The ordering of propositions then follows the simple rules of syllogistic logic, as Durkheim's theory of suicide illustrated; that is, certain propositions are logically deducted from other, higher-order, predictions. Durkheim's proposition 5, for example, is deduced from his propositions 3 and 4. (See Chapter 3 for additional discussion of ordering theories.)

Zetterberg (1955, pp. 533–40) has argued that the axiomatic method has the virtues of organizing previously unconceptualized data, permitting the location of strategic research areas, and allowing the construction of explanatory schemes through deduction. I do not quarrel with these points: Any theory should do exactly what Zetterberg says the axiomatic theory does. The basic problem with the axiomatic method—as Costner and Leik indicate (1964, pp. 819–35)—is that empirical reality seldom conforms to it. The axiomatic method as it currently stands does not adequately handle propositions with asymmetrically correlated variables. Nor does it satisfactorily treat situations of interactive causation. In the ideal axiomatic system, sufficient causes have been located to permit the direct deduction of propositions. Empirical reality seldom conforms to causal models where sufficient conditions can be located. For these reasons, the axiomatic method is of limited value. Its chief virtue is its ability to serve as a check for theorists as they formulate propositions. By following the rules of logical deduction, implicit or overlooked propositions can be formalized. Theorists, in general, employ a far looser and more imprecise model of theory construction; included in this activity is the method of insight, or introspection, as Cooley (1926) termed it.

Theory-Work and the Method of Insight

The assumption that significant sociological work does not occur within the confines of rigorous models of inference is best stated by Weber (1985, p. 136):

> Ideas occur to us when they please, and not when it pleases us. The best ideas do indeed occur to one's mind in the way in which Ihering describes it: when smoking a cigar on the sofa; or as Helmholz states of himself with scientific exactitude: when taking a walk on a slowly ascending street; or in a similar way. In any case, ideas come when we do not expect them, and not when we are brooding and searching at our desks. Yet ideas would certainly not come to mind had we not brooded at our desks and searched for answers with passionate devotion.

Once this view of the creative process is accepted, a major problem confronting any scientist is the stimulation of a psychological state in which new ideas can appear. In this sense no scientists can ever separate their personal and public lives. They are continually thinking about, puzzling over, and troubled about unsolved issues. As Weber states: "In the field of science only he who is devoted *solely* to the work at hand has 'personality' " (1958, p. 137). The scientist, like all humans, is forever conversing with himself, checking out plans of action, experimenting with new formulations, combining contradictory events, and judging future action against what has succeeded and failed in the past. It is in the arena of private conversations with the self that new ideas appear, propositions are constructed, and predictions take place. Only after these ideas are transferred to the written page, or communicated orally to others, does the scientific process become public. Zetterberg's axiomatic method leaps too rapidly from the private to the public arena of discourse.

Several features of this private side of science may be noted. First, scientist must accept the fact that their own experiences probably provide the most important sources of data for their theories. Blumer (1964, p. 121) has described the role of personal experiences in Mead's theory of interaction as follows:

> Mead was intensely preoccupied with cardinal matters which are present in every human society. He was concerned with such fundamental questions as how do human beings fit their lines of activity to another, what is the nature of communication, what is the nature of objects, how do objects come into being, how does the human being become an object to himself, . . . how is human action constructed. Mead worked out his answers to these fundamental questions not by postulating an ideal society, but by close and persistent observation of those around him and of himself. Where is there a more directly presented

and ever accessible area of empirical happening for inquiry into the nature of human communication than the daily conversations one has with one's fellows? Where does one have a richer body of recurring instances of human beings fitting their lines of action to one another than that which takes place under one's nose? . . . The natural happenings which set the cardinal problems of human action occur continuously in the area of immediate experience and observation. It was such natural happenings that constructed the empirical matters that Mead studied with care, with persistence, and with his unusual gifts of originality.

Blumer's description suggests that a closely related source of data is the experiences one shares with other acquaintances — whether they are friends closely observed or fellow colleagues. Indeed, theories of deviance, of labeling, or of socialization may be empirically grounded (initially at least) through observations of one's friends. Cooley (1922), for example, developed his theory of self and socialization through systematic observations of his own children. Gross and Stone (1963) expanded a theory of interaction and the functions of embarrassment partially in terms of experiences of embarrassment furnished by friends and colleagues. And while introspective moments of insight may suffer from biases of observation, it is the function of rules of inference and design to give them scientific rigor.

Mills has given perhaps the most complete statement on the creative frame of reference (1959, pp. 195–226). His suggestions call for continuous note-taking and introspection. Files and complex cross-referencing systems can be constructed; and whenever a new idea, reference, or finding is discovered, it is placed in the appropriate file. In Mills's system, the scientist is often involved in several projects simultaneously — thus all of his creative energies can be relevant to at least one of those projects. Mills also suggests the deliberate confrontation of contradictory elements, echoing Hughes's directive that a fundamental principle of social inquiry is the study of contradictory social types — for example, the comparison of prostitutes and psychiatrists, or physicians and plumbers (Hughes, 1956, pp. 42–55). This raises the related principle that one should continually think in a comparative manner. The experiences of patients in mental hospitals might profitably be highlighted by studying college students, since they also occupy positions in a total institution.

These suggestions of Weber, Mead, Blumer, Hughes, Glaser, Strauss, and Mills leave unanswered the basic question of how a researcher moves from insights to social theory. No pat answer can be given. Every scientist works somewhat differently. Some prefer complex filing systems; others never make so much as a marginal note in a book.

It has proved useful to interpret social experiences from the sociological perspective. Notes to oneself, predictions of forthcoming interactions, and after-the-fact explanations of what has just occurred become valuable ways of developing emerging theory. It is useful to test different social theories against the same body of experiences. Goffman's dramaturgical theory of interaction can be loosely tested by bringing Homans's exchange perspective or Parsons' functional theory to bear upon the same empirical event. The researcher can test the utility of each of these perspectives by forcing each to explain and predict what has just occurred.

If such a stance toward social experience is taken, the sociological imagination is stimulated. When an investigator attempts to fit propositions together into a theoretical system, all of her past experiences, predictions, and observations can be channeled toward the problem at hand. It no longer becomes necessary to check out unstated propositions; these should all be present in one's mind, in some form or another.

Mead's suggestion that the scientist should never accept prior interpretation at face value is useful. It demands that one's own achievement be measured by the degree to which new theory has been formulated. Each sociologist becomes his own theorist and methodologist. But above all, a critical view of all other work must permeate sociological activity; every sociologist is thus accountable for knowing, if only roughly, all that has been done before in the area under study. At some point, reviews of the literature must be conducted, and every sociologist must become a miniature, self-contained representation of the total discipline. Colleagues become sounding boards for new ideas, but their suggestions and interpretations are not taken for granted. A dialectic of respect and disrespect underlies this view of the sociological imagination: On the one hand, knowledge of the past is required; on the other, as Mead suggests, nothing is taken for granted.

The true test of insight is whether or not the researcher is troubled about the work. If it is impossible to relax, if problems keep appearing in one's consciousness, it is safe to assume that the imagination is at work. The sociological self is in process, but it is a self troubled over the development of new ideas and the resolution of problems.

A work schedule is important. Time must be set aside for thinking, for writing, and for reading. Time must also be allocated for interactions with other sociologists — whether in the classroom, the living room, the office, or a bar. It is useful to set a work and writing schedule; the activity of a day can be measured by the number of words written, the number of pages read, or the number of new ideas developed. Unfortunately, the researcher must be prepared for nonproductive periods; schedules will be interrupted or set aside. New ideas, as Weber suggests, do not come at specified times during the day. The best that can be hoped for is the creation of conditions conducive to work and insight.

The movement from insights to propositions and ultimately to theory follows from the continual focus on a core problem or set of issues. Problems and questions, not theory, create new perspectives.

At some point in the reflective process, a series of tentative solutions, often expressed as propositions, begins to emerge. The examination of these leads to other predictions, new concepts, and renewed empirical activity. As observations in the empirical world confirm tentative predictions, additional scope is added, and relationships with previous research are discovered. At this point theorists begin to consider the public nature of their formulations. When they move from self-conversations to public discourse, the medium of scientific communication forces alterations in their perspective; their presentation becomes formal. Propositions move from imprecision to precise statements; rules of evidence and inference are adopted; standard styles of exposition are utilized. Variations in the use of inference, propositions, and exposition give each scientist a personal style, but similarity between scientists will be present.

At some point in time researchers must, as Schatzman and Strauss note, "let go" (1973, p. 137). That is, researchers must move from the oral realm of ideas and conversation into the public realm of the printed page or the typed word. They must take a public stance on their own ideas and research findings. They must be prepared to present their own version of the social realities they have studied. They must be prepared to accept the fact that their work will be open to criticism and (in their own mind) perhaps unfair evaluation. It is unlikely that any reader of their work will fully understand or comprehend it or the energy and frustrations that were involved in the decision to "let go." But if researchers' published findings are to be of value to people other than the armchair sociologist, they must be recognizable and somewhat intelligible to research informants and respondents.

As the reflective process reaches completion, what began as an attempt to answer a specific question becomes a fully developed theory. Even if theory in the precise sense is not developed, interrelated propositions, clearly defined hypotheses, and bodies of data will be present. At no point in this process will the sociological imagination cease to work and give way to formal rules of inference and design. But unless rules of method are employed, insight suffers from a lack of direction. Conversely, theory does not arise from a knowledge of theory construction or data analysis, from the presence of typewriters, comfortable desks, and well-intentioned colleagues. Interaction must exist between all these elements.

ON THE VERIFICATION VERSUS THE FALSIFICATION OF THEORIES

How is it that theorists know their actions are valid? This is the question of theory verification. Several criteria can be employed to test or verify a theory.

The first and most basic test is the ability of a theory to generate valid causal propositions; if it cannot do this, it is not a theory. In Chapter 1 it was suggested that all causal propositions contain three elements: demonstration of time order, covariance, and the exclusion of rival hypotheses. Theories must also meet these criteria.

A second verificational test is logic. Once a system is constructed, the first test is that of logic.

The third test is the power of a theory to illuminate or make more understandable an area that has not been examined before or has been examined by another theory. If the theory cannot do as well as a theory that already exists, it fails this test.

But all these tests are of little value until it is realized that research methods provide the fundamental test of all theories. It is through their use that the data necessary to test any theory are gathered. Through the use of research methods elements of the causal proposition are brought together, and new observations are brought forth to modify, verify, and change the theory under examination. Methods work hand in hand with theories in the verificational process.

This inductivist position has several problems. First, it cannot provide the grounds for universal predictions, for every instance of a phenomenon can potentially refute a prediction. Second, the appeal to logic — that is, a prediction derived from a logically consistent proposition — cannot speak to empirical irregularities. Suppose a theory predicts that it never rains on Wednesday, and this observation holds for 100 Wednesdays in a row. On the 101st Wednesday, it rains. The theory cannot explain this variation. Third, this position fails to specify the circumstances under which a prediction will hold true (every Wednesday, for example, or only a certain percent of Wednesdays). The retreat to statistics and probability statements merely offers one verbal theory for another and does not address the basic underlying problem of when a theory is true or false (Chalmers, 1982, p. 17).

Some, including Popper (1968) and Lakatos and Musgrave (1970), have argued that theories can not be verified or established as true or probably true in light of observational evidence (Chalmers, 1982, p. 38). They can only be falsified. Falsification in this case refers to an empirical observation that fails to confirm a theory's prediction. If a theory predicts that all red leaves fall horizontally and a scientist observes a red leaf falling vertically, then the theory has been falsified. Here is an example of a falsifiable statement: "It never rains on Wednesday" (Chalmers, 1982, p. 39). This assertion is falsifiable because it can be shown to be untrue by observing rain falling on a given Wednesday. A hypothesis is falsifiable if there is a logically possible set of observations that are inconsistent with it. If these events occur, the hypothesis is falsified. Popper (1968) has offered this falsification approach as a corrective to the naive inductivist, logical-positivist view of science and the verification process. Good theories are falsifiable, he argues, because they make definite claims that can be refuted.

There are problems with this position. First, science appears to grow, change, and develop not necessarily because theories are falsified (Kuhn, 1977). For example, paradigms and interests change, and this has little to do with whether or not a theory has been falsified or verified. Second, what qualifies as a falsifiable observation? This is always open to interpretation. Third, the actual work that scientists do seldom conforms to the philosophies of science implied by either the logical-positivist or the falsificationist positions (see Latour and Woolgar, 1979). Scientists don't prove things right or wrong; they just make their findings interesting to one group or another (Becker, 1986, p. 2). Scientists socially construct their findings. Fourth, a fallible observation may be rejected, and a fallible theory accepted, when in fact the theory should be rejected. "Conclusive falsifications of theories are not achievable" (Chalmers, 1982, p. 61). Maines and Molseed (1986, 1988) have recently applied the aforementioned views on how scientists actually work to the body of research produced by the Stanford group of social psychologists. Their conclusions are devastating. Reasons such as the foregoing have generally led to considerable skepticism regarding both verification and falsification philosophies of science. More recent work has pursued what is called the "strong programme" in the philosophy of science (see Knorr-Cetina and Mulkay, 1983; Latour and Woolgar, 1979; Tibbetts, 1986). This approach stresses the pragmatic, socially constructed side of scientific activity, including how theory is constructed, and claims are made for the verification of hypotheses.

FEMINIST THEORY AND THE POSITIVIST CRITIQUE

Within the last decade, feminist theory has emerged as a major force in sociology. It has drawn upon various versions of Marxist, interactionist, psychoanalytic, phenomenological, and critical theory formulations (see Farganis, 1986, for a review and Denzin, 1985). Feminist theorists have articulated a methodology that is at odds with the standard and revisionist versions of positivism. It is useful to review these contributions. They have become a central part of contemporary interpretive methodology.

From the Frankfurt School, feminists take the following positions concerning contemporary positivist social science methodology: (1) It is unable to see itself as a human enterprise; hence it fails to understand its own inner, rationalistic biases; (2) it fails to raise central questions about human freedom, dignity, and purpose; (3) it sees knowledge as neutral (Farganis, 1986, p. 51), but this is a false neutrality, for positivists have no problem with those in power using their knowledge; (4) it fails to analyze the social context and ideological biases that shape research; (5) it does not grasp the fact that the methods of the natural sciences *cannot* be applied to the study of human beings; (6) scientific analysis cannot be value-neutral; (7) a critical theory of social life must be freed from false objectivism; (8) knowledge is always governed by special interests, be they technical, practical, or emancipatory; (9) critical-feminist theory must be emancipatory; (10) it must consider the focal place of gender and gender belief systems in the production and reproduction of human societies; and (11) gender structures the production of knowledge about society.

Methodologically, feminists articulate the following principles: (1) gender asymmetry must be reflexively studied as "a basic feature of social life, including the conduct of research" (see Cook and Fonow, 1986, p. 5); (2) consciousness-raising is a methodological tool; (3) the norm of objectivity must be challenged; (4) the ethnical, value-laden dimensions of feminist research must be paramount; (5) research can lead to the empowerment of women.

The *research strategies* used by feminist scholars include (1) a commitment to triangulation, or the use of multiple methods; (2) the use of visual techniques, including video cameras and film; (3) the use of linguistic techniques, including conversational analysis (see Thorne, Kramarae, and Henley, 1983); (4) the use of textual analysis methods, which involve the critical, deconstructive reading of social texts on and about women (see Smith, 1979); (5) a critical evaluation of quantitative research methods, including the phrasing of questions in social surveys; (6) collaborative research strategies involving the "collective" model of social organization. In 1983, the Nebraska Feminist Collective, for example, published a paper analyzing gender biases in the works of Erving Goffman. They found 5 dimensions of sexism in Goffman's work (see Nebraska Feminist Collective, 1983, pp. 535–43).

Feminist theory and research continues the critical appraisal of the human disciplines started by the Frankfurt School in the 1930s. It radicalizes the field as it opens the way for new, innovative approaches to the study of human group life. Most important, it recognizes the centrality of gender in the research act. Observers can no longer be regarded as passive, neutral agents through which knowledge flows. Observers are gendered beings, and the research act is a genered production. Feminism lays positivism to rest in the human disciplines.

THE FUNCTIONS OF THEORY

It is appropriate to conclude with a summary statement on the functions of theory for the sociologist. A theory must, of course, provide explanations and interpretations of the phenomenon under analysis. If it fails to do this, it is not a theory. It must also generate new images of reality, new hypotheses, and new interpretations; it must move sociologists toward the goal of explanation and prediction.

Theories serve as critical guides to future thought, research, and conceptualization. This, of course, implies a close working relationship with the research method and the research finding. Theories set problems for research, stake out new objects for examination, and direct empirical inquiry (Blumer, 1954). In turn, methods and research findings suggest new problems for theory (for example, the negative case), invite new theoretical formulations, and lead to the refinement of theories themselves. Theory, conceptualization, and empirical activity are interwoven in a contextual operation such that theory guides research while research guides theory.

CONCLUSIONS

I have offered an extended discussion of theory in contemporary sociology. I have addressed the politics of sociology and indicated that sociology cannot be value-neutral. I have shown how theory, method, and the research method interact with one another. Theory for its own sake was criticized. Interpretive, postmodern, critical, and feminist theories were discussed. I also indicated how a new view of theory in anthropology can shape the sociologist's conception of what theory does. This led to a discussion of the goals of prediction, explanation, and interpretation. Various models, metaphors, and images of sociology, including the physical science, the biological, and the humanities, were reviewed. The language and rhetoric of science were analyzed, as were various levels and forms of theory-work. Verificational and falsification views of proposition-testing were examined. The importance of the concept and the definition in sociological theory was stressed. In the next chapter, I will move from interpretation to method and discuss the strategy of naturalistic inquiry.

SUGGESTED READINGS

BOTTOMORE, TOM, *The Frankfurt School.* (London: Tavistock, 1984). A thorough discussion of the works of the key figures in the Frankfurt School (Horkheimer, Adorno, Marcuse, Habermas) and the relevance of their critical theory for contemporary social theory.

CHALMERS, A. F., *What Is This Thing Called Science?* (Milton Keyes, England: Open University Press, 1982). A highly readable presentation of the various positivist and postpositivist philosophies of science, including inductivism, falsificationism, Lakatos's picture of research programs, Kuhn's paradigms, Popper's objectivism, and Feyerabend's anarchistic theory of knowledge (what scientists do cannot be reduced to a few rules or principles).

GEERTZ, CLIFFORD, *Local Knowledge: Further Essays in Interpretive Anthropology.* (New York: Basic Books, 1983). This book and Geertz's earlier collection of essays, *The Interpretive of Cultures* (New York: Basic Books, 1973), clearly establish the centrality of the interpretive point of view in the human disciplines.

GIDDENS, ANTHONY, *Central Problems of Social Theory.* (Berkeley: University of California Press, 1979). A thorough review of the major developments in social theory, including hermeneutics, semiotics, structuralism, and poststructuralism.

WINCH, PETER, *The Idea of a Social Science and Its Relation to Philosophy.* (London: Routledge and Kegan Paul, 1958). A now-classic statement on the limits of positivism in the social sciences.

3

Naturalistic Inquiry

> Naturalistic investigation is what the naturalistic investigator does. . . . What is salient to us is that, first, no manipulation on the part of the inquirer is implied, and, second, the inquirer imposes no a priori units on the outcome. [Lincoln and Guba, 1985, p. 8]

In this chapter I will present the logic of naturalist inquiry. This approach to the interpretive process is a reaction to strict positivist views of the theory–research relationship, which were discussed in the last chapter. In particular, naturalistic inquiry objects to five central tenets of positivism: (1) objectivity, (2) hypothetical-deductive theory, (3) external lawlike relations, (4) exact and formal language, and (5) the separation of facts and meaning (Lincoln and Guba, 1985, p. 29). It takes these points from Habermas's (1971) critique of positivism.

The social sciences are in a postpositivist era, in which these traditional conceptions of positivism are being severely challenged. The central tenets of postpositivism "are virtually the reverse of those that characterized positivism" (Lincoln and Guba, 1985, p. 29). That is, postpositivist, interpretive inquiry assumes the social nature of the research process, takes account of interactive meaning, locates language centrally in the research act, incorporates values into research, and focuses on the gendered nature of social life (see Heron, 1981; and Lincoln and Guba, 1985, pp. 30–31). Naturalistic interactionism, which I develop in this chapter, is part of the postpositivist attack on positivism.

Three fundamental problems confront sociologists as they move from theory to observations. First, they must gather and record observations that have direct relevance for the theoretical questions they are exploring. If their observations lack theoretical relevance, then theory development, revision, modification, and verification become severely restricted. This first problem suggests that researchers must have a flexible set of guidelines that will take them to those situations in which they are most likely to observe the types of behaviors they are most interested in understanding. This leads to the second major problem, which is sampling. Researchers must have confidence that their observations are not typical only of those they have studied but could be generalized to other groups and individuals as well. Third, researchers must have confidence in the observations they gather. Observations must accurately, reliably, and validly reflect the behaviors that have been recorded. This third problem reflects the sociologist's concern for measurement.

Taken together, these three problems restate the issue of discovery and theoretical interpretation in the scientific community. They will be treated in this chapter as problems of observing, sampling, and recording. While Chapters 5 through 10 treat the analytic logic of six major sociological methods, it seems appropriate to offer a separate discussion of these critical elements in the research act. The discussion will not treat in detail types of sampling strategies. Nor will it focus on various measuring devices or levels of measurement per se. The concerned reader should consult such standard sources as Kish (1965) on sampling, Stevens (1951) Borgatta and Bohrnstedt (1981) on levels of measurement, and Upshaw (1968) on measurement and scaling devices. My intent is to develop the position of naturalistic inquiry and symbolic interactionism toward these matters. See Glaser and Strauss, 1967; Lofland, 1971, 1976; and Schatzman and Strauss, 1973 for similar statements from this perspective. See Cicourel, 1964, 1974b, for a discussion of these issues from the standpoint of "ethnomethodology." (Lofland and Lofland, 1984, and Lincoln and Guba, 1985, should also be consulted.)

OBSERVING, RECORDING, AND SAMPLING:
THE NATURALISTIC APPROACH

The *naturalistic approach* to observing, recording, and sampling involves the consideration of the seven principles from symbolic interactionism offered in Chapter 1. The researcher, as a naturalist, is committed to:

1. Combining a native's symbolic meanings with ongoing patterns of interaction.
2. Adopting the perspective, or "attitude," of the acting other and viewing the world from the subject's point of view, while maintaining a distinction between everyday and scientific conceptions of reality.
3. Linking the native's symbols and definitions with the social relationships and groups that provide those conceptions. Examining the place of gender and power in the social situation.
4. Recording the behavior settings of interaction.
5. Adopting methods that are capable of reflecting process, change, and stability.
6. Viewing the research act as an instance of symbolic interaction.
7. Using sensitizing concepts, which point to the construction of interactive causal explanations of social process.

Naturalistic interactionism, the logical method of the symbolic interactionist, turns on these seven principles, or directives. This methodological stance demands that the researcher actively enter the worlds of local people so as to render those worlds understandable from the standpoint of a theory that is grounded in the *behaviors, languages, definitions, attitudes,* and *feelings* of those studied. Naturalistic interactionism attempts to wed the covert, private features of the social act with its publicly observable counterparts. It works back and forth between word and deed (Deutscher, 1973). This version of the research act endeavors to move beyond pure ethnography to critical, interpretive theory (Manning and Fabrega, 1976, pp. 39–51; Manning, 1985). Naturalistic interactionism attempts to enter people's heads, recognizing that humans engage in "minded," self-reflexive behavior. Humans act in ways that reflect their unfolding and emergent definitions of themselves and the social situations they confront. Any research program that purports to be scientific must confront these features of human group life (see Blumer, 1969a; Mead, 1927, 1934). The term *naturalistic interactionism* is adopted from Mead's statement on *social behaviorism* (1934), which directs the researcher to link the symbol, or the attitude, with interaction — hence the term *symbolic interactionism.* In Blumer's (1954, p. 10) words, our research

> ... seeks to improve concepts by naturalistic research, that is to direct study of our natural social world wherein empirical instances are accepted in their concrete and distinctive form. It depends on faithful reportorial depiction of the instances and on analytical probing into their character. . . . While its progress may be slow and tedious, it has the virtue of remaining in close and continuing relations with the natural social world. . . . It also poses, I suspect, the primary line of issue in our discipline with regard to becoming an empirical science of our natural social world.

Seven considerations, then, provide the outline for this chapter. They are modified to fit the underlying features of face-to-face interaction discussed earlier (see Chapter 1). Naturalists focus their observations on selves, social objects, rules of conduct, social situations, and social relationships. They attempt to examine how the gender stratification system operates in the situations that they study.

Sampling

Sampling will be defined as following a set of rules that place the observer in a situation to record or elicit a set of behaviors which are presumed to have some degree of relevance for a specific concept, hypothesis, proposition, or theory. These rules specify a procedure that should be followed so as to increase the generalizability and theoretical relevance of the behaviors to be observed or elicited (Glaser and Strauss, 1967). They may take the observer to only one situation, or to a series of situations — as in a social survey, where the investigator may gather interviews from several hundred individuals. The researcher who samples selects from a larger set of behaviors, social situations, or historical documents a smaller number of behaviors, situations, or documents for intensive study. The larger set from which the researcher samples is termed a *population*. Before beginning to sample, the researcher must have an in-depth working knowledge of that population and must enumerate the units that make it up. (See Sudman and Kalton, 1986, on sampling special populations.)

In order to enumerate a population, researchers must have a clear definition of the population to which they wish to generalize. If we are studying the socialization of young children in preschools, for example, we must have a workable and operational definition of what a preschool is. Depending on our theoretical intentions, we might decide to include in the sample day-care centers, Montessori schools, and informally organized baby-sitting services offered by individual mothers. On the other hand, we might restrict our definition of a preschool to include only those agencies legally sanctioned by the state and subsidized by state or federal funds, as well as by tuition fees paid by parents.

Once the definition of the unit and population under study has been established, the researcher must then develop a complete listing of all the elements that make up that population. To return to the example of preschools, as researchers here we would be obliged to offer a complete listing of all the preschools that exist in the geographical area we wish to sample. The latter consideration suggests that any sampling procedure is constrained by the factors of time and place. The observer must ask, "At what point in time do I wish to observe?" And, "In what places, or geographical locales, do I wish to observe?" As researchers of preschools, we would often be constrained by the here and now. We can observe preschools only in the present, not in the past — although we might decide to consult historical documents and archive records that would give us a picture of what a given preschool was like 10 years earlier, or we might delve more deeply into the past and examine the historical development of preschools since the eighteenth century. Economic factors also constrain the investigator. A lack of funds may force an investigator to limit observations to only a given neighborhood, housing unit, city, county, state, or country. It can be seen that the enumeration of a population involves a set of complex decisions — not the least of which is the definition of the population itself. The basis of generalization often rests on a set of compromises that give something less than the desirable or ideal sampling frame.

Once the population has been defined and enumerated, the researcher may decide to *randomly* sample units from that population for observation. A *random sample* is one in which all sampled units have the same probability of being included in the final sample. The ideal random sample simply gives each sampled unit the same chance of inclusion in the final set of observations. As students of preschools for a given community, county, or state, we might decide to draw randomly from that list a fixed number of schools for study. We would have to be cautious in generalization, however, for our population might be constrained by factors unknown to us. That is, the factors that produced the preschools in the community from which we drew our samples might be unique to that community.

The method of randomly drawing a sample need not restrict the researcher to a single sampling frame. If, in the course of observing, factors or processes of high theoretical utility are found, the researcher should feel free to include those observations in the final data base. A logic of ongoing inclusion (Glaser and Strauss, 1967) underlies the sampling process. Often the investigator uses one sampling frame to produce another: This is called gathering a *snowball sample*. Mullin's study of theory groupings in American sociology (1973) employed a variation on this procedure. As he investigated separate theory groupings — ranging from structural functionalism to symbolic interactionism, ethnomethodology, small-group theory, the social forecasters, causal theorists, and radical-critical theory — he first located leading figures in each school of thought and then expanded his sample through interviewing and through examining published works. In this way he attempted to thoroughly exhaust, or saturate, the population of theorists that made up each school of thought. A snowball sample may move from a simple random sample (for example, 500 persons in a particular community) to a nonrandom sample. A researcher interested in patterns of friendship might ask a sample of randomly drawn respondents who their three best friends are, and then attempt to interview the persons named to see if they view themselves as the best friends of the persons questioned.

The snowball sample reveals another element of the sampling process. It should be *multistage* (Lazerwitz, 1968, p. 298); that is, the observational process should not be thought of in rigid, static terms. The researcher is continually seeking out new bodies of data that will potentially elaborate the observational framework. This may involve multiplicity, or network sampling, a variant on the snowball method (see Sudman and Kalton, 1986, pp. 411–13).

Often, the researcher employs a *stratified* sampling model, a *cluster* sampling model, or both. Rather than enumerating a population into single units — for example, all persons over the age of 21 in a given community — the researcher groups the population into strata, or classes. In our example of preschools, for instance, we might list all day-care centers, Montessori schools, licensed preschools, and home baby-sitting services in a given city. We would then randomly select a fixed number of socializing agencies from each stratum, or type. In this way our sampling frame would better represent the total range of socializing services offered in the city or area under study.

Observing and Recording

All sampling activities are theoretically informed. The aim of researchers is to place themselves in social situations where theoretically relevant observations can be gathered. Hence, sampling procedures provide the proper guidelines for the observational process. An *observation* may thus be defined as the recording of a unit or units of interaction occurring in a concrete social situation. The interaction that is recorded may be elicited, as in an interview. It may be experimentally produced, as in a social experiment. It may occur naturally and spontaneously, as in a participant-observation study.

Scales   What is observed is recorded. It may be recorded *in toto:* For example, the researcher tape-records or films an entire encounter between two individuals. Or it may be recorded within a specified format: That is, the researcher asks a respondent a question and records the answer on a scale that consists of several categories. When observations are recorded in the latter way, they may be said to be *measured.* They are assumed to exist along a continuum which consists of categories or positions. These categories are commonly presented as *scales,* and there are four levels or types of scales that correspond to a theory of numbers. This theory of numbers in turn permits certain mathematical operations to be performed on what has been observed. The act of measurement assumes that the observation of concepts can be transformed into statements concerning the degree to which they are present or absent in any given empirical instance.

It must be noted that this theory of numbers is entirely verbal, or symbolic. It does not refer to fixed, static, objective features of the social world. Bohrnstedt and Borgatta (1981, p. 17) comment, "Most of the variables in the social sciences are latent, unobservable constructs with no naturally occurring metrics." This theory is a set of constructions arbitrarily imposed on the social world. There is no way to test it except by another theory of numbers (see Cicourel, 1964; Collins, 1984; Maines, 1987). This has important implications for those social scientists who perform statistical manipulations of their data. Their findings can only be interpreted from within the basic theory of numbers they impose on the variables they measure. Their results are thus subject to considerable criticism.

It must also be noted that "measurement-minded" sociologists follow fads and fashions in the use of first one statistical method and then another. Maines (1987) has noted that in the 1940s factor analysis was employed. In the 1950s it was multivariate analysis; in the 1960s, path analysis; and in the 1970s, log-linear analysis. In the 1980s, it is the use of LISREL (Linear Structural Relations), which involves the analysis of linear structural relations. As one fad replaced another, the theory of numbers was modified to fit the new scheme of thought. (See, for example, Bohrnstedt and Borgatta, 1981, p. 36, who make a case for conceptualizing social science measurement as interval, and hence subject to the use of powerful parametric statistics.)

In the field of educational psychology, there is now considerable interest in classical test theory and item response theory as these theories relate to the theory of numbers just discussed (see Hulin, Drasgow, and Parsons, 1983). These discussions will probably soon appear in sociology. Given this brief background on measurement theory, the levels of measurement that have been used by social scientists can now be discussed.

Levels of Measurement

The simplest level of measurement is the nominal observation. A *nominal scale* places an observation into an "either-or" category. It consists of two mutually exclusive categories. A person is either a male or a female, black or white, married or not married, Catholic or Protestant.

The second level of measurement is the *ordinal scale.* An ordinal measurement assumes that objects can be placed within a rank order; however, the distance between the positions on the scale cannot be measured — that is, they are unknown. Thus a person's attitude toward the impeachment of a president of the United States might be measured on a scale that ranges from "strongly agree" to "agree," "neutral," "disagree," and "strongly disagree."

The third level of measurement is the *interval scale*. It contains all the elements of the ordinal scale but includes an additional factor: the ability to measure the distance between intervals, or rank positions (Stevens, 1951; Upshaw, 1968). If the researcher were to attach numerical values to the ordinal scale that measured individuals' attitudes toward impeachment (for example, "strongly disagree" equals 5 and "strongly agree" equals 1) and assumed that the scale met the requirements of the interval scale, then the differences between 1 and 5 on the scale could be mathematically interpreted. In the language of statistics, complex parametric operations could be performed on the data. Until the level of the interval scale is reached, only nonparametric operations can legitimately be performed on the data. (But see the controversy surrounding this issue as presented in Morrison and Henkel, 1970).

The highest level of measurement is the *ratio scale*. Such a scale assumes that a zero point of measurement exists. A person's weight can be measured on a ratio scale, as can her income and age. It can be shown that "4 pounds is 4 times as heavy as 1 pound" (Green, 1954, p. 337). Hamblin (1971) has further developed the logic of ratio scales to include the measurement of psychophysical behaviors, thus expanding the work of Stevens and his associates in the 1950s (but also see Stevens, 1975).

What can be observed?   What sociologists measure is directly linked to their sampling strategies. Indeed, the sampling procedure should permit the researcher to observe what a theory dictates or suggests. Thus theory is intimately connected with the sampling, observational, and measurement processes. Ideally, researchers attempt to gather, produce, or elicit interactions activities, and attitudes that will permit them to further develop their central concepts and propositions. In that sense all observations are observations of theoretical constructs. At the practical level, however, what is observed will be the actions and behaviors and attitudes of interacting individuals. From those behaviors and attitudes, sociologists then infer the existence of their central concepts and propositions. An inferential process underlies the processes of observational theory construction. A given behavior or elicited attitude is taken to be a representation of a concept and a proposition.

In practice, sociologists may observe *time* and its passage. They may, for example, study how individuals go about constructing their days. Or they may ask how a given group has rewritten its past into a coherent history. Researchers may study the social organization of *social situations* and ask how it is that individuals give different meanings to the situations they pass through and inhabit on a regular basis. Cavan's study of interactions in San Francisco bars (1966) focused almost entirely on how individuals transformed their drinking places from convenience bars to nightspots, and from marketplace bars to home territory bars. She was less concerned with the behaviors and attitudes of any given individual than with the social situation of the bar. At the time of her study there were "about two thousand establishments in the city of San Francisco licensed to sell alcoholic beverages for consumption on the premises" (1966, p. 23). From the spring of 1962 through the early part of 1965, she gathered participant-observation data in approximately 100 bars in that city. Cavan, (1966, pp. 15–16) describes her sampling strategies as follows. Her research properly displays the interactional nature of sampling and observational behavior.

> The observation periods in each bar ranged in length from a half hour to three hours and covered the lawful bar days as well as the entire week. I attempted to visit a number of establishments during a variety of times on a variety of days, although some establishments were visited only once and others as many as ten or twelve times.
>
> The establishments chosen for observation were selected in a number of ways. Some of the home territory bars were in the immediate vicinity of my residence, and this, in part, permitted me to patronize them — at least the first time — as might anyone else who lived in the neighborhood. Two of these were homosexual bars, and for my initial observations in them I was escorted by a homosexual acquaintance (who was one of the few people within the bar setting who knew that my concern was one of research). . . .
>
> Some establishments were selected because they were located in an area of the city of particular interest, such as the civic center, the financial district, the downtown shopping area, and the tenderloin; although the actual choice of bars within this area was frequently just a matter of convenience. I visited a large number of places because they had been mentioned in conversations either with patrons in some other bar or with acquaintances outside the bar setting. Some bars were visited because information was available about some change in them with respect to either the management or the patronage, and other bars were chosen because they had a "reputation" of one sort or another.

Cavan's sampling and observational strategies could not in any sense be described as random. Her study of bars within certain specified geographical locales — civic center, financial district, tenderloin — and the selection of homosexual bars revealed an attempt to make her sampling frame as theoretically informed as possible. Matters of convenience, personal knowledge, and emerging theoretical conceptualization guided her activity. Many naturalistic studies follow a similar format. To the best of their abilities, however, researchers are obliged to present some working picture of the broader social structure from which their observations are drawn. Cavan achieved this.

Researchers may study the structure of *social occasions*. They might study cocktail parties, as Reisman and Watson did (1964). They might study the focused interactions that emerge between physicians and nurses in hospital surgery rooms (see Goffman, 1961b). The study of social occasions directly links the observer's observations with the study of face-to-face interaction. It is one aim of naturalists to study interactions between individuals. Naturalists are less concerned with the behaviors and attitudes of persons who cannot be observed in some form of ongoing interaction.

Two types of social occasions may be noted. First, there are those that are the natural outcome of what persons do to and with one another. Interactions between husbands and wives, children playing in preschools, secretaries gossiping in a work pool, and the behaviors of street-corner gangs are spontaneously produced behaviors (see Liebow, 1967; Webb et al., 1981; Whyte, 1955). Their existence is not the result of some set of contrived, or "investigator-produced," set of conditions. Second, there are social occasions that *are* contrived. Such occasions are seen in the social experiment or the survey interview between an interviewer and a randomly selected respondent — investigator-produced occasions. While the data gathered from such contrived occasions are of great value, investigators should be encouraged to direct at least some of their efforts toward the study of the natural social occasion.

Observers may attempt to sample and record various classes or types of *social relationships*. They might, for instance, study the socializing, friendship relationship that exists in children's playgroups and contrast these relationships to those that occur in adult–child interactions (see the articles in Asher and Gottman, 1981). They might study the treatment counselor–alcoholic client relationship (Denzin, 1987b), and they might compare this relationship to the alcoholic–sponsor relationship that occurs in AA. Relationships of talking, which vary by physical proximity, medium of communication, and social context, might be examined. Goffman (1981), for example, offers a series of compelling and illuminating comparisons between these talking situations: (1) replies and responses to questions, (2) response cries (a person says "ouch" when he hurts himself), (3) lectures, and (4) radio talk. Manning (1988) has analyzed the telephone calls that go on between police stations and callers. He has developed a semiotic reading of these interactions, showing how the police organization creates its own theory of a call and its significance. A typology of talking, gendered interactional relations (friendly, collegial, intimate, hostile, therapeutic, cultivated, socializing, helping, exchange) could be constructed; researchers would then sample within each relational type in an effort to empirically ground the typology.

An investigator can focus on the meanings, ideologies, or values that a class or sample of individuals hold toward some specific object or set of activities (see Lofland, 1971, pp. 24-31). Many social surveys focus on the elicitation of attitudes. It should be clear, however, that any study of attitudes or meanings must be combined with some set of data which indicate how these attitudes are actually brought into play and used by interacting individuals (Deutscher, 1973).

Observational units reviewed: toward a merger   Five processes have been isolated for special observational attention. The investigator may focus on any of the following:

1.   Time — its social organization and passage
2.   Social situations — their encounters and uses
3.   Natural or contrived social occasions of interaction

4. Social relationships, including gender
5. The attitudes, meanings, languages, and symbols held by a group or sample of persons

The seven principles from symbolic interactionism, combined with the strategy of triangulation, suggest that a well-rounded investigation would combine all five processes (see Table 3-1).

Indeed, observations that are situated by time and place necessarily focus on the organization of time in social settings. Similarly, any situated observation will necessarily produce data on the social occasions of interaction that occur during the period of observation. Furthermore, a situated study of social occasions should properly yield data on the relationships that bind interactants to one another. Finally, the meanings or definitions each interactant directs toward himself should be revealed in the observer's records of the occasion. The meanings and utterances the interactant directs toward others should also be available for recording. Thus a naturalist's sampling and observational framework should produce material relevant for an analysis of how interacting individuals produce and give meaning to the interactions in which they find themselves involved.

Time and the observational process   Any investigation must take account of time. It must attempt to establish some link between the past, the present, and the future. Typically, researchers observe a process or set of events that occur in the present—in the concrete "here and now." On the basis of these observations, they offer a set of predictions about the future. It

TABLE 3-1   Principles of Symbolic Interactionsim and the Selection of Observational Units

		Units			
Principles	Time	Social Situations	Occasions	Social Relations	Attitudes, Meanings
1. Interactive explanations					
2. Embedded theory					
3. Flexible sampling strategy					
4. Attitudes and acts					
5. Sensitizing concepts					
6. Triangulation					
7. Situated observations					
8. Subject's perspective or perspectives					

is reasoned that if a group of individuals behaved this way in this situation, they are likely to behave in a similar manner in the future. It may also be reasoned that in past situations they behaved in a similar fashion. To adequately ground temporal predictions, researchers are under some constraint to gather data from the past (historical and retrospective accounts). They should also attempt to be present during future moments of interaction so as to check out their predictions.

THE LOGIC OF NATURALISTIC INQUIRY: BEHAVIOR SPECIMENS

In an effort to increase the likelihood that their theories and hypotheses will be better grounded in the actual experiences of interacting individuals, naturalists attempt to reproduce as fully as possible the actual experiences, thoughts, and actions of those they study. They achieve this reproduction through the collection of *behavior specimens*. Behavior specimens are slices of ongoing interaction that take particular behavior sequences from beginning to end. The behavior specimen reflects the actual temporal sequence or flow of behavior under inspection.

Specimen Format

The format for collecting and presenting behavior specimens is dramaturgical; that is, like the playwright, the naturalist endeavors to convey a working knowledge of the individuals recorded in the specimen.

First, the full specimen will give each individual studied a short biographical history that is relevant to the encounter at hand. This biographical history would consider such matters as the individual's age, sex, ethnic or racial identity, occupational, educational, and marital history, and any other pieces of information that would appear relevant to subsequent analysis.

Second, the specimen will describe how the interactants were dressed.

Third, the specimen will note any peculiar speech or behavior patterns associated with each interactant. If anyone stuttered, whined, or was abrasive or aggressive, this would be noted.

Fourth, the specimen will be recorded so as to indicate when each interactant came into the interaction sequence. The utterances of each individual would then be numbered in sequence, beginning with utterance (U) 1 and moving to the conclusion (perhaps U84). If the interactants speak in slurred, unintelligible, or ambiguous ways, the researcher would attempt to translate those utterance as accurately as possible. An unintelligible word or phrase would be followed in the specimen by the letters *tr* ("translation").

Fifth, many face-to-face encounters involve important nonverbal gestures. An individual might, for example, hit another person, shake a person's hand, pass a cup of milk, or spill a tray of cookies. Such gestures will be recorded in the behavior specimen and numbered: (G) 1, and so on. The specimen, then, would present a continuous flow of utterances and gestures, each recorded in precise sequence — for example, U1, U2, G1, U3, G2. As the specimen is collected and subsequently presented, the investigator takes pains to note when each utterance and gesture appeared in the overall specimen.

Sixth, the entire period of observation must be presented, and it must be dated. Observations in a preschool, for example, might be specified as follows: "May 8, 1974, 9:00 AM to 10:30 AM."

Seventh, the situation or settings of observation must be recorded. As observers in the preschool, we might confine our observations to a single area in the school—perhaps the kitchen or a dollhouse area. We would note, then, after the date and time of observation, exactly where we were when we collected the specimen or specimens. Furthermore, we would note how we were dressed for the occasion in question.

Eighth, the observer will record the salient social objects that were acted on during the occasion of interaction. In the dollhouse area of a preschool, it might be a kitchen table, a toy telephone, a highchair, plastic foods and fruits, a toy stove, a garment for dressing up. The objects that are acted on may be concrete pieces of equipment like those just mentioned. But such objects could also include talk and its production, or they might involve a group of individuals drafting a set of by-laws or listening to a tape recording of another person's conversations. The term *social object* describes anything that can be symbolically separated from anything else. It may be concrete (like a chair), ephemeral (like a thought, symbol, or dream), or abstract (like an ideology or a set of beliefs) (Blumer, 1966a).

Ninth, when describing each of the interactants in the specimen, the researcher should attempt to describe their relationships to one another. If they were related by kinship, by friendship, by the constraints of a superordinate–subordinate relationship, or by the constraints of the situation itself, this should be noted.

Tenth, the researcher should attempt to record, as well as possible, the rules of conduct that are displayed in the encounter, focusing on rules of polite ceremony, civil-legal rules, and rules unique to the individuals in question.

These ten procedural directives for recording and producing a behavior specimen rest on the elements of face-to-face interaction presented in Chapter 1 and at the beginning of this chapter. They provide a set of methodological directives for theoretically implementing the symbolic-interactionist perspective. The researcher who collects behavior specimens can, however, inspect and analyze these specimens from any of a number of differing theoretical points of view. The specimens, in this sense, simply reflect the interactions that have occurred between a specified number of individuals. They can be returned to, time and time again, for renewed analysis and interpretation. Yet, because the observations have not been collapsed into a set of precoded categories or recorded within the confines of a scale or a measuring instrument, the researcher reduces the risk of having lost (during the data collection process) valuable pieces of information.

One intent of the specimen is to establish *verisimilitude.* The goal is to produce for the reader the same perceptual and experiential states sensed by the original observer—and, it is hoped, to capture the feelings and moods experienced by those the observer has recorded in the specimens. The intent is to give the illusion that the same experiences could and would have been sensed if the reader had been present during the actual moments of interaction that are reflected in the behavior specimen. The behavior specimen captures a moment (or a set of moments) in chronological and interactional time. It is a small-scale record of ongoing behavior.

The form of the encounters—sociable, cordial, hostile, intimate —should be specified. The motives, or accounts the interactants give concerning their presence in the situation, should also be recorded. If there are subsettings within the total situation, this should be noted. If anyone's presence in the situation is involuntary, secret, public, or by invitation, this too should be detailed. The rule makers and enforcers and the method of enforcement should be listed.

Behavior specimens, as outlined, are much like the traditional field notes of the ethnographer. However, they are much more detailed and specific in nature. They ensure that the observer leaves any situation with a full-fledged account of the interactions that have just taken place. These specifications flow from a symbolic-interactionist perspective and reflect a concern for fine-grained records of social interaction. A hypothetical specimen would have the format shown in Table 3–2.

Examples of Behavior Specimens

A literary example of a behavior specimen can be taken from Robert Penn Warren's classic novel *All the King's Men* (1946). The actors in question are Jack Burden (the novel's narrator); Boss, Willie Stark (the Governor of the state); Sugar-Boy (Willie's driver); Lucy Stark (Willie's wife); and Old Man Stark (Willie's father). They are eating dinner in Old Man Stark's house. It is late on a Sunday afternoon. Warren (pp. 34–35) describes their interactions in the following sequence:*

I must have dozed off, for I came to with the Boss standing there, saying, "Time to eat."

So we went in and ate.

We sat down at the table, Old Man Stark at one end and Lucy at the other. Lucy wiped the perspiration-soaked wisp of hair back from her face, and gave that last-minute look around the table to see if anything was missing, like a general inspecting troops. She was in her element, all right. She had been out of it for a long time, but when you dropped her back in it she hit running, like a cat out of a sack.

The jaws got to work around the table, and she watched them work. She sat there, not eating much and keeping a sharp eye out for a vacant place on any plate and watching the jaws work, and as she sat there, her face seemed to smooth itself out and relax with an inner faith in happiness the way the face of the chief engineer does when he goes down to the engine room at night and the big wheel is blurred out with its speed and the pistons plunge and return and the big steel throws are leaping in their perfect orbits like a ballet, and the whole

*Excerpt from *All the King's Men,* copyright 1946, 1974 by Robert Penn Warren, reprinted by permission of Harcourt Brace Jovanovich, Inc.

TABLE 3-2   Format for Behavior Specimen

Date:
Time:

Setting:
Subsettings:
Observer's location:

Interactants (age, dress, demeanor, sex, education, race, occupation, relationship to one another, reasons for presence, form of encounter, rule enforcers, methods of enforcement):

Social objects:

Rules of conduct (polite-ceremonial, civil-legal, relationally specific):

Pecularities (special languages, gestures, phrases, flow of interaction, repetitions, special voice inflections):

Actual Sequence	Subject's Interpretation of Interaction	Observer's Interpretation of Interaction
U1:		
U2:		
U3:		
Etc.		

place, under the electric glare, hums and glitters and sings like the eternal insides of God's head, the ship is knocking off twenty-two knots on a glassy, starlit sea.

So the jaw muscles pumped all around the table, and Lucy Stark sat there in the bliss of self-fulfillment.

I had just managed to get down the last spoonful of chocolate ice cream, which I had to tamp down into my gullet like wet concrete in a posthole, when the Boss, who was a powerful and systematic eater, took his last bite, lifted up his head, wiped off the lower half of his face with a napkin, and said, "Well, it looks like Jack and Sugar-Boy and me are going to take the night air down the highway."

Lucy Stark looked up at the Boss right quick, then looked away, and straightened a salt shaker. At first guess it might have been the look any wife gives her husband when he shoves back after supper and announces he'll step down town for a minute. Then you knew it wasn't that. It didn't have any question, or protest, or rebuke, or command, or self-pity, or whine, or oh-so-you-don't-love-me-any-more in it. It just didn't have anything in it, and that was what made it remarkable. It was a feat. Any act of pure perception is a feat, and if you don't believe it, try it sometime.

In this excerpt, Warren has captured the vocal as well as the nonverbal gestures of Lucy and Willie. He has presented their actions in precise sequence, thus permitting the reader to gain a feel for what actually occurred during the meal. Warren's technique of having one interactant record as well as respond to ongoing interaction (for example, Jack's recording and then interpreting Lucy's response to Willie's statement. "Well, it looks like Jack and Sugar-Boy and me are going to take to the night air down the highway") deserves elaboration. As naturalistic observers, we are often participants in the behavior sequences we record and must blend as well as separate the activities of *interactional participant* and *interactional analyst*. We are forced to attend closely to the interactions of which we are a part. When writing up or transcribing our specimens, we are obliged to stand outside our own actions and record them, much as we record the actions of those we interacted with or observed.

An additional rule for the behavior specimen can now be noted. The researcher should attempt to reveal what each individual in the specimen was thinking about when he took part in the interaction under study. This may require interviews with the key participants after the specimen has been recorded. Often, however, persons will spontaneously reveal what they thought about a particular sequence of interactions. When the naturalist writes up the specimens, it is often useful to record beside each utterance a provisional interpretation of that utterance or gesture.

The psychologists Barker and Wright (1951, 1954) have pioneered in developing the methodology involved in specimen construction and analysis. Wright (1960, p. 84) describes how these specimens operate in the study of children:

> These [records] provide lasting *specimens* of behavior and immediate situations of children. . . . We shall call them *specimen records,* from which the name of the method as a whole follows, "Let us now get a segment thus-and-so long and as nearly complete as possible from the behavior continuum of Child X in Habitat Y. Then, later, we shall see what can be done with it." Such is the main idea of the specimen record.

Wright (1960, p. 85) goes on to present a specimen record collected by Gump and Schoggen (1955) on the behavior of a 9-year-old subject, Wally. The setting is a summer camp. Wally is just waking up:

> 7:23. Wally rolls over in bed, opens his eyes, props himself up on one elbow, and looks with a sort of bewildered stare at me.
> I am across the room from him.
> The he smiles briefly, as if he has caught on to what is going on.
> He says to me, but also to others around, looking at them intermittently, but more at me. "Gee, do you know what happened to me last night?" He says this again with more earnestness, "Do you know what happened to me last night? I had a dream." Wally now sits straight up in the bed and begins to tell his dream in a serious, impressed tone of voice. "I dreamed that my Dad and I were riding in this big truck and we were coming down this hill and the driver, he was knocked out, and we couldn't drive the truck and the truck was going faster and we landed in the river with a big crash! Jeeze!"

I nod but nobody else makes any comment on this dream, which was so vivid in Wally's mind when he woke up.

This specimen record is instructive, for as Wright notes, this method of observing describes actual behavior in context. The record has a sense of permanency. In Barker and Wright's research, the records are collected without theoretical bias. There is, however, a flaw in this specimen record, and this can be gleaned by asking, What is a "bewildered stare?" What does it mean to "smile briefly," to "look intermittently," to "say with more earnestness," to use a "serious, impressed tone?" Phrases such as these are judgmental. If they are included in this specimen, the researcher must give operational definitions for each judgment. This is by no means an easy assignment. Observers are better advised to delete such phrases from their behavior specimens.

Speier offers another version of the behavior specimen. In this case he has recorded a conversation that occurred between a mother and a neighborhood child. The child had come to the front door of the house to see if the woman's son could come out to play. Speier (1970, p. 193) has numbered each utterance in sequence:

1.   *Caller:* (Boy rings bell and waits for an answer to his ring.)
2.   *Mother:* Who's there?
3.   *Caller:* Can your son come out?
4.   *Mother:* What?
5.   *Caller:* Can your son come out?
6.   *Mother:* What do you want?
7.   *Caller:* Can your son come out?
8.   *Mother:* (Pause) Who is it?
9.   *Caller:* Jerry. Can your son come out?
10. *Mother:* Oh—No, he can't come right now. (Closes the front door.)
11. *Caller:* When do you think he could come out?
12. *Mother:* (Silence, since mother has not heard, having closed the door before the boy spoke utterance 11.)
13. *Caller:* (Leaves.)

In certain respects, Speier's specimen is superior to the record offered by Barker and Wright. His notation system, which numbers each statement in sequence, permits easy empirical analysis. This is especially the case when the researcher wishes to focus on only certain segments within the specimen (utterance 11, for example). Unlike Barker and Wright, Speier does not use judgmental phrases in the presentation of the specimen. However, a variation on Speier's method, as given in the following behavior specimen, is to be preferred.

"Juice and Crackers"

The following specimen was collected by the author. The time is 3:25 PM; the settings are the family's kitchen, dining room, and living room. The participants are three females (S, J, and R), ages 7, 6, and 5, respectively. E, the mother of J and R, is also present. The children have returned from school. R and J are sisters; they have been friends with S for three years. The observer (N) is not a party to the interactions. The specimen begins when J, R, and S enter the kitchen.

3:25 PM:

J, R, S−E: **U1**:"May we have juice and crackers?"

E−J, R, S: **U2**: "Yes. Wash your hands first." (The three leave to wash their hands.)

S−J, R: **U3**: "Let's play we're princesses. J, you be the King, R, you be the Queen."

R *and* J: **U4**: "All right."

R−J *and* S: **U5**: "Let's play the king died last night. Oh, dear, your husband is dead."

J, R, *and* S: **U6**: "What shall we do? Let's go for a walk through the woods and look for another king."

(The three leave the kitchen in search of a king. They enter the dining room and crawl under the dining room table.)

S: **U7**: "King, King, where are you?" (She moves under a chair and places a stuffed dog in front of her.)

S: **U8**: "Bow-wow, King, King, bow-wow!"

GI: S picks up the stuffed dog and bounces it along the floor away from the chair.

R−S: **U9**: "Oh no! Your doggie has to go to the bathroom."

(The three exit and go upstairs to the bathroom. They come back downstairs.)

R, S, *and* J−E: **U10**: "The king is dead and we found him."

3:45 PM: The episode with the king is concluded.

Detailed analysis of this specimen is not necessary at this point. It is offered as an illustration of the format for a hypothetical behavior specimen presented earlier in Table 3-2. An inspection of the specimen, does, however, reveal relatively young children engaged in rather elaborate verbal and symbolic forms of play. It is evident that "playing at princess" involves a form of interaction that can occur in any number of social settings. Their play moved from the kitchen to the dining room and upstairs bedroom, and concluded in the living room. In this sense, players can pick up their play and play it anywhere. The specimen also reveals the players dealing with matters of death and marriage. The entry of the dog into the episode provided a means of elaborating the search for the king. The announcement by R that S's dog had to go to the bathroom gave all three players an excuse to leave and go to the bathroom.

Recording the Behavior Specimen

Behavior specimens can be recorded on the spot, either by hand in a field notebook or by use of a tape recorder or video tape equipment. Tape recorders and video tape equipment are often expensive to acquire and operate, however; they may break down; and transcription from them is often time-consuming. Their use is purely optional. The user of the tape recorder is often lulled into less-than-critical self-awareness during the recording process. That is, there may be a tendency to think that the tape recorder will catch everything that is relevant. If a tape recorder is used, it is advisable to also keep a running notebook, noting significant gestures and so on.

Some users of the method have employed multiple observers. Barker and Wright often use teams of observers and randomly assign each observer a 30-minute observational slot. The use of multiple observers has resulted in reliability agreements as high as 92 percent. Reliability rates do vary by the specificity of what is being observed (Wright, 1960). With training and experience, the naturalistic observer should become skilled in writing up behavior specimens after they have occurred. Many social situations will not permit the open use of a tape recorder or a notebook.

Naturalistic Sampling Strategies

As was indicated earlier, the naturalist attempts to sample and record the ongoing interactions of individuals. Before actual observations begin, the researcher attempts to identify and form a rough working conceptualization of the interactions and individuals to be studied. A researcher studying the family as a socializing agent might select from a family's total set of behavioral repertoires only those actions that are most likely to bring the total family together as an interactional unit. Bossard and Boll (1960), for example, studied interactions at the evening meal table. A researcher might record the conversations that occur at such meals and then dissect them for what they reveal about the standing of children in the family unit, or compare and contrast the utterances and actions of mothers and fathers in order to isolate the main socializing effects each parent has on the children. Arthur J. Dyck (1963, pp. 78–98) performed such an analysis and reported that mothers initiate nearly two-thirds of all ritual-based actions toward their children. The father's impact, at least in the area of family ritual, was relatively low.

In a slightly different vein, West and Zimmerman (1983, pp. 102–3) report research on parent–child conversational interactions in a physician's office. They indicate that parents interrupted their children on 12 of 14 occasions. This pattern of an adult interrupting a child parallels male dominance in male–female conversations. In one study discussed by West and Zimmerman, males interrupted females in 46 of 48 (96%) conversational exchanges. This asymmetry in the initiation of interruptions in male–female and adult–child conversations suggests that an individual's standing in the gender and age stratification systems of our culture is reflected by whether or not she or he initiates conversational interruptions.

Once investigators have selected the interactional unit they wish to study, they next attempt to determine which members of that unit routinely engage in the behaviors that most concern them. The times and places of these activities will be recorded. Naturalists stratify, or classify, a study unit in terms of these theoretical constructs that are of greatest interest. They then *over*sample, so to speak, during those times when that behavior is most likely to occur.

Representational Maps

Before starting to collect behavior specimens, the investigator must develop a deep working knowledge of the settings that constitute the subjects' worlds of interaction. Coupled with this "setting knowledge" must go a knowledge of who it is that the subjects routinely interact with. This knowledge should yield a relatively detailed picture of the subjects' temporal, interactional, and situational activities. The researcher then links his subjects' behaviors to those situations routinely entered and acted in, constructing a *representational map* (or maps) of the subjects' world. Such a map details the temporal features of the subjects' world and indicates the network of interactive others who make up that world. It specifies the actual social settings in that world and the typical social objects that are acted on by the subjects. With knowledge of this order, the observer is in a position to selectively sample behaviors of high theoretical value.

Representational maps are simply frequency counts of acts, actions, and objects by setting and time. They give the researcher a working picture of the temporal, ritual, and routine features of the persons or social organizations under study.

Representational maps are also graphic. They pictorially display the recurrent and stable features of the social worlds under examination. Typically, these graphic maps will describe the ecological and physical layout of concrete social settings. A student of modern hospitals could offer maps of ward layouts and even describe specific nursing stations, corridors, and rooms on particular wards. A student of higher education could offer similar maps for college campuses, buildings, dormitories, public drinking places, and places for public entertainment. A student of race relations and community interaction in large metropolitan locales could offer a map such as "Peanut Park and Surrounding Area," which appears in Gerald D. Suttles's monograph *The Social Order of the Slum*. This map (see Figure 3–1) presents the ecological arrangement of a public housing system in the "Jane Addams" area of Chicago. "Peanut Park" provides a potential area for interracial recreational interaction, for it is surrounded by Italian residences, public housing (largely black), the playlot of a Greek school, a playlot used by young Italian children, and two baseball parks. Suttles (1968, pp. 55–56) discusses this park:

> "Peanut Park" . . . forms part of the boundary between the Negroes in the projects and the Italians to the north. . . . Until about 1961, the Negroes practically never used the park. Since then, the Negroes have progressively made inroads so that by now the question of who "owns" it is unsettled. Both the Negroes and whites make use of the southwest softball diamond, although they usually take turns. The northeast diamond is still used almost exclusively by the Italians. Map 5 [see Figure 3–1] gives a detailed picture of how the park is used.
>
> During the day, relations between ethnic groups are amicable enough, but at night each has some concern over its safety. The Negroes assume that the Italians will resist their invasion. The Italians assume that the Negroes want the park for themselves. In the meantime each group hesitates in an uneasy silence waiting for someone to make the first move.

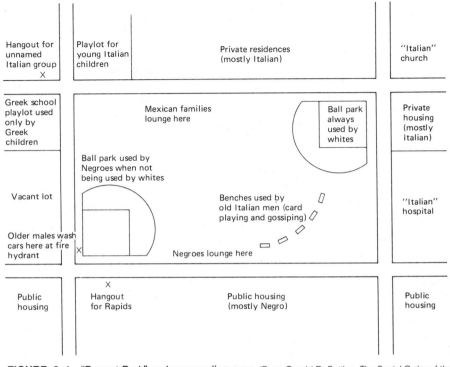

FIGURE 3-1   "Peanut Park" and surrounding area. (From Gerald D. Suttles, *The Social Order of the Slum*. Chicago: University of Chicago Press, 1968, p. 57, map 5. Used by permission of the publisher.)

Suttle's discussion of this map attempts to fit time to social settings and to the interactions that occur within those settings. It fits people together with the passage of time, as the interactions of those individuals are lodged within a specific social and ecological locale. The interracial tensions and accommodations that occur within the Addams area are vividly portrayed in Suttle's map of "Peanut Park." His analysis serves as a model for future investigators who might return to the area.

To summarize: Naturalists pay careful attention to the ecological (or spatial), temporal, ritualistic, and interactional features of the social organizations they are studying. They sample—that is, observe and record behavior specimens—at "peak" interactional times. They justify their observational and sampling strategies by presenting representational maps. If they have successfully entered the subjects' world of interactions, they should know when to be present to gather the observations they need. They are obliged, however, to inform the broader scientific community of the steps they went through when they made their sampling decisions. This is why the representational map is so crucial. It vividly reveals the extent to which an investigator is familiar with the phenomenon under study. It also serves as an observational aid, for the researcher may find that a particularly critical observational site has been unintentionally overlooked, or that sampling and observation have been done within a locale that is not representative of the social organization in question.

At another level, the representational map gives scholars in the future a firmer basis for replication. A student in 1988 could return to the Jane Addams area in Chicago and produce representational and interactional maps of the parks and places described and analyzed by Suttles in 1968. The extent to which interracial tensions have subsided or increased during this time period could be at least partially established by a systematic use of these maps.

"FIRST-TIME" AND IRREGULAR ACTIONS

Many behaviors central to a subject's world occur at irregular intervals, and some occur only once. The divorce, the first marriage, the first crime, the first homosexual encounter, and the first exchange with a drug dealer are examples. These behaviors cannot be experimentally reproduced. An observer who was not present when such an event occurred is forced to rely on the subject's reconstruction of it. One hopes that alternative accounts of the behavior in question can be secured, perhaps from the subject's peers, family members, or friends, or from members of official social control agencies. Ideally, the naturalist should be present when these irregular or "first-time" actions occur. In practice, this is often impossible. A compromise strategy is for the naturalist to secure a subject's account of a first-time or irregular act and then attempt to locate a class of individuals who are likely to experience that behavior at some point in the future. The observer then stations himself in the settings where that behavior is likely to appear and attempts to gather firsthand direct reports of its occurrence. In this way, past accounts direct ongoing observations.

Forming Generalizations

In the process of building up interpretations based on representational maps and behavior specimens, the naturalist must demonstrate how representative the behavior specimens actually are. That is, do these specimens faithfully reflect the nature and frequency of the joint acts and behaviors the investigator wished to generalize to and describe? An investigator concerned with gender differences in conversational interactions must offer a frequency of male–female and female–male interruptions in intimate, friendly, and stranger cross-sex relations. Similarly, male–male and female–female interruptions must be studied. It is not sufficient to record only male interruptions of females (see West and Zimmerman, 1983, pp. 105-7). Similar strictures would hold for studies of discrimination in high schools, for patterns of interracial contact in ghetto areas, for rates of crime and deviance for particular social groups, for the use of drugs by middle-class teenagers on weekends, for swinging or group sex among married couples, or for the hustling of whites by blacks in tourist sections of metropolitan areas. In short, the study of any class of behaviors must do more than record the fact that the behavior in question has occurred. The frequency, form, and content of these acts must be presented, analyzed, and shaped into an explanatory scheme that accounts for variations and stability over time and across persons and situations.

Unknown Populations

It is frequently the case that the population from which the behavior specimens have been drawn is unknown. While statistical-demographic data can be easily assembled to describe the age, sex, racial, educational, and occupational structure of, say, a community or a particular mental hospital, data on the *interactive relationships* among the members of those organizations are seldom available. They remain unrecorded. There are, for example, few concrete data on such matters as (1) how often members of families interact as total collectivities over a week's time; (2) the number of fights and arguments marital partners have in an average day, week, or month; (3) the number of hustling activities street gangs engage in during a week's time; (4) the number of focused conversational huddles police have with members of the criminal underworld during a month's time; (5) the number of "dropouts" preschools produce in a year's time. The frequency and form of interactive relationships are at issue in these examples. The unknown population is acutely problematic in the study of acts that go unnoticed by official recording agencies. Many acts and activities exist in a world that is neither systematically charted nor known. Students of these behaviors must modify, if not rewrite, the usual canons of sampling theory and develop alternative procedures for describing the populations they have sampled from (see Becker, 1970, pp. 31-36; and Sudman, 1986, pp. 424-26).

Alternative Sampling Units

Several approaches can be suggested.

The situation   As Becker (1970, pp. 35-36) suggests, the observer may employ the situation as an observational unit and argue that the sample is drawn from observations of all persons who passed through that setting for a specified period of time. Here the researcher must have data on how representative the situation is for the natives or persons who pass through it. Preschools, for example, are familiar worlds for preschoolers, yet preschoolers are not randomly distributed in preschools. Ghetto blacks will seldom pass through a Montessori school. Any situational study of interactive relationships in preschools would necessarily be biased in these directions. Hence, while the setting is a familiar and recurring one for natives, there are forces at work that make some more familiar than others. Similarly, while bars are recurring settings for sociable behavior in semipublic places, natives differentially transport themselves to different types of bars. Hence, any sample drawn from bars must demonstrate the distribution of persons across types of bars for the observational period. The naturalist, then, must have knowledge about the situated worlds of the natives: which are familiar and repeatedly entered, which are irregularly entered, which are entered voluntarily, which are entered involuntarily.

Time   Time can be employed as an observational unit. A particular day out of the native's week, month, or year can be selected for study. A ritual day, such as Thanksgiving, Easter, Christmas, New Year's Day, or Yom Kippur, may be designated, and then the sample is drawn from that day. The student then argues that the population is all persons acting on the day in question. Unfortunately, individuals give days unique meaning; so that while Christmas, for example, may be celebrated by all members of a particular community, its particular meaning may vary from family to family and from relationship to relationship. Members of social control agencies work on a calendar of days that may bear little relationship to other calendars (for example, a fiscal or political calendar). They may hasten or slow down their recording and labeling depending on where they stand in their overall calendar. Finding an excess of money in their budget as they approach the end of the fiscal year, they may inflate or increase their admissions of deviants (this appears to operate for many mental hospitals and drug clinics). The observer of official labeling encounters would find, then, that rates of institutionally defined deviance would vary temporally. Hence, time by itself may not be sufficient as a basis for gaining insight into the population to which the analyst wished to generalize.

Social organizations   Naturalists may attempt to hold time and setting constant by selecting as their observational unit a social organization that processes and produces the types of behaviors in which they are interested. Here the organization, not its participants, becomes the sampling unit. Police precincts, mental hospitals, prisons, schools, alcoholic treatment centers, and family counseling agencies may be selected for observation. But a researcher who lacks information on the frequency and distribution of such an organization throughout the native's world will be left with little more than an ethnographic account of one or more institutional settings.

Interactive relationships   The observer may decide to employ an *interactive relationship* as the unit of analysis, focusing on families, friendship groups, ghetto gangs, hustlers and pimps, teachers and students, police officers and juveniles, or labelers and those they label (see Cicourel, 1968, for a study of the last and Brede, 1971, for a study of police–juvenile encounters).

In a similar fashion, Power (1985, pp. 213–27) has examined how parents teach their children linguistic rituals. She recorded the interactions that occurred between children and children and adults and children in day-care and home settings. She timed and situated her observations to coincide with the natural interactional rhythms of these situations. She focused on those times when children were most likely to make requests of one another, or of adults.

There are advantages to selecting the interactive relationship as the sampling unit. It combines the variables of time and setting into a focused observational unit. It maintains the interactionist's commitment to study joint acts. Interactions between people — not people themselves — should represent the basic analytic and sampling unit for naturalistic studies.

Progress could be made through the careful construction of representative maps for different classes of acting units, or agencies (for example, types of families, gangs, police patrol teams, psychiatrists and social workers, teachers and students). The temporal rhythms of specific classes of social organizations could be detailed. The researcher, might, for example, isolate grocery stores, public drinking establishments, police stations, mental hospitals, wards in hospitals, schools, or neighborhoods for specific attention. Unfortunately, many of the encounters and interactive relationships we wish to study remain unrecorded. Neither their producers nor members of official control agencies keep records on their occurrences. Here investigators are left with no other recourse than to specify as rigorously as possible the temporal and spatial frames of sampling and observation.

Case Selection

The problem of representativeness is partially solved through the selection of cases for intensive analysis. As the researcher's theory begins to take shape, empirical regularities in the native's world emerge. It is the naturalist's task to identify these regularities and to forge interpretations that account for their shape and form. Similarly, irregular or episodic actions and first-time actions will appear. These behaviors occur only once or only a few times during the duration of the study. There may also emerge a class of behaviors that can be defined as deviant because they clearly challenge the theory the researcher is forming. These three classes of actions — regular, irregular, and deviant — must be detailed in the behavior specimens, and they must be theoretically taken into account. In short, the naturalist addresses the representational problem by categorizing behavior specimens into one of these three groupings. The majority of the specimens should reflect regular actions. From the behavior specimens, the researcher selects those cases that are most representative of the subject's behavior. These cases appear at a frequency sufficient to accurately cover the range of explained cases recorded in the unit under study. That is, they describe regular, routine behaviors. They are to be separated from, and compared with, the irregular or episodic cases and the deviant cases that will inevitably appear in the observer's field notes. As was argued in Chapter 2, the intensive analysis of episodic and deviant cases serves to highlight weak features of one's theory. Such cases also open up unexpected areas of inquiry and may lead to the refinement of research instruments. Their frequency of appearance over the observational period must be recorded.

Triangulating Data Sources, Methods, Perspectives, and Observers

Triangulation directs the observer to combine multiple data sources, research methods, theoretical perspectives, and observers in the collection, inspection, and analysis of behavior specimens.

Data sources Triangulating by data sources forces the researcher to go to as many concrete situations as possible in forming the observational base. It forces the researcher to *situationally* check the accuracy and repeatability of the specimens and emerging causal proposition. The attitudes a man expresses in private, for example, might be compared with those he offers when in the company of his larger social group (see Becker, Geer, Hughes, and Strauss, 1961). The use of multiple data sources also asks that the investigator *temporally* specify the nature of the interpretations. That is, when is it more likely that the subject in question will act in a particular way?

Methods The use of multiple methods means that the naturalist will use any and all research techniques that better unravel the processes under study. The researcher might, for example, combine demographic and ecological techniques with formal interviewing, unstructured interviews, and unobtrusive observing, and finally observe as a participant in a social group or a local community.

Perspectives Triangulation asks the observer to compare subjects' accounts of their experiences with alternative theoretical schemes. For example, in my AA study, I compared the reasons alcoholics give for slipping (relapsing and drinking again) with more formal sociological theories of relapse and the alcoholic's recovery (see Denzin, 1987b, pp. 124–34). It is inevitably the case (as was noted in Chapter 1) that the sociological explanation of any unit of behavior will differ from a subject's explanation of that behavior. Yet it is often the case that a subject's view of her behavior will be centrally relevant to any sociological explanation that is ultimately formed. The researcher must work back and forth between subjects' or natives' accounts and his own emerging theoretical scheme. The goal is to form a theory that rings true at the subjects' level, while conforming with accepted sociological rules concerning how a theory should be grounded. Contradictions in data and perspective will emerge during the course of any investigation. In part this is due to the low credibility of some data sources and of some informants. Many public relations documents—for example, those put forth by social movements and liberation groups—are deliberately proselytizing. They are aimed at gaining new recruits and convincing the public at large that the group's cause is a worthy one. The documents may be poor sociological accounts of the meanings and motives held by those who produce them.

Observers Often there is a *hierachy of credibility* (Becker, 1967a) at work in the social groups studied by the sociologist. The public statements of group leaders may not reflect the private feelings of other members. Furthermore, members often possess varying degrees of information about the inner workings of the group. Their opinions may reflect their standing in the overall hierarchy of persons that make up the group. Deviants, isolates, marginals, newcomers, old-timers, and past leaders may offer shifting interpretations of what is occurring in the group. These interpretations often vary widely. (See Simmel, 1950, pp. 330–76 on secrecy and group interactions.)

The use of multiple observers suggests that the researcher attempts to secure as many differing views as possible on the behavior in question and will not be content with the statements of just a few individuals who may be proclaimed experts. Furthermore, the investigator may utilize the insights and reports of multiple observers who are trained as social scientists. However, if multiple trained observers are used, the principal investigator must take steps to increase the likelihood that they actually observe what they report having observed. Roth (1966) has noted that "hired hand" researchers often generate the data they claim to have observed. Postinterview sessions may reduce this type of data reporting. A more practical stance would be to ensure that the "hired hand" researchers are actually a part of the research process—from beginning to end.

Naturalistic Indicators

Naturalists link their theoretical concepts to the empirical world through the collection of behavior specimens. They *operationalize* those concepts through a careful analysis of their specimens. Starting with loose sensitizing definitions of their concepts, they empirically operationalize the concepts only after having entered the worlds of interaction that they wish to understand. They attempt to secure several observations of their key concepts. They include as many behaviors as possible as indications of the concept in question, through the use of naturalistic indicators which represent any segment of subjects' behavior that reflects on, or describes, a sociological concept. An indicator is naturalistic if it derives (preferably spontaneously) from the subjects' world of meaning, action, and discourse—it is not imposed on that world by the observer. Such behavior is *interpreted* as being indicative of underlying sociological processes (see Lazarsfeld, 1972). It refers to a latent structure of meanings that are manifested in overt, measurable, recordable acts. Thus a man's image of himself as a worker can often be gleaned from an inspection of how he dresses for work. The reports he brings home at night about his work also reflect something about how he defines himself as a worker—for example, what he does is important enough to talk about (see Terkel, 1974). Similarly, studies of the development of self-awareness in early childhood could focus on the preschooler's use of personal pronouns, for the personal pronoun singles out the individual as a unique object (Bain, 1936, pp. 767–75); Cooley, 1922). It could be hypothesized that the more frequent the use of the personal pronoun, the more pronounced the child's degree of self-awareness. Additional naturalistic indicators of self-hood could include the attachment of a preference to a particular piece of clothing. The more active the children are in selecting their own clothing, the more self-conscious they are (see Stone, 1962). The researcher operationalizes central concepts through the use of these naturalistic indicators. It is hoped that there will be multiple indicators for each concept. Indeed, the strength of any empirical proposition is increased as the number of indicators for each concept in the proposition is increased. It is often the case that the researcher can combine indicators derived from behavior specimens with more formally structured indicators based on specific questions or items from an interview schedule. That is, the naturalist is not solely restricted to data drawn from behavior specimens.

Assessing Indicators

Behavioral validity   The first criterion for assessing a naturalistic indicator is its degree of behavioral validity. That is, how frequently does it appear in the subject's behavior repertoire? Furthermore, is its appearance influenced by matters of time and space? The greater its appearance across time and space, the greater its behavioral validity. The researcher should have multiple instances, or examples, of its occurrence; the lack of multiple instances detracts from the strength of an indicator. If the researcher is going to place a great deal of weight on a specific indicator, there *must* be multiple instances of it.

Frequency   This suggests a second criterion: The indicator must occur at a frequency sufficient to permit repeated observations. The researcher must be able to observe the same behavior over and over again for the same subject, or be able to observe its occurrence across a large class of individuals. Thus, if the measure of self-awareness in early childhood is based on the use of personal pronouns, the researcher must be able either to record the use of personal pronouns for a given child over a continuous period of time, or to study a large number of young children to see if they also use personal pronouns in their daily talk with one another.

The question of how often a given indicator occurs focuses on the repeatability of behavior and suggests that the more routinized a behavior becomes, the more likely it will be that the researcher can obtain multiple measures of it. For those behaviors that are episodic, or that occur infrequently, the observer can attempt to uncover multiple instances of similar behaviors across acting units. Novels, autobiographies, biographies, and journalistic accounts can be inspected for what they reveal about divorces, suicides, first births, marriages, marriage proposals, birthdays, anniversaries, and biological impairments (see Bossard and Boll, 1960). These documents record the occurrence of rare or infrequent events, yet a systematic sampling of them can give the researcher a data base otherwise not available. Thus if a behavior has a low rate of occurrence for one acting unit, the researcher simply extends the sampling base to include other units that also display the behavior in question.

Observability   A third criterion for evaluating a naturalistic indicator is the extent to which it is based on publicly observable acts and activities. The greater the public nature of the act, the greater its assumed validity. The naturalist places greatest weight on those behaviors that could have been observed and recorded by any other observer. Less emphasis is placed on those indicators that require the researcher to impute motives or intentions to those under study. If motives or intentions are imputed, verbal statements must be obtained from the subjects to support those imputations. Any thorough investigation will have a mix of public and private indicators. Indicators based on private acts — thoughts, dreams, fantasies, imputed intentions — should never exceed the number of indicators based on public acts; private acts must be blended with and balanced against public acts. When, for example, a person ruminates about a proposed future act, such ruminations are important and must be collected. They are of little use, however, until the future act is observed. Observers cannot confine their studies of interaction to covert, symbolic behaviors. They must move from attitudes to public acts so as to link the subjective side of social experience with the public world of face-to-face interaction (see Deutscher, 1973; Goffman, 1971).

Reliability and Validity of Naturalistic Indicators

The foregoing discussion suggests that the naturalist is concerned with the *reliability* and *validity* of observations.

A *reliable observation* is one that is not biased by idiosyncrasies of the observer, a research instrument, or a subject, or by the constraints of time and place. A reliable observation is an observation that could have been made by any similarly situated observer. The same, or nearly the same, behaviors would have been recorded in a behavior specimen or on a research instrument by any other observer. Observations that meet the three criteria just listed should be reliable observations.

A *valid observation* is one that is theoretically directed and is grounded in the actual behaviors of interacting individuals. Its degree of validity is assessed by its behavioral grounding. The more often it occurs in the actions of those studied, the greater its validity.

Repeatability of Naturalistic Indicators

Matters of reliability and validity lead to a focus on *repeatability*. This has to do with the frequency or rate at which a unit of behavior appears in the repertoire of an acting unit. The naturalist is concerned with faithfully producing reliable depictions of repeatable behaviors. From behavior specimens, the researcher culls, gleans, and analyzes those behaviors and representative cases that most faithfully describe and depict the actions of those studied.

Two questions are posed when the issue of repeatability is considered. First, the naturalist asks if repeated observations will clarify an emergent theory. If a theory is still in an ill-defined phase, then more observations are called for. Second, if the quality of the researcher's behavior specimens is weak and if the number of naturalistic indicators is low, then more observations are called for (see Schatzman and Strauss, 1973). If the researcher has carefully recorded the character of an act, or a series of acts, and determined that the collected behavior specimens are sufficiently representative of the acting unit in question, then repeated observations are unnecessary. If the behavior specimens lack in detail, are out of sequence, contain faulty biographical detail, are restricted to only certain times of observations, or are confined to only certain interactional locales, then new and additional observations are called for. Also, if the researcher's body of naturalistic indicators is small, or if the indicators fail to meet the three criteria noted above, then new observations are needed.

These general rules, it must be noted, *do not* impose a fixed time period for observation on the researcher. Nor do they demand that a certain number of behavior specimens, or a fixed number of pages in a field notebook, be generated. Observations end when the researcher has generated a theory, or explanatory account, of the subject or social organization in question that is naturalistically grounded in the routine, repeatable behaviors of that acting unit.

Two propositions concerning repeatability can be offered. First, acts of any consequence and importance to a subject will be repeated, time and time again. Observers need not be concerned if they have missed, or failed to record, one or more examples of the behavior in question. It will appear again in the future. Those acts that are not repeated, but that are assigned high importance, will be reconstructed and verbally replayed by the subjects. The researcher records those verbal reconstructions. Second, if behaviors are not assigned consequential and important meaning by the subjects, the researcher need not be overly concerned if such behaviors go unrecorded. A note of caution must be inserted, however. Behaviors that the subject takes for granted may be of high theoretical interest to the sociologist. In this case, the researcher must take pains to record such behaviors (see Garfinkel, 1967; Schatzman and Strauss, 1973).

Measurement

The naturalistic observer does not measure social behavior in the conventional way that sociologists define *measurement* (see Mueller and Schuessler, 1961). That is, naturalists seldom confine their observations to responses on fixed-choice questionnaires. Nor do they typically engage in index construction (Lazarfeld, 1972) or in the use of Likert, Guttman, or Thurstone scales (see Hamblin, 1971). Instead, they employ the more open-ended method of collecting behavior specimens. In this sense they do not measure behavior. They record behavior specimens and then subject those specimens to detailed causal analysis. Furthermore, they seldom confine themselves to one measuring instrument; they work with multiple measures, methods, and observations.

Their aim is to leave the field with actual records of behaviors that have naturally and spontaneously occurred. By continually sifting through these records, they progressively develop analytic models which may combine several types of data. They may, for example, collect records, accounts, documents, and specimens that yield data of the nominal, ordinal, interval, and ratio variety. They might relate age (ratio data) to sex (nominal data) to friendship network (ordinal data) to year in preschool (interval data), attempting to better understand and explain the processes of socialization that occur in preschools. They try to examine processes and events meaningful to their subjects and to classify and reclassify these processes in ways that reveal underlying causal processes. For both sampling and causal purposes, they are obligated to demonstrate the distribution of key processes in the social worlds under study. They must show how frequently such processes occur, which of the subjects produced them, and when and where they are most likely to appear. Such demonstrations specify the unique features of those studied and highlight deficiencies in the researchers' critical concepts and indicators.

Data Inspection and the Measurement Process

The researcher poses a number of questions when beginning to analyze behavior specimens. First, does a given unit of behavior exist in the subject's behavior repertoire? This is equivalent to making a nominal observation. Either the behavior exists, or it does not exist. Once the nominal question has been raised and answered, the researcher proceeds to ask how often, at what frequency, and at what rate the behavior in question appears for the subjects under study. The more frequently it appears, the more rigorous and detailed the observations become. Thus, the researcher records ongoing social processes and attempts to subject those processes to detailed analysis.

Causal Interpretive Analysis

Propositions gathered by the naturalistic method are assessed from several positions.

First, greater faith is placed in those which rest on observations that have been grounded in naturalistic indicators. The greater the naturalistic grounding, the greater the assumed validity of the interpretations.

Second, greatest weight is placed on those interpretations that have withstood the impact of triangulated observations. That is, do the multiple observers, data sources, and theories lead to the same analytic conclusions? (See Webb et al., 1966.) However, a single instance of a suggestive proposition need not be ignored. The fact that it has been observed only once, or only a few times, cannot be taken as justification for assigning it less theoretical significance. Possibly the behavior in question is repeatable but has never been noted before. Or possibly its repeatability was not assigned any significance by previous observers. A sociologist may assign it high theoretical meaning and assume that previous investigators were faulty analysts.

Third, naturalists assess the repeatability ratio of the acts they have observed and of which they have formed explanations. They give greater weight to those acts that have been observed more than once. As acts critical to the emerging theory are located and discovered, multiple instances and reconstructions of them are sought out.

Fourth, those interpretations that survive the test of multiple theoretical perspectives are given greatest credence and attention. It is hoped that the observer has not isolated a set of behaviors for explanation that could not be addressed by another theoretical perspective. That other perspectives might not, or have not, addressed the behaviors in question is irrelevant. They may have discovered a set of behaviors that will demand the total or partial reorientation of existing theoretical schemes (see Kuhn, 1977); in that case, the behavior specimens have more than adequately met minimal scientific demands.

Fifth, naturalists give greatest attention to explaining and forming interpretations about publicly observable behavior. They attempt to explain behaviors that any similarly situated observers could have noted and recorded. That previous observers have not given attention to a given class of behaviors is of little concern. Such actions could have been studied. They are public behaviors.

Many of the interpretations to be offered by the naturalist reflect attempts to develop sequential, phase-like explanations of the behavior under inspection. They rest on a common assumption. Few behaviors are the product of one variable or process. Children, for example, do not just become members of preschools. They pass through a series of interconnected phases, and what happens in one phase influences what happens in the next. The naturalist is obliged to identify these phases in the acting units' behavioral world of experience and to show how behaviors in each phase shape behaviors in the next. (See Chapter 2 in this respect, and see Lofland, 1971, and Lofland and Lofland, 1984, for a more general treatment of phase analysis.)

To identify the phases persons pass through (for example, the search for necessary and contributory, not sufficient, causes), the observer must have behavior specimens of the outcome, or final phase, of the act in question. It may be smoking marijuana, being a member of a preschool, getting married, learning how to play the "baby" game, or buying a new house. The researcher must empirically specify the outcome of the act in question and gather multiple observations of how it may vary. Becoming and being a member of a preschool can mean having one friend with whom one plays in the sandbox every day, or it may mean being the leader of the girl's group. Having secured behavior specimens of the act in question, the naturalist works back in time so as to uncover the actions that focal subjects undertook to get where they are now. At the same time, the naturalist attempts to follow new members into the situation so as to gather on-the-spot records of their behaviors (for example, new friends on the block). This problem of working back and forth between the past and the present established the cardinal significance of the behavioral specimens. They are like films that can be replayed and reanalyzed as new questions are asked and as new negative cases emerge.

Stage of Inquiry

Peirce (1965–1966) suggested that the research process moves through stages, or phases.

Abduction　　The first stage occurs after a substantial body of data has been collected; it is termed the *abductive insight*. The abductive insight forces the researcher to pause and ponder over the substance of the existing observational base. This insight suggests that there may be processes at work that are unknown, or unthought of, producing the behaviors he has recorded. Peirce (1965–1966, p. 181) describes this moment of insight as follows:

It is an act of insight, although of extremely fallible insight. It is true that the different elements of the hypothesis were in our minds before; but it is the idea of putting together what we had never before dreamed of putting together which flashed the new suggestion before our contemplation.

Deduction   The second phase is a period of rigorous *deduction*. In this phase the investigator is forced to systematically define critical concepts and inspect multiple instances of the behavior in question. Here the investigator explicates the tentative hypotheses formed in the abductive phase, reasoning that "if X was caused by Y, then future occurrences of Y should produce future occurrences of X."

Induction   If the reasoning is correct in phase 2, the investigator moves to phase 3, which is the period of *induction*. Here, one attempts to determine "how far those consequences (resulting from deductive application of the hypothesis) accord with experience" (Peirce, 1965–1966, p. 472). In the inductive stage of research, the investigator has to show that the causal processes that have been isolated are actually at work and, furthermore, to what degree they are operative. That is, how many behavior specimens can be explained, or accounted for, by the hypothesis? Negative cases force a reevaluation of the proposed causal sequence. (See Lindesmith, 1968.) This method is commonly termed *analytic induction*.

Asking questions: the method of abduction   Naturalists inspect and organize behavior specimens in ways which they hope will permit them to progressively reveal and better understand the underlying problematic features of the social world under study. They seek to ask the question or set of questions that will make that world or social organization understandable. They do not approach that world with a rigid set of preconceived hypotheses. They are initially directed toward an interest in the routine and taken-for-granted features of that world. They ask how it is that the persons in question go about producing orderly patterns of interaction and meaning (Garfinkel, 1967). They use a variant on what Peirce (1965–1966) termed the "method of abduction." That is, they do not use a full-fledged deductive-hypothetical scheme in thinking and developing propositions. Nor are they fully inductive, letting the so-called "facts" speak for themselves. Facts do not speak for themselves. They must be interpreted. Previously developed deductive models seldom conform with the empirical data that are gathered. The method of abduction combines the deductive and inductive models of proposition development and theory construction. It can be defined as *working from consequence back to cause or antecedent*. The observer records the occurrence of a particular event, and then works back in time in an effort to reconstruct the events (causes) that produced the event (consequence) in question.

At this point, the researcher may find that the existing body of behavior specimens is faulty or lacks the details necessary to inspect the interpretation. New observations are then gathered. The investigator may follow Peirce's suggestion and produce experiments, or quasi-experiments, that will better reveal the processes under study.

SUMMARY: STAGES OF INQUIRY

These three stages of inquiry mold the problems of observing, sampling, and recording into a coherent set of directives. The observer is not content with a single sampling, unit, with a single measuring or recording unit, or with a single set of theoretical interpretations. Rather, the observer's central interest is directed toward the discovery of the abductive insight which will make apparent that which was previously taken for granted. Investigators, then, are charged to free themselves from preconceptions so as to better see and understand those worlds of which they have become active students (Blumer, 1969a).

SUGGESTED READINGS

CICOUREL, AARON V., *Method and Measurement in Sociology.* (New York: Free Press, 1964). A classic critique of research techniques and measurement scales in the social sciences.

FIELDING, NIGEL, G. AND JANE L. FIELDING, *Linking Data.* (Beverly Hills: Sage, 1986). A sensitive and probing treatment of how the method of multiple triangulation may be employed in qualitative investigations.

LOFLAND, JOHN AND LYN H. LOFLAND, *Analyzing Social Settings: A Guide to Qualitative Observation and Analysis.* (Belmont, Calif.: Wadsworth, 1984). Valuable presentation of the major steps to qualitative, naturalistic inquiry.

LINCOLN, YVONNE S. AND EGON G. GUBA, *Naturalistic Inquiry.* (Beverly Hills: Sage, 1985). A comprehensive analysis of the latest developments in naturalistic inquiry as viewed from the field of educational psychology.

PATTON, MICHAEL QUINN, *Qualitative Evaluation Methods.* (Beverly Hills: Sage, 1980). An excellent discussion of how qualitative, naturalistic data are collected and interpreted.

4

The Sociological Interview

As long as the survey interview remains predominant, and we continue to accept the findings of research without a careful accounting of the social process of communication as well as our models of interpretation, sociology will continue to wander in an epistemological wilderness. [Manning, 1967, p. 312]

The interview, far from being a kind of snapshot or tape-recording—a simple report either of fact or of emotional response—in which the interviewer is a neutral agent who simply trips the shutter or triggers the response, is instead inevitably an interactional situation. [Kuhn, 1962, p. 194]

But the interview is still more than tool and object of study. It is the art of sociological sociability, the game which we play for the pleasure of savoring its subtleties. It is our flirtation with life, our eternal affair, played hard and to win, but played with that detachment and amusement which gives us, win or lose, the spirit to rise up and interview again and again. [Benney and Hughes, 1956, p. 138]

In the sociological interview, one version of the research act comes alive. Unlike the naturalistic observer, who seeks to record ongoing sequences of behavior, the interviewer elicits behaviors from a respondent. The interview is, as Kuhn (1962) and Benney and Hughes (1956) rightly note, the favorite "digging tool" of the sociologist. Indeed, it is commonly assumed that the interview is the sociologist's main data-gathering device. This has led some (Webb et al., 1966, 1981) to call for the use of multiple research strategies. They lament the overuse of the sociological interview.

The interview is like a conversation. A conversation is a give-and-take between two persons. It is an informal interchange of thoughts by spoken words. It often, but not always, occurs between intimates, or between the well-acquainted. The sociological interview, as a conversation, should not be the occasion for one person to do all the talking while the other only asks questions and listens. When interviews take this form, they become authoritarian exchanges in which the power and prestige of social science shape the information that is given. Douglas (1985, p. 15) has given the name "creative interviewing" to the process whereby two or more persons creatively and openly share life experiences with one another in a mutual search for greater self-understanding. This is one way in which interviewing should be experienced.

Interviews, as conversations, are typically "gendered productions." That is, the gender stratification of the larger society comes into play in the interview situation (see Thorne, Kramarae, and Henley, 1983). The usual rules of conversation between the sexes operate in the interview situation, but with a twist. Many social science interviewers are women. Thus there is an inversion of the usual dominance hierarchy, wherein males interrupt and speak more than do females in the talking situation. When women are the interviewers, this typical pattern of interaction is altered. Its effects on interviews are not well understood.

As the favorite research tool of the sociologist, the interview is beset with other problems (see Silverman, 1973, pp. 31–48). At one level, these problems derive from the fact that the interview is itself an instance of ongoing interaction. It is a focused, usually face-to-face encounter which must rest on rules of etiquette while at the same time eliciting intimate and private perspectives. The rules for such transactions and conversations vary from interviewer to interviewer. The dynamics of a given interview may also vary considerably during the course of the conversation that makes up the interview. Thus the ultimate basis of any interview is "talk" and its social organization (Silverman, 1973). Yet the talk that occurs is unlike everyday talk between friends, close acquaintances, spouses, or co-workers. It is gendered talk covering a wide range of topics, which are not selected by one of the talkers—the respondent. It is talk that is organized so as to give one person (the interviewer) greater control over the other (the respondent). It is talk that is (typically) furnished for someone else's benefit (see Goffman, 1981, pp. 1–77).

These and a variety of other matters will be taken up in this chapter. I begin with a discussion of various forms interviews may take.

FORMS OF THE INTERVIEW

An interview is "a face to face verbal interchange in which one person, the interviewer, attempts to elicit information or expressions of opinions or belief from another person or persons" (Maccoby and Maccoby, 1954, p. 499). Interviews may be classified by their degree of structuring, or standardization (Richardson, Dohrenwend, and Klein, 1965, pp. 32–55).

The Schedule Standardized Interview

At the most structured level is the schedule standardized interview (SSI), in which the wording and order of all questions are exactly the same for every respondent, the purpose being to develop an instrument that can be given in the same way to all respondents. All questions must be comparable, so that when variations between respondents appear, they can be attributed to actual differences in response, not to the instrument.

The rationale for this form of the interview rests on the belief that, for any study, "the respondents have a sufficiently common vocabulary so that it is possible to formulate questions which have the same meaning for each of them" (Richardson, Dohrenwend, and Klein, 1965, p. 40). In other words, it is assumed that each respondent will be presented with the same stimuli and that these will elicit the same range of meanings for each. Benney and Hughes (1956, p. 137) have called this assumption into question:

> Interviews are of many kinds. Some sociologists like them standardized and so formulated that they can be administered to large groups of people. This can be done only among large homogeneous populations not too unlike the investigator himself in culture. Where languages are too diverse, where common values are too few, where the fear of talking to strangers is too great, there the interview based on a standardized questionnaire calling for a few standardized answers may not be applicable. Those who venture into such situations may have to invent new modes of interviewing.

A second assumption of the standardized form suggests that it is possible to find a uniform wording for all questions equally meaningful to every respondent. Benney and Hughes's (1956, p. 139) critique indicates that this assumption is best realized in a homogenous sample—and typically, I would add, only in middle-class samples. That is:

> Probably the most intensive presocialization of respondents runs in roughly the social strata from which the interviewers themselves are drawn—the middle, urban, higher-educated groups, while at the top and bottom—though for different reasons—the appropriate role of the informant is apparently much less known.

A third assumption is that if the "meaning of each question is to be identical for each respondent, its context must be identical and, since all preceding questions constitute part of the context, the sequence of the questions must be identical" (Richardson, Dohrenwend, and Klein, 1965, p. 43). This assumes an order in which questions can be best placed to capture the interest and mood of the respondent. Questions are typically ordered as follows: those that elicit the interest of the respondent come first; once interest has been obtained, less interesting questions follow; highly emotional questions are embedded in the interview, often near the end. Placing the most threatening questions near the end ensures that, should the respondent "break off," a major portion of the interview will have been completed. Whether this outline for questions can be followed depends largely on the need and intents of the investigation.

The last assumption of the SSI is that "careful pilot investigation, development, and pretesting will provide a final schedule of questions that meets the requirements of assumptions (1), (2), and (3)" (Richardson, Dohrenwend, and Klein, 1965, p. 44). The pretest phase of the study consists of selecting a group of persons comparable to those who will be interviewed in the final study, but using these persons only to test hypotheses about the interview.

These four assumptions of the SSI are largely untested articles of faith. They are ideal guidelines which are seldom in fact met in any empirical investigation. Furthermore, they fail to point to the underlying interactional features of the interview encounter. There is some justification in attempting to meet them when the sample to be interviewed has similar characteristics and experiences. However, such an assumption is often difficult to justify. Certainly when the sample is known to be heterogeneous, the use of the schedule standardized form must be questioned.

The Nonschedule Standardized Interview

The nonschedule standardized interview, or unstructured schedule interview (USI), is the second basic type of interview. The "nonschedule standardized interviewer works with a list of the information required from each respondent" (Richardson, Dohrenwend, and Klein, 1965, p. 45). This form most closely approximates what has been called the *focused* interview (Merton and Kendall, 1946, pp. 541–52), in which certain types of information are desired from all respondents but the particular phrasing of questions and their order are redefined to fit the characteristics of each respondent. This form of the interview requires that each interviewer be highly trained in the meaning of the desired information and in the skills of phrasing questions for each person interviewed.

Becker, Geer, Hughes, and Strauss (1961, p. 29) describe their use of this interview form as follows:

> The student interviews, following as they did a great deal of "exploratory" work, were much more structured, being designed to get information on particular points for systematic analysis. . . . We used an interview guide, asking each student 138 questions. . . . But we left room for the free expression of all kinds of ideas and did not force the student to stick to the original list of questions or to answer in predetermined categories.

The assumptions underlying the nonschedule standardized interview are suggested by this quotation, First, if the meaning of a question is to be standardized, it must be formulated in words familiar to those interviewed. Medical students, for example, do not speak of patients as uniform types of persons. Some are "crooks," some are "good" patients, and so on. Lower-class people do not become mentally ill and suffer from anxiety syndromes; they "get nervous" or "go mental." The nonstandardized schedule indicates an awareness that individuals have unique ways of defining their world. To meaningfully understand that world, researchers must approach it from the subject's perspective. Second, this interview strategy assumes that no "fixed sequence of questions is satisfactory to all respondents; the most effective sequence for any respondent is determined by his readiness and willingness to take up a topic as it comes up" (Richardson, Dohrenwend, and Klein, 1965, p. 51). This assumption was reflected by Becker and his associates when they permitted each medical student to choose his own order of answering their questions. With this approach, the interviewer will often find that interviewees will raise important issues not contained in the schedule, or will even summarize entire sections of the schedule in one long sequence of statements.

A third, although unverified, assumption underlying the nonschedule strategy suggests that "through careful study of respondents and selection and training of interviewers, the necessary skills can be achieved to tailor the questions and their sequence so that equivalence of meaning is obtained for all respondents" (Richardson, Dohrenwend, and Klein, 1965, p. 51).

Not only will all respondents be given the same set of questions, but it is assumed that each respondent has been exposed to the same uniform set of stimuli (i.e., questions). This suggests a parallel to the schedule standardized approach, which also attempts to place all questions in a uniform context— the basic difference, of course, being that here questions and order are changed for each respondent.

The Nonstandardized Interview

The nonstandardized interview, or unstructured interview (UI), is the third major type of interview. In it, no prespecified set of questions is employed, nor are questions asked in a specified order. Furthermore, a schedule is not employed. This gives the interviewer a great deal of freedom to probe various areas and to raise and test specific hypotheses during the course of the interview. Lindesmith (1947, p. 6), who employed the nonstandardized approach in his study of opiate addiction, described his interviews as "informal friendly conversations." Similarly, Becker (1962, p. 592) described his interviews with marijuana users as follows:

> The interviews focused on the history of the person's experience with the drug, seeking major changes in his attitude toward it and in his actual use of it and the reasons for these changes. Generalizations stating necessary conditions for the maintenance of use at each level were developed in initial interviews, and tested against and revised in the light of each succeeding one.

The nonstandardized interview represents the logical extension of the nonschedule standardized interview and rests on essentially the same assumptions. It is clear, however, that there is no attempt to standardize either the interview setting or the format of the interview so that each respondent is presented with the same set of stimuli.

The Question and the Interview

Up to this point I have considered types of interviews in terms of their underlying assumptions. To complete the comparisons of these approaches it is necessary to return to the very basis of all interviews—the question. Kahn and Cannell (1957, p. 131) have suggested that the questionnaire or interview must serve two broad purposes: (1) It must translate research objectives into specific questions, the answers to which will provide data necessary for hypothesis testing; and (2) it must assist the interviewer in motivating the respondent, so that the necessary information is given.

It is to these two ends that the question becomes the major unit around which the interview is constructed. Hyman (1954, pp. 665–74) has argued that all questions should be comprehensive enough to cover all areas of the research and should elicit responses that can be validly and reliably quantified; that is, the questions should measure the areas intended to be measured by the investigation.

Lazarsfeld (1954, pp. 675-86) has argued that all questions should conform to the principles of specification, division, and tacit assumption. The *principle of specification* forces one to clarify and focus the function of each question. Each question should clearly tap a conceptual domain in the researcher's theory and should produce responses that would bear on one or more of the researcher's hypotheses. The *principle of division* states that the pattern of a sequence of questions should fit the actual experiences of those interviewed. The *meaning*, not the wording, of questions should be fixed; this gives interviewers flexibility, so that they can fit their questioning to the experiences of those questioned. The *principle of tacit assumption* involves determining the actual meanings that lie behind a respondent's answer to any given question. When a woman says that she thinks seeing a psychiatrist for emotional symptoms would be very likely to help her, how does she interpret the words *help, likely,* and *emotional symptoms?* Interviewers may "think" (tacitly assume) that they know what respondents mean, when in fact they are operating from a quite different point of view. This third principle forces a probing of the meanings that lie behind answers.

Garfinkel, in a series of papers, has taken the problem of tacit understandings one step further (1967). Indeed, he suggests that persons typically "act as if" they understand one another, when in fact they do not. Nods, shrugs of the shoulder, muttered yesses or nos — all convey an impression that one talker understands another. However, data gathered by Garfinkel's students and associates suggest that when persons are pushed to explain what they mean by a given utterance or set of exchanges, bitter reactions can be produced. Consider the following case (Garfinkel, 1967, p. 44):

> My friend [subject, S] and I [experimenter, E] were talking about a man whose overbearing attitude annoyed us. My friend expressed his feeling.
> (S) I'm sick of him.
> (E) Would you explain what is wrong with you that you are sick?
> (S) Are you kidding? You know what I mean.
> (E) Please explain your ailment.
> (S) (He listened to me with a puzzled look.) What came over you? We never talk this way, do we?

Placed in the context of the present discussion, Garfinkel's arguments support the proposition that many interviewers may in fact not adequately understand the responses given on their interview schedules.

Added to the problem of tacit understanding is the issue raised by Edwards (1957a) and Orne (1962) in their research on social desirability and demand characteristics as factors in scientific research. Edwards has observed that respondents in the interview situation frequently answer questions in terms that they perceive as having the greatest degree of social desirability. That is, the respondent attempts to present a credible and knowledgeable self to the interviewer. In the course of presenting a self—which in part involves answering the questions put to them—the respondents may selectively distort, mask, or lie about their attitudes on any given question.

Orne's study of experimental research (1962) noted that experimental subjects often attempt to discover what an experimenter has in mind, and then attempt to act in ways that are appropriate to that definition of the situation. It seems likely that respondents in the interview situation are also involved in attempts to understand what the interviewer wants from them. The demand characteristics of the situation, coupled with the social-desirability factor, often produce interview findings that do not accurately reflect the attitudes, definitions, and opinions held by the respondents.

These issues and criteria suggest that the interview should not be made up of ambiguous questions. Questions must be framed in ways that have meaning for the respondent.

Churchill (1971, p. 184) has suggested, on the basis of the work of Garfinkel and Sacks, that conversations that occur during interviews may be analyzed in terms of the *chain rule:*

> An American to whom a question is addressed should respond with a direct answer and then return the "floor" to the questioner. (The name "chain" rule derives from the possibility that the questioner, when he gets the "floor" back after an answer, may ask another question, and so on, thus explaining how sequences QAQAQA . . . can occur.)

Exactly why Americans should be led to conform to the "chain" rule is unclear. In fact, Churchill's data indicate that they seldom do. He does not mention the total size of his sample, but he reports that "only 17 percent of the immediate responses to questions in a set of transcribed conversations follow the chain rule" (Churchill, 1971, p. 184). In the remaining cases, "misfires" occurred—"What did you say?" Indirect answers were given; clarifications were called for; a sudden noise drowned out a question; a person's accent was too pronounced to be understood; the question contained words that were unfamiliar to the respondent. It may well be that an alternative set of conversational sequencing rules operates in the interview situation. For certain interviews—those with members of political and economic elites—it is evident that the higher-status person often controls all phases of the interview. Furthermore, many respondents may refuse to return the floor to the interviewer. In these senses the interview must be seen as an interactional and social production. The chain rule, then, may be an ideal type which operates only in courts of law, where lawyers and judges interrogate defendants and witnesses.

Questions should be presented in such a way that the respondent can actually get involved in the interview process. If they are ambiguous or open-ended, the interviewer should be instructed to follow up on those statements that the respondent leaves vague. If questions raise the possibility of the respondents' lying or fabricating (which is always a possibility), care should be taken to include questions that would catch them up or make it apparent that a previous answer contradicts a later one. If the interview is treated as a conversation, its demand characteristics can be reduced. Persons can often be interviewed unobtrusively, as though involved in everyday conversation.

Questions and Conversations

The interview should be approached as a conversation. It is a conversation between two or more persons where the main focus derives from the questions that make up the interview schedule. It is talk managed around a specific set of questions. It is a conversation that should not end until the interviewer has received satisfactory answers to the research questions. This suggests that the interviewer will often have to return to a specific respondent. Demands of time, work, family, and money may produce broken-off interviews. A skilled interviewer should be able to cultivate the interpersonal skills that would permit an interview conversation to be resumed at a later time that is convenient to both interviewer and respondent. It must be remembered, however, that the interview conversation is primarily a gift of time and information; and it is given by the respondent, not the interviewer. The respondent should have the upper hand in determining when and where the interview will take place. It must also be remembered that few sociologists willingly submit to interviews themselves.

Listening

Creative interviewing (Douglas, 1985) also involves creative, attentive listening. It is possible to learn a great deal about others just by listening to them talk. This requires immersing oneself in another's world and building a trusting relationship with him (Johnson, 1975). It involves a capacity to be quiet. In order to listen to another, one must also be able to project oneself into the other's situation. A sympathetic identification with the other's point of view is necessary. The listener must not pass judgment on the other's views. Listening creates the grounds for understanding, which is the process of interpreting, knowing, and comprehending the meaning intended, felt, and expressed by another (Denzin, 1984b, p. 284). Understanding draws upon shared experiences. Persons can't share experiences if they don't listen to one another.

The Three Types of Interviews Reassessed

Six Criteria   The issues just discussed suggest six criteria for evaluating the three interview formats: (1) conveying meaning, (2) securing respondents' interest, (3) ensuring the interviewer's clarity, (4) making intentions precise, (5) relating each question to overall intent, (6) handling the problem of fabrication.

Conveying meaning (criterion 1) in the SSI is difficult, because respondents are from different backgrounds and settings; therefore, a phrase or question frequently does not elicit a common meaning. With the USI, questions can be rephrased and reordered to convey meaning; in the UI, of course, this is even more true.

When the problem of *respondents' interest* (criterion 2) is considered, the SSI form again raises problems; but if extensive pretesting has been done, many of these problems can be avoided. When the USI and the UI forms are employed, it is up to the interviewer to reorder and rephrase questions so that they motivate a reply.

The third criterion, *interviewer's clarity*, is less of a problem with the SSI, because this has presumably been resolved before the interviewer is sent into the field; with the SSI form, there should be only predetermined rephrasing or reordering of questions by the interviewer. With the USI and UI forms, however, untrained interviewers will often reinterpret questions and restate them in a manner quite different from that intended by the investigator.

Precision of intent, the fourth criterion, should not be a problem with the most structured interview form, the SSI. Unfortunately, however, it often is. The problem of *interpretation* again falls on the interviewer.

The same is true of the fifth criterion, which demands that *each question be related to the overall intent*: This is not always the case, even in the SSI.

The problem of *fabrication* (criterion 6) looms largest with the SSI, for too frequently the interviewer has no specific set of questions with which to challenge the respondent's reply. With the USI and UI, it is relatively easy to challenge the respondents and check their replies.

Common deficiencies of all interview types   In their incisive comparison of interviewing with participant observation, Becker and Geer (1957, pp. 28–32) noted the following difficulties of all interview forms.

First, there is the difficulty of penetrating a group's language. In interviewing group members, sociologists are placed in the position of having at once to penetrate and understand the meanings and symbols of the group. While most Americans speak English, they do not all employ the language in the same way. This often leads to the first error in an interview — tacit assumption of understanding. All interview forms are susceptible to this error, and unless investigators can become firmly entrenched in a group's way of life, they have no assurance that they fully understand what is communicated.

The second difficulty is that people do not always tell interviewers what they want to know. Women are often reluctant to discuss their sexual relationships, for instance; drug addicts are unlikely to reveal to a stranger their sources of drugs; mental patients do not readily tell why they dislike other mental patients. This resistance to "telling all" may reveal insecurity in the interviewer's presence, may indicate a commitment to a sense of propriety unknown to the interviewer, may indicate a misunderstanding of the question, or may be deliberate resistance (see Paul, 1953, pp. 430–51). While it is easier to broach difficult "conversational topics" with the USI and UI interview forms, it may sometimes be impossible even with them. Becker (1954, pp. 31–32) has suggested as one tactic "playing dumb" and forcing respondents to become concrete when they appear unwilling to answer questions directly. This tactic, which forces respondents to make explicit what they might prefer to allude to, works best in the unstructured interview. Becker (p. 31) describes it as follows:

> The interview ordinarily started with questions at a high level of generality: "What are the problems of being a school teacher?" . . . Most teachers were able to talk about these relationships at this abstract level of discussion. . . . When a number of such statements had been made and we were well-launched on our conversation, I would assume a skeptical air and ask the teacher if she could give me any evidence for these statements. . . . This somewhat put the interviewee in the position of having to put up or shut up. . . . Once the interview area had been shifted in this way to personal experience, I used another strategy to elicit further information that was being withheld. I played dumb and pretended not to understand certain relationships and attitudes which were implicit in the description the teacher gave, but which she preferred not to state openly.

The third difficulty for all interviews relates again to the fact that groups create their own rules and symbols, a factor immediately complicated when it is realized that persons occupy different positions within their own groups and thus have their own interpretations and even distortions of what the group's values are. For this reason, interviews must be combined with other methods of observation.

Group Interviews

Because groups create their own structures of meaning and understanding, it is often useful to conduct group interviews or discussions. In a group context, the observer can elicit multiple opinions on the same issue. Points of agreement and disagreement can be clarified. The diveristy of perspectives in the group can be revealed. The researcher can verify hunches and interpretations with a willing group. If this method is to work, the researcher must become immersed in the group and build a degree of trust with its members. Blumer (1969a, p. 41) comments on the value of group discussions and interviews:

> A small number of individuals, brought together as a discussion or resource group, is more valuable many times over than any representative sample. Such a group, discussing collectively their sphere of life and probing into it as they meet one another's disagreements, will do more to lift the veils covering the sphere of life than any other device that I know of.

Douglas (1985, p. 46) calls the experts on a group's way of life "superinformants." These individuals are often the recipients of a group's secrets, and they know the lies of its members. They are valuable resources who should be sought out. If possible, they should be brought together for group discussions and interviews.

THE INTERVIEW AS AN OBSERVATIONAL ENCOUNTER

Whether the interview rests on complex interconnected sets of questions in the form of scales or relies on open-ended, unstructured questions, the investigator is obligated to report the reliability and validity of the items. I have established the centrality of these two problems of the measurement process. Validity, with its concern for what is being measured, and reliability, which points to the stability of observations over time, are directly relevant to the interview. The investigator must show the extent to which the questions measure what is intended as well as demonstrate the reliability of the instrument. I have suggested that these two problems are interactional in nature. To further extend this proposition, I wish to treat the interview as an observational encounter.

Characteristics of the Observational Encounter

An encounter (Goffman, 1961b) represents the coming together of two or more persons for the purposes of focused interaction. An encounter, then, is a form of the joint action and is represented in such divergent contexts as eating a dinner, making a purchase in a store, encountering another person in an elevator, or filling out an interview form. As interactions, all encounters are composed of two or more interacting persons, a situation for interaction, and a series of rules or standards of conduct that direct the behavior observed.

These rules may take three basic forms. First, they may be *civil-legal* in nature and find their expression in law, official morality, or codes of ethics. Second, they may be *ceremonial,* as seen in rules of etiquette; such rules govern polite face-to-face interaction among persons when they are in public or private behavior settings. They can range from statements on proper dress to how one introduces oneself to a stranger or leaves a party. Third, rules may be *relational* in form, as in long-term social relationships among lovers, co-workers, or friends. These rules redefine civil-legal and ceremonial standards, since participants have constructed their own meaning for what is right and proper. Thus the rules of polite conversation may be greatly relaxed in long-term relationships; profanity, speaking in a loud voice, and even silence may be common in such situations.

The importance of relational rules for the analysis of face-to-face interaction derives from the fact that they represent a synthesis of civil-legal and ceremonial standards. Consequently, all persons view the world of interaction from the peculiar moral complexion of their own relational standards. These standards go so far as to specify how selves are defined, how knowledge about the self is communicated, and how joint actions with others are organized. These rules do not exist on an abstract level, as is often the case with civil-legal and ceremonial standards; that is, they seldom find expression in law books or catalogues of etiquette. Rather, they are observed only through the process of interaction. Their relevance for the observational encounter should be apparent. Interviewers must work within the boundaries of polite etiquette as they probe into the relational rules and moralities of respondents. The problem arises when respondents either possess a set of interactional rules different from those of the interviewer or refuse to permit penetration into their relational worlds. In either case, the aim of the interview, which is focused interaction around the content of theoretically relevant questions, may be sidetracked, or even disrupted. The interviewer may also believe that she has penetrated the respondent's perspective and unwittingly be led astray by fabrication or differences in interactional rules.

Sources of Invalidity

If the interview, as an observational encounter, is analyzed by its constituent elements (observer, respondent, situation, and rules), the following sources of potential invalidity can be noted.

The interviewer's identity: self-presentation Beginning with the interviewers, it must be asked, "What rules of conduct direct their activity?" "Are they playing by polite rules of etiquette, or are they attempting to bring their relational rules to bear upon the perspective of the subjects?" It appears that many middle-class interviewers attempt a synthesis. They assume that all subjects will have a common perspective on such matters as annual income, patterns of sexual behavior, attitudes toward war, and so on; and they translate their stance on those issues into the interaction process, seldom questioning the legitimacy of that decision.

This is basically the problem of self-presentation. The rules one plays by structure the nature of one's presented self. Because the role of interviewer is relatively new and undefined, interviewers seldom have firm guidelines for selecting the proper set of rules and selves to present. Benney and Hughes (1956, p. 139) offer the following comment:

> The role of the interviewer, then is one governed by conventions, rather than by standards, rules or laws; it is a role that is relatively lightly held, even by professionals, and may be abandoned in favor of certain alternative roles if the occasion arises. *What* alternative roles is another matter. The interview is a relatively new kind of encounter in the history of human relations, and the older models of encounter — parent-child, male-female, rich-poor, foolish-wise — carry role definitions much better articulated and more exigent. The interviewer will be constantly tempted, if the other party falls back on one of those older models, to reciprocate — tempted and excused. For, unlike most encounters, the interview is a role-playing situation in which one person is much more an expert than the other, and, while the conventions governing the interviewer's behavior are already beginning, in some professional circles, to harden into standards, the conventions governing the informant's behavior are much less clearly articulated and known.

The relationship between interviewer and subject Paradoxically, I would suggest that interview schedules rest on multiple, conflicting identities, selves, and rules. The self established in the early phase of the encounter, when names are exchanged, is considerably different from the self that asks about a woman's belief in a higher being or about her sexual relationships. These selves may be in conflict, and the attendant data must be analyzed in that light.

The interview must be seen as a very special relationship, one often freely entered, and one in which information is exchanged. It is commonly assumed that information is more valid if it is freely given. As Benney and Hughes (1956, p. 139) note, this assumption stresses

> the voluntary character of the interview as a relationship freely and willingly entered into by the respondent; it suggests a certain promissory or contractual element. But if the interview is thought of as a kind of implicit contract between the two parties, it is obvious that the interviewer gains the respondent's time, attention and whatever information he has to offer, but what the respondent gets is less apparent.

There are two additional aspects of this relationship that warrant discussion. First, this is a relationship between two persons who meet as strangers and, except for the life of their encounter, are likely to remain strangers. There is nothing intrinsic in the fleeting relationship that will force the respondents to behave as they are supposed to. Observers have it on faith that respondents are telling the truth, that their opinions are well thought out, and that they are sincere. Yet encounters with strangers challenge these assumptions. Indeed, as Simmel (1950) has suggested, such relationships are often characterized by fiction and a strong sense of alienation. A participant can fabricate "tales of self" that belie the actual facts, and the other party lacks objective evidence to counter such tales. If the probability of future encounters is low, which is usually the case with interviews, the problem is amplified. Interviewers may not be able to penetrate private worlds of experience in such encounters. (This would be especially so with tightly structured interview schedules.)

Second, because interviewers are often forced to try to penetrate private worlds of experience—worlds characterized by a great deal of emotion and affect—a constant interactional tension is likely to be present in the encounter. The interviewer must encourage the expression of affect, not suppress it. If the fiction of equality and open exchange of information cannot be maintained, then the respondent is less likely to express attitudes on emotional issues.

These two features of the interview relationship give it a volatile and emergent nature. Suddenly, when questions become personal, the respondent may "break off" and force the interviewer to leave. Or, even worse, "flooding out" or embarrassment may occur (Goffman, 1961b). The respondent comes to a question that raises long-forgotten or even repressed attitudes, and cannot go on; and the interviewer may be ill-equipped to move on to other topics, or even to control the sudden appearance of affect. The life of the fleeting relationship drains away, and the interviewer leaves with an incomplete schedule.

This brings us back to subjects and their motivations. Benney and

Hughes suggest that the motives for participation in interviews are diverse (1956, p. 140), and I would add that this diversity contributes to a certain lack of comparability among interviews. Some respondents talk for the sake of self-expression in a relatively free atmosphere, as they might to a lawyer, physician, or psychiatrist. No reprisal is forthcoming, and so statements can go unmonitored. Others talk for money (this is not uncommon in many studies). Yet the interview remains a medium of self-expression between two parties, a medium where one listens and the other talks as Benney and Hughes observe (1956, p. 140):

> In this sense, then, the interview is an understanding between the two parties that, in return for allowing the interviewer to direct their communication, the informant is assured that he will not meet with denial, contradiction, competition, or other harassment.

A degree of muted equality permeates the interview. Even an interviewer who feels superior to the respondent must not express this feeling; the transaction must be seen as equal. Yet this sense of perfect equality seldom fits any interview. High-status respondents may, as Benney and Hughes suggest (1956, p. 140), talk past the interviewer (whom they view as lower-status) to a study director or a total discipline. And interviewers who contact lower-class persons may either force their morality upon the respondents or talk down to them. Thus if the fiction of equality is to be realized, a fit in backgrounds and status between interviewer and subject must be maximized. If it is not, the investigator runs the risk of having interviews conducted by selves talking past one another.

The problem of equality suggests that the interaction between an interviewer and subject may itself create sources of invalidity. Yet most, if not all, standardized interviews rest on what Benney and Hughes (1965, p. 141) call the "convention of comparability":

> Regarded as an information-gathering tool, the interview is designed to minimize the local, concrete, immediate circumstances of the particular encounter — including the respective personalities of the participants — and to emphasize only those aspects that can be kept general enough and demonstrable enough to be counted. As an encounter between these two people the typical interview has no meaning; it is conceived in a framework of other, comparable meetings between other couples, each recorded in such fashion that elements of communication in common can be easily isolated from more idiosyncratic qualities. However vaguely this is conceived by the actual participants, it is the needs of the statistician rather than of the people involved directly that determine much, not only the content of communication but its form as well.

This assumption justifies the use of standardized interviews, yet it ignores the interactional features of the interview encounter. If selves are multiply defined, if meaning is not consensual, and if the friction of equality cannot be maintained, then the assumption of comparability is better seen as a hypothesis to be tested than as an assumption accepted on a priori grounds.

Gendered Identities in the Interview Situation

Cross-gender interviews (female interviewer, male respondent; male interviewer, female respondent) become the occasion for the enactment of gendered identities. A gendered identity situates an individual in terms of masculine and feminine identities and the codes that organize these identities in the culture. The rules of conduct that organize the interview (civil-legal, ceremonial, relational) are filtered through and structure the gendered identities that are enacted in the interview. It cannot be assumed that "gender-free" information is obtained in interviews. That is, one's gender shapes how one experiences and sees the world. It is not sufficient for researchers to merely note the sex of the respondent. This only glosses over or downplays the significance of gender in structuring social experience. Furthermore, because interviews are gendered, interactional productions, the information given is itself constrained by the gendered identities that are enacted in the interview encounter. Gender filters knowledge.

The situation   The situations of interviewing must also be treated as potential sources of invalidity. Just as selves are defined through the process of interaction and the interpretation of rules, so too are situations. It is the combination of selves and rules that gives situations their definition, and it may be assumed that few interviews occur in situations defined in exactly the same manner. Indeed, situations within the same class — such as homes, offices, or laboratories — seldom share precisely the same interpretations. If it could be assumed that interviews always occurred within the same class of situations, the problem would be somewhat reduced. That is, the normative standards for behaving in homes, offices, or laboratories could be examined. Few studies succeed in locating interviews within the same situational class. Indeed, interviews may range from household settings to automobiles to the steps of a building, to jail cells, and so on. This raises the problem of between-class situational variance, and if the presence of divergent selves is added to the picture, it becomes difficult to justify the convention of comparability across interviews. I see no suitable solution to the problem other than the systematic recording by interviewers of their situations of observation. This at least gives other investigators some basis for evaluation and replication.

The act of observation   The act of making an observation must also be treated. It is axiomatic, I believe, that the process of interaction creates attitudes and behaviors that did not exist before the interaction. Or, if new attitudes are not created, old attitudes are reshaped. Applied to the interview, this axiom suggests that all observations have some reactive effect on what is being observed (Webb et al., 1966). It suggests that respondents may change attitudes, or even develop new ones, simply because they are being interviewed.

The reactive effects of observations raises the problem of demand-characteristic effects within the interview (see Orne, 1962, pp. 776–83) and suggests once again that the selves of interviewer and respondent cannot be ignored. That is, the knowledge that one is being observed, or interviewed, leads to a deliberate monitoring of the self so that only certain selves are presented. Because many interviews convey implicit demands to the respondent (social desirability, for example), there is often an attempt to present a self that meets these demands. This has the potential of creating a built-in, self-fulfilling prophecy within the interview: Subjects may tell the interviewer what they think the interviewer wants to hear.

It is possible also to speak of "reverse demand-characteristic" effects within the interview situation: Interviewers may develop their own interpretation of the research instrument and attempt to convey that interpretation to the subject. This often occurs among interviewers who want to please their study director by confirming his major hypotheses. In so doing, they destroy whatever reliability and validity an instrument has.

It becomes necessary, then, to strive for a close fit between the selves of the interviewer and the subject. Ideally, this fit will involve focused interaction around the main themes of the interview schedule. The difficulty of achieving this fit derives from the fact that interviewers and subjects are able to present a wide variety of identities at a moment's notice, ranging perhaps from husband to student, parent, intellectual, sociologist, enemy, and even interviewer or respondent.

Seldom will anything approaching an ideal fit of identities occur in the interview situation. Typically, the interviewer and respondent come from totally different social worlds. Often the respondent regards the interviewer as hostile, critical, or ignorant. It may take weeks and months before the interviewer is able to build up a working relationship with those being interviewed and studied.

Wax (1971, pp. 71–72) comments on her 1943 experiences as an interviewer for the War Relocation Authority at a relocation camp for Japanese-Americans who had been moved to a barricaded site in Arizona:

> Week followed week without any noticeable improvement in my "rapport" or my reports. Every letter I received from Dr. Thomas made it clear that I was not doing what she expected me to do. There was no one I could talk to in any meaningful fashion. . . . After about two months I began to see myself as a total failure. The anxiety I suffered was so agonizing that I still find it hard to describe. Every time I returned to my stifling room after a series of futile "interviews," I sat down and cried.

After a considerable period of time in the field, Wax succeeded in gaining what she regarded as some minimal acceptance from the Japanese-Americans. She believed this was because she had "learned" how to act like a Japanese woman. When she was recovering from a leg injury, she recorded the following conversation (p. 142):

> I did not know that the story of what had happened at the hospital had spread among the Japanese. A few days later when I was hobbling about, I ran into Mr. Yamashita and remarked that I would be over to see him again as soon as my leg healed. "Yes," said Mr. Yamashita in a loud, admiring tone, "We have all very much admired your *German* courage." I gulped and said nothing, for by Ger-

man courage Mr. Yamashita meant that I had behaved like a true Nazi. After this I gave up trying to behave like a "true Japanese" and began to meditate on the complexities of the images that we think we are presenting to other people.

Wax's experiences point up the problematic gendered and interactional nature of the interview and fieldwork situation. They suggest that the interviewer may be unaware of how these situations are being defined by the respondent. The interviewer may also have difficulty moving the respondent into the desired role. Success in this endeavor will of course vary with the characteristics of the respondent and the interviewer. Those who have been interviewed before, or who are familiar with or responsive to the purposes of the interview are more likely to make good respondents.

Interviewing as Participant Observation

Although Chapter 7 provides an analysis of the methods of participant observation, it is relevant at this point to note that a good interviewer is by necessity also a participant observer. That is, the interviewer is participating in the life experiences of a given respondent and is observing that person's report of herself during the interview conversation. The excerpts quoted earlier from Wax's excellent monograph on fieldwork illustrate how the interviewer attempts to become a part of the social worlds of experience he is studying. In short, it is erroneous to think of interviews and interviewing as atomized research techniques. Good interviewers should acquire an in-depth working knowledge of those they interview. Like naturalistic observers, they should have some acquaintance with the times and places of interaction that make up the subjects' world. Interviewers should acquire some feeling for the relationships that exist between their respondents. There should be an effort on the part of the interviewers to overcome the constraints of the "stranger relationship" that exists between so many respondents and interviewers. Such a commitment, which moves researchers into a multiple-methods approach to research, will be developed in Chapter 7. It is mentioned now in order to indicate that there is nothing intrinsic to the sociological interview that makes it susceptible to the problems thus far identified.

Rapport

The term *rapport* is frequently employed to describe the degree to which interviewers and the respondents are able to actually take one another's role. M. Kuhn (1962, p. 201) suggests:

> Rapport is probably by no means the intangible, mysterious thing it has been characterized as being. It involves, at the bottom, simply the sharing of a common language, so that through shared frames of reference each person in what he has to say, or in each posture he takes, calls out in himself, incipiently, the response that those gestures, postures and symbols call out in the other.

Rapport varies by class background, perceived social status, degree of consensual (that is, unambiguous) meaning conveyed by the interview, perceptions of the interview situation, and interpretations of roles of interviewer and respondent. The closer the fit between these dimensions, the greater the rapport.

Rapport can work to the disadvantage of the interviewer, however. Miller (1952, pp. 97–99) has reported a study in which excessive rapport between himself and members of a local union leadership hampered his ability to be objective and to obtain certain types of data. He comments:

> Many personal things were told to me in a friend-to-friend relationship; undoubtedly I gained information because of this relationship which would not have been available to me in any other way.
>
> On the other hand, once I had developed a close friendship to the union leaders I was committed to continuing it, and some penetrating lines of inquiry had to be dropped. . . . Friendship connotes an all-accepting attitude; to probe beneath the surface of long-believed values would break the friend-to-friend relationship. It may also be that development of a friend-to-friend relationship between the leaders and the participant observer was a means used by the former to limit the observer's investigations and criticisms. In a sense, the observer may be co-opted into friendship, a situation which may have prevailed in some studies of management–worker interaction.

Miller's second problem was that he became so attuned to the feelings and perceptions of the union leaders that he deemphasized the sentiments of the rank-and-file members.

Strictly speaking, Miller's observations go beyond the interview situation, for his problems developed in a long-term participant-observation study. They do indicate, however, that rapport can be developed too far; the observer must be on guard against cooptation and loss of objectivity.

The problem of excessive rapport, like that of reverse demand-characteristic effects, points to what I believe must be present in every observational act—a profound sense of self-cynicism. Observers can never take themselves and their own actions for granted, or too seriously. The possibility of being taken in, duped, or lied to is ever-present, as is the potential for thinking that one fully understands the problem, or interview, under analysis.

CONCLUSION

I have argued that the interview is a peculiar type of human interaction because it represents the coming together of two strangers. This gives the interviewer the large task of taking control of the situation and defining it so that the questions will be answered by the time the interviewer ends. While I am fully aware that interviews take place every day between strangers, and further realize that those directing these interviews are by and large satisfied with their results, I wish to call attention to the tremendous variability in the interview situation. If, as Benney and Hughes (1956) argue, sociology is the science of the interview, then I suggest that sociologists as yet know very little about it. I have no firm solutions to the problems raised in this chapter, but I suggest that interviewers be alert to them.

SUGGESTED READINGS

CICOUREL, AARON V., "The Role of Cognitive-Linguistic Concepts in Understanding Everyday Social Interaction," pp. 87–106 in R.H. Turner and J.F. Short, Jr., (eds.), *Annual Review of Sociology*, vol. 7. (Palo Alto, Calif.: Annual Reviews, 1981). Presents a thorough discussion of recent developments in "cognitive science" that are relevant to understanding the discourse that occurs in the interview situation. Contains a useful analysis of medical interviewing.

DEXTER, LEWIS ANTHONY, *Elite and Specialized Interviewing*. (Evanston, Ill.: Northwestern University Press, 1970). A somewhat dated but extremely valuable guide to interviewing powerful persons.

DOUGLAS, JACK D., *Creative Interviewing*. (Beverly Hills: Sage, 1985). Offers an exciting model of creative interviewing as a means of gaining greater understanding of life experiences.

ROBERTS, H. (ed.), *Doing Feminist Research*. (London: Routledge and Kegan Paul, 1981). Contains many valuable essays by feminist scholars on the research process. Ann Oakley's essay "Interviewing Women: A Contradiction in Terms" is useful in the context of the present chapter.

5

The Social Experiment and Its Variations

Within a laboratory, a specific type of interdependence can be constructed that retains fidelity to social life while simultaneously allowing for the control of the observer's observations. This interdependent environment can be viewed as a provocative stage wherein features constructed by experimenters precede the drama, but the social objective of the drama must be created by the participants. [Katovich, 1984, pp. 50–51]

Experimental results have no built-in validity. This means that some of the disdain with which psychological researchers customarily treat data obtained by sociologists and anthropologists working in the field is inappropriate. It might be profitably replaced by the study and application of their considerable literature on participant-observation methodology. For, whereas the ideal psychological experimenter is an immaculate perceiver of an objective reality, the real psychological experimenter is, to a far greater extent than he has expected, very much like his counterparts in the other social sciences. He too is a *participant observer*. [Friedman, 1967, p. 179]

In a fundamental sense, the experiment is the point of departure for all other research methods and for all other strategies of causal analysis. It offers the most rigorous solution to the problem of causality. It enables the investigator to directly control the three features of the causal proposition: time order between variables, covariance, and the exclusion of rival causal factors. The other research methods—the social survey, participant observation, historical and life history construction, and unobtrusive measures—represent strategies of decreasing control over these factors. They are best seen as strategies of causal analysis.

The experiment, however, is not produced in a scientific vacuum. It involves interactions between the experimenter and the subjects. The experiment is a "social occasion" that is staged in the laboratories of scientific investigators (see Friedman, 1967; Hood and Back, 1971; McGuire, 1969, pp. 21–51; Wuebben, Straits, and Schulman, 1974). As Friedman, (1967, p. 179), observes, experimenters are participant observers. They have an active hand in producing the findings that flow from their experimental designs and manipulations. Katovich (1984), Couch (1987a), and Couch, Saxton, and Katovich (1986) have argued that the traditional small-groups laboratory can be transformed into a setting where meaningful social interaction can occur. In their studies, and those of their associates, the laboratory is viewed as an interactional stage. Interactions in the laboratory will be discussed at the end of this chapter.

In this chapter the logic of the experimental model will be presented. Its causal assumptions will be compared with the modes of analysis that are used in the other four research methods. Types of experimental designs will be discussed. A major portion of the chapter will deal with the social psychology of experiments. A section on natural and field experiments will conclude the discussion. Quasiexperimental designs will be treated in Chapter 6. Surveys are properly seen as variations on the quasiexperimental method (Campbell and Stanley, 1963).

THE EXPERIMENTAL MODEL

In essence, the experimental model is the *true experimental design,* which is discussed further under "Experimental Designs" (p. 124) and diagramed in Table 5–1 (p. 129).

This design involves two sets of measurements, one before and one after exposure to the independent variable. Two groups are observed: One is exposed to the independent variable, and one is not exposed. The differences between the scores of the two groups at time 2 (second measurement) can be attributed to the independent variable if other factors are controlled. In this way, evidence relevant to the causal hypothesis is directly gathered. Concomitant variation is established by examining the scores of the subjects in the experimental group; time order between the dependent and independent variables is established with the first measurement. Both groups should score the same, because neither has yet been exposed to the experimental treatment. In order to ensure that no differences exist between the experimental and control groups before the experimental treatment, the typical strategy is to randomly assign subjects to one or another of the two groups. It will be remembered that random selection and assignment serve to normally distribute any differences between subjects, so that valid comparisons can be made. Randomization is an essential feature of experimental design simply because the investigator can neither know nor adequately control all the relevant factors that could influence causal analysis. (Camilleri, 1962, p. 173).

The problem of alternative causal factors cannot be ignored simply because randomization has been employed. If the same observer and the same set of subjects are employed throughout the experiment, changes they undergo may produce the differences observed between the first and last measurement. Maturation, instrument change, and subject–observer interaction can emerge as jeopardizing, intrinsic test factors. Randomization offers a basic strategy for controlling the effect of alternative extrinsic test factors, but it cannot directly control the effect of intrinsic variables. Their effects can be partially controlled by random selection of observers at time 1 and time 2, but the same set of subjects will typically have to be employed at both times. (Designs that minimize the effects of intrinsic variables will be discussed later.)

A simple logic underlies the experimental model. The experimental group is constructed in terms of the method of agreement, which makes the following assumption (Goode and Hatt, 1952), p. 74):

> When two or more cases of a given phenomenon have one and only one condition in common, that condition may be regarded as the cause (or effect) of the phenomenon. More simply, if we can make observation Z in every case that we find condition C, we can conclude that they are causally related.

The negative canon of agreement provides the logic for the control group (pp. 75–76):

> When condition non-C is found to be associated with observation non-Z, we may assert a causal relationship between C and Z. An example would be: Lack of social experience with ethnic stereotypes in childhood is followed by lack of ethnic prejudice in adulthood. In general this proposition, whether accurate or not, states that whenever, throughout all variations of other factors, an absence of factor C is associated with an absence of Z, it is possible to accept a causal relationship between C and Z.

The classical experimental design contains two observational groups observed at two points in time. The logic for this combination is termed the *method of difference* (p. 76):

> If there are two or more cases, and in one of them observation Z can be made, while in the other it cannot; and if factor C occurs when observation Z is made, and does not occur when observation Z is made; then it can be asserted that there is a causal relationship between C and Z.

The control group represents the combination of non-C and non-Z, while the experimental group represents the combination of C and Z. The logic is clear: A relationship cannot be established between two variables if they do not occur together.

The experimental model has certain weaknesses that are partially overcome with the use of randomization. But the method of agreement provides no evidence that other factors could not have caused the variations observed; it provides only a basis for inferring such a conclusion. Another problem is that the dependent variable may have been causing the independent variable. The method of agreement cannot clearly refute this claim, although if the first observation contains measurements on both variables, this could be established.

EXPERIMENTAL DESIGNS

It is possible to classify experimental designs into three groups: true experimental designs, nonexperimental designs, and quasiexperimental designs.

Nonexperimental Designs

Nonexperimental designs are those that lack one or more of the characteristics of true experimental designs: namely, the use of at least one control group and one experimental group; the making of two sets of observations; and, typically, the random assignment of subjects to observational groups. Designs in this category would include situations with no control groups, those with no "before" observations, and those which fail to place subjects randomly. These will be treated in Chapter 6.

Quasiexperimental Designs

The second major category of designs, the quasiexperimental formulations, will also be treated in Chapter 6. Quasiexperiments conform to the survey model of research, where repeated observations are often made under conditions of decreasing control by the observer (see Cook, 1983).

True Experimental Designs

Pretest-posttest one-control-group design   In its generic form, the experiment represents a situation in which the investigator controls some variables while manipulating the effects of others. This permits observation of the effects of the manipulated variables upon the dependent variable in a situation in which the effect of other relevant factors is believed to have been removed, typically by randomization. The generic experiment may be diagramed as shown in Table 5–1. As has been noted, in a true experimental design at least one control group and one experimental group are used, two sets of observations are made, and subjects are assigned to groups at random.

Two basic variations on the true experimental design can be noted: the Solomon four-group design and the posttest-only control-group design.

The Solomon four-group design   This design represents the addition of more than one control group to the pretest-posttest design. Its analysis will indicate the logic of employing more than one control group in any experimental design. It can be diagramed as shown in Table 5–2.

TABLE 5–1   Pretest-Posttest One-Control-Group Design

	Observed	Exposed to Independent Variable	Observed
Experimental group	Yes	Yes	Yes
Control group	Yes	No	Yes

TABLE 5-2 Solomon Four-Group Design

	Observed	Exposed to Independent Variable	Observed
Experimental group 1	Yes	Yes	Yes
Control group 1	Yes	No	Yes
Experimental group 2	No	Yes	Yes
Control group 2	No	No	Yes

The first two groups parallel the traditional pretest-posttest one-control-group design. The addition of the second control group allows the investigator to assess the reactive effects of the first measurement, as well as the effect of nonexposure to the experimental treatment. The second experimental group provides assessment of exposure to the first measurement upon a group that has received the experimental treatment.

The Solomon four-group design represents the purest of the experimental models. By stripping away, in a design fashion, as many of the possible threats to internal validity as possible, it permits the most accurate inference of causality. The investigator can directly answer the problem of temporal order between the independent and dependent variables by examining each control group in comparison with the experimental group. The exclusion of rival threats to internal validity is solved by the additional groups, and covariance of variables is solved by the "before-after" measurement on the first experimental group.

Posttest-only control-group designs   Although I have defined a true experiment as one in which before and after measurements are taken, after measurements on randomly assigned groups will often suffice as a control for the before observation. This is the solution proposed by the posttest-only control-group design. Often it is not possible to take "before" measurements on the subjects under analysis. While this design offers no data on what the "before" attitudes were, the fact that subjects are randomly assigned ensures that whatever differences did exist were distributed between the two groups in a random fashion. The factor of reactivity of initial measurements is removed, as are the problems of history, maturation, subject bias, differential subject mortality, and changes in the measurement instrument or the experimenter. These factors become irrelevant because initial measurements are not taken — thus removing the time period over which such factors as history, maturation, and experimenter variations could occur. Also, the factor of randomization removes the possibility of initial subject bias.

This design combines certain of the strengths of the pretest-posttest one-control-group design and the Solomon four-group design, but its use is recommended only when they cannot be employed. The investigator must still be sensitive to the fact that there is no substitute for "before" measures when the true and complete effects of experimental treatments are to be determined. Still, this design provides the minimal information on causal inference. The time order on variables can be determined by comparing the experimental and control groups. Covariance of variables should appear in the experimental treatment group, and the exclusion of other rival causal factors is minimized because of randomization and the use of two groups.

Steps in Experimental Design

The *first step* in designing an experiment is the development of a set of theoretically significant expectations. There must be some reason for conducting an experiment, and that reason must be theoretical (Couch, 1987a).

Conception of theory that produces hypotheses to be tested resolves the *second step,* which is determining the actual form of the experiment. A design will be selected, and experimental and control-group variations will be developed.

The theory will also specify the *third step* — selection of a population from which a sample will be drawn. The sample should be statistically rigorous and theoretically guided. If it is not, inferences to the broader population will be restricted, as will any theoretical analysis.

Fourth, a procedure for randomly assigning subjects to the observational groups must be employed.

Fifth, techniques for obtaining "before" and "after" measurements must be developed.

Sixth and last, given the resolution of foregoing conditions, the actual execution of the experiment follows. In this phase, the experiment will be conceived as a series of encounters between experimenter and subject. Introductions will have to be made, a setting for the experiment will have to be selected, and subjects for the experiment will have to be scheduled. Such interactional considerations as style of dress, mode of conversation, and experimenter–subject conduct must be considered. The ensuing interactions represent attempts to develop a common meaning regarding the experimental task. The job of the experimenter is to create consensus, and this leads to the consideration of interaction in the social experiment.

ON THE SOCIAL PSYCHOLOGY OF EXPERIMENTS

Conduct in the experimental setting represents a blend of the behavior Goffman (1963a) has termed "behavior in public places" with a very special form of dyadic interaction subject to its own rules of etiquette and propriety. Research by Rosenthal (1966), Friedman (1967), and Orne (1962) suggests that interaction in this context is influenced by the nature of eye contact between subject and experimenter, the mode of dress of the experimenter, and the definitions subject and observer bring into the situation.

Demand-Characteristic Effects

Orne (1962) has pointed to what he terms the "demand-characteristic effects" of experiment, referring to the fact that subjects cannot be viewed as passive objects upon whom the experimenter performs some operation and then observes the outcome. Orne (p. 777) notes that experimental subjects will perform tasks such as the following for more than 5 hours:

> One task was to perform serial additions of each adjacent two numbers on sheets filled with rows of random digits. In order to complete just one sheet, the subject would be required to perform 224 additions! A stack of some 2,000 sheets was presented to each subject—clearly an impossible task to complete. After the instructions were given, the subject was deprived of his watch and told, "Continue to work; I will return eventually." Five and one-half hours later, the *experimenter* gave up! In general subjects tended to continue this task for several hours, usually with little decrement in performance.

In an attempt to find a task the subjects would refuse to do, Orne increased the difficulty of the instructions. Subjects were instructed to compute additions for one page, tear that page up, and then take a new set of instructions from a large pile (which also told them to do the same task)—all as rapidly as possible. Again subjects persisted in the assignment. Explanations of this conduct emerged in a postexperimental inquiry period. Subjects invariably interpreted their performance as a meaningful part of an experiment on subjects' endurance, indicating that entry into the experimental setting may have effects manifestly different from those intended by the experimenter. In fact, the latent consequences of such interpretations indicate that an experiment can easily get out of hand. Subjects may have their own interpretations of the encounter and proceed in a manner quite divergent from that intended by the experimenter. Regardless of the direction this interaction takes, however, it is clear that subjects' conduct has reference only in the context of an interpretation that calls for them to "take part in an experiment."

Given the norms of the average experimental subject (the college sophomore, for example), taking part in an experiment typically represents a belief that the experiment will contribute to science and perhaps to human welfare in general. It appears that regardless of the motive for participation (a course assignment, money), both subject and experimenter share the belief that the experimental assignment is important (Orne, 1969, p. 778). Given this belief, it is not unusual to hear subjects asking experimenters: "How did I do?" or "Did I ruin anything?" The norm of the role of subject is to be a good subject; to be a good subject demands that one interpret ambiguous meanings and assignments in a context that values participation.

It is appropriate, then, to view behavior in an experiment as problem-solving behavior. The subject attempts to determine what the experimenter is up to and performs in a way that will best satisfy this interpretation. If subjects interpret an assignment as one in which their attitudes are supposed to change (the typical "before-after" design, for example), then they may see to it that their attitudes *do* change—and change in the way they think is expected (see Sherman, 1967). It is in this context that Orne (1962, p. 779) posits the assumption that subjects' behavior in any experimental situation "will be determined by two sets of variables: (a) those which are traditionally defined as experimental variables and (b) the perceived demand characteristics of the experimental situation."

The problem created by demand-characteristic effects   The extent to which an experiment can be replicated varies with the degree to which the subjects' behavior is determined by demand characteristics and not by experimental variables. The greater the influence of demand characteristics, the less the generalizability and the less likely it is that replication can occur.

Orne suggests that demand characteristics can never be totally removed from the experimental setting. It would appear evident that whenever two or more persons interact, some elements of the demand-characteristic variable will be present. The interaction process, as was noted in Chapter 4, involves individuals actively defining one another's behaviors and intentions on an ongoing basis. In this sense the experiment is just one variant on everyday interaction. It is not surprising that social psychologists have discovered that experimenters influence the behaviors produced in their laboratories.

Solutions to the problem of demand characteristics   A number of solutions to the problem of demand characteristics have been proposed (see Wuebben, Straits, and Schulman, 1974). Orne has suggested that in experimental settings in which instructions to subjects are unclear and highly ambiguous, the direction that subjects' behavior will take will also be unclear, because diverse demand characteristics will be at work. A clarification of instructions should serve to narrow the range of effects flowing from the demand characteristics. The number of misinterpretations of the experimenter's intentions should be significantly reduced.

It is clear that experimenters must be sensitized to this feature of the experiment and take steps to ascertain the diverse meanings subjects impute to the situation. Orne suggests the possibility of postexperimental inquiry wherein subjects are asked an open-ended question, such as, "What did you think this experiment was about?" Another strategy is to present subjects with the instructions of an experiment and then, before they have been exposed to the actual experiment, ask them questions "as if they had been subjects." The experimenter might ask: "If I had asked you to do all these things, what do you think the experiment would be about?" or "What would you have done?" These questions could then be given to a random sample of subjects in an inquiry period before the experiment; and on the basis of their responses, an experiment could be designed that took their interpretations into account—only now on a new pool of subjects. The investigator should be aware, as Orne cautions, that even inquiry sessions before and after experiments have their own demand characteristics; therefore, it is suggested that an investigator not acquainted or associated with the actual experiment conduct the sessions.

Orne has also proposed another means for dealing with this problem (1962, p. 779). This is the use of what he terms "quasicontrols." A *quasicontrol* subject is outside the usual experimenter–subject relationship. The investigator coopts the quasisubjects and makes them active participants in the experimental research. Orne (1962) suggests that quasicontrols can be created in at least three ways (see also Wuebben, Straits, and Schulman, 1974, pp. 249–53). First, subjects may be interviewed at different times during the experiment. Some might be interviewed before the experiment actually begins, others after it has concluded, others midway to completion, and so on. Each group of interviewed subjects would be asked what they felt the experiment was all about. The experimenter could thus gain some knowledge concerning his or her effects on the subjects' behavior. Second, a pool of subjects could be exposed to an "as if" experiment, but not subjected to the actual experiment. Their responses on the dependent-variable measure could then be compared with the responses of subjects who actually passed through the experiment. Third, experimenters could be exposed to "real" and "as if" subjects to determine whether or not demand characteristics were operating. A "double-blind" experimental model can be constructed, in which experimenters do not know which group of subjects they are working with; this can minimize or lower intentional actions on the part of experimenters to influence subjects in one way or another.

Wuebben, Straits, and Schulman (1974, p. 253) are skeptical of the use of quasicontrol subjects:

> Given our present state of ignorance about the experiment as a social system, the logic of demand characteristics suggests that any systematic change in the stimuli presented to subjects may alter the subject's definition of the experimental situation in unintended ways, and quasicontrol procedures as described by Orne do not represent a solution to this problem.

Alexander and Knight have suggested that subjects in the experimental situation attempt to present a situated identity that is most favorable to their self-conceptions; that is, they attempt to present a favorable image (1971, pp. 65–82). Thus the subject may be acting in ways that confirm an investigator's hypotheses, but, as these authors note (pp. 79–80):

> To the extent that desirable situated identities are associated with the responses derived from a particular theory, experimental data should show the "right" (predicted) results for the wrong reasons. The apparent confirmation of hypotheses may be produced by subject's concerns about self-presentation.

In another investigation, Alexander and Sagatun (1973, pp. 127–142) have expanded the situational identity hypothesis to include the behaviors of the experimenter. They proposed that a norm of reciprocity exists in the experimental situation such that a likable experimenter would be likely to elicit positive responses from the subjects. Their data indicated that student subjects feel that they are *expected* to respond favorably to the stimuli presented by a likable experimenter. In short, subjects will do what they think the experiment wants them to do. If they like the experimenter, they are even more inclined to do this.

It does appear, however, that the more deeply committed the subject is to the situated identity of subject, the more consistent will be the effects of demand characteristics upon his behavior. There does not appear to be any clear-cut resolution to the problem of demand characteristics. (But the disguised, or natural, experiment represents one possible solution; it will be discussed at the end of this chapter.)

Phases of the Experiment

Friedman (1967, p. 40) has shown that experimenter–subject interaction falls naturally into three phases; a face-sheet phase, an instructions phase, and the data-collection phase. It is appropriate to argue that the demand characteristics of the experiment will vary in each phase.

Face-sheet phase   The face-sheet phase consists of prefatory introductions between subjects and experimenter, as well as attempts by the experimenter to collect certain standardized information from subjects such as age, martial status, major in college, or other salient personal and social characteristics. Friedman has shown quite conclusively that the stance taken by the experimenter in this phase influences subsequent reactions of the subject. This phase consists, as Friedman argues, of a brief give and take of information, the subject giving and the experimenter taking. The interaction is strictly one-way — the experimenter asks questions and the subject answers. The forms this interaction takes vary from strict, ritualistic curtness to extreme informality. The following excerpt from Friedman (1967, pp. 80–81) indicates these two extremes.

Curtness

E: (never looking at the subject): Last name?
S: Ashton.
E: First name?
S: Carol.
E: Age?
S: Twenty.
E: Married?
S: No.

Informality

E: Have a chair.
S: Thank you.
E: How are you?
S: Fine, thank you.
E: Your name?
S: Joyce Dicholson.
E: Joyce, spell the last, please.
S: D-i-c-h-o-l-s-o-n. It's a Scotch spelling.

E: (looking up at her): Dicholson?
S: Yes, Dicholson.
E: Oh! Dicholson! Uh-huh.
S: Hm-hm.
E: Age?
S: (pause, then coyly): Ah-ah. . . . (E looks up.) Thirty-four. (E and S laugh.)
E: Marital status?
S: Single.
E: (who is single too [but male]); Single, huh. Major field?

That there is a wide degree of variation between these two ways of beginning an interview cannot be denied. The interest expressed by the second interviewer in his subject suggests a movement out of the role of experimenter and into a role more closely linked to marital status (in this case, bachelorhood). The impact of this informal stance upon the subsequent interactions of the experiment can only be surmised, but no doubt the second subject approached the experiment with quite different definitions of the experimenter and the task from the first.

Friedman also calls attention to the influence of such nonverbal gestures as smiles, eye contact, shrugs, and nods in setting an initial mood for subsequent interactions in the experiment. The data indicate that it is misleading to assume that all experimenters uniformly present the same self to subjects. Just as subjects approach the experiment with a conception of its demand characteristics, so too do experimenters. Some "play by the book" and refuse to depart from the printed instructions, while others introduce their own personalities into the encounter — thereby lending their own definitions of what an experiment is and what an experimenter does. Both experimenters and subjects bring to the first phase of the experiment a variety of definitions and meanings that become translated into the ongoing flow of conduct. The sum of these interpretations and behaviors constitutes the behavior called *experimental*.

Instructions phase   In the instructions period, the give and take between subject and interviewer has presumably ended. The experimenter reads a standard set of instructions, and the subject listens. In formulating the experimental design, the experimenter has presumably composed a set of instructions to which all subjects will be exposed before they enter the actual data-collection phase of the study. It is this set of instructions that sets the stage for subsequent behavior. This is the script for the future performance of experimenter and subject. If the experiment flows as it should, all subjects should receive the same instructions. However, as Friedman (1976, p. 91) observes, two contingencies may arise: Experimenters may not read the exact instructions (they may add, omit, or even change words), or it is possible that while the instructions are read as they stand, they are read in a way peculiar to the experimenter (with different emphasis on certain words, slurring over of others, and the use of smiles and winks to emphasize certain phrases).

Data-collection phase   The last period of the experiment, the task or instrumental (data-collection) phase, is also influenced by the interactions and selective presentation of selves by both subject and experimenter. Friedman (1967, p. 47) found support for the following conclusions from his observations of experiments in which subjects were asked to make ratings of the success or failure of persons who had been photographed doing a task: The more glances exchanged between experimenter and subject in the instructions period, the more likely the subject was to perceive success in neutral photos; the greater the number of glances directed by the experimenter to the subject (in all phases), the more likely the subject was to perceive success in neutral photos; the longer the duration of the instructions period, the more likely the subject was to perceive success in the photos; the longer the duration of the data-collection phase, the more likely the subject was to perceive success in the photos; the longer the duration of the face-sheet period, the greater the number of perceived successes; and the longer the duration of the experiment, the more perceived successes.

The experiment, then, is a face-to-face encounter, and simple variations in the temporal sequencing of action can produce significant behavioral differences, as can variations in nonverbal gestures. In this sense, interaction creates its own demand-characteristic effect.

The Experiment as an Encounter

The ideal experiment is one in which subject and experimenter respond exactly as the instructions read. Subjects do what they are told — they do not reinterpret instructions. Experimenters are supposed to act as experimenters, and not as persons who have other roles and selves. In the closed interaction of the experiment, subject and experimenter are to assume only those roles dictated by the experimental design.

Of course, in actuality experiments do *not* flow as they should. Subjects and experimenters respond in terms of their perceptions of the demand characteristics of the experiment. Each reinterprets the situation, adds to it, detracts from it, and in general acts in a manner that represents his definition of the situation. As I have shown, these interpretations and definitions may not always conform with those held by the person who has designed the experiment.

The relevant question becomes: "What accounts for experimenter–subject behavior if it is not the instructions on which the experiment is based?" Friedman (1967, p. 107) provides an answer when he argues that the ideal experimenter (and, I add, the ideal subject) "is . . . supposed to be a wooden soldier who thoroughly disciplines any nonrelevant role behavior (e.g., smiling at pretty girls)."

But Goffman (1961b, p. 143) warns:

Perhaps there are times when an individual does march up and down like a wooden soldier, tightly rolled up in a particular role. It is true that here and there we can pounce on a moment when an individual sits fully astride a single role, head erect, eyes front, but the next moment the picture is shattered into many pieces and the individual divides into different persons holding the ties of different spheres of life by his hands, by his teeth, and by his grimaces.

Applied to the experiment, this analogy suggests the falseness of assuming that subjects and experiments will respond in uniform manners during the course of an experiment. It is more appropriate to view the experimenter –subject dyad as "a tight little island of social interaction cut off from the mainland of everyday social gatherings, . . . an island to which the population of two carries its entire interpersonal repertoire" (Friedman, 1967, p. 108).

The experiment is what Goffman (1961, p. 89) terms an *encounter* or a *face engagement* in which

two or more participants in a situation join each other openly in maintaining a single focus of cognitive and visual attention — what is sensed as a single *mutual activity* entailing preferential communication rights. . . . Mutual activities and the face engagements in which they are embedded comprise instances of small talk, commensalism, lovemaking, gaming, formal discussion and personal servicing.

There is in the encounter a mutual awareness of each other's ongoing action, an attempt to maintain commitment and involvement, and an attempt to close the encounter to intruders. This is clearly the case with experiments. Each in her own way, experimenter and subject are involved in attempts to maintain (for a moment) that fleeting experience which has been transformed into a social gathering. Experimenters probe, reveal aspects of themselves, cajole or punish the subject, and even offer rewards in an attempt to carry out the instructions as they have defined them. Conversely (and simultaneously), subjects are defining these actions, attempting to bring a little bit of themselves into the setting, and generally acting in a manner that they think will make this encounter the best possible for the experimenter. The persons in this setting transform the sheer mechanical instructions of the experiment into a little world that represents (during the length of time they are together) their definitions of what the experiment should be.

THE RELEVANCE AND ADVANTAGES OF THE EXPERIMENT FOR SOCIOLOGY

The discussion of threats to internal validity and the detailed treatment of interaction in the experiment indicate the kinds of problems experimenters must be alert to. But such considerations are not reasons for not conducting experiments. My own position in this respect is that of Campbell and Stanley (1983, p. 34):

The average student or potential teacher reading the previous section of this chapter probably ends up with more things to worry about in designing an

experiment than he had in mind to begin with. This is all to the good if it leads
to the design and execution of better experiments and to more circumspection
in drawing inferences from results. It is, however, an unwanted side effect if it
creates a feeling of hopelessness with regard to achieving experimental control
and leads to the abandonment of such efforts in favor of even more informal
methods of investigation.

The formidable list of threats to validity of the experiment only attests to the
large amount of research psychologists have directed to the method. It is
incumbent upon sociologists to inquire into the usefulness of the method for
their purposes and to assess it against the criteria here presented.

The discussion of the problem of causality and the experiment pointed
to three factors that must be established before an acceptable causal inference can be made: the establishment of covariation between the independent and dependent variables; proof that the independent variables occurred
before the dependent variables; and the exclusion of rival causal hypotheses
and variables. The experiment, I argued, has become the model for causal
inference from which all other inferential strategies are derived or to which
they are compared. While open to criticisms, the experiment provides one of
the best methods that can be employed to answer questions of causal inference. What better way to establish time order between variables than to
control the presence of the dependent variable? Further, how can one show
covariance more accurately than by controlling the presence or absence of
those variables being observed?

In addition, the experiment provides the one research method that
allows the investigator to be both a participant and an observer of the
behavior being studied. By directing their own experiments, investigators
have at their disposal information on such factors as experimental demand
characteristics as well as the influence of their own gestures and interpretations on the experiment itself. The data collected are typically free from the
distortions of memory and recollection that so frequently occur with the
survey. Schwartz and Skolnick (1962, p. 138) phrase this as follows:

> In the field experiment, it was possible to see behavior directly, i.e., to deter-
> mine how employees act when confronted with what appears to them to be a
> realistic opportunity to hire. Responses are therefore not distorted by the
> memory of the respondent.

In the experiment, it is possible to remove those filters that too frequently
come between observers and that which they observe. The behavior is there
to be recorded. The use of tape recorders and films of experimental sessions
increases this ability to directly observe that which occurs.

A criticism that has frequently been lodged against the experiment is
that it is artificial (see Drabek and Haas, 1967, pp. 337–46). It is held that
because real life does not occur in the experimental setting, important
sociological issues cannot be brought there for analysis. But as an interaction
situation, the experiment represents a closed behavioral setting, a setting
from which certain persons are excluded, and, further, a setting in which only

certain kinds of conduct are permitted. This suggests that the dynamics of face-to-face interaction as they occur in such a situation could become the focus of serious sociological analysis. Within this situation the investigator can observe the transformation of a four-walled room into a setting for meaningful social conduct. The mechanisms by which selves are defined, projected, and alienated from one another becomes another topic of research in the laboratory. One of the recurring aspects of human conduct is the fact that when brought into another's physical presence, people interact. While the laboratory may not be a recurrent situation in the social arena, it is a situation that has enough in common with other behavior settings of its own class to be worthy of investigation in its own right. Just as physicians' offices have waiting rooms, so too do experimental laboratories. Just as patients leave a waiting room and enter an examination room, so too do subjects in experiments. The office of the physician is only one behavior setting that has similarities with the laboratory, and I am suggesting that society is replete with situations that have enough in common with the laboratory to justify the extensive study of conduct in laboratories.

Interaction in the Laboratory

Katovich (1984) has argued that the small group's laboratory is a provocative stage. On it, participants create a drama that has been scripted, in a sense, by the researcher. In the research of Couch and his students (see Couch, Saxton, and Katovich, 1986), dyadic and triadic interactional structures are videotaped. Participants are typically college students, who may be friends or strangers. Fraternity members were recruited in one study. Subjects are also selected on the basis of gender (Couch, 1987a; Molseed, 1986). Tapes are transcribed and analyzed sequentially in terms of the phases of interaction, negotiation, and planning that occur (see Katovich, 1984, pp. 57–58). The emergence of group structures, as well as partisan, representative-constituent relations and modes of cross-gender discourse, have been examined. In these studies the naturalistic method is brought alive in the laboratory. The charge of laboratory artificiality has been effectively met by this group of researchers.

In a sense, the laboratory becomes an interaction theatre. I have shown how experiments flow along a continuum that often deviates widely from the script laid down by instruction sheets. The laboratory is a behavior setting with its own rules and props for conduct. It is, then, a small stage on and in which the drama of interaction is presented. Sociologists must ask how it is that experimenters are able to stage performances in laboratories that manage to stay so close to the actual demands of the experiment. This suggests that the use of appointment rooms, the presentation of self in the guise of the scientist, and the communication of symbols that have meaning within the realm of science represent dramaturgical symbols and strategies employed by scientists as they conduct experiments. To conduct an experiment implies that one is engaging in a performance termed *scientific* in a situation that can have imputed to it scientific meaning.

NATURAL AND FIELD EXPERIMENTS

The problems of demand characteristics can often be avoided by studying naturally occurring events that either are deliberately produced or occur by accident (see Campbell, 1969, pp. 409-29). Administrative reforms, changes in official legislation, the institutionalization of educational programs, the development of new housing units, and the construction of new parks or recreational areas are all examples of events that could be studied from an experimental or quasiexperimental perspective. The researcher must be alerted to such changes and be prepared to move quickly into the field so as to gather the baseline data needed to establish whether or not changes are actually occurring in response to the new event.

Molotch (1970, pp. 131-44) and Molotch and Lester (1974, pp. 101-12) have argued that the sociological study of accidents provides yet another vehicle for uncovering underlying causal and social processes that are normally hidden by day-to-day routines. Events such as the Iran–Contra connection, the sudden death of a world leader, or environmental disasters (oil spills, burndowns at nuclear reactor sites), all bring to the surface events and processes normally hidden, or at least obscured, from the public and the scientist. They provide the setting for quasiexperimental study, for the sociologist can turn to public documents to determine the extent to which they have caused a change in social behavior. The sociologist can also compare other communities and individuals who were not victims of the accidents to assess their effects. Any student of accidents, however, must be alert to the problems of internal and external validity. An accident in and of itself may not yield valid sociological data that can be molded into sound causal propositions. Indeed, the sociological study of accidents may yield little more than poor journalism. Still, the accident may suggest experiments and quasiexperiments that could be carried out under more rigorous conditions.

If the experiment is the method *par excellence* for the social sciences, it is not without major flaws and weaknesses. Inevitably the experiment, whether ideal, quasi, natural, field, or accidental, involves individuals interacting with one another. Whenever individuals interact, norms of reciprocity, demand characteristics, and situated identities will be at work. Interaction can never be divorced from the research process. Researchers who employ this method must look more seriously at the interactions they produce when they bring subjects into their experimental settings.

SUGGESTED READINGS

COOK, THOMAS D., "Quasi-Experimentation: Its Ontology, Epistemology and Methodology," pp. 74-94 in Gareth Morgan (ed.), *Beyond Method: Strategies for Social Research.* (Beverly Hills: Sage, 1983). A thoroughgoing critique of the Campbell model of experiments and quasiexperiments, drawing on the recent criticisms of Campbell's formulations by such psychologists as Cronbach and Dunn.

COUCH, CARL J., *Researching Social Processes in the Laboratory.* (Greenwich, Conn.: JAI Press, 1988). A provocative presentation of the logic of naturalistic research in the laboratory. Details how such studies can be designed and implemented.

COUCH, CARL J., STANLEY L. SAXTON, AND MICHAEL A. KATOVICH (eds.), *Studies in Symbolic Interaction: Supplement 2: Parts A and B.* (Greenwich, Conn.: JAI Press, 1986). Contains the results of nearly 2 decades of research using the naturalistic, videotape approach to small-group interactional processes in the laboratory.

FRIEDMAN, NEIL J., *The Social Nature of Psychological Research.* (New York: Basic Books, 1967). A now-classic analysis of the effects of experimenters and subjects on experimental results.

6

The Social Survey
and Its Variations

Surprisingly, although most sociological research is based on nonexperimental data . . . (these) data are treated as far as possible *as if they were truly experimental data*. The data are sliced, chopped, beaten, molded, baked and finally artificially colored until the researcher is able to serve us proudly with a plateful of mock experiment. [Lieberson, 1985, p. 4]

From our point of view, the essence of a survey is that it is confined to, but can completely exhaust, all the possibilities inherent in a variable language.

The central problem . . . is thus the following: How does one translate ideas of social matters into variables, and how does one analyze the interrelations between these variables so that new ideas can be derived from them? It is not claimed, of course, that the procedures of variable language . . . cover all that the social scientist has to say or wants to say. It is not even clear whether all empirical research, let alone more general reflections, can be carried on in this kind of discourse. What additional "languages" are needed for well-rounded social science must be left to future methodological investigations. But such efforts will undoubtedly be helped if at least one such system has been clarified as far as possible. [Lazarsfeld, 1955a, pp. xii–xiv]

As survey research secured its dominance, its practitioners moved more forthrightly toward a focus on individual behavior. Dense community or organizational samples were replaced by national samples, snowball sampling died in its infancy, and the struggling effort to use survey research to make statements about communities, organizations, or social subsystems was overwhelmed by greater statistical rigor of characterizing "populations" and analyzing behavior of individuals as "independently drawn" members of the population. . . . The individual remained the unit of analysis. [Coleman, 1986, p. 1315; 1958, p. 28]

This chapter presents the basic rationales for the use of the social survey, which, because of its wide popularity among contemporary sociologists, deserves special attention. The discussion draws upon my earlier treatments of sampling, measurement, interviewing, and causal analysis. Like the experiment, the survey may be viewed both as a method of research and as a situation worthy of social-psychological analysis. Lieberson's (1985) recent criticisms of the experimental model that underlies survey analysis will be reviewed, as will Coleman's (1985, 1986) and Blumer's (1948) arguments that the survey research focuses primarily on individual behavior.

THE SURVEY

Definition

The survey can be defined as a methodological technique that requires the systematic collection of data from populations or samples through the use of the interview or the self-administered questionnaire. The investigator approaches a sample of persons who have been exposed to a set of events or experiences and interviews them with respect to these experiences. The survey parallels the preexperimental design defined as the "one-shot case study" (Campbell and Stanley, 1963, pp. 6–7). Observations are typically collected at one point in time. No "before" observations are made, no control is exercised over experimental variables, and no control groups are explicitly constructed; rather, a group of persons are observed at one point in time and questioned about their behaviors, attitudes, and beliefs with respect to a series of issues.

This extended definition is not intended to suggest that survey analysts make no attempt to simulate the true experimental design. In fact, they do; and they accomplish this through the use of multivariate analysis. After observations have been collected, the sample is divided into subgroups that differ on the variables or processes being analyzed. For example, if attitudes toward sexual relationships in marriage are being studied, the analyst might subdivide the sample into three groups: those never married, those currently married, and those married previously but now divorced or widowed. Such a division parallels an experimental design with two experimental groups and one control group. The two groups that were or had been married constitute those subjects exposed to the experimental variable, while the never-married group constitutes the control group. It is this strategy—the subdivision of a sample into contrasting control and experimental groups—that shows a general commitment to the experimental model of research and analysis (see Lieberson, 1985, pp. 4–5, 14–18).

Solution to the Problem of Causal Inference: Multivariate Analysis

Chapter 1 presented multivariate analysis as the basic model of inference underlying the survey. After data are gathered on those variables viewed as relevant to the development of causal propositions, multivariate analysis involves the following steps: cross-classifying two variables, one independent and one dependent; measuring the degree of association between them; and introducing a third variable to assess its affect upon the original association. The third variable becomes the test factor; it may be intrinsic or extrinsic in nature, and temporally it may be antecedent or contingent. The repeated introduction of test factors into covariant relationships becomes the major strategy of survey analysis.

It should be clear that before analysts can begin these operations, they must first demonstrate covariance between the primary variables. They must also have anticipated the causal status of the variables—that is, test, independent, or dependent. This anticipation must be theoretically directed, although there is an emergent quality to the analytic process that cannot be ignored. That is, relationships may not appear when they are supposed to, or they may disappear under the effect of unanticipated variables—for example, intrinsic factors. For these reasons, the survey process takes on a flavor of continuing analysis and emergence that the experiment lacks. In the experiment, the investigator can control those variables judged to be relevant; the survey analyst lacks this control. Multivariate analysis, then, is best seen as a strategy of analysis and not of design.

Both the survey and the experiment are strategies for uncovering causal relationships. But the survey takes the researcher to a natural field setting; the experiment typically does not. In addition, the experiment is based on the assumption that behavior is studied at two points in time in situations controlled by the investigator. The survey in its most popular forms lacks both of these qualities—hence the greater concern with the tentative nature of causal relationships.

A point of similarity lies in the survey analyst's attempts to construct ad hoc experimental and control groups. This strategy permits the analysis of causal relationships in situations or groups that have one characteristic in common—at least for the purposes of analysis.

An appropriate question is the suitability of multivariate analysis for resolving the problems of rival causal factors. Traditionally, survey researchers have given greatest consideration to extrinsic test factors in their causal analyses. This concern must be broadened to include the treatment intrinsic variables that flow from the research process. Every researcher is obligated to report the effects of the following variables upon causal propositions: the situations of observation; the attitudes and definitions of interviewers as they pertain to the interview process; variations in definitions and meanings observed among respondents or subjects concerning the research act; unique aspects of subject–observer interaction; time and its passage.

In a conventional sense, the survey analyst must treat internal validity as a basic feature of the research process. Because the survey method requires data collection in widely varying situations among dissimilar persons at different points in time, factors intrinsic to the process of data collection cannot be ignored. The survey researcher must become as rigorous as the experimenter in analyzing rival causal factors.

As a point of strategy, multivariate analysis can be easily adopted to these problems. Investigators need only expand their conception of rival causal factors to include the problems mentioned. Thus interviewers could be classified in terms of their styles of presentation (formal or informal, for example), and this dimension could be treated as an intervening test variable. This could also be the case for variations in subject presentation, for situational contingencies, and for the effects of temporal, or historical, events.

SURVEY DESIGNS

It is possible to distinguish several types of survey designs, each of which varies in some degree from the definition just given. Before we turn to these variations, it should be noted that as a methodological strategy, the survey rests heavily on the sampling considerations presented in Chapter 3, and that any classification of survey designs must consider approximations to the experimental model.

Surveys and Sampling Models

The survey begins with the assumption that a sample of theoretically relevant objects from a population will be studied. The choice of a sampling model (interactive or noninteractive, for example) becomes a prerequisite in the determination of what objects to include in the study design. Given the distinction between interactive and noninteractive sampling models, it is possible to differentiate survey designs that employ one or the other of these two models. These models seldom make assumptions about recurrent or repeated observations, however (though certain survey designs do employ repeated observations). For this reason, investigators must also consider the time base on which survey designs rest.

Surveys and the Experimental Model

It will be recalled that there are four key elements to the classical experimental model: control by the investigator over the treatment conditions; repeated observations; construction of two or more comparison groups (experimental and control); and the use of randomization as a technique for assignment of subjects to experimental and control groups. Nonexperimental or preexperimental designs may include any of these elements but will not combine all four. (The one-shot case study lacks all these elements, for example.) Quasiexperimental designs employ certain combinations of these elements but typically lack the important ability to control exposure or nonexposure to the experimental treatment condition.

Surveys approximate the experimental model through the use of multivariate analysis. The generic definition of the term given earlier, however, makes no assumptions about repeated observations or the use of random selection and assignment. In addition to the sampling model underlying the survey, I add to my classification those designs that in no way approximate the experimental model because of any of the following: failure to employ the principle of randomization; failure to construct comparison groups; failure to have repeated observations. Survey designs that fail to meet these criteria are called *nonexperimental.* I also distinguish those survey designs that attempt in some systematic fashion to approximate the true experimental model but because of their nonlaboratory nature are necessarily quasiexperimental. Those designs termed *quasiexperimental* are recognizable by (1) the use of repeated observations; (2) the probable use of comparison groups; and (3) the use of randomization (see Cook and Campbell, 1979).

It can be seen, then, that those survey designs not employing randomization are necessarily nonexperimental, even though they may permit repeated observations and the construction of comparison groups. Conversely, even though the design rests on probability sampling assumptions, it is not quasiexperimental if it lacks repeated observations or comparisons. In deciding which type of survey design to employ, the investigator should attempt to approximate the quasiexperimental model. The use of multivariate analysis to add experimental dimensions to the design is less desirable than employing a quasiexperimental model initially. (The reader will recall that the discussion of experimental designs distinguished three forms: nonexperimental, true experimental, and quasiexperimental.)

Types of Survey Designs

Nonexperimental designs   The following designs are distinguishable because they represent the most popular forms of the survey in use and they fail to incorporate one or more of the critical features of the experimental model: randomization, control groups, repeated observations, control by the investigator over experimental variables.

One-shot Case Study   In this nonexperimental design, the survey analyst randomly samples from a larger population a group of subjects who have been exposed to a series of critical events that can be causally analyzed by multivariate analysis. The sample will be theoretically relevant and representative. The sampling model must be random and may be either interactive or noninteractive. It may be stratified, or proportionate, in which case it would be termed a *weighted one-shot survey design.* If no weighting procedures are employed, it would be a *nonweighted one-shot survey.* It should rest on an interactive base so that natural social units are sampled.

These two variations of the one-shot case study constitute the bulk of modern survey research (Stouffer, 1950). They represent valid strategies for formulating causal propositions to the extent that theoretical guidance and randomization procedures are utilized. They are weakened to the extent that relevant comparison groups are excluded. Also, because "before" measures are not taken, inferences concerning time order are difficult. Because only one set of observations is gathered, problems of reactivity, time, and subject–observer changes are reduced. Still, these two variations represent the weakest form of the survey design.

One-group Pretest-posttest Design   The second nonexperimental survey design is the one-group pretest-posttest design. Here the investigator makes two sets of observation on the same group, but there is no control group. This restricts inference because the investigator has no way of knowing what would have occurred had the sample not been exposed to the critical event. This design is superior to the one-shot case study because of repeated observations. But repeated observations raise problems that are best resolved by adding at least one comparison group.

Static-group Comparison Survey The static-group comparison survey is the third nonexperimental survey design. Two groups are chosen for study (either randomly or nonrandomly), and each is observed at only one point. Its essential feature is an attempt to explain events that have occurred in the target sample by comparing them with the control sample. Unfortunately, there are no "before" observations. The analyst must infer what occurred before the observations were made. Valid comparisons and interpretations between the two samples become contingent on the demonstration that they differ only in that one group was exposed to a critical event and the other was not.

There are two ways to treat this factor of subject selection and bias. The first is to select the two samples randomly. With respect to the target sample (the one exposed to the critical event), however, the investigator may lack sufficient information about the larger population to gain a sufficiently representative and random sample.

The second method of treating subject bias is to match respondents in the target and control sample on personal-social factors presumed relevant. Matching, whether by precision or by control of frequency distribution (Selltiz et al., 1959, pp. 98–108), assumes that the relevant matching factors are known — but this may not always be the case. Furthermore, when matching target and control samples, investigators may soon run out of cases because they are forced to reject those persons who do not meet their criteria. This may lead to biasing in the final samples. This factor is magnified when the target population is so small that rejection of unmatched cases decreases the target sample to ridiculously low size. Another difficulty arises when the investigator selects small matched samples. The smaller the matched samples, the greater the likelihood that uncontrolled factors will invalidate meaningful comparisons.

Of the three nonexperimental survey designs presented, the static-group comparison design is preferred because it involves the use of comparison groups. I have pointed to the deficiencies in those designs that do not have "before" observations. Causal inference is always problematic, and the static-group comparison design is weakened because of the absence of "before" measures.

Quasiexperimental designs The essence of the quasiexperimental survey design is its emphasis on repeated observations, randomization, naturally induced experimental treatments, and the optional use of comparison groups.

Same-group Recurrent-time-series Survey without Comparison Groups The first such design is the same-group recurrent-time-series survey without comparison groups. The same group of persons are observed repeatedly in a "before-after" experimental fashion. No control groups are present. The initial sample of persons is randomly selected on either a weighted or unweighted basis. It is different from the one-group pretest-posttest survey because more than two sets of observations are made; in this respect it is superior to that design. But repeated observations raise the familiar problems of intrinsic test factors. Despite the potentially distorting impact of intrinsic factors, this design is favored because attempts are made to observe the same group of persons continually. This increases the investigator's ability to adopt the perspective of those studied, and ability that nonexperimental surveys restrict.

Different-group Recurrent-time-series Survey without Comparison Groups
In the different group design, recurrent observations are made on a population through the continual random selection of samples from it. The same people are not reobserved; instead, the investigator takes care to sample persons in each wave who are similar to those contained in the first sample. This strategy controls the effect of intrinsic factors but presents other problems. The Gallup and Harris public opinion polls are examples of this design; they trace, for example, voters' attitudes toward political figures or public issues over a specified time period. The essence of the design is to uncover changes in attitudes or behavior by repeated observations.

In the time-series study, the variables of maturation, mortality, instrument change, and subject–observer interaction and observation effects all become important. While recurrent observations reduce the problems of causal inference, the focus on events over time has the potential of introducing reactive factors that exist alongside the events assumed to be causing the change under analysis. The very fact that an investigator repeatedly presents himself before a group of persons introduces a dimension not ordinarily present in their lives, and this must be assessed. That is, repeated observations produce new behaviors. The observation of different groups at each point in time reduces these reactive factors, however.

Same-group Recurrent-time-series Survey with Comparison Groups
With a same-group recurrent-time-series survey with comparison groups, the investigator creates a comparison group each time observations are made on the target sample. The design begins with the random selection of a group of persons who will be observed over a long period of time. Before making observations on the target sample, the investigator randomly selects a comparison (control) sample whose responses are employed as checks for the reactive effect of repeated observations on the target sample. This feature of the design, which is often termed the *panel design*, builds in control for those internal validity factors to which other designs are most susceptible (for example, interview effects, maturation, and history). An investigator who identifies differences in response patterns between comparison and focal samples at any point will ask, "Are these differences due to my reinterviewing of the target sample, or are they differences arising from the natural events I am studying?" If the investigator concludes that differences are arising from the interviewing-observation process, then a potential source of error in all

surveys has been located and can be controlled by retraining interviewers, making sure the interview schedule has not changed, or more closely recording the interactions that do occur when the target sample is interviewed. It might be the case, for example, that certain interviewers are systematically eliciting unfavorable responses from certain types of subjects. If the same types of subjects in the comparison sample do not also give unfavorable responses, then it becomes a reasonable hypothesis that the interviewers are introducing the error. Without the use of a comparison sample, which is compared at each point of observation with the target sample, this could not be determined. For these reasons the same-group recurrent-time-series survey with comparison groups is the most sophisticated survey design.

Survey Designs: Review; Some Recurrent Problems

All six of the basic types of survey designs share the following features: the use of interviewing or questionnaires as the major mode of data collection; collection of data from large numbers of persons; and the use of multivariate analysis as the major method of data analysis. They differ by the presence or absence of the following: randomization; comparison groups created before or after data collection; repeated observations of the same group or equivalent groups. Two broad types of survey designs were presented: nonexperimental and quasiexperimental. I have suggested that the survey analyst should attempt to approximate the experimental model by using multivariate analysis. No survey is free from flaws, but when possible, the same-group recurrent-time-series survey with comparison groups should be employed.

The discussion of sampling models and the survey made only brief reference to the relevance of interactive and theoretically directed sampling procedures. However, it is clear that if the survey is to become a tool that permits the analysis of natural social units, interactive sampling models must be adopted. This is the first recurrent problem of surveys; thus the suggestions in Chapter 3 concerning the sampling of social relationships, social groups, encounters, and organizations take on central relevance for the survey analyst. By relaxing the formal rules of statistical sampling theory to permit greater theoretical guidance, investigators can make the survey a powerful tool for the large-scale study of natural interactive units.

A second problem (and one not peculiar to the survey) is that few investigators think beyond their own work to future studies. This short-sightedness often leads the analyst to conclude that a survey has raised more problems than can be answered—and unfortunately, the person who builds upon an earlier study seldom replicates it. The survey is one of the most widely used methods in sociology, but—paradoxically—it is seldom used for purposes of replication. As was indicated in Chapter 2, this is a reflection of the reward structure in sociology: Replication is not rewarded. As an alternative, I propose the following strategy (which would apply to all research endeavors): Each person who chooses to use the survey (or any other method) should regard his study as only one in a long series of interrelated investigations that may not be concluded in a lifetime.

A third problem with the survey is the frequent inability of the analyst to make statements about collectivities of individuals. Reliance on statistical sampling models that do not consider the sampling of groups leaves the investigator with observations of only individuals. In Chapter 3, group sampling models involving snowball, dense, and saturation strategies were considered. These methods can broadly be considered techniques of relational analysis. They represent one way to raise observation from the atomistic to the group level. Unless the survey is raised to this level, only statements about individuals can be made. This is acceptable if the goal is individual description; but if the survey is to be placed in the mainstream of modern sociological theory, relational methods of survey analysis must be made integral to the method.

These are three recurrent—but soluble—problems of the survey. A fourth problem is more difficult to solve; it is the question of whether or not the survey is appropriate for the analysis of complex forms of human interaction. While the survey permits statements to be made about large aggregates of individuals clustered in social units, it does not always provide clues about interaction (see Blumer, 1956, pp. 683–90). Human interaction is continually shifting and establishing new forms, as participants confront one another in concrete situations. Survey methodology, which relies on structured questionnaires, is ill-equipped to capture this aspect of human behavior. Certain interactional questions can be answered; when sociologists find themselves in settings where the meanings and forms of interaction are relatively ritualized, it is quite probable that their structured methods will satisfactorily record elements of the interaction. But in situations where symbolic meanings are in flux and where interactional forms are continually being redefined, the survey method will be found lacking because of its structured and relatively inflexible nature.

SOURCES OF ERROR IN SURVEY RESEARCH

The survey merges strategies of sampling and recording with the direct or indirect interviewing of individuals. This merger sets the stage for a number of probable errors that may ultimately distort the investigator's final results.

Demming (1944, pp. 359–69) has identified thirteen factors that may affect the usefulness of surveys. They flow from the elements that underpin the survey method: interviewers, respondents, sampling models, interview schedules, and procedures of coding and analysis. Like the experiment, the survey rests on the interactions of individuals who are engaged in the process of producing data that can be subjected to causal analysis. The presence of individuals in the research act inevitably creates sources of error that become topics of study in their own right. Demming's (1944, pp. 359–69) list of sources of error in the survey includes the following factors:

1. Variability in response.
2. Differences in forms of interviews: (a) mail, telephone, and direct interviews; (b) intensive and extensive interviews; (c) long and short schedules.

3. Bias and variation arising from the interviewer.
4. Bias arising from the agency supporting the research.
5. Imperfections in the design of the questionnaire. Lack of clarity in the interview questions; different meanings of the same word to different groups of people; eliciting an answer that is open to misinterpretation; the use of emotionally charged words.
6. Changes that take place in the universe before analysis is completed.
7. Bias arising from nonresponse.
8. Bias arising from late reports.
9. Bias arising from an unrepresentative selection of a date for the survey or of the period covered.
10. Bias arising from an unrepresentative selection of respondents.
11. Sampling errors.
12. Errors of processing, coding, editing, and tabulating.
13. Errors in interpretation: (a) misunderstanding the questionnaire and failure to take account of the respondent's perspective; (b) personal bias in interpretation.

Variability in Response

There are two kinds of variability in response: the same person can give different answers to the same question at two different times, or different persons sampled at the same time can give different answers to the same question. The source of this variability must be identified if the investigator is to develop any systematic explanation of the behaviors and attitudes in question.

Differences between Different Interview Forms

Too little is known about the effects of different interview forms on the data that are gathered by means of the survey. Will a self-report, mailed questionnaire produce the same answers as a direct, face-to-face interview? Does a telephone interview provide an adequate interactional format for intensive questioning? How long must an interview be before it bores a respondent? These questions and others are raised when differences in forms of interviews are considered (see Sudman, 1976; Sudman and Kalton, 1986).

Bias Arising from the Interviewer

As was indicated earlier, interviewers have different styles. Like experimenters, some are formalistic, others informal. Some interpret questions differently. Some skip certain questions and fill them in after the interview has been completed. Some actually forge interviews. Some belittle the respondent. The interviewer, as noted in Chapter 4, is a fundamental source of bias in survey research.

Bias Arising from the Agency Supporting the Research

Bias arising from the source of support largely rests on the respondents' inclinations to take sides for or against the supporting agency. Respondents may choose to protect their own interests and take a stand against the supporting agency. On the other hand, they may be impressed by the source of support and willingly cooperate with the interviewer.

Imperfections in the Design of the Questionnaire

Faulty design in the questionnaire can produce a fundamental source of bias in the final results of the survey. Faulty design often derives from a poor knowledge of the subject matter. Researchers may have spent too little time with the individuals they wish to interview. They may not have reviewed the research literature that would have given them clues about how their questions should be formulated. Their theoretical model may have been faulty. They may have failed to anticipate the analysis phase of their research; as a consequence, their questions may have been asked in such a way that certain forms of analysis become impossible. The questions on the questionnaire may have carried emotional overtures that could produce widely varying responses.

Changes in the Universe

The conditions described in the survey may have changed by the time the analysis is completed. Respondents' attitudes may have drastically changed after the interview. Historical and maturational factors can intercede and leave the researcher with little more than a set of data that are specific to a particular moment in time.

Bias Arising from Nonresponse

The nonresponders in any survey can serve to distort the final results. Those who refuse to respond or who cannot be located often exist in a special universe. If they are not located, researchers may be left with a highly selective sample of individuals. They may not have a *random sample* of the universe to which they wish to generalize.

Late Reports

Analysis in any survey typically must begin at a particular time. Interviews and questionnaires that come in after that time may represent biased reports.

Bias Arising from the Selection of a Date for the Survey

The day or time period selected for the survey can produce a bias in the final results. As Demming observes, a time coverage of weekly household purchases during any week in December would hardly be representative. A passenger-traffic survey near any national holiday would scarcely be representative. Similarly, a study of church attendance patterns conducted on Easter Sunday would be biased. The problem of dates and timing can easily be overcome. But the time of the survey must be given serious consideration.

Bias Arising from the Respondent

If researchers do not have a firm definition of the population from which they wish to sample, and if there is no updated list enumerating that universe, then they may end with an unrepresentative sample. As was noted in Chapter 3, the enumeration of the population is a critical step in the sampling and observational process.

Bias Arising from Sampling Errors

Modern sampling techniques virtually eliminate large sampling errors. If the researcher has successfully defined and enumerated the population, this source of error should be minimal. However, it is possible to have a scientifically sound sample that is not replicated during the interviewing process. Interviewers may be unable or unwilling to execute the researcher's sampling plan.

Processing Errors

Once the survey interviews have been completed, they must be processed and readied for causal analysis. This involves a process of coding which requires that individuals go through each interview schedule and translate the responses on that schedule into some set of categories, typically numerical in nature. Once the schedules have been coded, they must be processed for analysis. This involves either hand tabulations or the translation of the coding sheets onto computer cards. These two apparently simple activities introduce major sources of error in the final survey results.

Coders may not agree on how to classify responses. Interview schedules may be incomplete; this often forces the coder to take the perspective of the respondent and attempt to answer a question the respondent failed to answer. Often the coder is too rushed to do a good job of coding. Some coders are not really interested in the research; they may give less than careful attention to their coding assignments. If a response does not accurately fit a given category in the code book, many coders will treat the response as an instance of an open-ended category. That is, they "act as if" the response can be coded as an instance of the category in question. This tendency to let certain responses pass as instances of a category has been described by Garfinkel (1967, p. 20) as "ad hocing." Ad hoc considerations are after-the-fact considerations that involve the use of such phrases as *et cetera, unless,* or *let it pass.* That is, coders let uncodable responses pass as codable responses. Garfinkel believes that ad hocing occurs in all coding activities and regards such practices as invariant features of all social research. This is not the prevailing view. Garfinkel (1967, pp. 21–22) observes:

> Ordinarily researchers treat such ad hoc procedures as flawed ways of writing, recognizing, or following coding instructions. The prevailing view holds that good work requires researchers, by extending the number and explicitness of their coding rules, to minimize or even eliminate the occasions in which "et cetera" and other such ad hocing practices would be used.

Coding instructions furnish coders with a set of guidelines that permit them to produce codable data. Those data in turn constitute the basis for hypothesis formulation and subsequent causal analysis. In a very fundamental sense, the final data base of the survey becomes a social and interactional production. This fact cannot be denied. As the raw data from questionnaires are translated into codable responses and into numerical form, individuals must make decisions concerning how each response is to be coded. The sum total of these individual decisions constitutes a large source of bias and error in any survey.

Errors in Interpretation

Any causal analysis based on responses to survey interviews involves inferences derived from the raw data. As Demming observes (1944), there are bound to be errors in interpretation when the researcher moves from data to causal propositions. Differences in interpretation often arise from a misunderstanding of the questionnaire. A vague or poorly thought-out theory or proposition may lead the researcher to look for the wrong issues in the data base. A misunderstanding of the sample may also lead to misinterpretations. Personal and professional bias is bound to intrude in the analysis process. Facts do not speak for themselves. They must be defined and interpreted. This interpretational process can serve to distort the final results of the survey.

These 13 sources of error suggest that survey researchers cannot unthinkingly accept the results produced by interviewers and coders. They must be ever alert to the interactional processes that enter in at every step in the research.

Interpretive Problems: Lieberson's Critique

Lieberson (1985) has recently offered a critical interpretation of current sociological strategies of statistically analyzing findings from social surveys. The quotation from his book at the beginning of this chapter indicates that he believes that most sociologists attempt to pattern their survey analyses after the experimental model. This creates a number of problems, including (1) selectivity, (2) comparisons and counterfactuals, (3) asymmetrical forms of causation, (4) levels of analysis, (5) control variables, and (6) the place of theory in the analysis of data. A brief discussion of each of these problems follows.

Selectivity   As we have seen, a key feature of the experimental model is the random assignment of subjects to different test conditions. If the assignment is not random, the researcher must demonstrate that selectivity has no bearing on the study. Lieberson (1985, p. 14) notes that in the social sciences, we typically cannot meet the rule of random assignment. Some selective process is always operating. Researchers attempt to simulate the experimental model through the use of one or more of the quasiexperimental designs previously discussed. However, these designs cannot erase the fact that the subjects located in either the control or experimental group may be in those groups because of selective factors. The researcher does not know if the differences in outcome are attributable to the causal forces under consideration, or to unknown factors that placed the subjects in the control and experimental groups in the first place (Lieberson, 1985, p. 15). There is an additional problem with selectivity. The groups that are created are artificial; they are seldom, if ever, natural, interacting social groups or social collectivities.

Comparisons and counterfactuals   A true experiment rests on comparisons between the experimental and control group. Sociological research is inherently comparative, but nonexperimental. Sociologists like to act as if they are doing comparative, experimental, or quasiexperimental research. The comparisons that are made are often flawed by two problems: counterfactuals and contamination. When conclusions "are predicated on events that did not happen, philosophers call such statements 'counterfactual conditions'" (Lieberson, 1985, p. 45). Here is an example: "If Lincoln had not become president, blacks would still be slaves" (Lieberson, 1985, p. 45). Counterfactuals begin with untrue statements; hence one cannot verify or falsify a conclusion based on such arguments. However, quasiexperimental social science comparative research is based on such arguments. The researcher states, for example, that situations A and B are the same on all counts except for the existence of X, which is high in A and low in B. If Y (dependent variable) is high in A and low in B, then it is reasoned that if X were high in B (which it isn't), then Y would also be high. This is counterfactual logic; and social scientists are always making claims about acts and events that did not occur. Experiments and quasiexperiments are based on counterfactual conditions. But not everything can be controlled, and factors that are not studied may be creating the observed effects. Thus, comparisons between groups may be inaccurate (see the foregoing selectivity discussion).

Counterfactual logic may lead to conclusions that are also flawed because of the contamination effects of the independent variable that is operating in unstudied situations. For example, X, in our aforementioned A and B case, may also operate on D and E, which have not been studied. When this occurs, X's effects cannot be restricted to just the situations of A and B. Under these conditions, any theorizing about X's effects based just on the study of A and B will be erroneous.

Asymmetrical forms of causation   Lieberson (1985, p. 63) notes that many researchers assume a symmetric view of causation. For example, if X condition causes Y, which is defined as undesirable, then Y will disappear if X is removed. If segregated schools are associated with lower educational scores for minorities, then if schools are integrated, test scores should increase for minority group members. Much social policy is based on this view of symmetrical causation. Lieberson suggests that this is a flawed, narrow view of causation. Processes in the social world are not always reversible. For example, a given sequence of events can produce effects that cannot be nullified or reversed. The effects of the death of a father on a family cannot be reversed. Many claim that once a problem drinker becomes an alcoholic and loses control over alcohol, she can never drink socially again (see Denzin, 1987a, Chapter 2 for a review). Lieberson (1985, pp. 86–87) argues that social scientists and policy makers err to the extent that they employ symmetric causal models when asymmetric causation is operating.

Levels of analysis   Survey researchers often confuse levels of analysis when they formulate interpretations of their data. This is also called the "ecological fallacy" (Robinson, 1950), which occurs when the correlation of characteristics "on one level (spatial aggregates) is used to draw conclusions about the association of the same characteristics on another level (between individuals)" (Lieberson, 1985, p. 107). Sociologists cannot just move from the individual to the aggregate level (or vice versa) without considering the emergent interactional, and structural processes that connect persons to larger social structures. For example, it would not be correct to argue from crime rates in large American cities to the criminal behaviors of American minority groups. This is confusing the levels of analysis. Lieberson (1985, p. 117) contends that a theory must indicate the level of analysis appropriate to its testing. If it doesn't, the researcher may commit the level of analysis fallacy just discussed.

Control variables   It is common practice to apply control variables in the analysis of survey data. This practice reflects the attempt to model survey analysis after the experimental model, in which there is "control over the conditions under study" (Lieberson, 1985, p. 120). If two variables, X and Y, cause high values in variable Z, then it seems to make sense to determine the relationship between X and Z and Y and Z by controlling for the observed relationship between Y and Z. This is controlling for the effect of Y on Z. Lieberson (1985, p. 122) sees two basic problems with this procedure. First, if a control variable does affect a relationship between an independent and dependent variable, then the experimental model is not being approximated and the control variable should not be used. That is, the researcher has not created or isolated a truly experimental relationship between the independent and dependent variables. Second, if controls do not alter the original relationship between the independent and dependent variables, then — and only then — the quasiexperimental assumption is sound. In that case, the initial uncontrolled relationship is correct. One can only freely employ controls when the implicit experimental model is supported by the second criterion just discussed. Lieberson's criticisms of the strategy of control analysis warrant serious consideration because sociologists flagrantly engage in this practice.

Theory   Lieberson (1985, pp. 229–31) argues that sociologists lack a social theory of data. They do not know when to use controls, nor have they satisfactorily formulated answers for how to deal with selectivity, counterfactuals, asymmetric causation, or levels of analysis. A theory of data, he contends, should (1) specify the conditions under which a given phenomenon will appear as a measurable event, (2) indicate how a given set of measurements differ from the universe of events in which the phenomenon occurs, (3) suggest the conditions under which the independent variable varies, and (4) spell out how particular causal forces will affect the "control test" conditions (Lieberson, 1985, p. 231).

Lieberson's critique of current survey analysis practices calls into question the use of cross-sectional data. His argument calls for the use of longitudinal designs that will permit the examination over time of the relationships between independent and dependent variables. He suggests that cross-sectional data seldom allow sociologists to determine whether a relationship is symmetric or asymmetric. Furthermore, if cross-sectional analysis does not imply longitudinal change, then it cannot be causal analysis (Lieberson, 1985, p. 181). Lieberson's critique carries important implications for survey research. He calls for a serious rethinking of the entire conceptual-analytic apparatus which currently structures survey analysis (see Becker, 1986, p. 128; and S. Turner, 1987). More deeply, his approach suggests that data do not tell their own story. Data must be interpreted. Causal models of analysis underdetermine and fail to dictate the shape of a theory. These models are atheoretical, as well as extremely positivistic and inductive (for an example, see Blalock, 1984; and Turner and Martin, 1986; but also see Duncan, 1975).

Additional Problems with the Survey

A number of problems with the survey have recently emerged; Sudman (1976) offers a review. These problems include a growing refusal rate among respondents, the decline in the number of competent interviewers, inter-viewer's fears of interviewing in America's inner cities, the increased costs of surveys, and recent legal barriers accompanying the 1974 Federal Privacy Act.

Interviewing has traditionally been done by women who wanted part-time work. This means that gender has influenced the data upon which surveys are based. (We have shown how the gender of the interviewer shapes the nature of the information gathered in the interview.) As increasingly more women enter the labor force on a full-time basis, this labor pool has gotten smaller.

The 1974 Federal Privacy Act requires that prospective respondents be informed of the uses to be made of the data gathered in a survey. Many survey researchers fear that this act makes data collection more difficult. Critics feel the act is justified on the grounds that the social sciences already collect too much questionable data from the American public. These data are seen as invasions of privacy. Some researchers fail to protect the anonymity of the respondent. Many legal issues yet to be resolved in the courts are implied by this act (Sudman, 1976, p. 117).

ROLE OF THE SURVEY IN THE STUDY OF INTERACTION

The deficiencies and flaws of the social survey have been extensively dis-cussed. They were found to revolve around internal and external validity. The treatment of interaction, a circumscribed time period, aggregate-individ-ualistic bias, and failure to approximate the experimental model jeopardize causal inferences. A final word on causal inference: Multivariant analysis in conjunction with relational and contextual analysis partially solves the causality problem, because comparative data are necessarily gathered. Multivariate analysis in conjunction with statistical sampling models, however, is a poor second to the survey design that builds on theoretical sampling and the deliberate, ongoing selection of comparison groups. When comparison groups are constructed *after the fact*, as in the pure form of multivariate analysis, the investigator is manipulating data to create groups that should have been there initially. Systematically sampling comparison groups would be preferable.

The ideal survey would involve repeated observations, employ multiple comparison groups, combine theoretical with statistical sampling, and employ some form of relational analysis. I have said that the survey can contribute to symbolic interactionism. Despite the fact that survey designs necessarily involve commitment to a form of variable analysis just criticized, the survey can be employed as a method of determining the stable and routinized patterns of interaction that exist in social groups. Such patterns are often easily elicited. There is reason to believe that they will be accurately reflected when the survey method is used. National public opinion polls raise another issue, for—as Blumer has argued (1948, pp. 542–44)—the pollster too frequently fails to link opinions to their group context. There is reason to believe that opinions on such issues as a president's popularity or the desirability of entering a war cannot be accurately reflected in a social survey. Such opinions, tied as they are to small social networks, are often not clearly formed, perhaps not even existent. The forcing of a response into a "yes," "no," or "no opinion" continuum distorts the uncertain reality that opinion occupies in the symbolic world of the respondent.

Answers about which attitudes and interactions are stabilized and which are in flux can come only from intensive field work and close observation. Going to the field with a precoded, rigidly structured interview schedule, but without prior knowledge about the issues at hand, is inappropriate. If early observations indicate there are clusters of routinized meanings and interactions, then the survey becomes an appropriate instrument to measure the nature of these forms.

Many survey analysts will never encounter these problems, particularly if they deal with demographic or ecological data. The information is relatively solidified and constant and is not open to multiple interpretations. However, investigators who choose to analyze such problems as face-work among strangers, or the labeling process among deviants and normals, or the process of self-other definition in encounters, or the emergent and shifting reality of social groups, will find that the survey is ill-equipped to handle their questions. Its very emphasis on structure and regularity makes it best suited for the study of processes and events characterized by structure and regularity. To conduct a survey on the self-concept among a general population, or the process of labeling among the mentally ill, when such issues are theoretically defined as "in flux," is to misapply the survey method.

Thus far I have treated the survey basically as a method of research and have not discussed it as a situation created by the investigator that is worthy of study. In Chapter 4 it was suggested that interviewing represents interaction among the unacquainted. Typically, the survey involves the study of persons whom the investigator has not met before the interview and is unlikely to see afterward. A profitable line of inquiry for the interactionist would be the study of behavior as it occurs in encounters between the interviewer and the respondent. I suggest that, rather than focusing on interviewer bias and respondent bias in the interview, this interaction be systematically analyzed for what it tells and reveals about encounters between strangers. Sociologists could then examine such processes as how embarrassment is controlled or courted in the interview, how selves are defined and negotiated, how involvement is maintained, how illegitimate side activities arise and detract from the interaction, how the encounter is opened and ended, and so on. The survey, like the experiment, is both a method of research and a situation created by the sociologist. Its peculiarities are sufficiently different from those of the experimental laboratory to make its examination worth while.

SUGGESTED READINGS

HIRSCHI, TRAVIS AND HANAN C. SELVIN, *Principles of Survey Analysis*. (New York: Free Press, 1973). A thorough and highly readable discussion of the principles, methods, and pitfalls of survey analysis. Should be read in conjunction with the same authors' earlier work (1967), *Delinquency Research: An Appraisal of Analytic Methods*.

LIEBERSON, STANLEY, *Making It Count: The Improvement of Social Research and Theory*. (Berkeley: University of California Press 1985). Valuable reading of current survey analysis methods by a skilled practitioner of the method. The "It" in the title presumably refers not only to research, but also to data and "its" analysis.

SUDMAN, SEYMOUR AND GRAHAM KALTON, "New Developments in the Sampling of Special Populations," pp. 401–24 in R.H. Turner and J.F. Short, Jr., (eds.), *Annual Review of Sociology*, vol. 12. (Palo Alto, Calif.: Annual Reviews, 1986). Useful review of new survey sampling and interviewing techniques, including the mail questionnaire and the telephone interview. These methods of data gathering have become increasingly popular, due in part to the fear that interviewers have of interviewing America's inner cities.

7

Participant Observation: Varieties and Strategies of the Field Method

The concept of participant observation . . . signifies the relation which the human observer of human beings cannot escape — having to participate in some fashion in the experience and action of those he observes. [Blumer, 1966b, p. vi]

Personal narrative is a conventional component of ethnographies. . . . These . . . narratives play the crucial role of anchoring that description in the intense and authority-giving personal experience of fieldwork. [Pratt, 1986, p. 27]

Participant observation is a commitment to adopt the perspective of those studied by sharing in their day-to-day experiences. Participant observers do *ethnography*, which is the description, classification, and interpretation of a particular group's way of life (see Agar, 1986; Van Maanen, 1988). Participant observers are ethnographers, and part of what they do involves writing personal narratives about how they studied what they studied (Pratt, 1986).

Recent work in sociology and anthropology has begun to raise questions about the traditional activities of the ethnographer–participant observer (Adler and Adler, 1987; Bruner, 1984; Clifford and Marcus, 1986; Douglas, 1985; Geertz, 1973; Golde, 1983; Silverman, 1985; Turner and Bruner, 1986; Van Maanen, 1988). These questions, which will be reviewed in this chapter, involve the following: (1) How does theory structure inquiry? (2) How do past conventions determine how ethnographic narratives are written? (3) How does one write the experiences of the subject who is studied? (4) Can ethnographies be objective? (5) How does gender affect fieldwork? (6) How are ethnographies to be read?

It has become increasingly clear that participant observers and ethnographers *write culture* (Clifford and Marcus, 1986). They do not simply record an objective reality that is "out there." They create, through their ethnographic practices, the worlds that they study and then write about. How this is done is the topic of this chapter.

Defining The Ethnographic-Participant Observation Approach

The participation of the observer may be known to those observed, so that it is clear they are being studied, or the investigator may conceal the observer identity and attempt to become a "normal" member of the community, cult, organization, group, tribe, or club being studied. The goal of this participation is to produce an understanding of the group or culture being studied. Such an understanding should permit the student of the culture to know "Whatever it is one has to know or believe in order to operate in a manner acceptable to its members and to do so in any role that they accept for any one of themselves" (Goodenough, 1964, p. 36). The ethnographer attempts to discover the practices and meanings that the members of the group take for granted; in so doing, the culture of the group is grasped. Culture, which "explains how people act in concert when they *do* share understandings" (Becker, 1986, p. 13), becomes a resource for building an interpretation of the group. Some cognitive anthropologists (including Goodenough, Basso, Frake, Bloor, see Silverman, 1985, pp. 97–106) and conversational analysts (including Sacks, Schegloff, Jefferson, Atkinson, see Silverman, 1985, pp. 118–37) have attempted to write the formal cognitive rules that group members use when they put culture into practice. Such strategies often fail to produce in-depth understandings of the group in question. Some argue, however, that it is neither desirable nor possible to attempt to understand another person's situation. Such critics seek to build formal, cognitive models of culture and action (see Geertz, 1973, 1983, for criticisms of this approach).

In this chapter we will assume that understandings can be reached. These understandings build from the observer's participation in the daily round of life of a group. Whether the participation is known or concealed, the intent is to record the ongoing experiences of those observed, through their symbolic world. Such a strategy implies a commitment, however conscious, to basic principles of symbolic interactionism and to the naturalistic method. To comprehend the worlds of interacting individuals, sociologists must adopt the perspective of those studied—thereby avoiding the *fallacy of objectivism*. Adopting the perspective of those studied means that the evolution and unfolding of social action through time and across situations must be followed as completely as possible. This forces investigators to analyze events that occurred before their presence in the field and to record all the relevant events that occur after their presence. Obviously, events that occurred in the past can only be reconstructed by people who witnessed their occurrence. There is, then, a curious blending of methodological techniques in ethnography and participant observation: People are interviewed, documents from the past are analyzed, census data is collected, informants are employed, and direct observation of ongoing events are undertaken. For present purposes, *participant observation* will be defined as a field strategy that simultaneously combines document analysis, interviewing of respondents and informants, direct participation and observation, and introspection. (See Bogdan and Taylor, 1975, pp. 4–6.)

In participant observation, interviews are typically open-ended, as opposed to close-ended; census data, when analyzed, are usually not a central portion of the research process, but are used only to describe the characteristics of the population under study; and observation of ongoing events is typically less concerned with recording the frequency and distribution of events than it is with linking interaction patterns with the symbols and meanings believed to underlie that behavior. It is the thesis of this chapter that participant observation may be most profitably treated as a method of qualitative analysis which requires submersion of the observer in the data and the use of analytic induction and theoretical sampling as the main strategies of analysis and discovery. As such, the method, when appropriately employed, entails a continuous movement between emerging conceptualizations of reality and empirical observations. Theory and method combine to allow the simultaneous generation and grounding of interpretations. Participant observation is one of the few methods currently available to the sociologist that is well suited to an analysis of complex forms of symbolic interaction. In contrast to the survey, which may be best suited to the analysis of stable forms of interaction, participant observation can better handle forms of interaction that are in change. As is the case with all methods, however, it must be considered in terms of its ability to answer only certain kinds of problems—it is not a method that should be adopted every time a sociologist goes into the field. Deutscher (1975, pp. vii–viii) has noted that the method "is no panacea. It will not cure the ills of the discipline," and "there are . . . kinds of problems for which such methods seem inappropriate."

Existential Ethnography

Elsewhere (Denzin, 1988b) I have argued that interpretive studies begin with a biographically meaningful event that has transformed a subject's life. This may be the death of a loved one, divorce, losing a job, or becoming an alcoholic. The event may radically restructure an individual's life. This decidedly existential thrust of interpretive ethnography draws the researcher's attention to those moments, social situations, groups, and social structures in which lives are dramatically altered. Focus is then given to uncovering how persons live these experiences in their daily lives. (See Denzin, 1987b, for an example of how this may be done in studying the recovering alcoholic.) I shall draw upon this version of ethnography later in this chapter and in Chapter 8.

ESSENTIAL FEATURES OF PARTICIPANT OBSERVATION AND ETHNOGRAPHY

Handling of Hypotheses and Initial Interpretations

Participant observation is deliberately unstructured in its research design so as to maximize the discovery and grounding of theoretical interpretations. The attempt is to continually revise and test emergent hypotheses as the research is conducted. While this point will be discussed in detail when I turn to analytic induction, the following excerpt from Geer (1964, p. 337) points to the manner in which the hypothesis is treated with this method:

> My use of hypotheses falls roughly into three sequential types. The first operation consisted of testing a crude yes-or-no proposition. By asking informants or thinking back over volunteered information in the data ("nearly all students today" or "no student"), I stated a working hypothesis in the comments and began the second operation in the sequence: looking for negative cases or setting out deliberately to accumulate positive ones. At the second stage, working with negatively expressed hypotheses gave me a specific goal. One instance that contradicts what I say is enough to force modification of the hypothesis. It is a process of elimination in which I try to build understanding of *what is* by pinning down *what is not.*
>
> The third stage of operating with hypotheses in the field involves two-step formulations and eventually rough models. Hypotheses take the form of predictions about future events which may take place under specific conditions. . . . Needless to say, particularly in the first days in the field, the worker is never at the same stage with all his data; he may be operating at the yes-or-no level in one area and advancing to the model stage with another at any given time.

The hypothesis, then, in its final stage of development, frequently is not of the strict "A causes B" type. Instead, propositional sets of an all-inclusive nature are developed so that the total arena of experience under anlaysis can be incorporated in an explanatory network. Geer also suggests that the evidence presented for any given proposition are of a variety of types (for example, interviews, self-recollection, or use of informants). Further, she points to the ongoing and developmental nature of participant observation.

Thick Description and Thick Interpretation

Thick description and thick interpretation are central to the development of the understandings that the ethnographer comes to form about the group that is being studied. Thick description (Denzin, 1988b, Chapter 5; Geertz, 1973, p. 20) has two basic characteristics. First, it attempts to rescue the meanings, actions, and feelings that are present in an interaction experience. The interactional behavior specimens discussed in Chapter 3 are intended to do this. Second, thick description is interpretive. It captures the meanings persons bring to their experiences. It also attempts to record how these interpretations unfold during the interaction. Thick description creates the conditions for thick interpretation, which attempts to take the reader to the essential features of the experience that has been thickly described. Thick interpretation interprets the interpretations that are present in the recorded experiences. It attempts to uncover the "conceptual structures that inform our subject's acts" (Geertz, 1973, p. 27). Rosaldo (1984) offers an example; he details, in thick descriptive fashion, the emotions he felt after his wife's death, and then interprets those emotions within a framework that allowed him to make sense out of a particular problem in his fieldwork (see the following discussion).

Thick and Thin Descriptions and Interpretations

If I say, "X answered the phone and talked to his wife," I give a thin description of X's actions. I could say, "As X was working on his book, and listening to country music on the radio, he rose to get a cup of coffee when the phone rang. It was his wife. They discussed the fight they had had earlier in the morning and agreed that they shouldn't be fighting. They agreed to meet for lunch and talk in detail about their fight." If I said this, I would be on the way to giving a thick description of X's experiences with the telephone call. If I interpreted X's actions as "He answered the phone because it rang," I would be offering a thin interpretation of his conduct. If I said, "He answered the phone because he knew his wife would be calling; he had called her earlier and had left a message, because he wanted to make up after the fight," I would be developing a thick interpretation of his actions. This would be a thick interpretation built upon a thick description. Many social scientists build thick interpretations based on thin descriptions. Some offer thin interpretations of thick descriptions, and others do thin interpretations of thin descriptions. Psychologist B.F. Skinner is famous for doing thin description. *The interpretive, existential ethnographer seeks both thick descriptions and thick interpretations.*

Understanding and Interpretation

Perhaps more than other methods, the ethnographic–participant observation approach stresses understanding the experiences of those studied. Understanding refers to grasping and perceiving the meaning of a phenomenon. It assumes that the person has gained a thorough familiarity with the process in question. The researcher who understands, comprehends the meanings of the words and the experiences reported by another. Understanding rests on *interpretation,* which is the clarification of the meanings embodied in the words and language used by another person. Interpretation often involves *translation,* or moving from one language to another.

Understandings may be emotional or cognitive. A primarily cognitive understanding stresses logic and reason. Emotional understandings are based on shared and unshared social experiences. They are expressed as sudden awarenesses or flashes of insight about the meaning of an experience for another. (See the discussion of Rosaldo's experience, which follows.) Existential ethnographers seek emotional understandings of their subject matter (see Denzin, 1984, Chapter 5).

Assumptions of the Method

Sharing in the subjects' world   A central assumption of participant observation is that the investigator shares as intimately as possible in the life and activities of those under study. This may involve, as in the case of the ethnologist, moving in with a tribe of Indians and living with them for an extended period of time; or it may consist of joining in the daily rounds of activity of medical students as they attend classes, diagnose patients' illnesses, conduct laboratory experiments, attend social functions at fraternities, and drink at local bars. In a case like the latter, the investigator may not actually "live in" with the subjects, but does partake in as many of their activities as possible.

Direct participation in the subjects' symbolic world   Direct participation on the part of the observer in the symbolic world of those under study is also involved. This often entails learning their language, their rules of etiquette, their eating habits, and their work patterns. Direct participation in the subjects' symbolic world is not easy; learning a new language takes time, and acquiring a knowledge of what nonverbal gestures mean is often difficult. Wax (1960, p. 170) describes her difficulty in learning the meaning of Japanese conversational patterns:

> When I began to make modest progress in the Japanese language, informants drilled me in simple phrases and were delighted when I remembered their instructions. While my exuberant and energetic personality prohibited any attempt to conform to the ideal standards of Japanese female behavior, my forceful remarks were not resented if they were conveyed with a veneer of self-deprecation. It was good manners to apologize for anything which conceivably merited an apology.

Learning and sharing the meanings inherent in another person's symbolic world poses problems for the participant observer, who may cease to think entirely as a sociologist (or anthropologist) and, instead, begin to adopt the perspective of those under study. This "going native" can inhibit the development of hypotheses, for the observer may be defending the values of those studied, rather than actually studying them. Geer, for example, in the early days of her observation on college students, approached the field with a highly cynical attitude regarding the childish nature of the undergraduate college experience. As she began to make field contacts, however, her attitudes shifted, and she soon found herself defending the very values she had earlier defined as immature. To guard against this shift in perspective, field workers keep day-to-day field notes on their own reactions and attempt to record shifts in the own perceptions. (See Johnson, 1975, pp. 117–201.)

On the other hand, recent observers of the method (Adler and Adler, 1987; Douglas, 1985; Rosaldo, 1984) have argued that ethnographers can turn the experiences of "going native" to their own interpretive advantage. By drawing on shared emotional experiences, which can only come after one has deeply entered the native's world, the observer can develop insights and understandings that would not otherwise be possible. Rosaldo (1984, pp. 183–84) notes that he came to understand the grief and rage of Ilongot headhunters only after his wife slipped and fell to her death on a field expedition in the Philippines in 1981. By probing the powerful emotional feelings he experienced after this event, he came to see Ilongot headhunting in a different light. For these men, the rage of bereavement impelled them to headhunt. He shared in their rage and grief in a way that he previously had not.

Creating an identity   A third assumption of participant observation is that there will be a continual attempt by field workers to carve out an identity for themselves in the ongoing interactions they are observing. Cultures do not provide within their social structures a role called *participant observer*, and unlike experimenters, who have convinced at least one culture of the veracity of their role, participant observers must convince those they are studying to accept them and allow them to question and observe. Carving out an identity can be difficult, and may evolve through several phases (see Janes, 1961, pp. 446–50); Olesen and Whittaker, 1967, pp. 273–81). Wax indicates that she initially approached her study of Japanese relocation camps with a high degree of insecurity about her role as observer. As she began to define her own role, she found that the Japanese began to define her as an observer and thereby validated the very role she was initially unsure of—but the role of observer did not exist until she began to act as one (see also Berreman, 1962).

The role eventually settled on frequently represents a mix between the broad intents of the investigator and the personality and background of the observer. Wax, for example, was partially able to play the role of a Japanese female, but altered this role to fit her own personality. The general principle can be summarized by the dictum that *observers should not try to present themselves as something they are not and should use to advantage all the personal characteristics they possess to enhance their observational activity.* Depending on the investigation, this may include drawing on such diverse past experiences as violations of the law, experiences as a mental patient, associations with drug users, being a regular use of alcoholic beverages, or being an alcoholic.

Types of Observer Identities

Four participant-observer roles or strategies have been analyzed: the *complete participant,* the *participant as observer,* the *observer as participant,* and the *complete observer* (see Gold, 1958, pp. 217–23).

Complete participant   In this identity, observers are wholly concealed, their scientific intents are not made known, and they attempt to become full-fledged members of the group under investigation. A classic example is the study by Festinger, Riecken, and Schachter (1956) of a small group of persons who predicted the destruction of the world. The nature of the group led the authors to believe that if they presented themselves as sociologists, entry would be denied, so they posed as persons genuinely interested in the unusual prediction of the group and soon were able to penetrate its boundaries and become full-fledged members. This soon raised a problem because one of the observers had fabricated a biography involving previous occult and supernatural activities in Mexico. The members of the group had begun to believe their predictions about the destruction of the earth, and the joining of a person with similar experiences reinforced this belief. The problem of altering the patterns of behavior of a group through disguised entry soon became apparent, and the authors were never sufficiently able to counteract this influence. The problem was magnified when one of the observers was asked to lead a group meeting—an action for which he was ill-equipped and which he handled rather awkwardly.

A second problem confronting the observers was recording their observations. Obviously they could not make notes when in the group's presence, so they resorted to hidden tape recorders, writing up notes in restrooms and rushing back to their hotel late at night to tape their day's observations. As a result, doubt arose concerning the validity of certain of their field notes because of memory distortion, confusion of issues and speakers, and general field fatigue. Complete participation raises another problem—the issue of ethics in field research (this is given more complete treatment in Chapter 12).

As complete participants, sociologists find themselves confronted with contradictory role or interactional demands—playing the disguised role and playing the role of sociologist. *Role pretense,* as Gold terms it, is the basic theme of their activities; they know they are pretending. In effect, complete participants find themselves simultaneously responding to demands of the hidden self, the pretended self, and the self as observer (Gold, 1958, p. 219). If the disguise is successfully carried off, observers will achieve a sense of heightened self-awareness—an introspective attitude toward their own activities—because they must continually indicate to themselves that their experiences are due to the pretended self, not to the real self.

Participant as observer   The participant as observer is the second type of identity that may be assumed. Unlike the complete participant, the participant as observer makes her presence as an investigator known and attempts to form a series of relationships with the subjects such that they serve as both respondents and informants. The role is frequently employed in community studies, where an observer develops relationships with informants through time. While the observer is relieved of the tension that arises from role pretense, problems of establishing relationships, not going native, finding informants, and maintaining the observer–observed relationship must still be contended with. During early stages of fieldwork the investigator may encounter hostility. This may arise simply from misunderstandings concerning the observer's presence, or it may represent a resistance to divulging information to a complete stranger.

Investigations employing this strategy indicate that several phases are passed through as the investigator conducts observations (see, for example, Olesen and Whittaker, 1967, pp. 273–81). In the first stage, the investigator simply presents herself as a sociologist or anthropologist who is interested in making observations. The researcher is treated as a stranger and newcomer, and initial encounters are likely to be superficial. Subjects try to place the researcher in a recognizable social identity, and the researcher attempts to present herself in a role that is acceptable to the subjects. Few subjects are able to apprehend fully the meaning of the identity; Olesen and Whittaker have noted, for example, that on several occasions during the early phases of their study of nursing students, they were categorized as students, registered nurses, or faculty members — only infrequently were they recognized as sociological observers (1967, pp. 273–81). Because so few subjects are familiar with the observer identity, investigators find in this phase a greater reliance on roles that lie outside the boundaries of scientist or sociologist. For example, Olesen and Whittaker drew on their more global identities as previous students, as females, as music enthusiasts, and so on.

Once the parameters of the observer–observed relationship have been established, the investigator moves into a phase where she is accorded the status of provisional member. Respondents begin to recognize the investigator as a sociologist and may ask why they were selected for study. In this stage, as Wax has noted, there is a deliberate attempt on the part of the observer to teach the respondents how to act toward her. This includes convincing them of the confidentiality of their conversations, as well as teaching them to accept the presence of an observer during their daily rounds of activity. As this process unfolds, respondents are teaching the observer how to behave toward them. Backstage regions of behavior are pointed out, and acceptable topics for conversation are conveyed. In Olesen and Whittaker's (1967, p. 275) nursing study, the following observation was recorded:

> As I opened the door I caught sight of Mary Jones at the bedside of her patient, facing the direction in which I was looking. Mary caught sight of me and remarked so that I could hear, "We're having our bath now." I said that I was sorry to have disturbed them and would be back a while later.

In the third stage, the observer is accepted as a "categorical member" of the community. By this time rapport has been established, areas of observation have been agreed upon, and the identities of observer and observed are unambiguously defined. Certain modifications in these identities occur, particularly as the observer attempts to penetrate regions of observation initially defined as closed. Respondents and informants now bring and give information to the observer, who must take care that they do not define the boundaries of observation too narrowly.

The investigator is eventually confronted with the problem of removing himself or herself from the field, a process of identity *disengagement*. Field relationships are terminated, and though friendships established may linger, continuous interactions with those observed may cease. Janes (1961, pp. 446–50) has called this the phase of "imminent migrant," during which respondents and informants take on a sense of urgency concerning how they are going to be described by the investigator in the written reports, and may try to exert pressure regarding the total investigation.

Cultural Shock

Anthropologists who go into the field often speak of "cultural shock" (Golde, 1986, p. 11). Du Bois first used the term in 1951, crediting it to Benedict. It refers to a syndrome "precipitated by the anxiety that results from losing all your familiar cues, which includes frustration, repressed or expressed aggression against the source of discomfort, an irrational fervor for the familiar and the comforting, and disproportionate anger at trivial interferences" (Golde, 1986, p. 11). The four phases of this process parallel, in part, the phases through which observers pass during field work. These phases are as follows: (1) The honeymoon phase, during which everything goes well; (2) the crisis stage, during which the researcher may reject the entire field experience; (3) the recovery stage; and (4) adjustment. Cultural shock occurs in all ethnographic research, but, it is greatest when the observer travels to a foreign culture or country. Its effects appear to vary by the gender of the field worker.

Observer as participant   The observer as participant is the third type of identity. Investigations in which the researcher takes this strategy typically include only one visit — or interview — with the respondent. The nature of the contact is brief and highly formalized through the use of questionnaires, and there is no attempt to establish any sense of an enduring relationship with the respondent. This is the epitome of the encounter between strangers. It represents the fundamental thesis underlying the social survey and was treated in Chapter 6.

Complete observer   The complete observer is the fourth identity. It removes the field worker entirely from interaction and is best seen in experiments where observations are recorded mechanically or conducted through one-way mirrors in the laboratory. This identity is treated extensively in Chapter 5.

This brief discussion of observers as participants and complete observers is not intended to suggest that the participant as observer and the complete participant do not also employ these strategies. Generally speaking, however, the type of experiences and problems I analyze in this chapter are confined to the identities of complete participant and participant as observer. I treat most extensively the latter because what passes as participant observation and ethnography in contemporary sociology is largely of this variety, and the problems of this field strategy may also be generalized to the less frequently used method of complete participation.

SOLUTION TO THE PROBLEM OF CAUSAL INFERENCE: ANALYTIC INDUCTION

At the heart of a causal proposition lies the demonstration of time order and covariance and the exclusion of other causal factors. In the experiment this problem is explicitly treated by constructing two comparison groups — one exposed to the assumed causal variable and the other not exposed. The survey, I have noted, approximates the experimental model through multivariate analysis. In participant observation, the experimental model is approximated through the use of analytic induction, which is a strategy of analysis that directs the investigator to formulate generalizations that apply to all instances of the problem. This differentiates analytic induction from multivariate analysis, where concern is directed to generalizations that apply not to all instances of the phenomenon at hand, but rather to most or some of them.

Description of Analytic Induction

Strategically, analytic induction represents an approximation of the experimental model to the extent that explicit comparisons are made with groups not exposed to the causal factors under analysis. Conceptually, this represents the classic "before-after" experimental design, and when employed in participant observation it calls for the investigator to search for empirical instances that negate the causal hypothesis. This general strategy, which combines the method of agreement and the method of difference previously discussed in the context of the experiment, is described by Lindesmith (1952, p. 492) as follows:

> The principle which governs the selection of cases to test a theory is that the chances of discovering a decisive negative case should be maximized. The investigator who has a working hypothesis concerning his data becomes aware of certain areas of critical importance. If his theory is false or inadequate, he knows that its weaknesses will be more clearly and quickly exposed if he proceeds to the investigation of those critical areas. This involves going out of one's way to look for negating evidence.

Described abstractly, analytic induction involves the following steps (see Robinson, 1951, p. 813):

1. A rough definition of the phenomenon to be explained is formulated.
2. A hypothetical explanation of that phenomenon is formulated.
3. One case is studied in light of the hypothesis, with the object of determining whether or not the hypothesis fits the facts in that case.
4. If the hypothesis does not fit the facts, either the hypothesis is reformulated or the phenomenon to be explained is redefined so that the case is excluded.
5. Practical certainty can be attained after a small number of cases have been examined, but the discovery of negative cases disproves the explanation and requires a reformulation.
6. This procedure of examining cases, redefining the phenomenon, and reformulating the hypotheses is continued until a a universal relationship is established, each negative case calling for a redefinition or a reformulation.

Illustration: Lindesmith's Research

Lindesmith's research on opiate addiction (1947, 1968) provides an illustration of this method. The focus of his investigation was the development of a sociological theory of opiate addiction. He began with the tentatively formulated hypothesis that individuals who did not know what drug they were receiving would not become addicted. Conversely, it was predicted that individuals would become addicted when they knew what they were taking, and had taken it long enough to experience distress (withdrawal symptoms) when they stopped. This hypothesis was destroyed when one of the first addicts interviewed, a doctor, stated that he had once received morphine for several weeks, was fully aware of the fact, but had not become addicted at that time. This negative case forced Lindesmith (1947, p. 8) to reformulate his initial hypothesis:

> Persons become addicts when they recognize or perceive the significance of withdrawal distress which they are experiencing, and that if they do not recognize withdrawal distress they do not become addicts regardless of any other consideration.

This formulation proved to be much more powerful, but again negating evidence forced its revision. In this case persons were observed who had withdrawal experiences and understood withdrawal distress, but not in the most severe form; these persons did not use the drug to alleviate the distress and never became addicts. Lindesmith's (1947, p. 8) final causal hypothesis involved a shift on his part from "the recognition of withdrawal distress, to the use of the drug after this insight had occurred for the purpose of alleviating the distress."

The final hypothesis had the advantage of attributing the cause of addiction to no single event, but rather to a complex chain of events. This final hypothesis, which in reality represented a chain of propositions, involved the following (1947, p. 165):

1. Addiction rests fundamentally upon the effects that follow when the drug is removed, rather on the positive effects that its presence in the body produces.
2. Addiction occurs only when opiates are used to alleviate withdrawal distress, after this distress has been properly understood or interpreted—that is, after it has been represented to the individual in terms of linguistic symbols and cultural patterns that have grown up around the opiate habit.
3. If the individual fails to conceive of his distress as withdrawal distress brought about by the absence of opiates, he cannot become addicted, but if he does, addiction is quickly and permanently established through further use of the drug.

All the evidence unequivocally supported this theory, and Lindesmith (1947, p. 165) concluded:

> This theory furnished a simple but effective explanation, not only of the manner in which addiction becomes established, but also of the essential features of addiction behavior, those features which are found in addiction in all parts of the world, and which are common to all cases.

Before reaching the conclusion that his theory explained all cases of opiate addiction. Lindesmith explicitly searched for negative cases that would force revision or rejection of the theory. He describes this process as follows (1947, p.p. 9–10):

Each succeeding tentative formulation was not constructed *de novo*, but was based upon that which had preceded it. The eventual hypothesis altered the preceding formulations sufficiently to include the cases which earlier had appeared as exceptions to the theory postulated.

It may be asked whether the search for negative cases was properly conducted and if the observer has not neglected evidence of a contradictory character. To this, of course, there is no final answer. It is probable that somewhere in the course of any study unconscious distortion takes place. Concerning the central hypothesis and the direct lines of evidence, however, certain procedures were followed which may be said to exclude bias. For example, when the theory had been stated in an approximation of its final form it occurred to the writer that it could be tested in cases where an individual had had two separate experiences with morphine or opiates, each of which was sufficiently prolonged to produce withdrawal distress but with addiction following only the second episode. It was concluded that if the theory was valid, the person would report that he had failed to realize the nature of withdrawal in that experience from which he had escaped without becoming addicted. Thereupon a thorough search was made for cases in which an individual had undergone such an experience with the drug prior to becoming an addict. All cases of this kind which could be found, or of which any record could be located, were taken into account. Any of these cases might have contradicted the final hypothesis, but none did so. The inference or prediction which had been drawn on the basis of the theory was fully borne out. This procedure was followed throughout the study wherever possible.

Intent Of Analytic Induction

As Lindesmith's study reveals, a basic assumption underlying analytic induction is the search for propositions that apply to all cases of the problem under analysis. In other words, it is assumed that genuinely scientific causal propositions must be stated as universals. This belief forces the sociologist to formulate and state a theory in such a way as to indicate crucial tests of the theory and to permit the explicit search for negative cases. As Lindesmith notes (1947, p. 37), it is assumed

> that the exceptional instance is the growing point of science and that cumulative growth and progressive development of theory is obtained by formulating generalizations in such a way that negative cases force us to either reject the generalization or . . . revise it.

This strategy not only forces the careful consideration of all available evidence, both quantitative and qualitative, but also makes necessary the intensive analysis of individual cases and the comparisons of certain crucial cases. Thus, Lindesmith did not confine his study only to analysis of individual addicts; he also examined statistical reports on opiate addiction. In addiction, he explicitly studied nonaddicts who had regularly received drugs in hospitals in order to isolate the causal conditions present in addiction and absent among nonaddicted hospital patients. Of course, this represents the use of the method of difference that forms the logic for the construction of control groups in the experimental design.

Another central feature of analytic induction is its reliance on theoretical rather than strict statistical sampling models. While Lindesmith made use of previous statistical studies of opiate addicts, his main strategy was to sample theoretically in a continual effort to find crucial cases that would invalidate his theory. In one sense, the use of theoretical saturation as a criterion for concluding observations on a concept has its analogue in the dictum of analytic induction that a theory is complete insofar as negative cases which invalidate it are not identified.

The use of the concept in participant observation and analytic induction represents something of a departure from experimental and survey modes of research. Instead of an emphasis on strict variable analysis, concepts are used in a sensitizing fashion, as in Lindesmith's study, where opiate addiction was defined in terms of each crucial case. Such a strategy permits the investigator to work back and forth between theory and observations, altering when necessary both the theory and the definitions of central concepts.

Advantages of Analytic Induction

Analytic induction has at least six advantages.

First, it allows researchers to disprove theories while testing one theory against another. (Lindesmith was able to develop and test his theory of opiate addiction by testing it against psychological and physiological theories.)

Second, analytic induction provides a method by which old theories can be revised and incorporated into new theories as negative evidence is taken into account. (Lindesmith's initial theory was progressively refined in the light of each new piece of evidence.)

Third, this method, with its extreme emphasis on the importance of the negative case, forces a close articulation between fact, observation, concept, proposition, and theory.

Fourth, analytic induction provides one direct means by which theoretical and statistical sampling models can be brought together; that is, investigators will find themselves extending their propositions to representative cases not yet examined. One method of selecting cases will be the statistical sampling assumptions of randomization and representativeness. Theory will be of little use until it can be shown that the propositions apply to all cases of the phenomenon under analysis, and statistical sampling, or *enumerative induction,* provides one method of doing this.

Fifth, analytic induction allows the sociologist to move from substantive, or middle-range, theories to formal theories. Lindesmith, for example, hypothesized that the propositions in his theory would also apply to other forms of deviance such as alcoholism (see Denzin, 1987a, pp. 44–51). While this is not completely representative of a formal theory, it does indicate an attempt to work with a small number of generic concepts in a variety of different empirical settings to assess the range of utility of those concepts and the underlying theory.

Sixth, analytic induction leads to developmental or processual theories, and these are superior to static formulations which assume that variables operate in either an intervening or an antecedent fashion on the processes under study. If the assumption that social events occur in a temporal-longitudinal sequence is correct, then it is incumbent on the sociologist to develop theories that take this element into account. Sociologists need theories and models of proof and inference that interpret social process. (See Chapter 3.)

Deficiencies of Analytic Induction

First, as Turner has suggested (1953, pp. 604–11), analytic induction is too frequently employed in a definitional rather than a causal fashion. For example, predictions concerning who would take a drug and who would not, or under what conditions withdrawal symptoms would be severe or not severe, are not contained in Lindesmith's theory. Instead, it is a predictive system that explains the behavior of persons who have taken opiates.

Second, the emphasis on qualitative propositions of a universal nature creates problems when the processes studied are continuous variables that exhibit themselves in degree only. Lindesmith found that withdrawal symptoms had to be of a sufficient degree to cause the opiate user to become an addict. The precise amount of severity was never specified; hence, it becomes difficult to test this critical assumption in the theory. When the theorist identifies processes that do not present themselves in degree, this difficulty is avoided, but continuous variables occur frequently. The only reasonable solution to the problem, of course, is to measure these events quantitatively along a continuum of degree, but this solution has seldom been employed. In effect, then, if the theorist does not observe processes that have universal occurrence, they must be excluded from consideration. Such events, the province of enumerative or statistical induction, must be combined with the data of analytic induction. To fail to make this link is to forego the analysis of central pieces of information that would lead to greater specificity of the final theory.

A *third* disadvantage of analytic induction is an economical-temporal consideration. While relatively few cases will be analyzed, the time spent in the analysis typically will be much greater than that required in the ordinary experiment or survey. Lindesmith, for instance, intensively studied no more than 70 addicts, but spent several years in the collection, analysis, and presentation of his evidence. As sophisticated participant observers employ this method, they will use multivariate analysis to test alternative propositions and to identify the causal sequence of variables. The comparative method is central to the strategy because comparisons are made in situations where the causal propositions under development should not be present. In these senses, it can be said that *analytic induction represents an attempted synthesis of all the methods of inference treated thus far.*

PROBLEMS OF VALIDITY AND INTERPRETATION

Just as the experiment and the survey are subject to the problems of internal and external validity, so too is participant observation. Can the observations of the participant observer be generalized to other populations (external validity)? Do the observations represent real differences, or are they artifacts of the observational process (internal validity)?

External Validity and the Participant Observer

Ideally, the use of analytic induction frees the participant observer from the question of external validity. In practice, this issue has been one of the most frequent criticisms of the method. The criticism has taken the form that analysis of one case, or a series of cases, is not sufficient for scientific generalization because of the bias inherent in the cases chosen. The argument typically proceeds to state that at the essence of the scientific generalization lies a statistically representative sample of a large number of units from the population to which inferences are to be made.

Webb and associates (1966) have shown that the issue of generalizability to other populations involves three dimensions consisting of population restrictions arising from any of the following: (1) unique characteristics of respondents, (2) instabilities in the population over time, and (3) instabilities in the population arising from spatial or geographical differences.

It is incumbent on the participant observer to demonstrate that the cases studied are representative of the class of units to which generalizations are made. The sensitive participant observer is mindful of this demand, as the following statement from Burgess (1966, pp. 185–86) demonstrates:

> This one autobiography of a delinquent career is a concrete and dramatic exemplification of what a case-study may reveal about the causes and treatment of delinquency that can never be arrived at by more formal techniques like statistics, which must depend very largely upon external data.
>
> The case of Stanley appears also to be typical in a more real sense than can be verified by an statistical calculation. It is typical (i.e., belonging to the type) in the same way that every case is representative of its kind or species. This case is a member of the *criminal* species, and so of necessity must bear the impress of the characteristics and experiences of the criminal. It may not be the best specimen, perhaps only a good specimen or even a poor specimen. There can be no doubt that any case, good, bad, or indifferent, is a specimen of the species to which it belong. . . . Hence, the study of the experiences of one person at the same time reveals the life-activities of his group.

While Burgess's statement was formulated to defend the life-history method, it can be generalized to participant observation, which also involves intensive analysis of one case (an organization, a primitive tribe, a social club)—a position that, when coupled with the strategy of searching for negative cases, provides data bearing on the three types of instabilities in populations.

The participant observer must know intimately the social and personal characteristics of the subjects, and be sensitive to any biasing features they possess. Investigations also typically reveal characteristics of the cases studied that are not universally shared. For example, some opiate addicts may have college educations, while others may not have completed high school. The sample is not homogeneous, and the resulting theory must be reformulated to handle heterogeneity. It remains for the participant observer and the user of analytic induction to demonstrate that the problem of external validity has been solved.

Internal Validity and the Participant Observer

Internal validity sensitizes the observer to the biasing and distorting effects of the following seven intrinsic factors: (1) *historical factors,* (2) *subject maturation,* (3) *subject bias,* (4) *subject mortality,* (5) *reactive effects of the observer,* (6) *changes in the observer,* and (7) *peculiar aspects of the situations* in which the observations were conducted. Each of these factors is present in any participant-observation investigation. The earlier definition of participant observation stressed that it combines analysis of documents, interviewing of respondents and informants, direct participation, observation, and self-introspection. Each of these methods may be viewed as a source of data that reflect on the seven dimensions of internal validity.

Historical factors   History, especially in ethnographies, refers to several interrelated factors: (1) events that occurred before observations were made; (2) events that intervene between the first and last observation; (3) the larger historical social structure that surrounds the events in question; (4) the individual histories and biographies of the persons studied (see discussion of subject maturation which follows); (5) the researcher's personal history with the ethnography (see discussion of observer changes); and (6) the inner sense of history and process that adheres to the events studied.

In my ethnographic study of a community of recovering alcoholics in a large city in the northeastern United States, I attempted to address these dimensions of history.

Prior events: Before my study began, an Al-Anon social club was created for alcoholics and their families. This club was started by older members of the AA community. Its board of directors determined who could become a member, what membership rights were, and whose membership could be terminated. The club became a site of power and control in the local AA community. Persons who became sober after the club was established marked the beginning of their sobriety with their membership in the club. Hence, this event, which occurred before my study started, shaped events that I subsequently observed.

Intervening events: Three years after the club was established, its board of directors decided to move the club's location from its address in the center of the city to the far edge of the community. Its membership suddenly dropped, as did participation in meetings. People could no longer drive to the club for noon AA meetings. In reaction to this, a new meeting site was started by a group of dissident members. This site was near where the old club had been. This new group was then perceived as a challenge to the club, and conflicts developed within the AA community over where members went to meetings and to social gatherings. This intervening event (the moving of the club) created interactions that had to be studied.

The larger historical scene: The 1970, and then 1976, Comprehensive Alcohol Abuse and Alcoholism Prevention and Rehabilitation Act of the United States Congress mandated state and federal support of local, community treatment programs for alcoholism. When I started my study in 1981, there was one treatment center for alcoholism in the community. In 1987 there were three, and a fourth was being considered. These new treatment centers have brought new persons into the local AA community. The larger historical scene has intervened into the local community and created possibilities of experience and interaction that were not present when I started my study.

Inner history: The AA community that I studied in 1987 is not the same community I studied in 1981. A sense of shared, inner history exists within this community. It reflects events that occurred before my study started, events that have intervened since, and the larger historical context that now defines alcoholism.

The ethnographer must be alert to these historical factors and their effects on the events being studied. The researcher should make extensive use of interviews and existing documents to uncover the operation of these factors and processes.

Subject maturation: respondents and informants

This dimension is particularly important in participant observation, because the investigator will be establishing relationships that will lead to changes in the subjects themselves.

Consider the following statement from Whyte's *Street Corner Society* (1955, p. 301) concerning changes in his key informant, Doc:

> Doc found this experience of working with me interesting, and yet the relationship had its drawbacks. He once commented: "You've slowed me up plenty since you've been down here. Now, when I do something, I have to think what Bill Whyte would want to know about it and how I can explain it. Before, I used to do things by instinct."

Typically, subjects studied by the participant observer will be one of two varieties—either *respondents* or *informants*. Depending on which category the subject falls into, the issue of maturation will be different. By *informants* I refer to those persons who, ideally, (1) trust the investigator; (2) freely give information about their problems and fears and frankly attempt to explain their own motivations; (3) demonstrate that they will not jeopardize the study; (4) accept information given them by the investigator; and (5) provide information and aid that could jeopardize their own careers (Dalton, 1964, pp. 65–66; Naroll, 1968, pp. 265–67). These ideal characteristics distinguish the informant from the respondent, who functions primarily as the person filling out or giving answers to a questionnaire in a social survey. *Respondents* typically do not bring special information to the investigator; do not demonstrate special trust or give privileges of a special order; and answer only questions they are asked and no more. In short, the respondent performs as a stranger, while the informant performs and relates as an intimate, a confidant, and a friend (Dalton, 1964, pp. 65–66).

The primary functions of the informant are to act as *de facto* observer for the investigator; provide a unique inside perspective on events that the investigator is still "outside" of; serve as a sounding board for insights, propositions, and hypotheses developed by the investigator; open otherwise closed doors and avenues to situations and persons; and act as a respondent. Informants serve multiple purposes for the investigator, acting simultaneously as expert witnesses and as transmitters of information, and finally as informal sociologists in the field. In these various capacities the informant must be skilled at collecting, retaining, and transmitting information (Back, 1960, pp. 179–87). This implies that informants must be motivated to cooperate with the investigator. Furthermore, they will be knowledgeable in that they are exposed to the situations and topics central to the study. Whyte (1955, p. 301) describes his key informant as follows:

> My relationship with Doc changed rapidly. . . . At first he was simply a key informant— and also my sponsor. As we spent more time together, I ceased to treat him as a passive informant. I discussed with him quite frankly what I was trying to do, what problems were puzzling me, and so on. Much of our time was spent in this discussion of ideas and observations, so that Doc became, in a very real sense, a collaborator in the research.

The motivations underlying an informant's cooperation often range from curiosity to a belief that extrinsic rewards are forthcoming, to a commitment to science as an enterprise, or to the sheer fact that conversing with an investigator provides a release of pent-up aggression and hostility. Informants at any point in an investigation may be outsiders, frustrated rebels, "marginal" people, old hands, subordinates (such as secretaries), or even leaders of bureaucracies. The investigator must be sensitive to dual components of the informants (for example, their social position in the setting and their motivations for cooperating), because during the course of study motives will change, positions will alter, and the quality and nature of information given will be changing. (See Berreman, 1962.) Baseline interviews with respondents provide a standard for measuring the amount of change in them; day-to-day observations and their record in field notes measure changes in informants.

Subject bias   This is a major factor to be considered by the participant observer, particularly one who is developing propositions that apply to all persons under analysis. I have previously noted that nonhomogenous characteristics of subjects will often be uncovered. Baseline interviews and the day-to-day field notes provide the main measure for this bias. Standard biographical questions concerning educational background, occupational history, religious preference, and so on can be asked to attain a measure of the degree of subject bias present in the sample. Field observations supplement the interview, for here the observer will record interactional bias that emerges in the subjects.

Subject mortality   This factor is easily measured; the observer details those people who die, retire, move away, or in any other manner leave the research setting. Field notes supply data concerning the nature and motivation behind the departure, while interviewing and documents provide more standard means of measuring turnover rates, death statistics, and so on.

Reactive effects of the observer   Reactive effects of observation are the most perplexing feature of participant observation, since in any setting an observer is often a "foreign object." The creation of the identity of participant observer inevitably introduces some degree of reactivity into the field setting. The discussion of Festinger, Riecken, and Schachter's study of a small religious cult pointed this out: The presence of observers who had fabricated a social identity solidified the belief of the group that their prophecy was correct.

It is axiomatic that observers must record what they perceive to be their own reactive effects. The reactive effect will be measured by daily field notes, perhaps by interviews in which the problem is pointedly inquired about, and also in daily observations.

Changes in the observer   Changes in observers were noted earlier when it was suggested that many participant observers "go native" if they are in the field a long period. It is central to the method of participant observation that changes will occur in the observer; the important point, of course, is to record these changes. Field notes, introspection, and conversations with informants and colleagues are the major means of measuring this dimension. The observer who fails to record such changes risks losing the very objectivity gained by sharing in the events of those under study. The participant observer may just as easily commit the *fallacy of objectivism* as the survey analyst, for to be insensitive to shifts in one's own attitudes opens the way for placing naive interpretations on the complex set of events under analysis.

Peculiar aspects of situations   The last category of internal validity relevant to the participant observer is the situations in which observations are gathered. That all of human interaction is situated in social settings is fundamental to the analysis of observational data. The dynamics of these settings, the rules of etiquette that apply to them, the categories of participants who interact in them, and the varieties of action that occur within them must be recorded and analyzed. All the methods of participant observation should be brought to bear on this problem: formal documents to detail the nature of these settings and possibly even the persons who can and cannot enter them; behavioral observations to record their use and disuse; interviews to elicit the standard meanings persons hold toward them.

Becker and Geer (1960, pp. 267–89) have suggested that an important dimension of the behavior setting as a unit of analysis is the nature and number of participants present. They suggest that observations be recorded in terms of whether the investigator was alone with the subject or whether there was a group of respondents, since verbalized attitudes of respondents will be shaped by group influence. If subjects are alone, they may say things that run counter to group opinion; but in the presence of the group they may express group consensus.

STEPS IN PARTICIPANT OBSERVATION

The basic forms of participant observation were shown to share certain features: (1) the attempt on the part of the observer to carve out an identity, learn the culture of the group, and gain and maintain membership in the setting under study; (2) the use of multiple methodologies such as documents, census data, open- and closed-ended interviews, statistical and theoretical sampling, and behavioral observations; and (3) the development of complex causal propositions. The problems of role pretense, role disengagement, gaining entree, public recording of data, and "going native" are more difficult to control in the disguised-participant role than in the participant-as-observer role. but both methods — in the domain of data analysis — approximate the experimental model through the use of analytic induction. Neither method is free from errors of validity; the detailed treatment of internal and external validity was meant to establish the relevance of these dimensions for the observational method generally.

The following steps in participant observation may be noted. While these steps may not occur exactly in the order indicated, they are inherent in any investigation employing the observational, ethnographic method.

Step 1: Before actual field contacts and observations begin, a general definition of the problem is formulated. A theoretical perspective is adopted, the relevant research literature is reviewed, and an initial statement of research and theoretical objectives is written.

Step 2: Next, a field setting is selected, largely determined by the formulation of the problem as stated in step 1. The design is flexible, so that multiple settings can be considered for later observations (perhaps as dictated by analytic induction and theoretical sampling).

Step 3: Upon selection of the research setting, initial field contacts are made. Entree is established, the purpose of the study may be made public to certain persons, and initial observations are started.

Step 4: In this phase, the initial implementations of step 1 occur. Working definitions of key concepts are developed, and multiple research methods are employed. Statistical data on the setting and participants are gathered, documents are analyzed, and the historical context of the setting is documented.

Step 5: By this phase, field research is progressing. Informants have been selected, approached, and instructed, and interviews are solicited. Early theoretical formulations are now tested, reformulated, and tested again. Negative cases are sought as the general method of analytic induction is followed.

Step 6: General categories for data anlaysis are developed as hypotheses are formulated. Indicators of key concepts are now being developed and refined as a scheme for coding and analysis takes shape.

Step 7: Complex sets of propositions are developed and validated with multiple methods and varieties of data. Comparison groups are selected to further specify the causal propositions as a sequential, explanatory network is developed.

Step 8: This is the conclusion of the study, although additional observations may be made as necessary. Role disengagement occurs as the field workers begin to withdraw from continuous day-to-day observations. The actual writing of the research report now begins, and all earlier notes and observations are incorporated into a final picture of the events and processes studied. This phase is kept deliberately open-ended, since the observers may be drawn back for supplemental data.

WRITING AND READING ETHNOGRAPHY

At the outset of this chapter, I indicated that a number of questions have recently been raised about traditional ethnography. These include (1) how theory structures inquiry; (2) how conventions determine the narrative, written form of the ethnography; (3) how the experiences of the subject are written; (4) whether objectivity is possible; (5) how gender shapes the field experience; and (6) how we are to read ethnographies once they have been written. It is necessary to speak to each of these questions.

Theory   Two basic approaches structure the use of theory in ethnography. The first sees theory in terms of guiding hypotheses, propositions, and a priori assumptions dictating or guiding what the participant observer looks for in the field experience. Willis (1981), for example, used an English Marxist tradition in his analysis of how working-class youth learn to become laborers in the British school system. He states, "The role of ethnography is to show the cultural viewpoint of the oppressed, their 'hidden' knowledges and resistances" (Willis, 1981, p. 203). Here, Marxist theory guides inquiry. In a similar fashion, Becker, Geer, Hughes, and Strauss (1961, p. 19) based their book *Boys in White* on "the concept of symbolic interaction. ... This theory assumes that human behavior is to be understood as a process in which the person shapes and controls his conduct by taking into account ... the expectations of others with whom he interacts." The authors (p. 20) qualify this use of theory: "We are tempted to make our decisions seem more purposeful and conscious than in fact they were. ... The areas we found ourselves concentrating on were consistent with our theoretical formulations but did not flow logically ... from them."

I term this first approach to theory the *a priori stance*. Theory leads to inquiry. The second approach commits the researcher to writing the theory of those studied. It assumes that persons in the social world already have a theory that guides and directs their behavior. The ethnographer's task is to listen to that theory and to write it. Here the "prose of the world" (Merleau-Ponty, 1973) speaks through the ethnographer's text. This is the approach I took in *The Recovering Alcoholic* (Denzin, 1987b); I listened to the recovery stories of alcoholics and reported those stories in their words. I term this the "narrative" approach to theory. There is no attempt to fit the theory that operates in the social world into an abstract, a priori, second-order theoretical scheme.

Of course, all ethnography is guided by theory, or by a set of preconceptions. Even the view that no theory should be pursued is a theoretical position. What is at issue is who is in control and who has the power to write the interpretation the researcher or the person studied? My position says the person studied has this power. As a social scientist, all I can do is write, or make more visible that theory which is already at work in the social world.

Writing ethnography   At least four narrative conventions structure the way in which participant observers and ethnographers write ethnography (see Van Maanen, 1988). The *confessional tale* speaks to the trials and tribulations of the researcher in the field. It details the traumas, depressions, betrayals, illnesses, and successes of the field worker. It grounds the authenticity of the ethnography in the personal, emotional experiences of the researcher (see Douglas, 1985; Johnson, 1975). The *realist tale* or tradition attempts to depict in vivid, lived detail, the actual experiences of those studied. Realist ethnography may attempt a "wholistic" picture of the culture studied, or it may focus in strategic locales for intensive analysis (Marcus, 1986, pp. 171–73). In either case the goal is to reveal the inner workings of the system under study. In my AA study, I focused on the strategic sites of the treatment center and the AA meetings. I then told the alcoholic's story, based on my observations in these strategic locales.

The *impressionist tale* is the third narrative approach to ethnography. Here the writer conveys images and impressions of the setting and the persons studied, painting a picture of life in their social world. The writer may attempt to give an impressionistic sense of the daily round in a mental hospital, describe a cockfight in Bali, or attempt, as Margaret Mead (1923) did in Samoa, to portray the interplay of gender, sexuality, and stress in adolescence. Such writers often find that their ethnographic impressions are challenged by others (see Freeman, 1983, on Mead) and even termed "fables of identity" by some (Clifford, 1986b, p. 102).

The *scientific tale* is the fourth narrative strategy. In it, the author attempts to scientifically record, often with "objective" categories, the various sectors of experience that occur in the group or culture studied. A scientific ethnography heaps facts upon facts, tests hypotheses, presents statistical data, and builds or elaborates theory. (See Clifford, 1986, pp. 102–3, for a discussion of Freeman's "scientific" ethnography of Samoa.)

Authority and modes of discourse   Clifford (1986) has discussed four modes of authority that the ethnographer as writer may claim in his test: (1) the experimental, (2) the realist and interpretive, (3) the dialogic, and (4) the heteroglossic, or multivoiced. The first two modes correspond to the confessional and realist tales just discussed. The dialogic refers to the ethnographer's engaging the subject in dialogue and discourse, so that one voice (the observer's) is not privileged over another's (the subject's). Multivoiced discourse attempts to allow all points of view in the field experience to speak out. It does not give the author final authority over the text (see Krieger, 1983). It may tend toward fiction, or the fashioning of a textual story that conveys the essential nature of the experiences and points of view studied. Ethnographic writing has tended to suppress the dialogic and multivoiced model. The ethnographer writing as the authoritative observer of the field scene has tended to be the dominant mode of discourse.

The ethnographer writes culture. That is, a culture or a group does not just present itself to the participant observer in terms of a set of categories that can be objectively recorded. Accordingly, what is written is shaped by the narrative convention that is followed (confessional, realist, impressionist, scientific). This means that different versions of the culture will be depicted and different kinds of evidence will be used. The writing style (first person, third person) will also vary, as will the authority the author attributes to the text that it is written. Writing and research can no longer be reduced to method, or to "keeping good field notes, making accurate maps, 'writing up' results" (Clifford, 1986a, p. 2). Cultures are now seen as being composed of "competing codes and representations" (Clifford, 1986, p. 2). The poetic and the political now intertwine in ethnographic writing. Texts are made, or constructed. They are based on rhetoric, allegory, the choice of metaphors, writing style, the author's gender, politics, and ideology.

The subject's experience   Traditional ethnographers often wrote as if they could accurately reflect or depict the subject's experiences. In fact, what they wrote often reflected *their* interpretations of the subject's experiences, or at times *their own* experiences states as the subject's. Current anthropological writing argues that ethnographers create pictures of the subject that fit with their images of the culture or group. In short, subjects are created. Thus the writer may present adolescents in rebellion, alcoholics slipping, the dying members of a "primitive" culture, or Bali men betting at cockfights. In each of these cases a particular "type" of subject is presented, and this "type" may or may not be representative of other humans, in the culture. Furthermore, this "type" is seldom complete; it presents or contains only a slice of the person. An additional problem emerges when gender is considered. Many field workers in the past, ignored gender or only presented the male point of view in a culture or group. Gendered subjects must be represented in ethnography. This includes asking about how one is a man, woman, or child in a particular group.

When the ethnographer presents the subject's experiences, one of three narrative strategies can be followed. First, the researcher can present the life story of a single subject. Second, a collection of life stories or narratives grouped around a common theme can be presented. Third, slices of interaction from a strategic locale can be presented; in my AA study, for example, I presented samples of talk at AA meetings. Each of these strategies will be discussed in greater detail in Chapter 8.

Being objective   From the foregoing, it should be clear that an "objective" ethnography cannot be written. To think otherwise is to engage in the fallacy of objectivism. Such a belief also ignores the work that has appeared in the last decade in the ethnographical literature.

Gender   Gender enters into ethnography in two basic ways. First, ethnographers are gendered subjects who bring their experiences of maleness and femaleness into the ethnographic experience. (See Golde, 1986, for a discussion of women in the field.) Field work is a gendered social production. Women appear to have special problems in the field. These include (1) being sexually vulnerable; (2) raising suspicions if they are not married, or if they are married, why they do not have children or husbands who are present; (3) conforming to the culture's attitudes toward being a woman; (4) and resolving the cultural shock that sets in at the beginning of the field experience and creating an acceptable female identity in the culture. Wax's quotes speak directly to this point. Second, the subjects who are studied are themselves gendered beings. As noted earlier, each group or culture's constitution of a man or a woman requires special study.

Reading ethnography   Ethnographies and the reports of participant observers have traditionally been read as "windows" into another group or culture's way of life. The foregoing discussion has been an attempt to challenge this conception. Granted, ethnographies are not novels or pure fictions or just travelogues. They are, however, "tales from the field" and must be read as one author's version of what he experienced and then wrote about. Ethnographic texts do not just speak for themselves; they have to be read and interpreted. This means that readers create the texts that they read. They do so, in part, on the basis of their own experience with the phenomenon discussed in the text. For example, recovering alcoholics who read my book *The Recovering Alcoholic* bring their own recovering experiences to the text; nonalcoholic readers bring a different set of experiences to it. It is not the same book for the two different types of readers.

CONCLUSIONS

I began this chapter with the claim that participant observation, broadly defined, is a method well-suited to the analysis of complex forms in interaction. This is but one way to conceptually distinguish this method from the survey, which I view as more appropriate for the study of stable, routine forms of behavior. Unfortunately, this theoretical advantage has many empirical flaws, for whenever a method proposes to study change and process, factors jeopardizing internal validity must be carefully treated. In one sense, then, earlier criticism of participant observation as being narrow and impressionistic becomes irrelevant, at least until the investigator answers the problems of internal validity.

I have attempted to show how the observational method is conducted, what its major forms are, how it can use analytic induction, and how the issues of internal and external validity were resolved in one illustrative case. It seems appropriate here to reconsider Trow's (1957, pp. 33–35) dictum that sociologists must carefully analyze each of their methodologies in terms of the kinds of questions they can best answer. To proclaim participant observation as *the* method of sociology is equivalent to stating that the experiment is *the* method of psychology. Obviously, every discipline can and must employ more than one method, just as any theoretical perspective can and must employ more than one method as it moves from vague hypotheses to observations and empirical tests. I have, then, broadly defined participant observation as a method that combines several other methodologies in the hope that sociologist will take the best from it as they work from their theories to the level of empirical reality. The foregoing discussion of reading and writing ethnography suggests, however, that traditional conceptions of participant observation have undergone radical revisions in the last decade. It remains for sociologists to incorporate these new views into their own understandings of this and all of the other methods they use when they leave their offices and engage in the research act.

SUGGESTED READINGS

BECKER, HOWARD S., BLANCHE GEER, EVERETT C. HUGHES, AND ANSELM L. STRAUSS, *Boys in White: Student Culture in Medical School*. (Chicago: University of Chicago Press, 1961). Remains a classic accounting of how four symbolic interactionists used participant observation and open-ended interviewing in the study of a medical school.

GOLDE, PEGGY (ed.), *Women in the Field: Anthropological Experience*, 2nd ed. (Berkeley: University of California Press, 1986). An outstanding collection of essays by female anthropologists interpreting their field experiences in a variety of cultural contexts.

SILVERMAN, DAVID, *Qualitative Methodology and Sociology: Describing the Social World*. (Hants, England: Gower, 1985). Chapters 5 through 8 are critical and informed readings of ethnography, conversational analysis, and the reading of social texts.

TURNER, VICTOR AND EDWARD BRUNER (eds.), *The Anthropology of Experience*. (Urbana: University of Illinois Press, 1986). Excellent treatment of the "new" interpretive approach to ethnography in anthropology. Should be read in conjunction with Clifford and Marcus's (1986) *Writing Culture: The Poetics and Politics of Ethnography* and Bruner's (1984) collection, *Text, Play and Story: The Construction and Reconstruction of Self and Society*.

VAN MAANEN, JOHN, *Tales of the Field*. (Chicago: University of Chicago Press, 1988). An illuminating and powerful exposition of the various narrative strategies ethnographers use when they write their stories of being in the field.

8

The Biographical Method

The world is crammed full of personal documents. People keep diaries, send letters, take photos, write memos, tell biographies, scrawl graffiti, publish their memoirs, write letters to the papers, leave suicide notes, inscribe memorials on tombstones, shoot films, paint pictures, make music and try to record their personal dreams. All of these expressions of personal life ... can be of interest to anyone who cares to seek them out. They are ... "documents of life." [Plummer, 1983, p. 13]

Criteria drawn from the experimental model and used to evaluate single studies in isolation, however useful they may be in a variety of contexts, have had one bad by-product. They have led people to ignore the other functions of research and, particularly, to ignore the contribution made by one study to an overall research enterprise even when the study considered in isolation, produced no definitive results of its own. ... We can perhaps hope that a fuller understanding of the complexity of the scientific enterprise will restore sociologist's sense of the versatility and worth of the life history. [Becker, 1966, p. xviii]

In the 1930s and 1940s, under the influence of Park and Burgess, sociologists trained at the University of Chicago employed the life history, case study, case history, and biographical method extensively (see Becker, 1955; Park, 1952, pp. 202-9; Plummer, 1983). With the rise of quantification and rigorous empirical measurement, sociologists in succeeding decades turned away from the method. However, the last 10 years have seen a resurgence of interest in the life history, life story, biographical method (see Bertaux, 1981a; Bertaux and Kohli, 1984; Denzin, 1986a, 1986b; Plummer, 1983). In 1986, a new research committee devoted to this method was approved by the International Sociological Association. Called "Biography and Society," it publishes an international journal, *Life Stories/Recits de vie*, and a quarterly newsletter. The journal *Oral History* also publishes materials using this method. In this chapter I present the major forms of the life history, life story, bibliographical method, detail the steps by which data are collected, discuss the analytic forms of the method, and present what I feel are its unique advantages for contemporary sociology. The problems of the method will be treated, but my main thrust will show that, like ethnography and participant observation, the life history method closely approximates the fit between theory, method, and interpretation advocated in earlier chapters.

DEFINITION

The life history, life story, biographical method presents the experiences and definitions held by one person, one group, or one organization as this person, group, or organization interprets those experiences. Life history materials include any record or document, including the case histories of social agencies, that throws light on the subjective behavior of individuals or groups. These may range from letters to autobiographies, from newspaper accounts to court records. A careful transcription of an interview, provided it does not intermix the interviewer's own interpretations, is as much a form of life history data as a personal diary.

Every human being, symbolic interactionism suggests, defines the world differently. If sociologists are to accurately explain these different definitions and relate them to action, they must penetrate this subjective world of concepts, experiences, and reactions. Park (1931, p. 167), perhaps more than any other sociologist, was sensitive to this methodological principle:

> In the case of human beings, it is the wide range of subjective life of mental and imaginative behavior which intervenes between stimulus and response, which makes human behavior fundamentally different from that of lower animals. It is this, too, which makes human behavior, particularly in the case of certain persons, so problematic and so difficult to understand. It is the purpose of the life history to get a record of this inner life.

ASSUMPTIONS

A central assumption of the life history is that human conduct is to be studied and understood from the perspective of the persons involved. All materials that reflect upon this perspective should be employed. Clearly this is a case for taking the role of the "acting other" and actively sharing in the subject's experiences and perspectives. These notions, of course, lie at the heart of participant observation, which is one life history expanded many times, and are traceable to symbolic interactionism.

A second assumption is that the sensitive observer employing the life history will be concerned with relating the perspective elicited to definitions and meanings that are lodged in social relationships and social groups. Additionally, the variable nature of these definitions across situations will be examined.

Third, concern will be directed to recording the unfolding history of one person's, one group's, or one organization's experiences. This feature becomes a hallmark of the life history—the capturing of events over time. The sociologist employing the methods becomes a historian of social life, be it the life of one person or the life of many persons similarly situated.

Fourth and finally, it should be noted that because the life history presents a person's experiences as he or she defines them, the objectivity of the person's interpretations provides central data for the final report. The investigator must first determine the subject's "own story." In fact, the subject's *definition* of the situation takes precedence over the objective situation because, as Thomas and Thomas (1928, pp. 571–72) have argued:

> There may be, and is, doubt as to the objectivity and veracity of the record, but even the highly subjective record has a value for behavior study. . . . Very often it is the wide discrepancy between the situation as it seems to others and the situation as it seems to the individual that brings about the overt behavior difficulty. . . . If men define situations as real, they are real in their consequences.

In obtaining a life history, definitions of the situation will be gathered first, and then the perspective of others who bear directly upon those definitions will be studied. This triangulation permits the analysis of varying definitions as they relate to the same experiential unit. To understand definitions of the situation, the sociologist will first place the subject within the total range of units which this single case represents.

Clarification of Terms

The terms *life, self, history, fiction, biography, story, discourse,* and *narrative* require clarification because they are each, in some fashion, embedded in the life history, life story, biographical method. A *life,* for present purposes, will refer to the lived experiences of a person, a *person* being a cultural creation (see Frank, 1979, pp. 75–82). The Bali, for example, have six different classes of terms for individuals, including "Father-of," "First Child," and "Chief," while a person's first name is seldom, if ever, used (Frank, 1979, p. 80). A *life* is an unfinished project belonging to a person, given meaning by the person and his cultural and emotional associates (Denzin, 1984b, pp. 87–88; 1986a, p. 9). *Self* is a "process that unifies the stream of thoughts and experiences the person has about herself around a single pole or point of reference" (Denzin, 1984b, p. 81). *History* is the account of an event and involves finding out how something occurred (see Titon, 1980, p. 278). *Fiction* does not necessarily mean falsehood or something opposed to truth. A fiction is something made up or fashioned. Good ethnographies are "true fictions" (Clifford, 1986, p. 6). A fiction is a making of something, usually a story, while a history finds out something (Titon, 1980, p. 278). A *biography,* after Dryden, who defined the term in 1683, is "the history of particular men's lives" (Titon, 1980, p. 280). A biographer is a historian. A *story* is fiction.

It is a "sequence of actions or events, conceived as independent of their manifestation in discourse" (Culler, 1981, pp. 169–70). *Discourse* refers to the "discursive presentation or narration of events" (Culler, 1981, p. 170). A *narrator* reports a story as a *narrative*. Every narrative has a double logic: a plot and sequence of events that exist independent of the narration, and a set of justifications for relating the elements of the story in a particular way (Culler, 1981, p. 187; Labov, 1972, p. 366). All stories and narratives are temporal productions. They are either tales or stories of time, or stories about time (Ricoeur, 1985, p. 101). Furthermore, all stories deal with a temporal order of events, some events being anterior to or simultaneous with other events, while some are posterior, or come after other events (Culler, 1981, p. 171).

Varieties of the Biographical Method

Given the foregoing definitions, it is now possible to distinguish the meanings of several interrelated concepts, including life history, personal history, case history, case study, life story, oral history, self story, and personal experience story. A *life history*, as discussed earlier, focuses on the experiences of a person, group, or organization. (See discussion of its forms which follows.) Life histories have also been called *personal histories* (see Titon, 1980, p. 283). A personal history is "a written account of a person's life based on spoken conversations and interviews" (Titon, 1980, p. 283). Chambliss's *Box Man: A Professional Thief's Journey* (1975) is a personal history, or life history, as is Heyl's work, *The Madam as Entrepreneur: Career Management in House Prostitution* (1979). Life histories attempt to find out how something happened in the life of a person, or a group. A *case* refers both to an event or happening and to the actions and experiences of a person or a collectivity. A *case history* is a "full story of some temporal span or interlude in social life — a biography, an occupational career, a project, an illness . . . a ceremony, and so forth" (Strauss and Glaser, 1970, p. 182). A case history differs from a life history because it focuses on a process and not a person. A *case study* is the analysis of a single case or multiple cases for the purpose of description or generation of theory. The case history focuses on a process. The case study analyzes a case or body of cases for what can be said about an underlying or emergent theory or social process (Strauss and Glaser, 1970, p. 183). A case study will often merge with a case history; that is, case studies are based on case histories. My study of the American liquor industry merged these two approaches (Denzin, 1977a, 1978). I combined a case study of the industry with case histories and life histories of particular individuals and units within the industry (see also Denzin, 1979).

A *life story* focuses on a life, or a segment of a life, as reported by the individual in question (Bertaux, 1981a, pp. 7–9). It is "a person's story of his or her life, or of what he or she thinks is a significant part of that life. It is therefore a personal narrative, a story of personal experience" (Titon, 1980, p. 276). It may take the form of an autobiography. It is based on fictions or fictional accounts of what happened. It exists as a story, somewhat independent of its telling. It is of and about time and time's meaning to the narrator. The intent of the life story is to contain within a single sweep the relevant objective details and subjective experiences of a single person's life. A life story is different from a life history. The former deals with an entire life or a segment of a life. It deals with fictions, while histories deal with what happened and how it happened. Obviously, the two merge in the telling. The latter deals with the experiences of not only persons, but also groups and organizations. It studies how these units interpret and relate to a particular body of experience—for example, prohibition, the economic depression of the 1930s, World War II, the Viet Nam War, or being a hostage.

The poet W.H. Auden is reported to have said that "for a pence you can get the details of any person's life. For present purposes the eliciting of these details will be called the life history. The meanings of those details can not be so easily purchased." These meanings are contained in the life story told by the person. This brings me to the self story. *Self stories* are told by an individual in the context of a specific set of experiences. Self stories position the self of the teller centrally in the narrative that is given. They are literally stories of and about the self in relation to an event or an experience. Self stories build on the position that each individual is a story teller of self experiences, an oral historian of his own life. To collect self stories is to collect oral histories of the self. These self stories are personal narratives, and may take the form of personal experience narratives.

The term *personal experience narrative* partially describes what I am calling self stories (see Stahl, 1977; Dolby-Stahl, 1985). Personal experience narratives are "stories people tell about their own personal experience" (Dolby-Stahl, 1985). They often draw upon an oral storytelling tradition and may be related in some fashion to the traditional folklore of a group (Stahl, 1977, p. 17). These narratives are based on personal experience and have the structure of a story. They have a narrative structure (beginning, middle, end, point of view) which details a set of events conceived as independent of their manifestation in discourse. When they are performed or told, they draw on private but shareable experience. They create an emotional bond between listener and teller. "They express a part of the 'inner life' of the storyteller" (Dolby-Stahl, 1985, p. 47). The personal experience narrative is a genre, or form, of storytelling. It is dependent on the "private" folklore of the person or the group, although it may draw on broader cultural and ideological themes (Dolby-Stahl, 1985, pp. 49, 61). Such a narrative draws on everyday experiences, and may be a "true" story which identifies core, shared values of the teller and the listener. They may be based on single-experience episodes or be multiepisodic. Their significance lies in their ability to create an intimate bond between teller and listener. They connect selves in a context of shared and shareable experience.

These narratives are not *oral histories.* An oral history deals with factual accuracy. "Its focus is chiefly on events, processes, causes and effects, rather than on the individuals whose recollections furnish oral history with its raw data." Oral histories proceed "from a historical rather than a fictive stance" (Titon, 1980, p. 281). Oral histories are not to be confused with *personal histories,* which, as just noted, reconstruct a life based on interviews and conversations. Nor are they life stories, life histories, or, strictly speaking, self stories.

Self Stories and Personal Experience Narratives

Personal experience narratives differ from self stories in the following ways. First, these narratives do not necessarily position the self of the teller in the center of the story, as self stories do. Second, self stories are often mandated by a group. Alcoholics in AA, for example, are expected to be able to tell such stories and to base them only on their experiences. Personal experience narratives are seldom culturally mandated in this manner. Third, self stories are often told to groups, while personal experience narratives may involve only one or two listeners. The stories told at AA speaker meetings are told to large groups of recovering alcoholics. Fourth, personal experience narratives are more likely to be based on anecdotal, everyday experiences, while self stories involve pivotal, often critical self experiences. Fifth, self stories, unlike personal experience narratives, need not be coherent, or delightful, or recreate cherished memories of a group. (See Stahl, 1977, p. 19, and Hall, 1977, p. 31, on these dimensions of personal experience narrative.) However, these two biographical forms are alike in that they both rest on personal experience.

Combining Biographical Methods

In my AA study (Denzin, 1978b), I examined the history of AA in the United States. I also studied the lives of AA's two cofounders, Bill Wilson and Robert Smith. I used each of the previously described biographical methods. I presented a life history and case history of AA. I examined the life stories of Wilson and Smith. In my study of AA in the local community, I listened to the oral histories of old timers. I also offered a brief case study of AA and compared it to other socializing agencies in our society. I analyzed the self stories of AA members as they talked around the AA tables. In addition to these self stories, I listened to and collected personal experience narratives that did not contain involved self stories per se.

Figure 8-1 summarizes the basic distinctions between the several forms of the biographical method. A detailed discussion of each of the variants on the biographical method is beyond the scope of this chapter (see Titon, 1980, for a comprehensive discussion and Plummer, 1983). Because the life history is the generic form of the biographical method—that is, other variants derive from it—I shall primarily confine my discussion to this approach. It must be noted, however, that a fully triangulated biographical investigation combines case histories, case studies, life stories, personal experience stories, oral histories, and personal histories.

TYPES OF LIFE HISTORIES

Three basic forms of the life history can be distinguished: the complete, the topical, and the edited (see Allport, 1942, Chapter 6). All the forms, however, contain three central features: the person's own story of his life; the social and cultural situation to which the subject and others see the subject re-

Figure 8-1.   Forms and Varieties of the Biographical Method

Term/Method	Key Features	Forms/Variations
1. History	What happened? How?	Oral, life, personal
2. Fiction	An account, something made up, fashioned	Story (life, self)
3. Biography	History of a life	Autobiography
4. Story	A fiction, a narrative	Life, personal experience
5. Discourse	Telling of story	First, third person
6. Narrative	A story, having a plot and existence independent of the teller	Fiction, epic, folklore
7. Narrator	Teller of a story	First, third person
8. Life History	Account of a life based on interviews and conversations	Personal history, edited, complete, topical
9. Case	An instance of a phenomenon	Event, process
10. Case History	History of an event or social process, not of a person	Single, multiple, medical, legal
11. Case Study	Analysis and record of a single case	Single, multiple
12. Life Story	A person's story of his or her life, or a part thereof	Edited, complete, topical, fictional
13. Self Story	Story of self in relation to an event	Personal experience story, fictional, true
14. Personal Experience Story	Stories about personal experience	Single, multiple episode, private or communal folklore
15. Oral History	Recollections of events, their causes and effects	Work, musical, family
16. Personal History	Reconstruction of life based on interviews and conversations	Life history, life story

sponding; and the sequence of past experiences and situations in the subject's life.

Complete Life History

The complete life history attempts to cover the entire sweep of the subject's life experiences. It will necessarily be long, many-sided, and complex. Shaw's (1966) life history of a juvenile delinquent, for example, initially ran some 200 pages and was followed by a sociological interpretation.

Topical Life History

The topical life history shares all the features of the complete form except that only one phase of the subject's life is presented.

Sutherland (Conwell and Sutherland, 1937), for example, in a presentation of the life of a professional thief, was concerned only with the experiences of one thief as they related to the social organization of professional crime; his purpose is described as follows (p. iii):

> The principal part of this book is a description of the profession of theft by a person who had been engaged almost continuously for more than twenty years in that profession. This description was secured in two ways: first, the thief wrote approximately two-thirds of it on topics and questions prepared by me; second, he and I discussed for about seven hours a week for twelve weeks what he had written, and immediately after each conference I wrote in verbatim form, as nearly as I could remember, all that he had said in the discussion.

There was little attempt by Sutherland to "objectify" the statement of his subject by reference to other sources or documents. What the reader finds is simply one man's conception of his profession with interpretations and annotations offered by Sutherland to clarify unusual terms and phrases. This is not to imply that the topical life history never employs additional sources, however.

Edited Life History

The edited life history may be either topical or complete. Its key feature is the continual interspersing of comments, explanations, and questions by someone other than the focal subject. Sutherland, for example, approached an edited life history by adding annotations and interstitial passages. For purposes of theory construction and hypothesis testing, some degree of editing and interspersion of comments by the observer must be present. Without such intrusions, the life history must stand as its own sociological document.

LIFE HISTORY MATERIALS

I began this chapter by noting that life history materials consist of any documents that bear a relationship to a person's ongoing definitions and experiences. Two basic forms of these data may be noted: public archival records and private archival records (see Webb et al., 1966, Chapter 3; 1981, Chapters 4, 6). *Public archival records* are to be distinguished by the fact that they are prepared for the express purpose of examination by some set of others, often legally defined, as in the case of court records. *Private archival records* typically are not prepared for an audience. With the exception of published autobiographies, they seldom reach more than a few readers.

It is possible to introduce a classification of these two types of records, noting those that are primary in nature and those that are secondary in nature. *Primary records* have direct reference to the subject. *Secondary records* represent reports that do not directly pertain to a specific subject, but instead pertain to the class the subject represents. In addition, they may be writings about the subject by a third person; it is possible to speak of letters written about a person, records of the person's family but not of himself (or herself), and so on. The statements prepared by the subject are the personal documents of the life history. A complete life history will combine as many primary and secondary sources as possible, while focusing the report around the subject's own personal document.

Public Archival Records

Generally speaking, the public archive is secondary in nature, although there will be occasions when court testimony, prison records, or newspaper accounts will directly refer to the focal subject. In these cases they become primary data sources. Four basic varieties of the public record may be noted (see Webb et al., 1966, Chapter 3; 1981, Chapters 4, 6).

Actuarial records   First are actuarial records concerning the personal and demographic elements of the population served by the record-keeping agency; these will range from birth and death statistics to records of marriages and divorces.

Political and judicial reports   Second are political and judicial records concerning court decisions, public votes, budget decisions, and so on.

Governmental documents   Third are other governmental documents (national, state, or local) such as weather reports, crime statistics, records of social welfare programs, and hospitalization records of the mentally and physically ill.

Media accounts   Last are productions of the mass media pertaining to such issues as shifting political or social problems and instances of collective behavior. Mass-media data may in addition involve the study of letters to editors, advertisements as business documents, comics and caricatures as works of fiction, and editorials and syndicated columns as expressions of opinion.

Private Archival Records

The most important data for the life history are private records or documents. In these materials, the subject's definitions of the situation emerge; it is precisely these definitions that the sociologist wants to juxtapose against the public document. Private documents include autobiographies; questionnaires, interviews, and verbatim reports; diaries and letters; and artistic and projective materials. While no one of these sources is likely to provide a complete picture of the subject's life experiences, a combination of them will approach it closely.

Autobiography   The most common form of the personal document is the autobiography (see Allport, 1942, Chapter 6). It is often written on the basis of questions provided by the investigator and, of course, represents the subject's own interpretation of his life experiences. Two types of the autobiography may be distinguished: one that has been previously published, and one written at the request of the sociologist. With the previously published autobiography, the analyst must be aware of publication restrictions arising from canons of good taste and literary merit, and perhaps from the goal of profit. On the other hand, the published autobiography has the advantage of prior editorial criticism, which usually makes it easier to read. If it is the life of a distinguished and articulate person, it may also possess artistic and social significance. The unpublished autobiography will more strongly bear the imprint of the sociologist requesting it and will reflect the life of persons not ordinarily accorded social recognition or prestige.

Allport (1942, Chapter 6) has distinguished three types of the autobiography that correspond to the three types of the life history: *comprehensive* (complete), *topical,* and *edited.*

Comprehensive Autobiography   The comprehensive autobiography covers the subject's life from the earliest memory to the time of writing. It will deal with a relatively large number of lines of experience, giving, Allport suggests, a picture of the variety, roundness, and interrelatedness of life.

Topical Autobiography   The topical autobiography — for example, Sutherland's treatment of a professional thief — is an excision from the life of the subject. As such it invites comparison with other kinds of lives. Sociologists, for instance, might profitably compare the life of the professional thief with the professional experiences of the burglar, the con artist, or the embezzler on the basis of similarly constructed topical life histories.

Edited Autobiography   The edited autobiography, the third type, has as its virtue the elimination of the length and repetitiousness of the comprehensive and topical autobiographies: The sociologist deliberately monitors the statements of the subject, selects certain materials for amplification, deletes others, and so places her own stamp on the final product. (In a sense, all autobiographies bear this imprint because the subject probably would not have written a life history without prodding from the sociologist.)

But which portions of the material should be edited, and which should stand as stated by the subject? Allport (1942, p. 78) proposes the general guideline that unique styles of expressions (argot and colloquial phrasing) remain unedited; editing for the sake of clarity or to remove repetitious material would seem justified.

Advantages of Autobiographies   When confronted with an articulate subject, the sociologist is able to test and refine hypotheses through successive questions and probing. A single case or a series of such cases can then be employed to develop a grounded theory. This was Lindesmith's strategy (1947) as he refined his theory of opiate addiction. Each statement of the subject and each phase of the subject's life represent a universe of experiences that potentially confirms or negates hypotheses. As was noted earlier, Sutherland monitored and edited, and each modification and interpretation was subsequently presented to the subject, who then responded to it.

The great merit of the autobiography, as Allport states (1942, p. 77), is that it provides an "inside picture" of the subject's life, a side that is neither fully apparent nor fully public. It happens, however, that the author of the autobiography may not always be fully aware of what has occurred in his or her life. Furthermore, the subject may dress up, beautify, or hide certain things. It is the sociologist's job to probe and uncover such topics. What our subject's acts have been and what his habits are, we can know, as Park tells us. It is more important to learn, "What is it that habitually engages his attention? What are the subjects of his dreams and reveries? . . . In addition to these facts of his history, it is important to know, however, his incompleted acts: what he hopes; what he dreams; what his vagrant impulses, 'temptations,' are" (Park, 1952, p. 204).

Triangulation   In the autobiography, the sociologists must keep the record of experiences separate from the interpretation given them. Here the triangulation of perspective becomes relevant. The sociologist hopes to discover the differences in definition and meaning attached to those events that form the core of the subject's experiences. This was the line taken by Shaw (1966, p. 32), in the case of Stanley:

> An important initial step in the study of the delinquent child is to procure a rather complete and accurate description of his delinquencies and other behavior difficulties. Among other things this description should show the specific offenses in the order of their occurrence, the chronological age of the child at the time of each offense, the immediate circumstances in which each offense occurred, and the number of persons involved. . . . In the present chapter materials are presented to give an objective picture of Stanley's difficulties. . . . The subjective and personal aspects of these problems (without which the picture is necessarily incomplete) are revealed in the boy's "own story" which follows in subsequent chapters.

The final life history is not a conventional autobiography. Life histories and the autobiographies they rest on "have rather the character of confessions, intimate personal documents intended to record not so much external events as to reveal sentiments and attitudes" (Park, 1952, p. 204). The sociologist who incorporates autobiographies into a life history should take steps to minimize the slighting of any relevant event and must also ensure that the subject's interpretations are accurately reported. These are two features often not present in the published autobiography, because the subject may deliberately distort the life history to bring it into line with present behavior. Further, the sociologist tries to keep the subject "oriented to the questions sociology is interested in, asks . . . about events that require amplification, [and] tries to make the story jibe with matters of official record and with material furnished by others familiar with the person, event, or place being described" (Becker, 1966, p. vi).

Diary   While few sociologists have employed the diary as a source of life history data, Allport has suggested that the spontaneous, intimate diary is the personal document *par excellence* because in it "the author sets down only such events, thoughts, and feelings as have importance to him; he is not so constrained by the task-attitudes that frequently control the production in letters, interviews, or autobiography" (1942, p. 95).

In the diary the author may express feelings that otherwise would never be made public, and in its ideal form the diary is unsurpassed as a continuous record of the subjective side of a person's life. Ideas are set down; disappear with age; are replaced with new thoughts, new feelings, new experiences. Turning points and reactions to personal tragedies may be recorded, and in the long-term diary sociologists may find a record surpassing the autobiography.

In contrast to the autobiography, the diary represents the immediate recording of experiences, unimpaired by reconstructions and distortions of memory. Because of the reconstructed nature of the autobiography, it may suffer from the *fallacy of motive attribution*; the diary is less susceptible to this. Observers frequently find the author of an autobiography constructing motives to explain past behavior which, while plausible at the moment, may not be correct. In William Wordworth's poetic autobiography *The Prelude,* there is a deliberate attempt to reinterpret childhood experiences with nature from the literary and philosophical positions of Romanticism and pantheism. The interpretations are forced and inconsistent. Had Wordsworth kept a diary, critics would have another criterion by which to assess the credibility and authenticity of his autobiography.

Diaries may take several forms. Allport (1942, Chapter 7) proposes the following classification: The *intimate journal,* the *memoir,* and the *log.*

Intimate Journal   The intimate journal is perhaps the most useful of the three types, for it contains "uncensored outpourings"—the entries being written discontinuously, either daily or at longer intervals of time. The biography of Dylan Thomas (Read, 1964) contains portions from his personal diary, notes kept by Thomas on poems he was writing, reflections on his financial status, and comments on his acceptance in the artistic world. For the sociologist interested in the private life of a public figure, the intimate journal provides data not elsewhere available.

Memoir   The memoir is the second form of the diary. It is basically impersonal in nature and may be written in a few sittings. In this respect it may resemble the autobiography, although it typically contains much less about the subject and his or her personal life. It becomes more of an objective "accounting" of the subject's affairs. Records kept by foreign correspondents represent the memoir—Shirer's *Berlin Diary* (1943) is an example. Faris's accounting (1967) of one phase in the history of the University of Chicago Department of Sociology takes on the flavor of a memoir, although it draws on the perspectives of more than one person. Still, its data are mainly career biographies, records of publications, courses taught in the department, and so on. The impersonality of the memoir substantially reduces its sociological significance for many interactional purposes.

Log   The log is an "account book," a record of events or happenings, a list of meetings, visits, trips, and so on. It may also contain time-budget accounts, but its typical form is depersonalized. This is not to degrade its importance as a personal document. When placed against a topical auto-biography, the log may fill gaps concerning the subject's day-to-day patterns of interaction that would not otherwise appear. Barker and Wright (1954) have made excellent use of the log in depicting the ordinary patterns of interaction of members in one small community. Time budgets on a large number of like-situated persons—in an organization, for example—can provide a vibrant picture of the daily rhythm of conduct in the setting. Again, however, logs taken alone are too depersonalized to suffice as complete life history data.

Letters   In contrast to diaries and autobiographies, which are directed (initially at least) to only one person (the author), the letter has a dual audience—the writer and the recipient. This fact introduces an element that must be considered in analyzing letters, for the document may reveal more about the relationship between the author and the recipient than about either alone. The analyst of letters (Allport, 1942, pp. 108–10) must consider who the recipient is, what the relationship is between the writer and the recipient, and who the author is. This topic of a letter and the nature of the relationship represented by it must also be considered. In many senses, letters may be said to reveal as much about the letter writer as they do about the person receiving them. The style of address, the mode of presentation, the topics covered, and the frequency of writing all reveal elements about one person's perception of another. In the letter, the author raises his own experiences up for examination and presents them to another in a fashion intended to be acceptable and interpretable. Allport (1942, pp. 108–9) comments:

> If they are defective in revealing many sides of one personality, they are undoubtedly successful in revealing the tie between two personalities. Dyadic relationships, tapped by letters, constitute a neglected chapter in social psychology.

This seems almost too restrictive, for the letter may reveal a good deal about the personality of the author, particularly if observers have access to a cross-section of letters that go to more than one person. The published letters of Dostoevsky (Mayne, 1964), for example, reveal his conception of his friends and family while presenting the emergent personality of the author over a period of 50 years. In Dostoevsky's letters, the reader finds the purest form of his autobiographical memoirs. Put with the sometimes thinly veiled auto-biography of his novels and stories, his letters provide a major source for reconstructing his private life, for in the letters the reader finds the progressions Dostoevsky underwent from moody adolescent to budding author, to convict, to successful author.

Sociologists have been prone to ignore the value of the letter as a source of data, but historians and literary critics have made extensive use of such data as they attempt to reconstruct the lives of important literary and historical figures (see Gottschalk, Kluckhohn, and Angell, 1945, Chapter 2). With few exceptions, sociological uses of the letter have dealt with the products of the deviant, the immigrant, and the social outcast. Thomas and Znaniecki (1927), for example, made extensive use of letters of the Polish peasant to uncover the transitional problems involved in moving from one social setting to another.

Family letters represent another version of this type of interpersonal communication. In a study of the rise and fall of family solidarity within extended family networks, I collected all the letters received by one family member from all other members over a 15-year period. They reveal not only the play of family jealousies, but also the multiple effects of illness, death, bequests, and growing alienation upon the life of an extended family group. Such letters, if systematically collected, would shed new light on the modern family.

Questionnaires, interviews, and verbatim reports   Earlier, I pointed out that for a life history to have a broad sociological significance, it necessarily must be oriented to "the questions sociology is interested in." Obviously, these questions will vary according to the theoretical and research orientations of each sociologist, but the point stands: Extensive use must be made of the questionnaire, the interview, and the verbatim report. The reason for including these is to keep the subject mindful that many life experiences are of sociological importance even though they may appear unimportant to him. The questionnaire—or "life history guide," as it more properly becomes—serves as a guide to the subject who is ordering her thoughts and conveying them to the sociologist. It also ensures that topics will not be forgotten or overlooked. In addition, it will become the major source of operationalization for the concepts contained in the theoretical framework under analysis.

Guidelines for Gathering and Interpreting Biographical Materials

If life histories, life stories, and biographical materials in general are to be compared, some guidelines must be established; at this point, there seems to be little consensus in the psychological, sociological, and anthropological literature on the form these guidelines should take. However, such standards must not sacrifice "the spontaneity of self-written accounts produced by the subject in his own way, in solitude, and at his own convenience" (Allport, 1942, p. 94). In this context it is useful to review several proposals for ordering life history, life story, biographical materials. For convenience I have divided these proposals into two categories: (1) objective formats, and (2) subjective, interpretive formats.

Objective approaches   A variety of objective approaches have been proposed (see Denzin, 1978, pp. 229-32 for a review). These include those offered by Dollard (1935), Helling (1987), Kohli (1986), Langness (1965),

Lemert (1951), Plummer (1983), Schutze (1983), Titon (1980), and Young (1952). The most recent development within the objective approach has been carried out in Germany under the direction of Schutze and his associates (see *Biography & Society Newsletter,* 1987). This approach combines narrative interviewing, "objective hermeneutics," and the grounded theory approach of Glaser and Strauss (Kohli, 1986, p. 106).

This work has the following characteristics. First, these scholars begin with an objective set of experiences in a subject's life, often connecting these events to life course stages (childhood, adolescence, early adulthood, adulthood, middle age, old age, and so on), and to life course experiences (schooling, sports, sexuality, deviance, family crises, work, marriage, illnesses, and the like). Second, they secure narrative accounts of these experiences, often through interviews. Third, they subject these interviews to careful readings and interpretations, usually by a group of researchers. Fourth, they generate a set of narrative segments and categories within the interview, looking for orderly patterns of experience and interpretation. In this phase they reconstruct the subject's biography and detail the structural factors that have shaped his life experiences. Fifth, they write an analytic abstraction of the case, which includes (1) the structural processes affecting the subject's life, (2) the different kinds of autobiographical theories that relate to the life history experiences, and (3) the features of the life that are case specific and general. Sixth, when the researcher has finished this phase of interpretation, a second case is selected. This phase proceeds through the same phases as the first: differentiation of the text into units, structural descriptions, and analytical abstractions. Seventh, when this case has been analyzed, the researcher formulates comparisons between it and the first. Eighth, theoretical interpretations are generated which may stress any of the following: (1) career models, (2) structural processes of the life course, (3) relational models of biography and structure, (4) models of social worlds, and (5) natural history models of the life course. The intent of this research is to connect biographical experiences to sequences of objectively determined social-structural processes. From such materials sociological theories are built, tested, and reformulated.

This work has the following advantages. First, it treats each case as a totality. Second, it attempts to extract the multiple meanings that are given in the interview narratives. Third, it involves a careful working back and forth between cases as general theory is built. It has the following disadvantages. First, it assumes a linear, developmental model of life experiences — that is, that event A causes experience B, and so on. Lives are not lived or experienced in a linear manner. Second, it assumes that the meaning of interview narratives can be extracted by skilled analysts. In fact, analysts create the meanings that they impute to the texts that they interpret. Third, the preoccupation with theory places the researcher's interpretations over those of the subject. There will always be a tension on this point — that is, whose interpretation to favor, the subject's or the researcher's? The search for theory belies a commitment to an objective view of life histories and life stories that is not completely warranted by the method. Fourth, in writing interpretations, "objective" researchers too often resort to a style of writing that objectifies the subject's life and thereby diminishes the subjective meanings in that life. Fifth, a concern for "data" analysis, often couched in questions that involve reliability, validity, representativeness, and generalizability, belies a "positivistic" bias of the objective approach. It is questionable whether human experiences as given in biographical documents can or should be reduced to "data." Too often objective researchers tape and video record the words and actions of their subjects, and these documents are then treated as if they are (or were) "the actual remains of something that once appeared in the actual world" (Goffman, 1974, p. 69). In fact, these recordings of accounts and documentations of past actions are not the original actions themselves. These documentary bits of material inhibit the original meaning of the behavior or experience in question. Interviews turned into "narrative texts" and read as documentary evidence of past experiences objectify the past in ways that are not warranted.

Interpretive formats   There are several interpretive approaches to biographical analysis. These include Sartre's progressive-regressive method, Thompson's (1978) oral history approach, my own critical, hermeneutic approach (Denzin, 1984b), and, with modifications, Dolby-Stahl's (1985) literary folkloristic methodology for the study of meaning in personal narrative. I will briefly discuss each of these strategies.

Sartre   Sartre's method (1963) begins with *the* pivotal event in a subject's life and then works forward and backward from the event. This event or problem is defined as the subject. In my AA study, it was the person's public admission of alcoholism to an AA group. I then worked forward in the person's life experiences as he or she began to attend AA meetings and talk more and more about past life experiences. I worked backward, identifying how the person came to AA in the first place. Sartre's method (and mine) involves a sympathetic identification with the subject. The researcher must live his way into and through the life of the subject. This allows the researcher to come back on the subject's experiences from the double vantage point of having been where the subject has been while being able to see her experiences through her eyes. In this process, the researcher utilizes any and all materials (including letters, diaries, personal experience stories, oral histories) from the subject and his or her relevant others. The intent is to draw an interpretive circle around the subject's life and to grasp the meaning of that life as it has been lived by the subject (see Dilthey, 1900/1976, pp. 259–60). Abstract and particular theorizing about the life is not pursued as a goal.

Paul Thompson   The oral historian Thompson (1978) has distinguished three strategies for analyzing, presenting and interpreting life story and life history materials. (These were briefly discussed in Chapter 7 under the section "Writing and Reading Ethnography." The first strategy focuses on single life-story narratives along with oral history materials and personal experience narratives. Here the emphasis is on a single case. The second method involves the collection of several life stories grouped around common themes (for example, life stories of persons in the same occupation). The third strategy involves a cross-case analysis of oral and life story materials as theory is built. This is similar to the method used by Schutze and his colleagues. Thompson's method combines interviewing with conversations, as a life history and life story is pieced together.

Dolby-Stahl   Dolby-Stahl (1985) has developed a literary folkloristic methodology for the study of meaning in personal narrative. Although her work is designed to deal with the analysis of personal narrative stories, it can be fitted to the analysis and interpretation of personal documents. Her strategy involves the following steps: (1) locating the subject or case within a generic social category (female college student, unwed mother, recovering male alcoholic); (2) identifying the salient themes and experiences in the subject's life (seeking an abortion, going to an alcoholism treatment center, getting a college degree); (3) connecting the subject's life history and life story to larger social meanings, including communal and private folklore; (4) understanding that the subject's life story reflects a set of meaningful experiences which, when told, create an emotional bond between the teller and the listener; (5) realizing that the private, inner meanings of these experiences to the subject can never be fully revealed or illuminated; (6) interpreting the materials by sharing in the world of experiences of the subject. This involves (7) bringing the interpretive approaches of literary theory and criticism (reader-response theory, deconstructionism, semiotics, psychoanalysis, feminism) to bear upon the life story materials. This means (8) that the interpreter creates the document that is interpreted.

Dolby-Stahl (1985) argues that her methodology must meet 5 prerequisites: (1) the document analyzed must be a part of a life story or personal narrative; (2) the method must make the interpreter responsible for hearing and listening to the document in question (that is, others can't do the interpreter's work); (3) the interpreter must share the narrator's point of view; (4) the interpreter must be knowledgeable in the methods and theories of literary criticism; (5) the interpreter must be willing to take the responsibility for the interpretation that is formulated. Here Dolby-Stahl draws upon her own shared experiences in the culture with the subject. She analyzes, for example, a personal experience story told to her by her mother. Her interpretations are based on her shared biography with her mother.

While designed for the analysis of personal experience stories, this framework can be fitted to the reading and interpretation of self stories, life histories, oral histories, and life stories. It places the burden of interpretation on the researcher, not a research group. It locates interpretation in shared experience. It does not seek to build theory nor does it trouble itself with the validity or truthfulness of the account or story. It simply accepts the story (and its documentation) as material for interpretation.

The Natural History, Interpretive Approach
to Life Histories and Life Stories

A life is an unfolding production, marked by critical, turning point experiences. These experiences build on one another and become part of the person's biography. The natural history, interpretive approach to life histories seeks to combine each of the foregoing methods. It isolates critical experiences and locates them in the subject's social world. It isolates the critical others in the subject's life. It secures personal experience narratives from the subject and his or her significant others, using these stories to fill in the subject's life and bring the subject alive. This approach recreates the subject's life history and then illuminates that history with life stories and self stories. These narratives are fitted to the oral history of the subject. The subject then becomes a case study, whose personal history is compared with the histories of other subjects. This approach realizes that lived time is not linear; it is circular and interactional. The objective temporal division between past, present and future blurs in the telling of a life story, or personal experience narrative. Lives are lived in the present. This method aims to uncover how the subject lives time and its meanings in the present. Hence the natural history approach is relevant only at the beginning of the research. It allows the researcher to establish the guideposts, or key markers, in the life study.

Summary   There has obviously been considerable development in the use and analysis of life history, life story materials over the last decade. No single approach dominates. Since the hallmark of this method is its reliance on personal experience and its meanings, the interpretive approaches just outlined seem to carry the greatest promise for future work with this approach.

ANALYSIS OF LIFE HISTORIES

Thus far I have discussed the major forms of the life history and the various materials upon which it rests. Remaining to be treated are the forms of analysis employed in the method and categories of internal and external validity as they relate to life history analysis.

The Causality Problem

Analytic induction   In solving the problem of causality, I recommend that the sociologist employ analytic induction in analyzing life history materials. The thrust of analytic induction, as was noted in Chapter 7, is to formulate, through progressive revisions of the research hypothesis, a series of propositions that have universal application (see Manning, 1982). The life history method becomes the paradigmatic form of this analysis, for the investigator *assumes* that the case, or cases, which have been intensively analyzed portray the universe from which they were selected.

Idiographic and nomothetic analysis   Analytically (Allport, 1942, Chapter 4), the sociologist may choose to formulate either *idiographic* or *nomothetic* propositions and explanations. A researcher who chooses the latter will attempt to generalize the cases analyzed to the total population; one who chooses the former will relate the analysis only to the case under study.

Idiographic analysis is the intensive study of one case, with the attempt being to formulate lawful statements that pertain only to that case. The rationale for it rests in the assumption that because no two lives are the same, causal propositions will never be identical from case to case. Therefore, the laws of science must rest fundamentally on the idiographic mode of analysis.

Nomothetic analysts, on the other hand, claim that the only scientific laws are statistically derived from the analysis of a large number of cases; they disparage the case-study method. Lundberg, for example, calls the case document "a helpless tail to the statistical kite" (1926, p. 61). Lundberg's position is quite clear—the life history—case method (the idiographic method) is unscientific, impressionistic, and of use only in the exploratory phases of research. Allport (1942, p. 57) replies to this interpretation by offering the following rationale of the method:

> *What for the nomothetist is hard to contemplate is the very real possibility that no two lives are alike in their motivational processes.* To assume that causation is identical from case to case is to overlook the point that Lewin has emphasized, namely that *lawful determinism* need not be based upon the frequency of occurrence in multitudes of cases, but may apply to one-time happenings (to the single life). If each personality harbors laws peculiar to itself; if the course of causation is personal instead of universal, then only the intensive idiographic study of a case will discover such laws.

Unfortunately, this dialogue has ignored the fact that it is possible to discover propositions that pertain to a total population by the use of a single life history or a small set of life histories. This is the solution offered by analytic induction. Each case studied, and each event within each case, becomes a critical source of data that either validates or disconfirms a previous hypothesis.

Etic and emic investigations   The contrast between nomothetic and idiographic investigations may be further illuminated by a discussion of the *etic* and *emic* controversy in recent anthropological theory (see Ulin, 1984, pp. 91–125 for a discussion). *Etic* investigations are external, comparative, and cross-cultural, or cross-societal. The researcher does not explicitly seek to understand the meaning of cultural terms from "within" a culture. Distance from particular cultures is sought so that general patterns can be discovered. Cross-cultural universals are sought. *Emic* investigations are particularizing. They do not search for cross-cultural universals. They study cultural meanings from "inside." They are not generalizing, as etic studies are. Emic research uses thick descriptions, while etic investigations rest on thin descriptions and interpretations.

The progressive-regressive method of Sartre   Sartre (1963, pp. 85–166) proposed a method of inquiry that synthesizes the foregoing discussion. The progressive-regressive method of research seeks to situate and understand a particular subject or class of subjects within a given historical moment. rogressively, the method looks forward to the conclusion of a set of acts or ects undertaken by a subject (for example, becoming sober in AA). Regressively, the method looks backward to the conditions that shape the projects and actions of the subject (coming from an alcoholic family, for example). By moving forward and backward in time, the subject and his projects are located in time and space. The unique differences in the person's life are revealed, while the commonalities and similarities shared with others are illuminated. The method positions the subject within the social structure and the culture that impinges on his or her life. It shows how these structures both constrain and free the subject to act in one way but not in another. The progressive-regressive method is a critical, interpretive approach to biographical research. It draws upon the emic, idiographic, analytic induction strategies previously discussed.

Problems of Internal and External Validity

In the discussion of participant observation, the factors of internal and external validity were intensively treated. In many respects it is unnecessary to repeat that discussion, for nearly every statement concerning that method has direct relevance to the life history.

All persons, located as they are at various points in their own moral careers, construct a personally convenient and socially acceptable picture of their life up to and including the future. Goffman (1961a, pp. 150–51) has suggested:

> Given the stage any person has reached in a career, one typically finds that he constructs an image of his life course — past, present, and future — which selects, abstracts, and distorts in such a way as to provide him with a view of himself that he can usefully expound in current situations. Quite generally, the person's line concerning self defensively brings him into appropriate alignment with the basic values of his society, and so may be called an apologia. If a person can manage to present a view of his current situation which shows the operation of favorable personal qualities in the past and a favorable destiny awaiting him, it may be called a success story. If the facts of a person's past and present are extremely dismal, then about the best he can do is to show that he is not responsible for what has become of him, and the term sad tale is appropriate.

The sociologist must be aware that a subject is likely to present some variation on the success story in the life history. Under unusual conditions a subject may focus on a sad tale, but it is likely to cover only certain areas of his life. Quite obviously, an accurate life history lies somewhere between these two extremes. It is the function of the sociologist to bring the subject around to this middle ground — around to a picture of his life that includes more than only the good or only the bad.

Further Problems in the Analysis of Life Histories: Some Comments on the Historical Method

The sociologist compiling a life history is confronted with many of the same problems that historians resolve through the use of what is termed the *historical method* (see Gottschalk, Kluckhohn, and Angell, 1945). Examples of such problems include imputing a motive to the deceased author of a crucial document (for example, the suicide note); analyzing a document that appears inauthentic; establishing the fact that the author of a document is in fact the author; and discovering the meaning of a document after its authenticity has been established. These are issues that lie at the heart of any form of document analysis. Sociologists are aided by the fact that their subjects are typically "before" them and hence some of these problems can be overcome. But on many occasions the author or the sources of critical documents may not be present.

Any method that attempts to collect, record, and analyze documents from the past and to weave these documents into a meaningful set of explanations is historical. The reconstruction of the past from such data is termed *historiography* (Gottschalk, Kluckhohn, and Angell, 1945, pp. 8-9). Clearly, the sociologist compiling a life history engages in some form of historiography.

The sources of data employed by the historian parallel those of the sociologist (contemporary records, confidential reports, public reports, questionnaires, government documents, and expressions of opinion in editorials, essays, fiction, song, poetry, and folklore). The historian classifies these data as primary sources (those involving the testimony of an eyewitness) and secondary sources (those involving the testimony, or report of a person not present at the time of the events recorded) (see Gottschalk, Kluckhohn, and Angell, 1945, pp. 10-14). The historian classifies as a primary source any document directly related to the subject (for example, a letter written by the subject); the historian's secondary sources are those that refer not directly to the subject but to the class of persons the subject represents (for example, court records on juvenile delinquents). Accordingly, I term the historian's primary sources *firsthand* reports, and secondary sources *secondhand* reports. This permits me to classify primary sources by whether they are prepared by the subject or by some other person.

It is necessary to consider the delay between the occurrence of an event and the time at which it was reported. The majority of life history data will, of course, be primary and firsthand. When the reports of others are brought in, however, then their secondhand nature must be considered. Thus, while a document by a focal subject may be contradicted by another's statement, observers would be led to suspect that statement if it was secondhand, perhaps based on hearsay.

The problem is further complicated when we consider what literary critics and historians term the *reality-distance problem*. That is, the analyst is often several times removed from the problem under study. This may be stated in the following form: *reality* (subjectively perceived) leads to *subject's* interpretation, which is *translated* into a document (poem, letter, and so on) *perceived, interpreted, and analyzed by the investigator* (art critic, historian, sociologist). A chain of interpretations can thus be envisioned. Each person who reads the document brings to it her general bias and feelings, which may further distort its meaning. Analysts are thus brought back to the difficulty of communicating unambiguous meaning. It is impossible to escape Thomas's dictum regarding definitions of the situation—each person's statement initially has as much validity as any other person's. Furthermore, it must be recognized that no statement is ever interpreted exactly as it was intended by the speaker or author. All symbolic statements, Camus tells us, "always transcend the one who makes use of it [the author] and makes him say in reality more than he is aware of expressing" (1960, p. 92). Camus suggests, "In this regard, the surest means of getting hold of it [the work] is not to provoke it, to begin the work without a preconceived attitude and not to look for its hidden currents" (1960, p. 92). Even this cautioning principle is difficult to abide by: All observers approach their "realities" with preconceptions. The point, however, stands: When analyzing ambiguous documents, analysts must try to permit them to speak for themselves.

Still, there must be some general rules for judging the reliability and validity of a document. Following Gottschalk's discussion (Gottschalk, Kluckhohn, and Angell, 1945), I state the following. *First,* the closer a subject is to the event he reports, the greater the validity and reliability. *Second,* because documents differ in *purpose* (some being intended purely as records or aids to one's own memory, some as reports to other persons, some as apologia, some as propaganda, and so on), the more serious the author's intention to make a mere record, the more dependable the source" (Gottschalk, Kluckhohn, and Angell, 1945, p. 16).

This rule presupposes the fact that analysts can infer the reason behind a document's preparation—a point that will be considered shortly. The *third* principle is based on the number of persons for whom the document is intended. Because, as Gottschalk notes, the tendency to embellish and dramatize a document may increase as the number of persons it is intended for increases, the greater the confidential nature of the report, the greater its probable validity. *Fourth,* because the testimony of schooled or experienced observers is generally superior to that of the untrained and casual reporter, researchers must give greater validity to those reports prepared by the more expert observer. Essentially this rule suggests that analysts give greater credence to reports prepared by persons who are either closest to the event under study or trained at observation. Sociologists suspect the naive reports of a person who learns of an event at a distance. Similarly, the greater the familiarity of the author with the event, the greater the validity of her statements.

External criticism   Thus far I have assumed that the documents that come under analysis are authentic (that is, are what their author and their content claim them to be). It may often be the case that the authenticity of a document is doubtful, however. For example, observers may come upon forged or garbled documents and may be forced to accept the subject's claim for their meaning and authenticity. Establishing the fact that a document represents what it is claimed to represent is the goal of external criticism (Gottschalk, Kluckhohn, and Angell, 1945, p. 29).

To distinguish a hoax or a misrepresentation from a genuine document, first, the sociologist (or historian) establishes the date of the document (as nearly as possible) and then examines the materials to see whether or not they are anachronistic. (Anachronisms may appear as physical features of a document—in the material on which the document is written, for example, or in the medium in which it is written. A typewritten document that purports to date from a time before typewriters were common may be suspect. There may also be anachronisms in the content. A letter would be invalidated if, say, it described a labor strike that had not occurred at the time the letter was supposedly written.)

Second, making the best guess as to the author of a document, the sociologist tries to identify the handwriting. If observers have handwritten documents from their subjects, they can place these specimens against other letters or materials.

Third, the style of presentation will be examined. Peculiar phrases, spelling patterns, the use of proper names, and , most important, signatures can be analyzed and compared with authenticated documents.

Fourth, having authenticated a text as well as possible, the sociologist is then "faced with the task of determining its meaning" (Gottschalk, Kluckhohn, and Angell, 1945, p. 33).

To achieve all this, a sense of "historical-mindedness," or the ability to accurately take the role of acting others and view the world from their perspective, is necessary (Gottschalk, Kluckhohn, and Angell, 1945, p. 33). It is inappropriate to analyze documents out of context, or to analyze only portions of them; they must be situated and analyzed in their completeness (see Garfinkel, 1967). Failure to do so may lead to a misinterpretation of a document's meaning or intent.

The meaning of a document will never be completely established, because symbols are never interpreted exactly as they were communicated. Observers can only infer meaning, but the closer they are to the subject, the easier this becomes.

Internal criticism   Having established an authentic text and discovered as completely as possible what the author intended, the sociologist or historian has "established what the [witness's] testimony is" (Gottschalk, Kluckhohn, and Angell, 1945, p. 34). It remains to be determined whether that testimony is credible and, if so, in what parts — the job of internal criticism. In asking, "Is this document credible?" sociologists are not really concerned with whether or not what it describes is what actually happened. Rather, they ask, "Is this as close to what actually happened as we can learn from a critical examination of the best available sources. The historian thus establishes credibility or verisimilitude ... rather than truth" (Gottschalk, Kluckhohn, and Angell, 1945, p. 35).

Sociologists recognize, then, that a completely accurate rendering of the event under analysis will seldom be achieved; instead, they strive for approximation and valid inference.

Interrogative Hypotheses   In approaching a document, the analyst begins with a series of questions that may be noncommittal, such as, "Did this subject really attempt suicide?" or "What were the details of the subject's life before the suicide attempt?" Or the analyst may have full-fledged hypotheses, "though only implicit and in interrogative from" (Gottschalk, Kluckhohn, and Angell, 1945, p. 35). Putting the prediction in the interrogative form makes it easier for researchers to progressively modify and reformulate their hypotheses as they become more familiar with the data.

Criteria for Evidence   To admit any piece of evidence as pertinent to the interrogative hypothesis, the historian demands that it pass the following four tests (Gottschalk, Kluckhohn, and Angell, 1945, p. 38):

1. Was the ultimate source of detail (the primary witness) *able* to tell the truth?
2. Was the primary witness *willing* to tell the truth?
3. Is the primary witness *accurately reported* with regard to the detail under examination?
4. Is there any *external corroboration* of the detail under examination?

Any detail that passes these tests is good historical and sociological evidence.

ORGANIZATION AND SYNTHESIS OF LIFE HISTORY MATERIALS

The organizational and synthetic steps of preparing a life history report are briefly as follows:

> *Step 1:* Select a series of research hypotheses and problems to be answered or explored in the life history. Formulate tentative operationalizations of key concepts.
>
> *Step 2:* Select the subject or subjects and determine the form the life history is to take.
>
> *Step 3:* Record the objective events and experiences in the subject's life that pertain to your problem. These events should be triangulated by source and perspective so that contradictions, irregularities, and discontinuities can be established.
>
> *Step 4:* Obtain the subject's interpretations of these events as they occurred in their chronological, or natural, order.
>
> *Step 5:* Analyze all reports and statements collected thus far in terms of internal validity, internal criticism, external validity, and external criticism.
>
> *Step 6:* Resolve the validity of the foregoing sources, and establish the priority of sources for subsequent tests of hypotheses.
>
> *Step 7:* Begin testing hypotheses that have emerged to this point, search for negative evidence, and continue to modify, generate, and test these hypotheses.
>
> *Step 8:* Organize an initial draft of the entire life history and submit this to the focal subjects for their reactions.
>
> *Step 9:* Rework the report in its natural sequence in light of the elicited reactions. Present the hypotheses and propositions that have been supported. Conclude with the relevance of the report for theory and subsequent research.

Rather than viewing these as inflexible steps, we should see them as relevant criteria against which any life history may be assessed. There is a built-in bias here: Theory is assumed to be the major guiding force in the organization of the materials. In this respect I disagree with those who feel that life histories cannot be employed to generate and validate theory (see Blumer, 1939; Elkin, 1947, pp. 99–111).

EVALUATING LIFE HISTORY, LIFE STORY MATERIALS

The foregoing discussion has enumerated a number of points of evaluation of life history and life story materials. It is clear that this approach is receiving considerable attention in the contemporary literature. It is appropriate to review once more the criticisms that have been lodged against the method. It has been called unscientific, novelistic, unreliable, journalistic, and of use only for exploratory purposes. Some charge that it is costly and too time consuming.

Blumer's Critique of Personal Documents

Herbert Blumer (1939, 1979) argued, in his famous critique of *The Polish Peasant in Europe and America,* that the personal documents used by Thomas and Znaniecki suffered from the following problems. First, the authors did not base their theoretical scheme on the personal documents they collected. Second, the documents did not offer decisive tests of the theory. Third, the documents did not offer an adequate basis for generalization. Fourth, the documents did not pass the tests of validity, representativeness, adequacy, and reliability (Blumer, 1979, p. xii). Fifth, the authors did not offer an adequate scheme for fitting subjective data into a generalizable theory.

Elsewhere (Denzin, 1986f), I have argued that these criticisms are not appropriate. They attempt to evaluate the personal document from a "scientific" perspective that is antithetical to the method itself. The more correct approach is to read and evaluate life documents in terms of their ability to shed light on lived, human experience. As long as sociologists bring the evaluative criteria of "positivism" to bear on these materials, they will be seen as existing on the margins of sociological inquiry. It is time, then, to dispense with these outmoded readings of life documents.

FUNCTIONS OF THE LIFE HISTORY FOR SOCIOLOGY

Exposure to Other Viewpoints

Given the stereotypes commonly ascribed to the method, what are its most appropriate uses for the contemporary sociologist? Shibutani (1961, p. 4) aptly states one:

> Whatever else social psychologists must know, it appears obvious that the effective study of human behavior requires some familiarity with the intimate details of the lives of a variety of people. But many students have been so well protected that they know little of what goes on outside of middle-class communities. One economical way of overcoming this handicap is the extensive reading of first-person documents—autobiographies, letters, diaries and the clinical reports of psychiatrists.

The relevance extends beyond sheer exposure to other points of view, however.

Interpretation of Social Acts from the Perspective of the Actors

If sociologists take Mead's social behaviorism seriously, they are obligated to formulate methodologies that begin with overt, observable human interactions, and to interpret these acts in terms of the meanings and definitions attached to them. Mead (1934, pp. 7–8) states:

> Social psychology is behavioristic in the sense of starting with an observable activity—the dynamic, ongoing social process, and the social acts which are its component elements—to be studied and analyzed scientifically. But it is not behavioristic in the sense of ignoring the inner experience of the individual—the inner phase of the process or activity. On the contrary, it is particularly concerned with the rise of such experience within the process as a whole. It simply works from the outside to the inside instead of from the inside to the outside, so to speak, in its endeavor to determine how such experience does arise within the process.

This ability to interpret ongoing social acts from the perspective of the persons involved has been one criterion I have brought to bear against all methodologies. The life history becomes an excellent method in this light because it rests on the assumption that records of human subjective experiences form the core data of sociology. Sociologists should, then, view life histories as points against which data from interviews, questionnaires, and observations would be assessed. If analysts can obtain meaningful statements of the "subjective" life from an interview that cannot be excelled by a life history document, then they have a triangulated piece of data. But if they find that the interview is lacking in this regard, then they must turn to a form of the personal document as supplementary data.

Evaluation of Theories, Hypotheses, and Propositions

Becker (in Shaw, 1966, pp. x–xviii) has extended the functions of the method beyond this. He suggests it may serve as a "touchstone" by which theories, hypotheses, and propositions may be evaluated. (When Lemert applied Sutherland's theory of professional crime to the systematic check forger, he uncovered a negative case that led to a revision of Sutherland's original formulations.) The life history can function, then, as a negative case against which existing theories may be assessed.

Subjective Provision of Data on Institutional Experiences

Becker also notes that life histories can be useful in providing data on the subjective side of routine institutional experiences and processes. Although criminologists have elaborate theories concerning the effects of prisons on convicts, they frequently lack data concerning the subjective side of such experiences. By explicitly focusing on the subjective, the life history can extend their theories further into this realm of organizational experience.

New Exploration of Apparently Resolved Issues

Becker suggests that the life history method may open avenues of inquiry into areas that appear resolved. Thus while small-group research appears to have run its course in such areas as leadership and group process, a set of life histories on the actual experience of group leaders might well expand existing theories and raise problems that heretofore have appeared to be resolved.

Establishing of Links between Subjective and Objective Data

Finally, Becker states that the method has the potential of providing the data observers are presently unable to obtain from the more behavioristic experiments and retrospective surveys. That is, if analysts assume that a full-blown naturalistic methodology must link overt interactions with subjective experience, then they can employ life histories to establish the links other methods are incapable of providing.

Analysis of Social-Psychological Processes

To the functions just listed I add three more. First, the life history may be the best available technique for studying such important social psychological processes as adult socialization, the emergence of group and organizational structure, the rise and decline of social relationships, and the situational response of the self to daily interactional contingencies. It is easy to conceive of life histories carried out on entire organizations, social groups, or even communities. Indeed, this is one strategy employed by the cultural and social anthropologist in writing the history of a community. Key community leaders can be interviewed, their trajectories of public experience can be noted, and the objective career points in the community's history can be described by persons in varying social positions.

"Sensitizing Concepts"

Second, on a more methodological level, life histories represent a major approach to the "sensitizing concept" strategy of theory development and verification. Beginning with vague, yet generic concepts, sociologists can derive operationalizations from the subject's point of view — thus allowing the subject's meanings to be attached to a conceptual framework. In addition, because the life history requires demographic reports, data from interviews, analysis of documents, and participant observation, it permits the merger of several discrete methodologies into a single strategy.

Relationship to Symbolic Interactionism

Third, a theme running through this discussion has been the close relationship between the life history and symbolic interactionism. I have argued that a theory that stresses the "subjective" side of social experience demands a methodology that explicitly focuses on such data. Herein lies the tremendous value of the life history: It permits sociologists to balance the "objectivism" of the experiment, the survey, and participant observation with the internal, covert, and reflective elements of social behavior and experience.

SUGGESTED READINGS

BERTAUX, DANIEL (ed.), *Biography and Society: The Life History Approach in the Social Sciences.* (Beverly Hills: Sage, 1981). Contains a number of seminal papers on the life history approach as it is currently being used in Europe and the United States.

BLUMER, HERBERT, *Critiques of Research in the Social Sciences: An Appraisal of Thomas and Znaniecki's The Polish Peasant in Europe and America.* (New Brunswick, N.J.: Transaction Books, 1979). This is the classic evaluation of personal documents in sociology. In his new introduction, Blumer modifies somewhat his earlier, harsh interpretation of Thomas and Znaniecki's work.

PLUMMER, KEN, *Documents of Life: An Introduction to the Problems and Literature of a Humanistic Method.* (London: George Allen & Unwin, 1983). An outstanding analysis of this method, with a comprehensive bibliography.

9

Film, Photography, and Sociology

I was taught that one picture was worth a thousand words, weren't you? [Friedlander, 1972, p. 10, quoted by Becker, 1986, p. 242]

An anthropo-sociology of everyday life is inconceivable without an anthropo-sociology of the cinema . . . An anthropology of the cinema is inconceivable without an anthropo-sociology of everyday life. [Morin, 1984, p. 39]

Photography and sociology have approximately the same birth date . . . 1839 . . . From the beginning, both worked on a variety of projects. Among these, for both, was the exploration of society.[Becker, 1986, p. 223]

Every culture creates its own perceptual worlds . . . This means that *every culture must be seen in its own terms* . . . As the Colliers state, "Through photography it is possible to see through native eyes. Verbally we can interview natives and share the realism of their visual context." [Hall, 1986, p. xvii]

In this chapter I explore the use of film and photography by sociologists. A visual sociology — or a sociology that relies upon photography, audio-video film records, and the analysis of film — has recently come into existence. The methods of visual sociology include still photography, audio-visual recordings, documentary films, and Hollywood-made movies. Visual sociology can be defined as that method of research which deals with two problems: "how to get information *on* film and how to get information *off* film" (Hall, 1986, p. xiii). It struggles with the problem of how observers see and record what they perceive. What is perceived and then recorded with the camera is structured by cultural and contextual meanings (Hall, 1986, pp. xvi–xvii). The information that is read off film is also shaped by cultural and contextual processes. Accordingly, as a method of research, visual sociology deals simultaneously with the grammars of vision, perception, and interpretation.

There is a double need for analyzing film and photography. First, everyday life is structured and given meaning by visual records, including film photographs, and advertisements. How these representations structure reality demands analysis. Second, visual representations are interactional productions. "Pictures do not simply make assertions . . . rather we interact with them in order to arrive at conclusions" (Becker, 1986, p. 279). Visual representations of society are both methods of research and resources, or topics to be studied in their own right. These two assertions organize my discussion in this chapter. I will keep asking, "How do these methods represent society?" and "How may sociologists use them?"

I will examine the following topics. First, a brief review of the use of film in the social sciences will be offered. Second, the essential features of the method will be presented. Third, the problems of causal inference, validity, and interpretation will be addressed. Fourth, I will discuss how film and photography, as research tools, can be used to explore and examine society. Fifth, I will treat the problem of how films and photographs are to be read. I conclude with the principles of visual research.

PRIOR USES OF FILM

The use of film and photography has a long history in the human disciplines. Educational films have been used for instructional purposes in United States grade schools since 1918, in high schools since the 1930s, and in college since the 1960s (Worth, 1981, p. 111). Anthropologists have been producing films and experimenting with photography at least since the 1940s, when Bateson and Mead (1942) produced their famous photographic study of Balinese character. In the 1930s, Arnold Gesell, the child psychologist and psychiatrist, pioneered in the production of photographic records of the development of young children. In 1976, Richard Sorenson, the founding anthropologist of the National Field Research Archives, published, in the tradition of Bateson and Mead, *On the Edge of the Forest,* a "photographically researched text of child development in New Guinea" (Collier and Collier, 1986, p. 12). In 1975, the journal *Studies in Visual Communication* was founded.

Birdwhistle (1970) has used photography and film for over 3 decades to study culturally patterned forms of posture and gesture, which he calls "kinesics." Hall (1959, 1966) has employed ethnographically gathered photographs and films in the study of nonverbal communication. Anthropologists Worth and Adair (1972) used 16-millimeter film as a means of obtaining an insider view of how the Navajo's structured their visual world. Collier and Collier (1986) report on a professional lifetime of experience with film and the methods of visual anthropology.

Sociologists have recently entered the field of film and photography. Becker's essays on photography and sociology (1981; 1986) and Goffman's (1976) study of gender advertisements are important examples. In 1982, *Video Sociology Quarterly* was founded. At the University of Minnesota,

Stephen Spitzer has created a number of commercially available films on "visual sociology." Couch's work with students in the "New Iowa" School (Couch, 1984; Couch, Saxton, and Katovich, 1986) has employed video film records of interactions in small-group laboratories since the early 1970s. McPhail and his students (see McPhail and Wohlstein, 1986, for a review) have been using wide-angle and telephoto cameras since the early 1970s to record collective behavior and collective locomotion in public settings.

Photography, film, and sociology complement one another, for each seeks to explore and make statements about society. Indeed, in the first 15 years of its existence, "the *American Journal of Sociology* routinely ran photographs in connection with its publication of muckraking reformist articles" (Becker, 1986, p. 225). As sociology became more scientific in the decades after World War I, however, it became less interested in photography and film. At the same time, photography moved in artistic and political directions and, until recently, carried out few direct sociological explorations of society (Becker, 1986, p. 229). Morin (1984) has recently argued, as the quotation at the beginning of this chapter indicates, that a sociology of everyday life requires a sociology of film. Morin goes further: He also argues that an understanding of film demands a sociology of everyday life. Morin's demands are beyond the scope of this chapter (see Denzin, 1988).

ESSENTIAL FEATURES OF THE METHOD

The methods of visual sociology rest on the principles of triangulation. They combine the production of a visual record of an event with an accompanying text, which may include (1) audio-voice recordings, (2) transcriptions of the audio-visual text, (3) interviews using what Collier and Collier (1986) call the "photo elicitation technique," with the persons photographed or filmed, (4) historical information on the site, event, or persons photographed, and (5) a title or interpretive framework that surrounds the photographic or filmed text. Before discussing the assumptions of visual sociology, a number of distinctions must be made.

Clarifying Terms

Three different forms or types of film and photographic activity must be distinguished. Amateur, or lay, film and photographic conduct is the kind of representational work ordinary people who have cameras do. Family photo albums are an example. Professional filmwork includes the representations made by professional filmmakers and photographers. These professional may work in academia or for Hollywood, television, or news magazines. I divide them into four categories: artists, Hollywood professionals who work in film, those who work for television, and photojournalists who work for national magazines. This third category can be subdivided into content areas: fashion, news, commercial art, and so on. Ethnographic and sometimes experimental filmwork references the film and video records made by ethnologists, sociologists, anthropologists, psychologists, historians, and other social scientists. When discussing how sociologists may use film, I will draw my examples primarily from the latter two categories of filmmakers, although any photographic record, whether amateur or professional, can be of sociological use.

Assumptions of the Method

Theory   A central assumption of the visual method is that what can be seen can be recorded, but not everything that can be seen is worth recording. Hence all photographic records are theoretically informed. They carry theoretical, emotional, biographical, historical, or scientific meaning for the observer, and sometimes for those recorded.

Heider (1983, pp. 5–8) has distinguished two approaches to theory and to what is filmed. *Descriptive realism* reflects those films or photographic records in which events are assumed to speak for themselves. *Interpretive realism* describes those records in which theory guides what is filmed, including the organization of shots and the location of the camera.

Prior to Heider's formulations, Mead and Bateson (1978) debated these two positions. Mead argued that the only safe way for anthropologists to take pictures was to put the camera on a tripod and not touch it. She felt that if the anthropologist touched the camera, personal bias would enter into the research process. Bateson contended that it was necessary to move the camera to photograph what was of theoretical interest.

Of course, events don't speak for themselves, they must be interpreted. One's choice for location of the camera represents bias and choice (Becker, 1986, p. 299). All ethnographic film is, in this sense, oriented by theory, and hence should be termed *interpretive realism*. Heider's first term is of little use, for no film or photograph is purely descriptive.

The mirror with a memory   A second assumption holds that the camera doesn't forget, get tired, or make mistakes. The last photograph in a series is as good as the first. The phrase "mirror with a memory" is Collier and Collier's (1986, p. 7). They suggest (1986, p. 7) that "the camera's machinery allows us to see without fatigue." This assumption argues that the camera allows the researcher to produce reliable, shareable observations (Couch, 1987a, Chapter 1). Of course, the camera is not really a mirror; it does not just copy what is photographed. It transforms three-dimensional phenomena to a flat plane, "severing their ties with the surroundings" (Kracauer, 1960, p. 15). But like a mirror, the camera reflects what the photographer wants to see.

Pictures tell the truth   Becker (1986, p. 250) remarks the following:

> a photograph or group of them purports to be "true." . . . Photographs minimally claim to be true in that what they show actually existed in front of the camera for at least the time necessary to make the exposure.

Photographs in the social documentary style claim that they accurately capture events that routinely occur. This is the third assumption: Film is truthful and captures the essence of the phenomenon in question. There are problems with this argument, as I will soon show (see Becker, 1986, pp. 250–52, 273–301). The "myth of total cinema" (Bazin, 1971, pp.

17–22)—the belief that film can offer a "total and complete representation of reality . . . a recreation of the world in its own image . . . unburdened by the freedom of interpretation of the artist or the irreversibility of time"—is closely related to the assumption that photographs tell the truth. Of course, the world cannot be recreated in its own image. The photographer's interpretations structure what is seen.

Entering the subject's symbolic world   A fourth assumption involves the visual sociologist directly and indirectly participating in the symbolic and visual world of the subject. The camera sees what the subject can see, although what the camera sees may not be of symbolic importance to the native. By photographing and filming the subject's world, the observer symbolically and representationally enters that world.

Taking the subject's point of view   A fifth assumption of the visual method is that there is a continual effort to take the subject's point of view: to see and record the world as the subject sees it. Worth and Adair (1972), for example, gave Navajos cameras and told them to record what they saw. In this way they produced an insider version of the native's world.

The decisive moment   Cartier-Bresson (1952; Becker, 1986, p. 237) coined the phrase "the decisive moment." It refers to that instant when everything falls into place in the viewfinder (or in the film). In this moment the right way to tell the story, to capture the truth or the essence of the phenomenon is discovered (Becker, 1986, p. 237). This is the sixth assumption: The decisive moment will occur and the researcher will be able to capture it on film.

Creating an observing identity   Seventh, the visual sociologist must, like the ethnographer and participant observer, create an observing, photographing, filming identity in the field setting. Not all groups include within their identity structures an identity called photographer or filmmaker. AA, for example, has no place for photographers in their meetings. United States college and professional football teams have official photographers, for the identity is not problematic in these groups. The camera is not a foreign object in many segments of American culture, especially in urban places. Picture-taking has become a taken-for-granted practice in many public and semi-public locales.

Types of Observer Identities

Four observer identities may be created: the complete participant, the participant as observer, the observer as participant, and the complete observer.

Complete participant   In this identity the observer passes as a member of the group who happens to have a camera and likes to take pictures. His or her identity as a social scientist is not made known to the group members. This identity raises ethical problems, for persons have a right to refuse to have their picture taken or published.

Participant as observer   The photographer as observer makes known her presence as an investigator and attempts to form a series of relationships with those studied. Informants are sought out, and permission to take pictures or to film is requested. The observer may have to agree to refrain from photographing faces or particular activities. The photographer in the participant-as-observer identity will pass through the honeymoon, crisis, recovery, and adjustment stages of experience. These stages are the same as those through which the ethnographer passes.

Observer as participant   In this identity there is no attempt to create a relationship with the photographed subject. The contact is brief and highly formalized. A sports fan at a football game who takes pictures of players and spectators acts out this identity.

Complete observer   The news photographer who takes pictures at the site of a fire or automobile accident acts as a complete observer, as does a social psychologist who sets up recording equipment in a laboratory and films subjects in experiments. The researcher-observer is completely removed from interaction. The camera does all the observing work.

PROBLEMS OF CAUSAL INFERENCE, VALIDITY, AND INTERPRETATION

Pictures and films tell stories. These stories presume causality. They assume that some set of past events cause or are related to events, happenings, and experiences in the present. These texts or documents also assume that an invariant ordering of events has been, or can be, established. These events, as they have been recorded, exclude or rule out the effects of other events or processes. In short, photographs and films make causal claims. How do they do this?

Causal Assumptions

Visual sociology rests on the biographical, case study method. It assumes that the subject of a photograph or film record represents a universal instance of the phenomenon in question. Thus a photograph, or series of photographs, of the face, poses, and experiences of a famous person (for example, the president of the United States and family) is presumed to tell all there is to tell about this person. His essence has been captured. These pictures universalize the subject and make claims to telling all that is worth telling about him. Since only cases can be filmed, the logic of case study analysis underlies and structures the visual method.

Analytic Induction

In Chapters 7 and 8, I discussed the logic of analysis contained in analytic induction. Analytic induction organizes the visual method in the following ways:

1. The observer creates and formulates a rough definition of the phenomenon in question. This involves taking pictures, whether it be of a tribal ritual, medics at work, drug users taking drugs, or children playing.
2. The observer formulates a working interpretation of the phenomenon and decides when the "decisive moments" that reflect what is to be captured and interpreted occur.
3. One case, or set of photographs, is examined in light of this interpretation. A series of "decisive moment" photos is taken. Either the interpretation fits the case or it is reformulated.
4. More cases are examined to see if they fit the interpretation. If they do not fit, the interpretation is modified. A progressive refinement of photo-images occurs as the researcher seeks those images that best depict the phenomenon in question.
5. This process of refining interpretations continues until all the cases, or photos, have been explained. The researcher then makes a claim for having produced a universal causal analysis of the phenomenon in question.
6. A set of "decisive" photographs or filmed sequences are then presented as documentations of the interpretation that is offered.

PROBLEMS OF VALIDITY AND INTERPRETATION

A viable interpretation based on visual materials must be tested against rival explanations. Two generic classes of rival hypotheses, or explanatory structures, repeatedly treated in this book have been factors deriving from internal validity and those deriving from external validity. These factors, to repeat, deal with the populations or settings to which observations can be generalized (external validity) and the effects of observations on the findings (internal validity). To summarize these earlier discussions, challenges to the validity and interpretation of visually produced documents may arise from the following sources (see Webb, 1966, p. 36; Webb et al., 1981, pp. 49–77):

1. Reactive Measurement Effects

Awareness of being observed
Role playing, staged performances
Disruptions of natural sequences of action

2. Effects of Investigator

Observer–observed interactions
Change in observer
Intentions, preconceptions, and theory

3. Sampling Errors

Population idiosyncracies
Population instability over time
Population instability over areas

Access to Content

>Restrictions to content or settings
>Stability of content over time
>Stability of content over areas

Truth Claims and Authenticity of Documents

>X is true about something; X is all that is true (Becker, 1986, p. 252)
>Fakes
>Artistic productions
>Censorship
>Thick and thin documents
>Actors
>Transcriptions and interpretations

These five categories of invalidity are some of the major sources of error treated in earlier discussions of internal and external validity. I have fitted them to the special problems that arise when visual documents are produced. A brief discussion of each is required.

Reactive Measurement Effects

The awareness that one is being observed or photographed may alter mood, intention, and performance (see Smith, McPhail, and Pickens, 1975). The person "plays" to the camera. Becker (1986, pp. 255, 258) has argued that when people are engaged in serious activity, they often will not change their behavior because of the observer's or camera's presence. He reports an incident in which a photographer was taking pictures of a woman fighting with her child in a playground. The photographer stationed himself very close to her, but she continued arguing with her screaming child. Reactivity is a function, in part, of how involved people are in their on-going activities. When they can be free to be self-conscious, they can role-play, or stage performances. In these instances, the authenticity of a photograph—that is, the degree to which it reflects what is "really" going on, is challenged. McPhail and his students have found, however, that the reactive effects of the camera are no greater than those that can be attributed to paper-and-pencil modes of observation in a natural setting.

Photographers often find it necessary to disrupt a natural sequence of action in order to take pictures. Some do this in order to reveal how the disruptions bring to the surface what persons take for granted. Photographs or films made in these circumstances become documents that explicitly study reactivity and the taken-for-granted structures of situations (see Becker, 1986, p. 258).

Effects of the Investigator

Observer effects are covered, in part, under the discussion of reactivity. Interactions between the observer and the observed can alter a photographic text. The observer may call forth in the subject reactions that would not have occurred naturally.

Changes in the observer over time can alter the validity claims of a visual document. Couch (1987a, p. xiv) notes that a great deal of time was wasted in the first few years of his making audio-visual tapes in the laboratory. He didn't know what he was looking for, or how to tape it. Later, as his ideas took shape, he learned how to design and set up laboratory interactions that met his theoretical needs. He also learned how to record and transcribe the tapes that were made.

As the observer's intentions and preconceptions change, his or her theory also changes. This means that items photographed at one stage of a study might not be photographed at a later stage. Theory shapes what is recorded. An object, if photographed from a different angle, becomes a different object. In addition, as the researcher becomes committed to an interpretive position, she may slant the photographic record so that a particular story is told. Thus, a selective bias enters the research process.

Sampling Errors

Sampling errors, which include temporal, situational, and population instabilities or idiosyncracies can also challenge a visual document's claim to validity. Researchers may present a set of photo-essays that they claim makes statements about a particular process, setting, or population, but because of sampling errors, their claims are challenged. The time period that is studied may be unique and nongeneralizable. For example, pictures taken of a small community after a disaster has occurred may present a story of community solidarity and unity that is not ordinarily present.

In a similar fashion, the situations that are photographed may be nongeneralizable or unstable. Pictures taken of American families in public shopping malls do not tell the full story of American family life. To argue that they do is to overextend the claims the photograph can make about the phenomenon in question. (Further discussion of this subject follows.)

Population instabilities can also create problems. Returning to the example of the pictures taken of a community after a disaster, the persons who are photographed may not be representative of the general community; they are likely to be persons present when the disaster occurred. Thus, social structural factors determine who is present in a given situation at any moment in time. To make generalizations without this knowledge is to risk building a biased picture of the processes and events under study.

Access to Content

The observer may confront restrictions concerning access to particular interactional processes; these restrictions may bear on content, settings, and time. Official White House photographers, for example, can seldom take pictures of the president's family during family fights; this is a restriction of content. Interactions in bathrooms and bedrooms are also typically not allowed; these are situational restrictions, which intersect with temporal restrictions. Thus the American public sees only particular pictures of the first family. Any generalizations about first family life are restricted by these factors.

Truth Claims and Document Authenticity

Becker (1986, p. 252) has argued that a photograph—and, I would add, a visual document—can make two different types of truth claims about the phenomenon depicted. It can argue that X is true about something, or that X is all that is true about something. Obviously, a visual document can say many different things at the same time. No single truth statement or assertion need be the whole truth about the phenomenon in question. The researcher must specify the range of the truth claim. If this isn't done, critics can claim exceptions. For example, photos that show the White House family smiling and happy can be countered by the claim that they can't be happy all the time. The 1987 made-for-television movie *The Betty Ford Story* made this point.

Seldom can a truth claim be verified by a single visual document (Becker, 1986, p. 280). Furthermore, what is true from one point of view is false from another standpoint. This means that every visual document is simultaneously both true and false. It is true because what was recorded did in fact exist. It is false because it cannot be the whole truth about what was recorded (Becker, 1986, p. 275). The meanings of a visual document lie in the interpretations brought to it. Triangulated evidence must be used in order to strengthen the authenticity of the document and its claims. Truth, as Becker (1986, pp. 280–81) notes, is always partial, incomplete, and based on a group or viewer's perspective.

Two Additional Types of Truth Claims

Subjective and objective truth claims need to be distinguished from the two claims just discussed (that is, "X says all there is to say about something" and "X says something about something"). Subjective truth claims speak to the personal meaning the photo-image or visual document has to the photographer and the viewer. Objective truth claims refer to the belief that the visual document in fact accurately depicts a segment of reality (in other words, something that actually happened). Photographers and visual researchers often confuse these two types of truth statements, leading them to take photographs that are subjectively meaningful, and perhaps aesthetically pleasing and artistic, but objectively incorrect (see Becker, 1986, p. 251).

Threats to Validity and Authenticity

There are a variety of challenges to the truth claim of a visual document. Several of them have just been reviewed (reactive effects of observation and of the observer, sampling errors, and restrictions in access to content, settings, and time). At least three other threats to validity can be raised.

Fakes   Photographers can fake pictures. They can retouch them and can move objects around to make a good picture, thereby altering the natural relationship between the objects. They can dress subjects in ways that fit popular understandings of them. For example, photographers of the old West dressed Indians in ways that Indians did not ordinarily dress; these photos took on a reality that viewers regarded as real. Photographers can fake authenticity (Becker, 1986, p. 291). For example, they can place heavy black lines around the edges of a negative, suggesting that the negative has not been cropped (Becker, 1986, p. 291).

Artistic style   Photographers and visual researchers may alter their pictures to fit current artistic fashion (Becker, 1986, p. 285). This desire to create art may lead to the suppression or alteration of facts and details. It may lead to pictures of only "interesting" things. As a result, the more mundane, taken-for-granted features of the subject's world are ignored. The result, as just noted, may be an aesthetically pleasing artistic image that is objectively and factually incorrect. The researcher's "artistic" intentions should be stated so that the viewer knows what interpretation to bring to the visual document.

Censorship   Becker (1986, p. 288) notes that some form of censorship may prevent certain pictures from being taken. Censorship can be imposed by the state, an official agency of the state, or a private group or organization. It can also be imposed by the photographer. Ideology structures the creation of visual documents. When censorship occurs, only officially sanctioned pictures of the phenomenon in question are produced. This leads to bias and to threat to validity.

Thick and thin documents   A *thick* visual document is visually and conceptually dense (see Becker, 1986, p. 243). It shows that a number of important things are going on in a situation. It also shows that these things have been documented in a variety of ways. Furthermore, a thick document reveals a conceptual grasp of the situation, the social relationships, and the social structure that organizes the images in question. *Thin* visual documents lack these features. They often rest on single images, and on underdeveloped theoretical schemes that inform the documenting process. Stereotyped pictures of Indians in the old West were thin visual documents. They presented a naive theory of Indian–white relations. They presented Indians in poses, representing an idealized picture of the American West. Thick visual documents have stronger claims to validity and authenticity and thus have greater value to social researchers.

Actors   Another threat to validity and authenticity arises when photographers or researchers use actors or instruct the people they are photographing about how they are to appear. The picture that depicts actors, instead of ordinary people acting, raises the same question as the "faked" image. That is, what is going on here is not real, it is staged. Hence the truth claim of the image or visual document is challenged. The question is, Do ordinary people act this way? If actors are used, the researcher must substantiate the claim that the actors are only doing what ordinary people do anyway.

Transcriptions and interpretations   A final threat to a document's validity claim lies in the problems associated with transcription and interpretation. When an audio-visual record is made, the researcher must make a transcription of the audio recording. This is not easy to do. Couch (1987a, Chapter 6) discusses the problem. Transcribers must be trained to take note of verbal as well as nonverbal actions that occur on the tape. The sequential ordering of acts must be carefully noted and recorded. Rapid interactions are often difficult to transcribe the first time through; hence multiple drafts of a transcription must be made. It is often hard to hear what was said. Phrases in an audio tape sometimes cannot be understood. Mumbles and grunts are common utterances. Mutual, simultaneous actions are difficult to record and capture. Transcribers may miss these actions.

A transcribed audio-video text is an interactional production. It is a document made from a document. It is a printed text that describes a visual and audio recording. Hence it suppresses the nuances of interaction, meaning, and mood that are present in the visual and audio text. It is one level removed from the actual experiences captured on the audio-visual tape.

Transcriptions are subject to the accounting problems that Garfinkel (1967, pp. 11–24) has located in research situations. Transcribers are under the demand to produce a warrantable, valid, and reliable transcription of an audio tape. In order to produce such a document, they engage in practices that involve deciphering utterances and placing them in orderly sequences. They are led to gloss over unclear statements, to make judgments about who spoke or acted first, and to perhaps indicate that utterances have ended even when relistenings indicate that they haven't. Perfect, error-free transcriptions of audio-visual tapes are virtually impossible to produce. This means that the interpretations of such documents are always open-ended and inconclusive.

Assessing Visual Documents

The interpretation of any visual document can be challenged by any of the foregoing dimensions. In general, more credibility is given to documents that take account of the reactive effects of observation, of the observer, of sampling, of access, and of truth claims restrictions. Another set of criteria also influence the validity judgments that are brought to bear on a visual document. These involve the evidence presented in the document. If the evidence is naturalistically generalizable (Stake, 1987)—that is, if it evokes images that the person has seen before—it is given more credibility. If the document has been made in a public place, then more credibility may be attributed to it, because any other observer could have made the document. Such documents can be independently checked. If the document has been made by a reputable observer and published in a reputable journal, then it is given more credibility (see Becker, 1986, p. 251, on these points).

Given the problems just mentioned, along with the limitations of the visual method and the documents it produces, I now turn to a more positive note and discuss how these methods and procedures can illuminate features of everyday social life.

EXPLORING SOCIETY WITH FILM AND PHOTOGRAPHY

Film, photography, and audio-visual tapes describe ways that people use to represent to others their knowledge, feelings, and insights about society and social experience (see Becker, 1986, p. 122). Each of these methods may be used to illuminate various facets of society. In this section I discuss how this is the case for photography, Hollywood film, ethnographic, experimental film, and audio-video tapes and recordings.

The Camera

Becker (1986, pp. 224–25) has suggested that photography can be used in the following ways to explore and examine society. First, it can offer a record of far-off societies and cultures. This is what Bateson and Mead did in their 1942 study of Bali. More recently, Bruner (1985) has used the ethnographic camera to record tourist–native interactions and experiences in Kenya, Africa. Second, the camera can be used to expose the "evils" and social problems in society — for example, urban slum life or poverty in rural America. Third, photographers produce pictures of newsworthy events for newspapers and magazines, and contribute to the understandings of these events. Fourth, cameras can record the life and life-style of the rich and famous in a society. Fifth, important social events, including wars, political speeches, and nuclear and natural disasters can be captured on film or in pictures, becoming part of the historical record of a society. Sixth, photographers can map the social and geographical terrain of a community, showing key interactional sites. Such work can reveal how a way of life is structured by its fixed places of interaction. Seventh, photographers can capture social relationships, including families, work groups, children at play, and physicians at work (see Becker, 1986, p. 287, for a photograph of emergency medical care in a rock concert setting). Eight, photographers can record the significant ritual events in a group, including birth, marriage, and death. These records historically document how a group aligns itself to the major turning-point experiences in the life cycle.

Hollywood Film

Films, in contrast to still photography, can better illuminate the processual, interactional features of a society or a culture. I will first discuss Hollywood films. These texts can be read as defining everyday cultural experiences in the following ways. First, they reflect and define problematic social experiences, including war, divorce, incest, alcoholism, drug abuse, political corruption, love, birth, and death. Think, for example, of a Hollywood family melodrama like *Terms of Endearment* (1983). This popular award-winning film dealt with adultery, love, marriage, birth, and death. It represented two American families going through crises, and showed how they resolved their problems.

Second, Hollywood films document key historical moments in the life of a society. *Grapes of Wrath* (1940) translated John Steinbeck's famous novel into a moving account of American Okies moving from the dust bowl to California during the depression of the 1930s. *Apocalypse Now* (1979) and *The Deer Hunter* (1978) forcefully brought before the viewing public the effects of the Viet Nam War on young American men. In these films, Hollywood recorded the effects of war on the family, on friendships, and on a foreign nation.

Third, film can expose problems in key social institutions. *Mass Appeal* (1984) dealt with alcoholism and homosexuality in the Catholic Church. Francis Ford Coppola's 1983 films *The Outsiders* and *Rumble Fish* turned S.E. Hinton's best-selling books into visual treatments of how the American high school and family system fail to deal with the pain of love, loss, and rebellion in adolescence.

Fourth, Hollywood films express and convey political ideology and core cultural values. *Terms of Endearment,* for example, is about the value of love in the American family. Frank Capra's social-message films of the 1930s and 1940s, including *Mr. Deeds Goes to Town* (1936), *Lost Horizon* (1937), *You Can't Take it with You* (1938), *Mr. Smith Goes to Washington* (1939), *Meet John Doe* (1941), and *It's a Wonderful Life* (1946), dealt with social myths. They recreated an imagined social past in the United States, with comfortable homes, close-knit families, friendly neighborhoods, prosperous communities, and bountiful farms located on the edges of a benign wilderness (Sklar, 1975, p. 210). The Walt Disney films have also kept fantasy and folklore before the viewing public with such characters as Mickey Mouse, Alice In Wonderland, Bambi, and Cinderella. The family western film, including *Stage Coach* (1939), *Duel in the Sun* (1947), *High Noon* (1952), *Shane* (1953), *Cat Ballou* (1965), *The Cowboys* (1972), and *Silverado* (1986) has served to keep alive a particular romantic, partriarchial version of the West, American Indians, women, men, honor, and heroism. These films, like Capra's, speak to core American values (see Wright, 1975). These films also reproduce the gender, race, ethnic, and class relationships in society. They inevitably place white males in positions of power, locate women in the family, and cast racial and ethnic minorities in servile positions or attach violent, antisocial attitudes and behaviors to them. In so doing, these films create representations that structure reality. They keep alive the myth of the autonomous individual in the modern mass society. They also create inaccurate pictures of American history.

Fifth, films illuminate the underside of everyday life, taking the viewer into scenes and social worlds that might otherwise not be visible. *Grapes of Wrath* recorded the American depression, which no person born after 1940 experienced. Unless one is a Catholic priest, the behind-the-scenes pictures of priesthood shown in *Mass Appeal* are unknown. War films show viewers the underside of armed combat. Alcoholism films, including *The Lost Weekend* (1945), *Come Fill the Cup* (1951), *Come Back, Little Sheba* (1952), *Days of Wine and Roses* (1962), and *The Morning After* (1986), take the viewer into the realities of alcoholism. These films show the terrors and destruction that alcoholism can bring to families and individuals. Unless the viewer is an alcoholic, comes from an alcoholic family, or knows an alcoholic, he or she may be unable to relate to these experiences.

Sixth, films create emotional experiences for viewers. Indeed the hallmark of the movie is to "fascinate the observer and draw him into the drama. . . . the forté of motion pictures is in their emotional effect" (Blumer, 1933, p. 198). Such being the case, films create viewer identifications with characters who embody the central cultural values of honor, individualism, will power, valor, and self-control. Few viewers, for example, can be unmoved by

George C. Scott's performance as General George Patton in the film *Patton* (1970), or by Vivien Leigh's performance as Scarlett O'Hara in *Gone With the Wind* (1939). Films can also create incarnations of deceit and evil—for example, Bette Davis in *The Little Foxes* (1941).

Seventh, films can create idealized versions of the male–female, husband–wife, intimate relationship. Spencer Tracy and Katharine Hepburn, and Elizabeth Taylor and Richard Burton enacted these relationships in a variety of films, including *Pat and Mike* (1952), and *Who's Afraid of Virginia Woolf?* (1966). These films create larger-than-life depictions of gender relations in society.

Eighth, films provide interpretive structures for dealing with problematic everyday events. Blumer's (1933) study of movies and conduct revealed how young men and women learned how to date, kiss, make love, dress, smoke, drink, rob, and fight by watching Hollywood-made movies.

Hollywood films thus reveal, illuminate, and explore society. The reading and analysis of these films (to be discussed shortly) allows the sociologist to see things about a society that might not otherwise be visible. By studying these interactional, processual representations, including how they are made, distributed, and given meaning by the viewing public, the sociologist is able to engage in a level of cultural analysis that other sociological methods do not allow. I turn now to a brief discussion of ethnographic, documentary, video, and experimental film.

Ethnographic, Video, and Experimental Film

Couch (1987a, Chapter 1) has argued that audio-visual tapes made in the experimental laboratory permit the researcher to make more complete and refined observations of social processes than can be made by unaided observers. He also argues that these tapes allow for the accumulation of new types of interactional data that can be brought to bear on key sociological problems. For example, authority relationships can be constructed, videotaped, and analyzed in terms of the processes that lead to the development of power relationships in dyads and triads. Videotapes are shareable; other researchers can study them. These tapes are processual and record interaction. They can be replayed, slowed down, stopped, and carefully studied, and high observer agreement on what is occurring on the tape can be reached (see McPhail and Wohlstein, 1982, p. 354).

Audio-visual tapes and films do not necessarily reveal phenomena not previously observable. Rather, they allow more precise and processual observations of "naturally" occurring events to be made. Couch and associates have used audio-visual recordings to study and illuminate such phenomena as power and authority relationships, the negotiation and bargaining process, the effect of gender on conversations, openings and closings in interactions, mood and intimacy, solidarity in partisan groups, the temporal stages of situated action, and intergroup negotiations.

Conversation analysts (see Schegloff, 1987, p. 103; Maynard, 1987) have employed the audio-video tape method in their studies of talk-in-interaction, By securing detailed records of "natural" talk, they have been able to describe some of the underlying structural dimensions that organize conversations.

Analysis of the transcripts of these tapes have aided in the construction of rather formal theories of conversation and talk in everyday life.

Ethnographers such as the Colliers (1986) have used ethnographic, documentary film to study Indian and Eskimo interaction in schoolrooms. Heider (1972) has produced a film showing the Dani building a pig sty. Smith (1983) has made in-depth ethnographic films of modern Mayan survival.

VISUAL METHODS AS RESEARCH TOOLS

The foregoing discussion has demonstrated a number of ways in which film and photography can illuminate social processes. It is now necessary to discuss visual methods as research tools. Visual methods can be used in the following ways: (1) as part of a strategy of triangulation; (2) as tools for preserving key social processes; (3) as a way of putting the sociological imagination into practice; (4) as the basis for interviewing; (5) as techniques for enhancing rapport in the field situation; (6) as a means for mapping a social structure; and (7) as tools for studying social relationships and social interaction.

Triangulation

In general, visual methods can be used in conjunction with any of the research methods thus far discussed in this book (including the interview, experiments, surveys, participant observation, ethnography, and biographical analysis). Indeed, they complement the triangulation strategy that I have repeatedly advocated. Interviewers, experimenters, biographers, and ethnographers can film what they do and show photographs or films to the persons they study. For example, Spradely (1979, 1980, p. 33) advocated the taking of photographs in participant-observation research.

Preserving and Documenting Social Processes

Becker (1986, p. 231) suggests that photography can be used as a tool for (1) preserving nonverbal data for later analysis; (2) recording how natives see their world; (3) producing historical documents; and (4) studying social groups, institutions, and communities. Illustrative work under each of these categories includes Birdwhistle's use of film to study kinesics, the Worth--Adair study of the Navajo, Bateson and Mead's study of Bali, and Becker's photographic work on community life in the San Francisco Bay Area. Couch's audio-video tapes of dyadic and triadic interactions in the laboratory can be studied by anyone. They are records that preserve the interactional text.

The Sociological Imagination

Becker (1986, pp. 248–49) argues that every photograph raises the following sociological questions: (1) What are the different kinds (and types) of people in this situation? (2) What common understandings do they share, and not share? (3) What would deviance or a breach of understanding look like in this situation? (4) What would happen if an understanding was violated?

These traditional sociological questions can become topics that the camera (and film) can explore and capture. I have already discussed how Hollywood films speak to issues like these. The theoretically informed sociologist can take her camera to situations in which these phenomena are likely to occur. Or the researcher can create these conditions in the laboratory and video-tape them (Couch, Saxton, and Katovich, 1986a, 1986b). In both cases, the camera becomes a research tool for exploring problems informed by the sociological imagination. Without the sociological imagination, the camera (or the audio-video tape) becomes another uninteresting research method.

Interviewing and Rapport

Photo-interviewing, or the photo-elicitation technique, can be a means of bridging a communication gap between strangers (Collier and Collier, 1986, pp. 99–115). Photographs of natives at work or pictures of citizens in their community can serve as a starting point for discussions of the everyday lives of the individuals being studied. By bringing the familiar in front of a person, the researcher can establish a common ground of interaction.

Photographs "can sharpen the memory and give the interview an immediate character of realistic reconstruction (Collier and Collier, 1986, p. 106). The photograph may locate the informant in a work or leisure situation. In so doing, it creates the context for interviewing about the processes in question. This use of the photograph changes the interview-respondent relationship. It makes both individuals collaborators in a discovery process. Group interviews can supplement individual interviews. In groups, the multiple meanings of an event, activity, or problem can be secured (see Collier and Collier, 1986, p. 104). These strategies develop and build upon the interpretations of the native. They anchor the research in concrete, lived situations.

The uses of a camera and the production of a visual record in a community often extends beyond research purposes. Heath (reported in Collier and Collier, 1986, pp. 25–27) details how the members of a Camba community in Santa Cruz, Bolivia, constructed a whitewashed wall as a projection screen for showing the films he had made of them. The building of the wall soon expanded into a community effort which resulted in the building of a stage for school, church, and civic functions.

Blumer (1933, p. 3) pioneered another photo-interviewing method, termed the "motion-picture autobiography." Subjects were asked to "write in narrative form their motion-picture experiences" (Blumer, 1933, p. 3). Over 1,800 motion-picture autobiographies were gathered from office and factory workers, and from university, college, junior college, and high school students. A detailed analysis of these narrative texts was then offered in terms of the effects of movies on the emotional fantasies and social relationships of these subjects. In this method, the subject recalls experiences connected with films. More recently, Davis (1988) interviewed subjects immediately after they had seen films. Employing group- and individual-interview methods, he contrasted the differences in interpretation that occur when a group, as opposed to an individual, reconstructs the meaning of a film. Like the photo-elicitation interview method, the film-elicitation technique locates the researcher and the subject in a common field of experience.

Mapping Social Structures

The camera can be used to map and record the social, economic, technological, and family life of a community. Collier and Collier (1986, p. 108) state:

> The box camera is capable of distinguishing houses and counting the number of cars and people on Main Street. The functions of counting, measuring, and identifying that have proven to be scientifically reliable depend on relatively simple elements that any novice with the camera can record.

Such photo-records can later be used in interviews. They preserve a picture of community life that later researchers can build upon, Aerial and ground-level mapping can also be collected, as well as black-and-white and color films.

Interiors—lobbies, offices, banks, private homes, and health clubs can be photographed. People decorate and furnish interiors. How they do this reflects the life-style they wish to live and project to others (Becker, 1986, p. 306). By studying these photographs, an understanding can be gained of how a status group or domestic group lived.

The ways in which a group does its work can also be photographed. Collier and Collier (1986, p. 67) offer a scheme of observation that includes the following:

1. Environmental location of technology and work
2. Raw materials
3. Tools
4. Steps in production
5. Conclusion of a process
6. Functions of technology
7. Social structure of technology

Consider the writing of this page of text. The environmental location is a sun room. The raw materials are ideas, blank sheets of paper, and computer disks. The tools are pens, pencils, a personal computer, and a printer. These tools are being used on an oak table. The production of this page concludes when I have a satisfactory text on the screen, which I then print. My technology allows me to be both a writer and a printer. I have become my own secretary.

My work could be photographed. Indeed, I could have a picture of myself working on the word processor hanging on the wall in front of me.

Studying Social Relationships and Social Interaction

Visual records of interaction and social relationships must contain the following elements: (1) *proxemic* information on the spatial distance and relationship between people; (2) the *context*, or situation, of the interaction;

(3) the *temporal flow* of interaction; (4) *kinesics,* or the postures, gestures, and nonverbal interactions that transpire in the situation; (5) sufficient detail to permit the identification of differences in manner of *dress* and *appearance;* and (6) background information on the *social relationships* that connect the participants to one another. Audio-visual records must, of course, include *verbal recordings* of the spoken utterances in the situation.

The study of interaction and social relationships can be keyed to certain social and cultural events in the group. Collier and Collier (1986, pp. 82–83) suggest that the researcher might be guided by programmed public events, ceremonial occasions, and the occurrences of disasters. In each of these contexts, different interactional, power, and relational structures in a group or collectivity are made apparent. The researcher can, when permission has been granted, also enter private homes and photograph families (see Collier and Collier, 1986, p. 97). Such photographs and films lay bare the ritual, proxemic, kinesic, contextual, and temporal features of family life.

Couch and his students, as noted earlier, have studied dyads and triads in the laboratory. And Hollywood films almost invariably depict social relationships and social interaction.

READING PHOTOGRAPHS AND FILM

How are the languages and texts of film and photography to be read and interpreted? This is the problem of getting information off a film or a visual document.

A film or a photograph offers an image or set of images that are interpretations of the real. The real, or the slice of reality that is captured can never be reproduced, for what is represented can occur only once. Visual documents are records of events that have occurred in the past.

Film (and photographs) speak a language of emotion and meaning. They present a vocabulary and a set of framing devices that mediate and define reality for the viewer. Four meaning structures exist in any film or set of photographs: (1) the visual text, (2) the audio text, including what photographers say about their photographs, (3) the narrative that links the visual and audio text into a coherent story, or framework, and (4) the interpretations and meanings brought by the viewer (including the social scientist) to the visual, audio, and narrative texts. Take the film *Terms of Endearment,* for instance. The visual text consists of the pictures and images, connected to scenes, which tell the film's story. Memorable examples include Jack Nicholson and Shirley MacLaine eating oysters for lunch, and Nicholson entering MacLaine's bedroom. The audio text consists of the words spoken in the film; the narrative that connects the visual and audio texts consists of the story that the film is telling. *Terms of Endearment* is the story of a mother and daughter coming to terms with the meanings of their own lives in relation to each other. The men in their lives are obstacles they have to overcome as they find their way back to each other.

READING THE VISUAL

No visual text evokes the same meanings for all viewers. In the process of interacting with the text, viewers develop readings and interpretations that are uniquely their own. Some famous film theorists disagree with this position. They claim that outstanding movies do in fact have common emotional effects on all viewers, and that these effects can be determined by the director. Viewers bring interpretations to texts, however, and they are not always those intended by directors. Viewer interpretations must be studied, For example, I do not like horror films; I will not watch Hitchcock's *Psycho*. I'm not sure why I don't like horror films, but I know I don't. If I am trapped into watching one, I become anxious. Of course, these are some of the effects such films are supposed to produce.

Theories of Film

The literature contains many theories of film and film interpretation (see Andrews, 1984, for a review), including psychoanalytic, Freudian, and Lacanian theories, and semiotic (or the analysis of the sign systems in a film), hermeneutic, phenomenologic, realist, feminist, cultural, Marxist, and institutionalist theories. Books have been written on each of these approaches. Rather than review them here, I will discuss how I, along with a group of students (Krug, Davis, Kray, Louisell, Elke), have been reading and interpreting alcoholism films (see Denzin, 1988a).

READING FILM

A film or photograph always tells two stories. The first is the one that can be literally read off the text (for example, this is a picture of a young child playing). The second is the story that is not directly told but can be inferred from the film or photograph (for example, this is a middle-class child playing in a park for middle-class families). From this reading, if one can locate (and date) the park in a city, a political economy of parks can be developed. One could examine (or take) pictures of ghetto children playing in streets and rundown buildings, and then compare those "play" places with the faces and experiences of the children who play in middle-class settings. In this way, one contextualizes the photograph, locates it within the social structure, and begins to make sociological statements about the questions the picture raises.

Two Levels of Meaning

A film or a picture can be read as having two different levels of meaning. The first, as the foregoing example suggests, is the literal, or "realist," level. It says, "This is a picture of X." A literal reading takes a picture on "face value." It asks, "What does this picture (or film) say about X?" The second level of meaning is the one below the surface. It is the one that suggests that there is more going on here than just a picture of X. Readings at this level are called *subversive*. They challenge, go beneath, and go beyond, the surface, literal interpretations of a text.

Realist Readings

A realist reading of a visual document has four characteristics. First, it treats a visual text as a realistic, truthful depiction of some phenomenon. Realist readings assume that pictures are windows to the real world. Second, a text is viewed as establishing truth claims about the world and the events that go on it; that is, tells the truth. Third, the meaning of a photo-visual text can be given through a close reading of its contents, its attention to detail, its depiction of characters, and its dialogue. Fourth, these readings validate the truth claims that the film or text makes about reality. A traditional realist reading attempts to discover how visual texts speak to the "universal" features of the human condition.

What would a realist reading of a film look like? Here is a realist description and interpretation (Maltin, 1986, p. 966) of the alcoholism film *Tender Mercies* (1983):

> Winning but extremely low-key film about a country singer who finds the inspiration to put his life back together when he meets an attractive young widow and her little boy. Duvall's Oscar-winning performance is the real attraction here. Horton Foote's screenplay (also an Oscar winner) is not so much a story as a series of vignettes. . . . Duvall wrote his own songs for the film.

This statement conforms to the four features of the realist reading of a film. First, it treats the film as a work of art that truthfully describes the world of a country singer who meets a young widow and puts his life back together. Second, it suggests that the film's strength lies in Duvall's performance. He makes what happens seem real and truthful. Third, the meaning of the film is given, in part, in the songs that Duvall wrote. Maltin suggests that a close reading of these songs will reveal the messages in the film. Fourth, a close interpretation of the movie confirms the position that it is a winning but low-key film.

This realist reading stays close to the surface of the film and keys primarily on its dominant storyline, and on the performances of its major actors. A subversive reading, which I have offered elsewhere (Denzin, 1989), challenges this realist interpretation. It focuses on the three women in Duvall's life (his ex-wife; his adult daughter, who is killed; and his new wife). It argues that the film is about these women and not about him. It is also about alcoholism, good and bad women, and alcoholism's effects on family life. These interpretations are not given in the realist reading.

Subversive Readings

Subversive readings challenge realist interpretations. They suggest that the realism in visual texts is always filtered through preconceptions and biases. Hence a work's claim to being a truthful reflection of "reality-as-it-really-is" must always be challenged. A subversive reading argues that the truth statement that a realist claims for a text are always biased. That is, they reflect the viewer's point of view on the topics contained in the text. A film makes claims only about the photographer's or filmmaker's vision of reality.

A film, under subversive reading, does not speak to the universal features of the human condition. It speaks only to limited versions of human experience — that is, those captured by the photographer or filmmaker. A close reading of a film or photograph reveals features that a realist reading ignores. It focuses on minor characters, not just major characters. It contrasts the positions of men, women, and children in the narrative. It looks at how the film idealizes certain key cultural values, like family, work, religion, and love. These features are the ones that will be highlighted in a subversive reading. By illuminating them, the reader then argues that the film's dominant message presents only one view of reality. The goal of the subversive reading is to discover the multiple meanings that can be found in a film's text.

A film creates its particular version of truth by suppressing particular contradictions that exist within its text. These contradictions appear at those junctures in the narrative when the film (or visual text) answers cause-and-effect questions. In *Tender Mercies* such a moment includes Duvall's asking why he "wandered out to this part of Texas and you (his new wife) took me in?" By examining how a film answers these causal questions, a subversive reading illuminates the underlying values that the text is attempting to promote.

Of course, a subversive reading can be challenged by a realist reading. It should be clear that the second level of meaning in a visual text can be discovered only after the surface, literal levels of meaning have been interpreted. Any text should be read both ways. There is never a correct reading of a visual text; there are only multiple interpretations. It is erroneous to confine interpretations to just the realist or subversive levels. To do so misses the other layers of meaning that are always present in a text.

THE PRINCIPLES OF VISUAL RESEARCH

It is necessary to state a number of principles that organize visual research, including the production and analysis of visual documents. The following guidelines are provisional and should be fitted to the needs of the researcher (see Collier and Collier, 1986, pp. 178–79).

1. Phase 1: Looking and Feeling

Observe the visual documents as a totality.
Look and listen to the materials. Let them talk to you. Feel their effects on you.
Record these feelings and impressions.
Write down questions that occur to you. Note patterns of meaning.

2. Phase 2: What Question Are You Asking?

State your research question.
What questions does the text claim to answer?

How does it represent and define key cultural values?
Inventory the evidence and note key scenes, photos, and so on.

3. Phase 3: Structured, Microanalysis

Measure, count, and take quotes from the text.
Form and find patterns and sequences.
Write detailed descriptions.
Keep a focus on the research question.
If analyzing a film, do a scene-by-scene microanalysis.
Identify major moments in the film when conflicts over values occur.
Detail how the film takes a position on these values.

4. Phase 4: Search for Patterns

Return to the complete record.
Lay out all the photographs, or view the film in its entirety.
Return to the research question. How do these documents speak to and answer your question?
Contrast literal and subversive readings of the text.
Write an interpretation, based on the principles of analytic induction (pp. 215–16) and the threats to interpretation (pp. 216–21) discussed previously.

These steps will aid in the production and organization of a research statement based on visual documents. They will allow your readers to visually enter the field situation you have studied. They can then judge whether or not your interpretations are naturalistically generalizable to their fields of experience.

CONCLUSIONS

I have examined how sociologists may use film and photography as research methods. The methods and problems of visual sociology were reviewed, including the problems of causal analysis and interpretation. Film is simultaneously a means of communication and a method of inquiry. Films are cultural and symbolic forms that may be used to reveal and illuminate important features of social life. Visually recorded documents are of use "so long as we are aware of how and by what rules we choose our subject matter, and so long as we are aware of and make explicit how we organized the various units of film from which we do our anlaysis" (Worth, 1981, pp. 193–94). I have attempted to clarify some of these rules in this chapter.

SUGGESTED READINGS

BARTHES, ROLAND, *Camera Lucida.* (New York: Hill and Wang, 1981). Barthes offers a semiotic and interpretive reading of photography and locates the practice of taking pictures in the political economy of contemporary societies. He discusses film as an instrument of social and political domination.

BECKER, HOWARD, S., *Doing Things Together: Selected Papers.* (Evanston, Ill.: Northwestern University Press, 1986). The articles in Part 4 of this book are on photography. I have drawn a good deal of the discussion in this chapter from these papers.

COLLIER, JOHN, JR., AND MALCOM COLLIER, *Visual Anthropology: Photography as a Research Method.* (Albuquerque: University of New Mexico Press, 1986). This outstanding book takes the reader step by step through the use of photography in fieldwork.

WORTH, SOL, *Studying Visual Communication.* (Philadelphia: University of Pennsylvania Press, 1981). Excellent collection of essays on the use of photography and film in visual research.

10

Strategies of Multiple Triangulation

We should combine theories and methods carefully and purposefully with the intention of adding breadth or depth to our analysis, but not for the purpose of pursuing "objective" truth. [Fielding and Fielding, 1986, p. 33]

Advocating triangulation, or the combination of methodologies in the study of the same phenomena, has been a basic theme of this book. I have repeatedly suggested that the sociologist should examine a problem from as many methodological perspectives as possible. The use of multiple measures and methods to overcome the inherent weaknesses of single measurement instruments has a long history in the physical sciences. The concept of triangulation, as in the action of making a triangle, may be traced to the Greeks and the origins of modern mathematics. The metaphor of radio triangulation, "determining the point of origin of a radio broadcast by using directional antennas set up at the two ends of a known baseline" (Lincoln and Guba, 1985, p. 305), aptly illustrates this concept.

My definition of each research method has implied a triangulated perspective. Participant observation was seen as combining survey interviewing, document analysis, direct observation, and observer participation. Similarly, the experiment, the survey, the biographical method, and film and photography were defined as involving multiple approaches to gathering data and empirical materials. Interpretive sociologists who employ the triangulated method are committed to *sophisticated rigor*, which means that they are committed to making their empirical, interpretive schemes as public as possible. This requires that they detail in careful fashion the nature of the sampling framework used. It also involves using triangulated, historically situated observations that are interactive, biographical, and, where relevant, gender specific. The phrase *sophisticated rigor* is intended to describe the work of any and all sociologists who employ multiple methods, seek out diverse empirical sources, and attempt to develop interactionally grounded interpretations.

Two topics remain to be treated. The first topic involves the strategies by which the sociologist may meaningfully combine these methods so that fully grounded interpretations can be generated. The second involves a critical discussion of triangulation as a research approach. A number of authors have identified problems and weaknesses with this strategy as it has been discussed in earlier editions of this book (see Fielding and Fielding, 1986; Lincoln and Guba, 1985; Patton, 1980; Silverman, 1985). These criticisms will be taken up throughout this chapter and in a separate section at the end.

RESEARCH METHODS AS ACTIONS ON THE ENVIRONMENT

Research methods represent lines of action taken toward the empirical world. Many sociologists assume that their research methods are neutral, "atheoretical tools" suitable for valid scientific use by any knowledgeable user; I have attempted to indicate that, on the contrary, research methods represent different means of acting on the environment of the scientist. The reality to which sociologists apply their methods is continually in a state of change, and you find, as Shibutani (1966, pp. 170–71, 182) has argued,

> that what is called "reality" is a social process; it is an orientation that is continuously supported by others. . . . Societies, no matter how stable they may appear, are ongoing things. The world is in a state of continuous flux, and as life conditions change, knowledge must keep pace. In this sense all knowledge is social.

THE "NEGOTIATED REALITY" OF SOCIOLOGY

Lack of Consensus

When I speak of triangulated research strategies oriented toward common units of observation, I mean that these units of observation are social objects in the environment of the scientist. These objects represent the reality of the scientist, and their meaning arises out of the scientist's experiences. It is to be hoped that the definitions attached to these objects will be public and agreed upon. Indeed, scientists demand a certain degree of agreement, but consensus will never be reached, for several reasons.

First, each method implies a different line of action toward reality — and hence each will reveal different aspects of it, much as a kaleidoscope, depending on the angle at which it is held, will reveal different colors and configurations of objects to the viewer. Methods are like the kaleidoscope: Depending on how they are approached, held, and acted toward, different observations will be revealed. This is not to imply that reality has the shifting qualities of the colored prism, but that it too is an object that moves and that will not permit one interpretation to be stamped upon it.

A second reason that consensus cannot be attained arises from the users of methods. Each sociologist brings to these lines of action her own interpretations of them, and to an extent these interpretations are unique.

A third reason that agreement can never be complete arises from the definitions brought to bear upon the units observed. Each user approaches these units from a unique perspective that reflects past experiences, personal idiosyncrasies, and current mood. If, for example, one were examining the stratification system in a local community, past experiences would condition the persons observed, the questions asked, and ultimately the results. Vidich and Shapiro (1955, pp. 28–33) have shown that in one community study, the participant observer systematically overobserved middle-class, professional males; females and persons from the working class were underrepresented in the final analysis. While Vidich and Shapiro suggest that the observer's position in the community dictated this sampling strategy, it seems fair to conclude also that his own preferences and abilities to interact with persons most like him may also have contributed to his choice.

The fourth reason is that the world of observations is in a state of continuous change. This necessarily makes observations at one point in time different from any other set of observations. What Campbell and Stanley have termed "population instabilities arising from time and space" refers to this factor of change. To summarize, the sociologist *creates* the world of observation; it does not exist independent of actions taken toward it.

Rules of Method; Triangulation

The activities of the sociologist are in many ways no different from those of the persons studied. All humans are involved in the process of making sense out of this social object called *reality,* and they do so by agreeing on the definitions attached to it. Until sociologists recognize the fundamental elements of symbolic interaction embedded in their own conduct, sociology will not move closer to the status of a mature, self-aware discipline that understands its own activities and subject matter.

Triangulation, or the use of multiple methods, is a plan of action that will raise sociologists above the personal biases that stem from single methodologies. By combining methods and investigators in the same study, observers can partially overcome the deficiencies that flow from one investigator or one method. Sociology as a field of inquiry is based on the observations generated from its theories, but until sociologists treat the act of generating observations as an act of symbolic interaction, the links between observations and theories will remain incomplete. In this respect, triangulation of method, investigator, theory, and data remains the soundest strategy of theory construction.

TYPES OF TRIANGULATION

It is conventionally assumed that triangulation is the use of multiple methods in the study of the same object (see Campbell and Fiske, 1959; Webb et al., 1966, 1981). Indeed, this is the generic definition I have offered, but it is only one form of the strategy. It is convenient to conceive of triangulation as involving varieties of data, investigators, and theories, as well as methodologies.

There are four basic types of triangulation. (1) *Data triangulation* has three subtypes: (a) time, (b) space, and (c) person. Person analysis, in turn, has three levels: (a) aggregate, (b) interactive, and (c) collectivity. (2) *Investigator triangulation* consists of using multiple rather than single observers of the same object. (3) *Theory triangulation* consists of using multiple rather than single perspectives in relation to the same set of objects. (4) *Methodological triangulation* can entail within-method triangulations and between-method triangulations.

Data Triangulation

Observers triangulate not only by methodology; they may also triangulate by data sources. In a very loose sense, theoretical sampling is an example of the latter process; that is, researchers explicitly search for as many different data sources as possible that bear upon the events under analysis. *Data sources*, in this sense, are to be distinguished from *methods of generating data*. The latter term refers to research methods per se, and not to sources of data as such. By triangulating data sources, analysts can efficiently employ the same methods to maximum theoretical advantage. Thus, in studying the social meanings of death in the modern hospital, it would be possible to employ a standard method (for example, participant observation) but deliberately take this method to as many different areas as possible. Researchers might examine different groups within the hospital and then turn to family members of dying persons. Death rituals in other settings might also be examined by the same process. Primitive societies could be studied. Highway deaths, deaths at home, deaths at work, and even deaths at play are other examples. Each of these represents significantly different data areas within which the same generic event (death) occurs. Basically this would be the use of *dissimilar comparison groups* as a sampling strategy, but it more properly reflects a strategy of triangulation. By selecting dissimilar settings in a systematic fashion, investigators can discover what their concepts (as designators of units in reality) have in common across settings. Similarly, the unique features of these concepts will be discovered in their situated context.

Subtypes: time, space, person   All sociological observations relate to activities of socially situated persons—whether they are in groups or organizations or aggregately distributed over some social area. A focus on time and space as observational units recognizes their relationship to the observations of persons. A major focus in time observations will be its relationship to ongoing interactions; observers can sample activities by time of day, week, month, or year. Similarly, they can also sample space and treat it as a unit of analysis (for example, ecological analysis), or as a component of external validity. Personal data point, of course, to the most common unit of analysis—the social organization of persons through time and space. These three units—time, space, and person—are interrelated. A study of one demands a study of the others. Returning to the instance of dying, an investigation could be designed that triangulated data by these three dimensions. Death in the early morning in the emergency room of the hospital, for example, could be compared with deaths at midday in the presence of nonhospital personnel.

Levels of person analysis   Three distinct levels of person analysis can be treated.

Aggregate Analysis   The first is what is commonly found in the social survey; individuals are selected for study, not groups, relationships, or organizations. I term this *aggregate analysis* because of the failure to establish social links between those observed. Random samples of homemakers, college students, and blue-collar workers are instances of aggregate-person analysis.

Interactive Analysis   The second level I term *interactive.* Here the unit becomes interacting persons in either laboratory or natural field settings. Small groups, families, and work crews are examples. What sociologists commonly associate with participant observation, small-group experiments, and unobtrusive measures represents this form of analysis. The unit is interaction rather than the person or the group. Goffman's studies of face-to-face encounters in hospital surgery rooms (1961b) are excellent examples. Surgeons, nurses, and the hospital social structure were studied only as they interacted in generating a series of interactive episodes.

The Collectivity   The third level, the one commonly associated with structural-functional analysis, is the collectivity. Here the observational unit is an organization, a group, a community, or even an entire society. Persons and their interactions are treated only as they reflect pressures and demands of the total collectivity.

Example   The three levels of analysis can be illustrated by returning to the example of dying in the hospital. An aggregately oriented investigation might simply sample the various attitudes held by hospital personnel toward the dying process. An interactional study would examine how these attitudes are generated out of the encounters between personnel. Last, the collectivity-oriented investigator might examine how the structural features of the hospital (for example, its organizational chart, its work positions) dictate certain attitudes and practices on the part of its members.

Synthesis of levels and types   Any one investigation can combine all three levels and types of data; in fact, those studies commonly regarded as classic make these combinations: Time, space, and persons are alternatively analyzed from the aggregate, interactive, and collective levels.

Boys in White (Becker et al., 1961) represents such a synthesis. Medical students were randomly sampled and interviewed, groups of interacting students were observed, and the work demands of hospital staff, as they related to these interactions, were analyzed. Situation and time sampling were also used. Students' study patterns during critical examination periods were compared with patterns during other times. Study habits in laboratories, fraternities, and the classroom were also compared.

It must be noted that data triangulation seldom yields a single, coherent, consistent picture of the situation being studied (Patton, 1980, p. 331; Silverman, 1985, p. 105). This is the case because reality is always conflictual and socially constructed. The "situated character of action" (Silverman, 1985, p. 105) means that data triangulation is always indefinite and open-ended. (See Cicourel, 1974a, pp. 128–29 on the indefinite triangulation of accounts and the impossibility of ever obtaining an "objective" reading of a situation.)

Investigator Triangulation

Investigator triangulation simply means that multiple, as opposed to single, observers are employed. Most investigations, in fact, do employ multiple observers, although all of them may not occupy equally prominent roles in the actual observational process.

What Roth (1966, pp. 190–96) has termed "hired-hand" research represents an inappropriate use of multiple observers: The act of making observations is delegated to persons who lack the skill and knowledge of the primary investigator. The use of undergraduates as coders, graduate students and homemakers as interviewers, and computer specialists as data analysts represents a delegation of responsibility that places the least well-prepared persons in crucial positions. When multiple observers are used, the most skilled observers should be placed closest to the data.

Triangulating observers removes the potential bias that comes from a single person and ensures a greater reliability in observations, a rationale well illustrated by Strauss and colleagues (1964, p. 36) in their observational study of interactions in mental hospitals:

> There were three fieldworkers subjected for the most part to the same raw data. Search for pinpointing and negative evidence was abetted by the collective nature of our inquiry. If the colleague reported the same kind of observation as another without prior consultation, confidence grew. If after hearing the report of an observation, a colleague was himself able unquestionably to duplicate it, it indicated that our observational techniques had some degree of reliability. If no colleague did corroborate an observation—which did happen—if it seemed important then, or later, further inquiry was initiated. Something like a built-in reliability check was thus obtained because several fieldworkers were exposed directly to similar or identical data.

Multiple observers may not agree on what they observe, for each observer has unique interactional experiences with the phenomena that are observed (Lincoln and Guba, 1985, p. 307).

Theory Triangulation

Theoretical triangulation is an element that few investigations achieve. Typically, a small set of hypotheses guide any study, and data are gathered that bear on only those dimensions; but there would seem to be value in approaching empirical materials with multiple perspectives and interpretations in mind. Data that would refute central hypotheses could be collected, and various theoretical points of view could be placed side by side to assess their utility and power (see Westie, 1957, pp. 149–54). Such strategies would permit sociologists to move away from polemical criticisms of various theoretical perspectives. Pitting alternative theories against the same body of data is a more efficient means of criticism—and it more comfortably conforms with the scientific method. Of course, this last statement must be tempered with the understanding that sociologists never have "the same body of data," for the meaning of any body of empirical materials is always socially constructed and subject to multiple interpretations.

Necessity for theoretical triangulation   The necessity of considering theoretical triangulation as an integral feature of the research process is shown in those areas characterized by a high degree of theoretical incoherence—contemporary theory in the area of small-group analysis, for example. Some sociologists argue that exchange theory explains interaction in groups, while others stress a functionalist perspective; at the same time, theorists of interpersonal attraction and balance debate the efficacy of their approach, while symbolic interactionists propose their own framework. Empirical data go unorganized, and each theorist searches for data appropriate to his hypotheses. As a consequence, no solidly grounded theory has emerged in this area.

Each new investigator has typically taken one of three lines of action. Some resort, as Westie has shown in the field of race relations, to "a rigid empiricism in which the 'facts' (meaning the empirical findings) are seen to speak for themselves. The utility of such research is often bound to the particular moment, place and project (1957, p. 149)".

A second strategy is to select from among the "many contradictory propositions already held in the field, a particular proposition or set of propositions, which are relevant to the problem at hand and which appear to make sense in terms of what the investigator already knows about the aspect of society under investigation" (Westie, 1957, p. 149). The obvious difficulty with this approach is that what one "already knows" is limited in scope and range and hence hardly reliable enough to provide a solid basis for selecting propositions and hypotheses.

The third line of action leads the investigator to develop her own propositions and theory. These represent additional formulations to those currently existing in the area and hence detract from any ongoing synthesis of theory and research. These small theories come close to what Merton has termed "middle-range" theory; more properly they must be viewed as small ad hoc theories that pertain only to the data under analysis. Glaser and Strauss (1967) have called for grounded, substantive sociological theories, a position more in line with my criticisms. Their theory of dying in the hospital is one example (see Strauss, 1987).

Steps in theoretical triangulation   Westie's arguments for theoretical triangulation fail to take account of Lincoln and Guba's (1985, p. 307) point that

> facts are, in the first instance, theory determined; they do not have an existence
> independent of the theory within whose framework they achieve coherence. If

a given fact is "confirmable" within two theories, that finding may be more a function of the similarity of theories than of the empirical meaningfulness of the fact.

If facts are determined by theory, then theoretical triangulation is best seen as a method of widening one's theoretical framework as empirical materials are interpreted. The recommended procedure is to use all the interpretations that could conceivably be applied to a given area. It involves the following steps:

1. A comprehensive list of all possible interpretations in a given area is constructed. This will involve bringing a variety of theoretical perspectives to bear upon the phenomena at hand (including interactionism, phenomenology, Marxism, feminist theory, semiotics, cultural studies, and so on).
2. The actual research is conducted, and empirical materials are collected.
3. The multiple theoretical frameworks enumerated in Step 1 are focused on the empirical materials.
4. Those interpretations that do not bear on the materials are discarded or set aside.
5. Those interpretations that map and make sense of the phenomena are assembled into an interpretive framework that addresses all of the empirical materials.
6. A reformulated interpretive system is stated based at all points on the empirical materials just examined and interpreted. (See Westie, 1957, pp. 150, 153; Denzin, 1978, pp. 298–99).

ILLUSTRATION: READING THE EMOTIONS IN THE ALCOHOLISM FILM

The foregoing process can be illustrated by my ongoing research on film and the American alcoholic. In one study I offered a reading of how two films, *Come Back, Little Sheba* (1952) and *Days of Wine and Roses* (1961), represented the emotional experiences that occur in alcoholic marriages. In the first film, Burt Lancaster plays "Doc," a recovering alcoholic chiropractor married to "Lola" (Shirley Booth). In the second film, Jack Lemmon plays "Joe," an alcoholic public relations executive married to "Krysten" (Lee Remick). I wanted to offer multiple readings, or interpretations, of these movies. I located them within the postmodern period of American life (post–World War II) and, following Mills's (1959) lead, attempted to understand what kind of men and women this period of history produced. I located the marriages within the postwar economic and family systems and noted that both women in the movies were housewives, although "Krysten" had worked as a secretary prior to her marriage to "Joe." I attempted, in this respect, to bring recent feminist historical research on the American family to bear upon the experiences of the women in the two movies.

I also drew upon recent work in cultural theory and media studies. I wanted to see how these films created cultural meanings about alcoholics and alcoholic marriages in the 1952–1961 period. At this level, I looked at their theories of alcoholism and at how they presented AA. I contended that these texts drew upon early postmodern experiences in alcoholic and nonalcoholic families, in which women defined themselves in terms of their marriages and not their work. I also suggested that the films presented patriarchal father figures who dominated the women, even after they had left home and married.

At the level of emotions, I drew upon theories of negative symbolic interaction, love, bad faith, and intimacy. I showed how alcoholism destroys love in a marriage. I also contended that these movies used alcoholism as a metaphor for violent emotionality.

I thus brought several theoretical perspectives to bear upon the movies. The theories that I used included feminism, cultural Marxism, symbolic interactionism, phenomenology, and the sociology of emotions. I used what I could from each perspective and discarded what I couldn't use. In this way I attempted to develop a conceptually dense interpretation of the two movies. This is how theoretical triangulation works. It must be noted, however, that each perspective led me to see certain things and not others. Feminist theory tells me little about alcoholism, for example. It does alert me to the position of women within the gender-stratification system of postwar American society, however, and it tells me that a woman's experience in an alcoholic marriage is shaped by her relative autonomy, or lack thereof, in the workplace.

The foregoing example indicates that theoretical triangulation has two requirements: (1) a body of empirical materials — in my case, two movies; and (2) a working knowledge of a number of theoretical, interpretive frameworks at the same time. This strategy uses interpretations as *sensitizing* structures for the production of understanding (see Blumer, 1954, 1956). A theory sensitizes the researcher to relationships and structures of experience. It does not dictate facts, nor can it be confirmed or disconfirmed. It can only be relatively useful or unuseful in the development of interpretations. A sound interpretation, in this sense, is one that illuminates, discloses, and engulfs the phenomenon at hand. A sound interpretation is thickly contextualized, historically embedded, processual, and sensitive to gender, and incorporates prior understandings and interpretations. It will also be incomplete, subject to revision the next time the researcher returns to the subject matter.

Advantages of theoretical triangulation   The advantages of this theoretically triangulated strategy are several. First, as Westie notes, it "minimizes the likelihood that the investigator will present to himself and the world a prematurely coherent set of propositions in which contradictory propositions, however plausible, are ignored" (1957, p. 154). The procedure demands that all relevant propositions be considered and made explicit before the investigation begins, a stricture that should lead researchers away from particularistic explanations of their data.

A second advantage is that triangulation permits the widest possible theoretical use of any set of observations. Sociologists can move beyond theory-specific investigations to generalized-theoretical studies. The strategy makes the investigator more broadly aware of the "total significance of his empirical findings" (Westie, 1957, p. 154). Westie states:

> Where, as in the usual procedure, the investigator is concerned with upholding or refuting a particular theory, he may be completely unaware of the fact that his empirical findings actually add confirmation, or doubt, as the case may be, to numerous other theoretical propositions extant in the area or in related areas.

Third, triangulation encourages systematic continuity in theory and research. At the moment it is rare for one sociological investigation to unambiguously support or refute a set of propositions. Similarly, as Westie (1957, p. 154) notes, when there is little in the way of theory to guide interpretation,

> subsequent empirical investigations of alternative interpretations are often necessary. Where alternative interpretations are made explicit from the beginning of the project they are more likely to survive as alternatives after the fact of investigation: The present procedure encourages research programs rather than isolated projects.

Rather than searching only for support of their propositions, investigators should deliberately seek negative evidence, a parallel to the strategy from analytic induction that directs the observer to view each data unit as a potential negative case that must be explained before further observations are gathered.

Sociologists should also think in terms of a theoretical synthesis. It may well be that each interpretation contains a kernel of truth. A final interpretive network might combine features from interpretations that were initially contradictory. If so, the final framework should reflect the discriminatory power of each perspective.

Methodological Triangulation

This is the last generic form of triangulation, and the one stressed in earlier chapters.

Types   Two forms can be noted: "within-method" triangulation and "between-method," or "across-method," triangulation.

Within-Method Triangulation   This form is most frequently employed when the observational units are viewed as multidimensional. The investigator takes one method (the survey) and employs multiple strategies within that method to examine data. A survey questionnaire might be constructed that contains many different scales measuring the same empirical unit. For example, in the famous case of alienation scales, many recent investigations have employed five distinct indices. The obvious difficulty is that only one method is employed. Observers delude themselves into believing that five different variations of the same method generate five distinct varieties of triangulated data. But the flaws that arise from using one method remain, no matter how many internal variations are devised. As Webb (1966, p. 35) states:

> Every data-gathering class — interviews, questionnaires, observation, perfor-
> mance records, physical evidence — is potentially biased and has specific to it
> certain validity threats. Ideally, we should like to converge data from several
> different data classes, as well as converge with multiple variants from within a
> single class.

Between-Method Triangulation   A much more satisfactory form of method triangulation combines dissimilar methods to illuminate the same class of phenomenon — what I call *between-method,* or *across-method,* triangulation. The rationale for this strategy is that the flaws of one method are often the strengths of another; and by combining methods, observers can achieve the best of each while overcoming their unique deficiencies.

Between-method triangulation can take many forms, but its basic feature will be the combination of two or more different research strategies in the study of the same empirical units. With seven distinct research methods that overlap in design, a variety of combinations can be constructed; a completely triangulated investigation would combine all five. Thus, if the basic strategy was participant observation, researchers would employ survey interviewing with field experiments, unobtrusive methods, film, and life histories. Most sociological investigations can be seen as stressing one dominant method (any of the seven), with combinations of the others as additional dimensions (see Cook and Fonow, 1986, p. 16).

CRITICAL DISCUSSIONS OF MULTIPLE TRIANGULATION

As indicated at the outset of this chapter, a number of authors have recently offered informative and critical discussions of the strategy of multiple triangulation.

Data triangulation   Silverman (1985, pp. 105–106) has argued that a positivistic bias underlies the triangulation position and that this is most evident in the concept of data triangulation. He argues that a hypothesis testing orientation is present when authors argue, as Webb and colleagues (1966, p. 174) do (see previous quotation), that hypotheses that survive multiple tests contain more validity than those subjected to just one test. He also suggests that to assume that the same empirical unit can be measured more than once is inconsistent with the interactionist view of emergence and novelty in the field situation. If (as Silverman argues, and I agree) all social action is situated and unique, then the same unit, behavior, or experience can never be observed twice. Each occurrence is unique. Accordingly, data triangulation better refers to seeking multiple sites and levels for the study of the phenomenon in question. It is erroneous to think or imply that the same unit can be measured. At the same time, the concept of hypothesis testing must be abandoned. The interactionist seeks to build interpretations, not test hypotheses.

Patton (1980, p. 331) has correctly noted that the comparison of multiple data sources will "seldom lead to a single, totally consistent picture. It is best not to expect everything to turn out the same." Patton goes on to argue that different types (and levels) of data reveal different aspects of what is being studied. The point is not to ignore these differences, but to attempt to understand and interpret them. Lincoln and Guba (1985, p. 283) extend this point, while stating the general principle that "no single item of information (unless coming from an elite and unimpeachable source) should ever be given serious consideration unless it can be triangulated." This means that the researcher must have multiple occurrences or representations of the processes being studied.

Investigator triangulation   No two investigators ever observe the same phenomenon in exactly the same way. Lincoln and Guba (1985, p. 307) suggest that it is a mistake to "expect corroboration of one investigator by another." The argument that greater reliability of observations can be obtained by using more than one observer is thus indefensible. This does not mean, however, that multiple observers or investigators should not be used. When possible, they should be (see Douglas, 1976, pp. 189–225). Their use expands the interpretive base of the research and reveals elements of the phenomenon that would not neccessarily be seen by just one researcher. In some cases, a researcher does not have access to a particular site because of gender. For example, in my study of AA meetings, I had no access to women's meetings, which excluded men. Had I been working with a female investigator, a window into this world of AA would have been opened.

Douglas (1976, pp. 204–12) has suggested that team research, a similar term for the use of multiple observers, allows an investigator to gain multiple perspectives on a social situation. Research team members have a multiplier effect on the research, each adds more than just his presence to the knowledge that is gained about the situation being studied. Some team members have special talents that can be drawn upon. They may be good at sociability or at observing people and remembering what they say, or they may be members of the social worlds under investigation (Douglas, 1976, p. 212). These skills can be drawn upon in investigative, team research.

The triangulation of observers may extend, as Patton (1980, pp. 331–32) notes, to *triangulating analysts*. It is possible to have "two or more persons independently analyze the same qualitative data and then compare their finds." This approach has been employed in my research on alcoholism films (see Denzin, 1987d). A team of film-viewers have been viewing films together, forming interpretations as we watch the films, checking them out against the film's text, and reformulating them as we watch the films more than once. Our intent is not to build a consensual interpretation of the film. Rather, we are seeking the multiple meanings that can be located in the viewing experience. In so doing, we adopt an adversary–advocacy model of interpretation (Patton, 1980, p. 332). Each member, working with the same film, marshals evidence to support different, and often opposing, conclusions.

Theory triangulation   Lincoln and Guba (1985, p. 307) state, in regard to theoretical triangulation, that "The use of multiple theories as a triangulation technique seems to us to be both epistemologically unsound and empirically empty." They base this harsh conclusion on a narrow reading of this strategy. As previously outlined, theoretical triangulation simply asks the researcher to be aware of the multiple ways in which the phenomenon may be interpreted. It does not demand, nor does it ask, that facts be consistent with two or more theories. Such a demand is of course, absurd.

Methodological triangulation   This strategy asks only that researchers use more than one method. It takes the position that single-method studies (that is, only surveys, only experiments, and so on) are no longer defensible in the social sciences. Patton (1980, p. 330) notes that "There is no magic in triangulation." This is true. The researcher using different methods should not expect findings generated by different methods to fall into a coherent picture (Patton, 1980, p. 306; Lincoln and Guba, 1985, p. 306). They will not and they cannot, for each method yields a different picture and slice of reality. What is critical is that different pictures be allowed to emerge (Trend, 1978, pp. 4352–53). Methodological triangulation allows this to happen.

Multiple triangulation   Fielding and Fielding (1986, p. 33) offer a critical interpretation of this strategy:

> Multiple triangulation, as Denzin expounded it, is the equivalent for research methods of "correlation" in data analysis. They both represent extreme forms of eclecticism. Theoretical triangulation does not . . . reduce bias, nor does methodological triangulation necessarily increase validity. . . . In other words, there is a case for triangulation, but not the one Denzin makes. We should combine theories and methods carefully and purposefully with the intention of adding breadth or depth to our analysis, but not for the purpose of pursuing "objective" truth.

I agree with the last sentence. The goal of multiple triangulation is a fully grounded interpretive research approach. Objective reality will never be captured. In-depth understanding, not validity, is sought in any interpretive study. Multiple triangulation should never be eclectic. It cannot, however, be meaningfully compared to correlation analysis in statistical studies.

SUMMARY

I began this chapter with a statement on the inherent difficulties of formulating coherent, comprehensive sociological interpretations when only one method is employed. The shifting, conflictual, emergent, constructed nature of the social world, coupled with the unique problems that arise from theories, methods, and observers, make the doing of sociology fundamentally difficult. I have suggested that the resolutions to this difficulty are twofold. First, sociologists must recognize these basic features of the research act.

Second, multiple strategies of triangulation must become the preferred line of action when theory-work, research, and interpretation are undertaken. By combining multiple observers, theories, methods, and empirical materials, sociologists can hope to overcome the intrinsic bias and problems that come from single-method, single-observer, single-theory studies.

The triangulated method is not without problems. A number of issues that have been raised about the approach were discussed. There is no empirical world independent of observations. No two theories will ever yield completely compatible images of the phenomenon at hand. Every method reveals a different slice of the social world. Every researcher sees different qualities. Triangulation is expensive. Weak designs may result from its implementation. However, its use, when coupled with sophisticated rigor, will broaden, thicken, and deepen the interpretive base of any study.

SUGGESTED READINGS

ADLER, PATRICIA A. AND PETER ADLER, *Membership Roles in Field Research.* (Newbury Park, Calif.: Sage, 1987). A sensitive reading of how researchers push beyond research identities to full participation in the worlds of lived experience. Such a position implies—indeed, requires—a triangulated stance toward one's life and one's research activities.

DOUGLAS, JACK D., *Investigative Social Research: Individual and Team Field Research.* (Beverly Hills: Sage, 1976). Outstanding discussion of the "mixed" research strategies involved in the triangulated approach advocated in this chapter.

JOHNSON, JOHN, *Doing Field Research.* (New York: Free Press, 1976). Probes beneath surface representations of field research and takes up in depth the problems of truth, misrepresentations, and field relations.

MANNING, PETER, K., *Semiotics and Fieldwork.* (Newbury Park, Calif.: Sage, 1987). Bold synthesis of semiotics and the methods of fieldwork. An implied triangulated strategy, which illuminates the underlying linguistic foundations of field work, is thus proposed.

PATTON, MICHAEL QUINN, *Qualitative Evaluation Methods.* (Beverly Hills: Sage, 1980). Valuable treatment of the triangulation approach developed in this book as applied to evaluation research.

11

On the Ethics and Politics of Sociology

The question is not whether we should take sides, since we inevitably will, but rather whose side are we on? [Becker, 1967a, p. 239]

Truth isn't outside power. . . . Truth is a thing of this world; it is produced only by virtue of multiple forms of constraint. . . . Each society has its regime of truth . . . the types of discourse which it accepts and makes function as true. [Foucault, 1980, p. 131]

A single theme has guided my discussion in this book: I set out to show that sociological methods represent different lines of symbolic interaction taken toward the social world. Each sociologist constitutes, through his or her actions, the worlds of experience that are studied. The research act is a process of symbolic interaction. It involves interpretation, the definition of social objects, and the formation and carrying out of lines of action. It is a dialectical act that turns back upon itself, negates itself, affirms itself, and moves forward into uncharted fields of experience. The research act is a *gendered* social act. It is shaped by the researcher's gender and personal biography. It is also a political act, involving values and ethics. When sociologists do research, they inevitably take sides for and against particular values, political bodies, and society at large. That is, they act as agents for the state, for interest groups, or for themselves. In so doing, they take sides, for it is impossible to do value-neutral research (see Silverman, 1985, pp. 178–79; Gouldner, 1962, 1968).

The research act is embedded in larger units of social organization, for sociology, as Becker and Horowitz (1986, p. 102) remind us, "is part of society." Every society, including American society, has its regimes of truth and its disciplines that produce truth statements about society and its problems. Sociology functions as a truth-producing regime. It produces findings and truth statements about social institutions and their social problems. Criminologists, for example, study prisoners in prisons and delinquents who commit crimes. Medical sociologists study healthcare professionals and healthcare delivery systems. Demographers chart the contours of birth, death, and marriage statistics and make predictions about the age structure of societies. In these capacities, sociologists produce information that the state uses for its political, educational, and social control purposes.

It is impossible, then, to view research methods as "atheoretical," "apolitical" tools suitable for use by any knowledgeable sociologist. Each method implies a different reality of empirical materials for sociological interpretation. These realities and their attendant lines of action were indicated in each of the chapters on methodology. I fear, however, that this discussion may have presented an overly "idealized" picture of the research process. In this chapter I hope to remedy this. I shall treat the following topics: (1) common methodological misconceptions, contingencies, and problems; (2) the subject–researcher relationship; (3) the political context of research; and (4) values, ethics, and the research act.

METHODOLOGICAL MISCONCEPTIONS AND PROBLEMS

The sociological enterprise of theory and research has been presented as an idealized process, immaculately conceived in design and elegantly executed in practice. My dicussions of theory, measurement, instrumentation, sampling strategies, resolutions of issues of validity, and the generation of valid causal propositions by various methods proceeded on an assumption. This assumption was that once the proper rules were learned, adequate theory would be forthcoming. Unfortunately, of course, this is seldom the case. Each theorist or methodologist takes rules of method and inference and molds them to fit her particular problem—and personality.

If I have made the process of theory construction too public and rational, then, a further deficiency has been the implication that the researcher carries on a dyadic relationship with subjects and data, that each sociologist learns a method and then goes out and designs a study to which that method is applied. This is not the way research gets done.

Few studies are conducted in entire isolation. Sociologists are involved in a complex web of social relationships that formally and informally influence their actions. The following may be noted (see Sjoberg, 1967, pp. xi–xvii). If a project is funded by government or university sources, there is an obligation to produce results. This may imply that only certain problems will be studied (often those currently in vogue). Further, it implies that only certain findings will be reported. Negative results seldom go into final grant reports; researchers tend to show positive findings. To produce negative findings suggests a faulty sociological self; good sociologists do not design studies that fail (see Record, 1967, pp. 25–49).

Obligations also fall upon sociologists from their formal positions in an organizational hierarchy. Sociologists employed by universities are expected to do research and regularly publish their findings. They are also expected to demonstrate their ability to do research. Also, many sociologists at a university are evaluated by the amount of money they bring in to do research; these funds are then used to hire graduate assistants and secretaries—to build research organizations.

Location in an organizational setting also creates problems for the principal investigator and his associates. When the problem of allocation of rights to data (who can publish what) arises, there may be arguments because initially no agreements were made. If investigators of equal status are directing a project, personalities may come into conflict, with each feeling that he has responsibilities and skills not possessed by the other.

Then there is the question of ethics (see Shils, 1959, pp. 114–57). To whom do sociologists owe the greatest moral obligation? Can they study persons with hidden recorders? Must they obtain permission from subjects before a study begins? Must they maintain anonymity in their final reports? Do they owe society at large a responsibility not to pry into private behavior settings? These questions represent ethical issues of the highest order, and they must be answered at some point in every investigation.

A further problem is the sociologist's involvement in value decisions. Can sociologists legitimately view their research as free of value implications, and can they avoid making value commitments as they do research? Some persons argue that values have no place in the scientific process, while others say that value commitments are made every step of the way (see Becker, 1967a, pp. 239–48; Gouldner, 1970).

The problems of ethics, organized research, responsibility to subjects, value positions, informal demands on the investigator, and misconception of the subject are issues that lie at the heart of doing sociology and science in general, yet they are not adequately treated in most methodology texts. In the remainder of this chapter these problems will be examined. I have held a discussion of them to the last, because to begin with them might have given a distorted view of the sociological enterprise.

TOWARD A RATIONALIZATION OF UNPLANNED CONTINGENCIES IN THE RESEARCH PROCESS

Consider the researcher doing a study of organizational records. She may be studying death statistics, juvenile court records, or rates of admission into a hospital for treatment of an emergency illness. Such a researcher might well employ an *unobtrusive measure of observation*, which is any method of observation that directly removes the observer from the set of interactions or events being studied. Public archival documents represent one major class of unobtrusive measures: The conditions that lead to their production are in no way influenced by an intruding sociological observer. These documents include valuable information about an organization. Prepared by a person in a given organizational position, archival records represent a peculiar stance toward the issues contained in it. Observers must be sensitive to such elective bias and ambiguity as these dimensions are introduced into the documents being analyzed. This is the first of three contingencies I will discuss.

Problems of Bias and Ambiguity

Analysts must realize that any public archival document represents the imprint of the organization that produced it, and thus bias arises simultaneously from both the author and the organization. The problem is further compounded when changes over time are considered; shifts in language, in population characteristics, and in organizational personnel all lead to potential dissimilarities across time in any report from an agency and in reports from agencies of the same class.

Observers must realize that the reality of any agency that produces archives is a reality representing that agency's interpretations of what has occurred, what is to be reported, and what is to be saved for future generations. The "agency perspective" becomes particularly acute when sociologists propose temporal analyses of such matters as crime rates, birth and death statistics, marriage and divorce rates, hospitalization statistics, and the like (see, for example, Garfinkel, 1967; Kitsuse and Cicourel, 1963, pp. 131–39).

If the problem of death is considered, the ambiguity of official, archival statistics becomes more clear. All persons understand what it means to die and what the word *dead* means, but Sudnow (1967, p. 65) has shown that:

> The actual occurrence of a death involves the operation of a rather specific set of mechanisms, none of which is currently understood in great detail. To "die," some say, the heart must cease beating, and that can occur as a direct result of one or more of a series of quite specific biochemical-physical occurrences, e.g., the heart can burst open in certain kinds of trauma, the nerve tissue which provides the heart with its electrical stimulation can be damaged, or weakened through a loss of blood supply, etc. Yet cessation of the heart is currently considered by some to be merely a "sign" of death, and not definitive of it.

Medical experts cannot agree on when death has occurred, nor can they agree on what definition will be attached to that biological and social status termed *death*. The problem is further complicated when the question is under what conditions a newborn is considered to have died. Citing observations from one hospital, Sudnow (1967, pp. 109–11) reports the following definitions that are used to describe *newborns*:

> At County Hospital, there is a system of definitions and weights intended to describe the status of fetuses. According to its weight, length, and period of gestation at the end of which it is delivered (or "expelled"), a fetus is either considered "human" or not. At County, the dividing line is 550 grams, 20 centimeters, and 20 weeks of gestation.

Not only do hospitals have different problems to confront when a human, as opposed to a "thing," is born, but they must also prepare official statistics to report such occurrences. If a fetus is not accorded "human" status, then a death statistic is not generated; however, the conditions that generate such data are ambiguously determined and subject to a great deal of modification and negotiation. Sudnow notes, for example, that Catholic parents are more likely than Protestants to have their fetuses defined as human (even if they immediately die). These observations challenge the generalizability of archival data on birth and death rates from one hospital to another. More broadly, of course, they suggest that similar organizations processing the same set of events (for example, police departments, mental hospitals, courts of law) may not generate comparable data on those events.

Before observers can confidently make valid comparisons across organizations and through time, they must consider the potential bias that arises from differing "organizational perspectives" on those events. It is a plausible hypothesis (and one that must be answered before analysis proceeds) that variations in such matters as delinquency rates or shifts in birth and death statistics do not represent true differences in the occurrence of those events. They may represent only differences in organizational bookkeeping.

Cicourel's analysis　This problem was sensitively treated by Cicourel (1968) in a study of juvenile courts in two communities. He found that the social organization of juvenile agencies in the two communities accounted for variations in their recorded rates of delinquency. Political pressures, previous experiences with juvenile officers, the presence or absence of lawyers, and the social status of the potential delinquent's family all affected the decision of whether or not a given adolescent would be defined as delinquent.

Cicourel (1968, p. 330) suggests that a meaningful analysis of public archival data (at least data on delinquency rates) cannot proceed until the investigator has "taken the role" of the members in the organization that is producing the records under analysis. He states, "Attempts to estimate crimes now known to the police are exceedingly difficult, but it is also difficult to evaluate the cases that are uncleared in police files and for which there are no suspects."

Cicourel suggests that observers study the generation of organizational records as they would study the formation of rumor, gossip, and history in everyday activities (see Shibutani, 1966). In analyzing such records, sociologists are dealing with the transformation of conversations, haphazard observations, and negotiated interpretations into formalized and unambiguous statements concerning the occurrence of a particular set of events, the motivations underlying such occurrences, and the actions of the recordkeeper toward them.

These issues return the discussion to the problem of ever achieving a complete and accurate rendering of any set of events, a problem further complicated because sociologists work with imperfectly constructed records as they elaborate their own interpretations and explanations. The meanings they bring to bear upon those records, the coding procedures they go through, and their final explanations represent still more steps away from the actual events being analyzed. Cicourel (p. 333) states:

> The policeman's conception of "typical" juveniles, "punks," "good kids," his recognition of typical sociological arrangements, family organization, and the like, are integral to understanding how behavior comes to be labeled "delinquent." ... The "delinquent" is an emergent product, transformed over time

according to a sequence of encounters, oral and written reports, prospective reasonings, retrospective readings of "what happened," and the practical circumstances of "setting" matters in everyday agency business.

The existence of delinquents, dead children, married women, and psychiatric patients assumes that such "objects" have an objective social existence uniformly perceived by all qualified persons. The position I am advocating holds that the occurrence of such "objects" in a social reality is always a negotiated existence subject to alternative interpretations, definitions, and symbolic meanings. Therefore, their reported existence in public and private archives must be treated as a "peculiar" interpretation that may or may not have been reported in the same fashion by another agency or another person at another time. Each archival report must be interpreted within its own "situated" context. The failure to achieve this "situated interpretation" can only further challenge the internal validity and more greatly distort the authenticity and meaning of such analyses.

Failure to Consider Subjects' Social Context; Relationship of Subjects and Researchers

A second major contingency that may arise during the research process is a failure to consider the social context within which subjects are located. Closely related to the contextual location of subjects is the type of relationship observers establish with them. (This latter point raises the broader question of values and ethics and will be discussed shortly.) A continuum of effects that subjects may have upon research activities can be constructed. Persons randomly selected in a social survey seldom influence total research efforts, of course, but at the other extreme recalcitrant informants, persons who refuse interviews, or even entire communities and nations, can tremendously influence individual studies and indirectly affect the total discipline.

Analysis of the effects of subjects first demands an analysis of the types of subjects whom sociologists conduct research *on, toward,* and *for.* Some subjects remain strangers to us, and for them our research is of little importance. Shils (1959, p. 141) has described the typical small-group experiment as one in which little feedback occurs because of the nature of this relationship:

> In the first place, the groups on which experiments are carried out are small. The situations are very often no more than quasi-real at best. They are contrived by the experimenter; they are seldom recurrent, and they are usually of brief duration, falling mainly between a half-hour and two hours. The stimuli or the variables in the situation are rarely of great significance to the experimental subjects and as far as is known — it has never been followed up — leave no lasting impression on the personality or outlook of the subject. Since, furthermore, the groups that are the objects of the experiment usually have had no anterior life of their own, they disappear from memory with the end of the experiment.

In these circumstances few alterations in the research design would be expected, but there are subjects with whom observers establish an in-depth relationship. They may be students who become subjects, friends who formerly were subjects, or colleagues from whom data are gathered. Analysts can expect demands from such subjects. They may, for example, ask that certain features of their behavior not be reported; some may quarrel with the researcher's interpretations; others may attempt to ingratiate themselves. If prior agreements have not been made concerning the research relationship, severe repercussions can occur.

Vidich and Bensman (1964, pp. 313–49) report on a community study that focused on stratification, prestige, and political patterns of interaction, but soon became an investigation that commanded the attention of the American Anthropological and Sociological Associations. Their book, *Small Town in Mass Society,* received negative reviews in the newspaper of the small town they studied; it was likened to the book *Peyton Place.* The townspeople charged that Vidich and Bensman had violated their research agreements and had misrepresented themselves to the town.

It has become commonplace for researchers to have subjects sign "informed consent" documents in which they agree to be subjects in the research that is undertaken. The U.S. federal government requires that these forms be signed before funded research begins. The intent is to protect subjects' rights and to ensure that they will not be subjected to ethical, psychological, or physical harm and danger. Many universities have followed suit. The 1974 Federal Privacy Act also speaks to this problem. It stipulates that prospective respondents be informed about the existence of data systems that contain, or will contain, information on them. In this way, a subject's right to privacy is supposedly maintained.

The lesson should be clear: An investigator who makes promises to a subject, no matter how implicit, will be held to them. Such promises can take a number of forms, depending on who the subject is, what the relationship between investigator and subject is, and what the investigator's intents and purposes are. It is nearly axiomatic that all subjects expect something in return for their cooperation. Except for small amounts of money, the sociologist has little to offer. An investigator can show subjects the final report (knowing they may not understand it) and occasionally may be able (and willing) to make policy recommendations concerning a social problem, but that is about all. Sociologists must always be aware that subjects do indeed talk back, however, and the nature of this dialogue can significantly shape final results.

Political Context of Research; Impingement of Pressure Groups

A third, and highly variable, contingency in the research process is the political and social context in which sociologists find themselves—a complex, political world of competing, conflicting, and only infrequently complementary values, perspectives, and ideologies. In short, it is a world of settings defined differently by each of many competing reference and pressure groups. The existence of such perspectives means that sociological activity in some way reflects the interpretation given them. When researchers attempt to meet the needs of a client while satisfying the goals of their own profession, they find themselves compromising the demands of each when they try to bring their own goals into the process.

The following groups may impinge on the sociologist's actions: clients, subjects, respondents, informants, research organizations, granting agencies, academic communities, students, colleagues, scientific and professional societies, and even local, national, and international political communities (see Sjoberg, 1967, p. xiii). To the extent that these groups and their perspectives are differently recognized and brought into the sociologist's lines of action, it is possible to speak of differing social relationships and interpretations emerging between them and the sociologist. A researcher may be simultaneously responding to the demands of a client, a network of colleagues, and a university while engaging in a single act of research. What is the effect of these variously recognized pressure groups upon one's activities as a sociologist?

The literature abounds with instances in which one pressure group was ignored to please another. In such cases, sociologists run the risk of endangering the project, if not their own careers.

Unless sociologists are of such eminence that clients will feel fortunate to receive their services, they find themselves compromising these competing perspectives, and too often the compromise shifts in the direction of the client or granting agency, with sociology taking second best. This would not be so unfortunate if it were not for the fact that the client's money is typically tied to the analysis of social problems. The sociological analysis of social problems is appropriate, of course; but what is a social problem one year may not be so the next, and in such cases sociologists find their research being directed by another's perspective. It would seem that a more reasonable strategy for building a science of sociology would be long-term programmatic research projects that permitted the sociologist to pursue problems in an atmosphere free from a client's demands and needs.

Ethics: The Value-Laden Context of Sociological Research

I have thus far argued that all sociological activity occurs within a context of shifting political pressures. It follows that a fourth major contingency shaping sociological activity is the values and ethical stances sociologists either voluntarily or involuntarily assume. While most sociologists now agree that it is impossible to conduct research in the absence of personal and political values, few agree upon the exact nature of these values and the precise role they should occupy in their activities. My previous comments on social relationships suggest that sociologists may have as many values and ethical stances as they have relationships. Thus, clients may expect certain findings, while colleagues expect another.

Definition   In this respect, I must make clear what is meant by the term *ethics*. There seems to be general agreement that ethics (and values as well) refer to an "ought" world. When researchers make a decision to study prisoners and not prison officials, they are making a value decision. But when they say that the relationship between X and Y is negative, they are making a scientific statement. Science is "an *is world*, a set of facts growing out of consensus among a small group" (Dalton, 1964, p. 60). When I say that all sociologists *should* honor their relationships with subjects, I am making an ethical statement. When some sociologists do not honor these relationships, they are branded as unethical. It must be remembered that ethics and values, like scientific findings, are not statements that come from an invariant source. They do not reside in a world of abstract ideals. Rather, ethics (like all plans of action) consists of symbolic meanings subject to the most complex political arguments. Hence, when I speak of values and ethics in the scientific process, I refer to meanings that are subject to negotiation and redefinition. What is ethical in one period, one university, one profession, or one group may be unethical in another.

It is impossible not to take ethical and value stances in the process of research. When analysts choose to enter one social setting and not another, they have made an implicit value decision that one is better than the other for their purposes. When I state that sociology should be scientific, I make a value statement. Values and ethics are with sociologists at all times. According to such spokesmen as Lundberg and Parsons, values have no place in the scientific process; they say that science studies the world of facts, and that scientists do not make value decisions. To the contrary, I would agree with Becker, who suggests, as the quotation at the beginning of this chapter indicates, that it is not whether we take sides, but rather, whose side are we on?

Ethical questions

Accountability   A consideration of values and ethics in sociology must first answer this question: "To whom are sociologists accountable when they make observations?" My position is that they are responsible to many differing groups. A good deal of the debate today over the uses of sociology represents an inability to agree on which pressure group should take precedence. Shils (1959, p. 147) states:

> Ultimately, the ethical quality of social science research—i.e., the ethical quality of the relationship of the investigator to the person he interviews or observes—is derived from the social scientist's relations, as a person and as a citizen, with his society and with his fellow man.

I would reject Shils's treatment of ethics; it denies the important and significant part played by the variety of pressure groups considered earlier. Sociologists find themselves in a complexly variegated world of changing values, ethics, and political perspectives. No one value, ideology, or system of ethics uniformly applies to their activities.

Consequences   A second major question is: "What are the ethical consequences of sociological activities?" For example, do certain methodologies raise different moral and ethical questions from others? Is it reasonable to state that participant observation in a disguised role is more unethical than a public survey (Erikson, 1968, pp. 505–6)?

Implication of Findings   Closely related to such questions about methodology is the question: "What stance should sociologists take toward the implications of their findings?" Are sociologists obligated to move into the outside world and actively promote social change? Or is their position more restricted, primarily involving the pursuit of knowledge? In my discussion of these questions, the main interest will be in demonstrating that unless sociologists recognize the role played by values and ethics in their daily affairs, closer ties between theory, method, and data will not be forthcoming.

Ethical absolutism and ethical relativism   Two incompatible solutions to the question of how sociologists resolve their obligations to those observed may be distinguished. On the one hand, there are what may be termed *ethical absolutists*, who argue that one set of ethics uniformly applies to all sociological activity. On the other hand, there are the *ethical relativists*, who suggest that the only reasonable standard is the one "dictated by the individual's conscience" (Becker, 1964, p. 280; Dalton, 1964, pp. 50–95).

The ethical absolutist's position was best summarized by Shils (1959, pp. 114–47) and repeated by Erikson (1967, pp. 366–73). Before I present this position, a word on my own position is in order. Briefly, I disagree with those who suggest that the sociologist has no right to observe those who have not given their consent. I suggest that sociologists have the right to make observations on anyone in any setting to the extent that they do so for scientific purposes. The goal of any science is not harm to subjects, but the advancement of knowledge. Any method that moves us toward that goal without unnecessary harm to subjects is justifiable. The method employed cannot in any deliberate fashion damage the credibility or reputation of the subject, and the sociologist must take pains to maintain the integrity and anonymity of those studied — unless directed otherwise. This may require the withholding of certain findings from publication entirely, or until those observed have moved into positions where they can be done no harm. My position holds that no areas of observation should be closed a priori to the sociologist, nor should any research methods be defined a priori as unethical, a position clearly at odds with that of the ethical absolutists.

Ethical absolutism begins with the assumption that one can ascribe to modern Western society a value structure that stresses individual autonomy. The dominant moral theme of this social order is the fundamental right of privacy and autonomy for each individual. From this basic assumption a number of ethical principles can be derived for the social scientist (Shils, 1959, pp. 114–47). *First,* social scientists have no right to invade the personal privacy of any individual. Thus, disguised research techniques such as participant observation or unobtrusive methods are defined as unethical when they invade this private order and hence potentially challenge the right of individual autonomy. *Second,* sociologists as scientists are morally obligated to contribute to their society's self-understanding. In this respect they can manipulate subjects and intrude into their private quarters only when such activities have therapeutic or genuinely scientific purposes, such as increasing knowledge. *Third,* because intrusions into private quarters and the deliberate disguising of the intentions of research potentially cause harm to subjects, sociologists can legitimately practice their science only in public spheres with openly defined methods (for example, public surveys).

This ethical system does contain a number of qualifications. Shils (1959, pp. 138–39), for example, suggests that under certain circumstances it is permissible to invade private spheres of conduct. That is, he suggests that sociologists can legitimately study public institutions such as the law and polity when they do not unduly challenge the moral order and sacredness of those institutions. He states:

> I myself see no good reason, therefore, other than expediency, why these "sacred" secular subjects should not be studied by social scientists or why they should not be studied by legitimate techniques. I can see no harm that can come from such inquiries, carried on with judicious detachment and presented with discretion. I can see no moral issue here, such as I can see in the case of manipulation by interviewers and observers or in the case of intrusions of privacy.

Despite this, Shils argues that excessive publicity given to sacred-secular institutions "not only breaks the confidentiality which enhances the imaginativeness and reflectiveness necessary for the effective working of institutions but also destroys the respect in which they should, at least, tentatively, be held by the citizenry" (1959, p. 137). That this position contradicts his other ethical mandates seems not to bother him, however, for he goes on to state (pp. 137–39):

> The former consideration is purely empirical and has a reasonable probability of being right. It restricts the freedom of social scientists. The second consideration is genuinely conservative, as it implies that authority must have some aura of the ineffable about it to be effective.

To summarize, Shils — as an ethical absolutist — argues that there are only two conditions under which sociologists can legitimately engage in their science: when the results contain some potential therapeutic value (the alleviation of a social problem), or when they contribute to the total body of scientific knowledge. It is clear, however, that the value of science for science's sake takes a position subordinate to science for purposes of therapy. Shils seems to see the function of all human activity as upholding the morality of the attendant social order. This deliberately conservative bias contradicts what I regard as the necessary stance of modern social science. It must also be noted that Shils's position can lead the sociologist into support for clearly unethical state practices, as evidenced in Nazi Germany in the 1930s and '40s. On this Becker observes (1964, p. 273):

> The impossibility of achieving consensus, and hence the necessity of conflict, stems in part from the difference between the characteristic approach of the social scientist and that of the layman to the analysis of social life. Everett Hughes has often pointed out that the sociological view of the world — abstract, relativistic, generalizing — necessarily deflates people's view of themselves and their organizations.

Becker states that sociologists inevitably take someone's side to the potential injustice of another, and hence inevitably present things as some people do not wish to see them; to this, Shils would reply that sociologists should simply avoid circumstances in which such consequences could arise. This, of course, represents an irreducible conflict. If sociologists true to their calling represent the seamier sides of life, then how can it be proposed that they examine settings where no injustice to any perspective would occur?

It seems to me that the ethical absolutists share many of the biases of their counterparts in philosophical idealism, who presume that it is possible to have a complete knowledge of the values of a society. The idealists claim to have an image of good and bad, and hence to be able to construct one set of ethical mandates. What they ignore is that ethics, like values and other lines of action directed toward social objects, are symbolic meanings that emerge out of a political context. Morality, ethics, and values emerge out of interaction. The absolutist disregards this fundamental feature of human interaction.

It is totally indefensible to state that sociologists ought not to challenge the sacred order of their secular institutions, just as it is indefensible to define beforehand what methods, goals, and strategies sociologists ought to employ. While my position on this matter is clearly value-laden, I feel it is justified by the interactionist perspective. Further, it seems to be supported by the activities sociologists routinely engage in. Sociology is abstract, and sociological observations necessarily reveal elements of social behavior that persons in everyday life would prefer not to have revealed.

What, then, is the solution? I have suggested that each sociologist necessarily determines his or her own ethics. If no one set of standards will apply to sociological activities, then in each situation encountered, a slightly different ethical stance will be required. This position, of course, entails a view of the sociological process which assumes that each sociologist is committed to "telling it as it is" and is relatively free to make such statements. That is, I assume that despite the existence of multiple competing pressure groups, the sociologist can manage to maintain scientific integrity. I further assume that the social location of sociologists in this political world is such that they are free to make value and ethical decisions.

Several conditions will affect the translation of this ethical standard into daily sociological conduct. In the simplest cases, as Becker notes, the sociologist may be "taken in" by those under study and thus may be unable to tell it "as it is." Let us take research in organizational settings as an instance of this situation. It is possible to note cases in which observers are permitted access to certain behavior settings, but those giving this permission may structure the situation so that researchers see only what they want them to see. To counteract organizational management of the situation, the researcher must have a thorough knowledge of the field situation and an awareness that things are often not what they are presented to be. The researcher may also be taken over by the values of those under study and lose sociological objectivity. To guard against this, I have earlier recommended periodic absences from the field by the observer so that a renewed perspective may be established.

The sociologist may be forced into an undesirable ethical stance because of promises made to subjects. This was the problem confronted by Vidich and Bensman: In order to secure the right to observe, they had to make promises that were later violated. Commenting on these promises, Becker suggests that most sociologists specify "that they have the final say as to what will be published, though they often grant representatives of the organization the right to review the manuscript and suggest changes" (1964, p. 278).

Ostensibly, the solution to this problem lies in the kinds of agreements observers make with those studied. Upon analysis, however, this can be seen as sidestepping the issue. Ultimately, the kinds of bargains sociologists should strive for are those that give complete freedom to study what is deemed necessary. Few subjects will agree to this, feeling always that they know more than sociologists about their problems—a conviction that conveniently permits them to limit researchers' access to settings that might be viewed as crucial. In situations in which subjects grant complete freedom, it is likely that they will not understand the full implications of such an agreement: "The people who agree to have a social scientist study them have not had the experience before and do not know what to expect, nor are they aware of the experiences of others social scientists have studied" (Becker, 1964, p. 280).

Making a proper research agreement, as a solution to the problem of publication and one's obligations to those studied, is insufficient, because each scientist must ultimately decide for herself what to do or not to do, what to publish or not publish. These decisions must rest with the conscience of the individual researcher, who, more than any other person, has intimate knowledge of the consequences of his or her actions. Abstract ethical rules cannot solve the issues that daily arise in sociological research. For example, certain officials in an organization may have access to researchers' manuscripts and daily observations, while low-level line workers are not even aware of the investigators' presence. To those officials made aware of such studies, are observers ethically obligated to reveal how line workers avoid certain forms of work? Must observers tell all persons they study that they are sociologist? Can they tell line workers that their managers care little about the quality of their products? These are only a few of the problems that arise in any investigation. Their resolution must come from the persons involved—the individual scientist and the subjects.

One mandate thus governs sociological activity: The absolute freedom to pursue one's activities as one sees fit. This rule will be variously translated into individual projects; it is ultimately contingent on the researchers' conscience and on what those in the field situation permit them to do and see.

When making an agreement, an additional line of action may be of value. *First,* researchers can warn those studied of the effect of publication and help to prepare them for possible consequences. As Becker suggests (1964, pp. 270–83), a carefully thought out educational program may help those studied to come to better terms with what the sociologist reports. Such programs might take the form of seminars, small-group discussions, and even the circulation of the final report before it is published. In presenting results to the group studied, the investigator can make clear the kinds of consequences that may be forthcoming. As Becker notes, the investigator can point out the effect of the study on other groups with which those studied are in interaction (the press, national organizations, clients, citizens, and the like) and show them that the findings may endanger their standing with respect to these groups. But in so doing, the investigator can make clear that their problems are not unique — that they are shared by many other organizations and communities. Given this perspective, the subjects can better defend their own difficulties and perhaps move in directions for needed social change.

Second, sociologists can make clear the kinds of interpretations a report may generate. They can make their own value judgments clear and indicate what their biases were. With this information, the subjects can better defend their own setting by making reference to the scientific document generated on and about them.

Third, the investigator may open new avenues of action and perception among those studied. Organizational leaders may be ignorant of the repressive, dysfunctional aspects of certain programs, and an exposure to the sociologist's findings may correct their misconceptions.

Dangers to sociologists' integrity may arise during this process of education. Hostile factions of which they were previously unaware may come forth and challenge their credibility. Faced with this pressure, a researcher may be inclined to alter certain elements of a study. Although it may appear that deletions from a report would appease certain parties, under no circumstances should such deletions be sanctioned. It may appear that certain features of a report can be deleted without changing its significance. Embellishments on a point previously well established can be removed if their presence would unduly jeopardize some person. If, however, their presence is necessary to establish the credibility of a point, they should remain. In this situation, if it appears to the investigator that the findings will bring harm or loss of respect to some subject, publication may be withheld until the subject has moved into a situation in which such harm would not occur, or at least would be minimized. The sociologist must know field situations thoroughly in order to resolve these ethical issues adequately and confidently. Theory and data must be well in hand, so that when the problem of deciding what to publish arises, the researcher can defend deletions and inclusions with full confidence.

Closely related to the foregoing issues is the question of whether or not various research methods have differing ethical implications. Basically, the ethical absolutist argues for the exclusion of all research strategies that hide or disguise the true nature of sociological activities. To an absolutist, disguised observer roles and many unobtrusive methods are unethical because permission for their use has not been obtained from those studied. A strong proponent of this absolutist position is Erikson (1967, pp. 366–73). In this presentation of his argument, the counterperspective of the ethical relativist will also be discussed (see Ball, 1967; Denzin, 1968, pp. 502–4; Polsky, 1967, pp. 117–49).

Erikson's first argument against disguised observation is that it represents an invasion of privacy. Such an interpretation of course assumes that the sociologist can define beforehand what is a private behavior setting and what is a public behavior setting. Cavan's findings (1966) suggest that any given behavior setting may, depending on the time of day and categories of participants present, be defined as either public or private. The implication is that "privateness" of a behavior setting becomes an empirical question. To categorically define settings as public or private potentially ignores the perspective of these studied and supplants the sociologist's definitions for those of the subjects. Erikson continues this argument by suggesting that when sociologists gain entry into private settings by taking on disguised roles, they potentially cause discomfort to those observed; and because sociologists lack the means to assess this induced discomfort, they have no right to disguise their intentions or roles in the research process. If the research of Goffman is taken seriously, the statement that wearing masks or disguising one's intents raises ethical questions and causes discomfort during the research process may be challenged, for the proper question becomes not whether wearing a mask is unethical (since no mask is any more real than any other), but rather, which mask should be worn? There is no straightforward answer, for sociologists assume a variety of masks, or selves, depending on where they find themselves (the classroom, the office, the field). Who is to say which of these are disguised and which are real? My position is that any mask assumed intelligently and not deliberately to injure the subject is acceptable. To assert that an assumed role during the research process is *necessarily* unethical and harmful is mistaken.

Second, Erikson argues that the sociologist who assumes a disguised role jeopardizes the broader professional community, because exposure could simultaneously close doors to future research and taint the image of the profession. My position is that any research method poses threats to fellow colleagues. A community surveyed twice annually for the past ten years can develop an unfavorable image of sociology and refuse to be studied just as easily as a local AA group studied by a disguised sociologist can. Every time sociologists venture into the outside world for purposes of research, they place the reputation of the profession on the line. To argue that disguised observations threaten this reputation more than the survey or the experiment ignores the potential impact these methods can, and often do, have.

Third, Erikson argues that sociologists owe it to their students not to place them in situations in which they might have to assume a disguised research role. The assumption of such roles, Erikson suggests, poses moral and ethical problems for the investigator, and students should not have this burden placed on them. My position, based on my own experiences and experiences related by other colleagues, is that this feeling of uncertainty and ethical ambiguity can just as easily arise from the circumstances surrounding the first interview with an irate subject in a social survey. Certain persons feel more comfortable in the role of disguised observer than in the role of survey interviewer, known participant observer, or laboratory observer. The belief that encounters with subjects when in the role of disguised observer cause more investigator discomfort than other kinds of investigation may be questioned. I suggest there is nothing inherent in the role that produces ethical or personal problems for the investigator.

Erikson's fourth argument is that data gathered by the disguised method are faulty because sociologists lack the means to assess their disruptive effects on the setting and on those observed. I propose that sociologists sensitive to this problem of disruption employ the method of postobservational inquiry recently adopted by psychologists; the investigator asks the subjects what they thought the experiment entailed. After completing observations in the disguised role, the researcher's presence could be made public and those observed could then be questioned concerning the effect on them. Such a procedure would provide empirical data on these perceived disruptive effects, thus allowing their assessment, and it would permit sociologists to measure empirically the amount of discomfort or harm their disguised presence created. Further, investigators might make greater use of day-to-day field notes to measure their own perceived impact. Every time sociologists ask a subject a question, they potentially alter behavior and jeopardize the quality of subsequent data. It seems unreasonable to assume that more public research methods (surveys, for example) do not also disrupt the stream of events under analysis. To argue that disguised roles cause the most disruption seems open to question.

Erikson concludes by noting that sociologists never reveal everything when they enter the field. I suggest that not only do they never reveal everything, but frequently it is not possible for them to reveal everything; they themselves are not fully aware of their actual intentions and purposes (in long-term field studies, for example).

Summarizing his position, Erikson offers two ethical dictates: It is unethical for researchers to deliberately misrepresent their identity to gain entry into private domains otherwise denied them, and it is unethical to deliberately misrepresent the character of research. My reactions are perhaps in the minority among contemporary sociologists, but they indicate what I feel is a necessary uneasiness concerning the argument that sociologists are unethical when they investigate under disguise or without permission. To accept this position has the potential of making sociology a profession that studies only volunteer subjects. I suggest that this misrepresents the very nature of the research process; sociologists have seldom stood above subjects and decided whom they had the right to study and whom they were obligated not to study. Instead, they have always established their domain during the process of research, largely on the basis of their own personal, moral, and ethical standards. (In retrospect this can be seen to be so, given the fact that such categories of persons as housewives, homosexuals, mental patients, and prostitutes are now viewed as acceptable and legitimate persons for investigation.)

Finally, I suggest that in addition to these ethical questions, sociologists might also concern themselves with the fact that at this point in the history of their science they lack the automatic moral-legal license and mandate to gain entry into any research setting; nor do they have the power to withhold information from civil-legal authorities after their data have been obtained. Sociology as a profession has little stature in the eyes of the public and the broader civil-legal order. To put ourselves in a position that sanctions research only on what persons give us permission to study continues and makes more manifest an uncomfortable public status. Certainly this need not be the case, as the current status of psychiatry, medicine, the clergy, and the law indicates (see Bulmer, 1982).

I have placed the burden of ethical decision on the personal-scientific conscience of the individual investigator. My own position should be clear: I feel that sociologists who have assumed those research roles and strategies Erikson calls "unethical" have contributed more substantive knowledge to such diverse areas as small-group research, deviant behavior, and medical and organizational sociology than those who have assumed more open roles. But again, this is a matter of individual, as well as collective, scientific conscience and standards. The entry into any scientific enterprise threatens someone's values — be it another sociologist or a member of some society. As Becker said, sociologists must always ask themselves, "Whose side are we on?" (1967, p. 239). I feel that Erikson's position takes away from the sociologist the right to make this decision. Perhaps rather than engaging in polemics and debate, the best course of action would be for sociologists as a profession to open these matters to public discussion and empirical inquiry.

SILVERMAN'S THREE ANSWERS TO THE QUESTION "WHOSE SIDE ARE WE ON?"

Silverman (1985, pp. 178–96) has offered three answers to Becker's question, Whose side are we on? His statement not only criticizes the one I have taken in this chapter, but, more important, it also thickens the problem and anchors its discussion more firmly in the postmodern period of American sociology (post–World War II). Table 11-1, adapted from Silverman, articulates three ethical positions.

Scholar

The liberal stance of the scholar assumes that no absolute set of ethical values can be applied to the research act. Each researcher must search his or her conscience and develop an ethical stance that reflects the highest standards he or she can attain. This will necessarily be a critical, value-laden stance. In my own work, I have argued that the sociologist should not merely record and describe human experience; the sociologist's voice can be one of the props to help men and women endure and prevail (see Faulkner, 1967, p. 724). I have also argued that sociologists should study significant, turning-point human experiences in which biography and society existentially merge. In so doing, it should be possible to develop a meaningful, interpretive sociology which speaks to real, consequential human experience.

Becker and Horowitz (1986, pp. 83–102) state, in regard to good sociology:

> [It] is sociological work that produces meaningful descriptions of organizations and events, valid explanations of how they come about and persist, and realistic proposals for their improvement or removal.

TABLE 11-1   The Ethics of Involvement in Social Research*

Sociological identity	Politcal stance	Ethical commitment	Example
Scholar	Liberal	Knowledge for knowledge's sake, protected by scholar's conscience	Weber, Denzin
State counselor	Bureaucratic	Social engineering	Popper
Partisan	Feminist, Marxist, conservative	Praxis, political theory, political practice	Marx, Foucault, Silverman, C.A. MacKinnon, Hoover Institute

*Adapted from Silverman, *Qualitative Methodology and Sociology: Describing the Social World.* Hants, England and Brookfield, Vt.: Gower, 1985, p. 180, by permission of the publisher and the author.

Elsewhere, Becker (1967b) has argued that sociology can assist in the study of social problems in five ways. First, it can help sort out competing definitions of a problem. Second, it can expose and illuminate the underlying assumptions that support competing definitions of a problem. Third, it can check these assumptions against social facts. Fourth, it can suggest strategic points of intervention in problem situations. Fifth, it can propose alternative moral definitions of the problem.

I followed such a strategy in my research of alcoholics. I examined competing social science theories of alcoholism. I checked these theories out against the lived experiences of alcoholics. I suggested various ways of intervening in the alcoholic situation. I proposed making a distinction between the alcoholic and alcoholism, and I argued against negative moral judgments of the alcoholic's conduct.

Sociologists must be free to do good sociological work. Such work, as Becker and Horowitz observe, produces meaningful descriptions of situations and problems, builds interpretations of action in these situations, and offers realistic proposals for their improvement or removal. If this work is directed to existentially meaningful human problems, then the higher ethical value that guides such work is the betterment of the human condition. This stance requires freedom to do research, skepticism concerning those in power, an identification with those who live social problems, and a willingness to criticize both those in power and those who live the problem.

Perhaps an example will illustrate. Alcoholic treatment centers create alcoholics. They teach persons who have problems with alcohol how to call themselves alcoholics. It is not always clear that persons who end up in treatment centers need to learn how to call themselves alcoholics. In my research, I suggested that large classes of persons are treated as alcoholics, when in fact they suffer from other problems, including mental illness. Therefore, closer attention must be given to a person's biography before the label "alcoholic" is applied to him.

At the same time, I argued that many AA-affiliated groups organize themselves in ways that work against the alcoholic's recovery. Some social clubs punish and expel members who drink and relapse, thus pushing them back into the worlds of drinking experience. Some AA groups exclude blacks and homosexuals. Others exclude persons of lower social status. In these actions, AA as a self-help organization perpetuates discrimination and works against the recovery of certain types of alcoholics. By addressing treatment centers, which are sites of power, and AA groups, also sites of power, I attempted to show how the lived experiences of alcoholics are shaped by enduring social stereotypes. I think that this is how good sociological research conducted under the scholarly label works.

State Counselor

In the identity as state counselor, the sociologist will often conduct research that is used by policymakers; indeed, the research is often paid for by the state or one of its agencies. In this identity the sociologist becomes a state bureaucrat and engages in social engineering. He attempts to implement studies that conform to or address agency needs and policies. State counselors may, as Bulmer (1982) and Silverman (1985) argue, follow one or more combinations of the following models.

Empiricism: Here it is assumed that facts speak for themselves. The researcher merely collects facts that an agency wants or needs. Of course, facts do not speak for themselves; they are theory-based and are shaped by the ideological stances of the researcher, the agency, and sometimes the method employed.

The Engineering Model: State counselors as social engineers often conduct research that moves through four stages: (1) identification of the required knowledge (Silverman, 1985, p. 182); (2) gathering of relevant data; (3) interpretation and analysis of data; and (4) proposed changes in policy at the intervention level. Too often, engineers study what bureaucrats want studied. They become ideological agents of the state. They supply information that supports the state's desire to perpetuate or terminate programs that they want continued or abolished.

The Enlightenment Model: Under this identity, the researcher attempts to enlighten bureaucrats (Silverman, 1985, p. 183). He or she does not just collect facts, supply political ammunition for programs, or evaluate policy. Instead, the effort is to help policymakers think through new conceptualizations of problems so that they can be viewed in a new and different light.

This is a flawed model, for, as Silverman notes (and he cites Project Camelot to support his case), the researcher still acts as a handmaiden of the state. The United States "Star Wars" program, which is supposed to prevent the nuclear annihilation of the world, is a product, in part, of the enlightenment model.

Partisan

Silverman (1985, p. 184) defines this identity in terms of the following dimensions:

1. The partisan does not suffer under the delusion (as the scholar does) that the world can be held at arm's length and that no accountability toward social problems need be taken.
2. The partisan, unlike the state counselor, does not become an agent of the state.
3. The partisan seeks "to provide the theoretical and factual resources for political struggle."

Partisanship can be of the right or the left. It can take the form of feminist discourse, Marxist thought, socialist theorizing, or conservative posturing. It can be mechanistic and simply apply "proven truths," often ideologically based, to a social situation — in which case little is accomplished, except for the reaffirmation of a political position. Too often the partisan "makes claims to know how things really are while all too often ignoring what people are actually saying and doing" (Silverman, 1985, p. 188). Such self-righteousness is all too common in academia.

Silverman concludes his discussion of these three answers to the question "Whose side are we on?" with an approving discussion of Karl Marx's inventive inquiry method. This method, in the hands of Marx, he contends, shows how research can create a dialogue between researchers and subjects so that a research method can become a "didactic and political instrument" (Silverman, 1985, p. 195) for social change.

CONCLUSION

All sociologists are partisans. There is no pure scholarly identity; nor is there a pure social engineering identity. Silverman does not answer Becker's question; he merely charts three ways in which we can take sides. If we must take sides, and there is no choice about the matter, then our partisanship must lie in the direction of "the reign of freedom," in which all humans are free to become who they can be (Sartre, 1960/1976, p. 818). In such a regime, the sociologist's duty, like the poet's, will be to show that such freedom is possible. On the writer's duty, Faulkner (1967, p. 724) writes:

> It is his (and her) privilege to help man (and woman) endure by lifting his (her) heart, by reminding him (her) of the courage and honor and hope and pride and compassion and pity and sacrifice which have been the glory of his (her) past.

But there is more. Postmodern, interpretive sociology must expose the social problems that modernist, positivist sociology helped create. The sociologist has an obligation to become free of the positivist preconceptions of the research act so that a fully interpretive, existentially relevant sociology can be written.

SUGGESTED READINGS

MILLS, C. W., *The Sociological Imagination*. (New York: Oxford University Press, 1959). A classic statement on how to connect the research act to the sociological imagination. Should be read as an agenda-setting statement for contemporary sociologists.

SILVERMAN, DAVID, *Qualitative Methodology and Sociology: Describing the Social World*. (Brookfield, Vt. and Hants, England: Gower, 1985). Outstanding discussion (pp. 178–96) of values, ethics, and partisanship in sociological research. Chapter 5 offers a thoroughgoing critique of the interactionist position taken in this book.

ENDNOTE

Ultimately, sociological analysts must return to the fact that their discipline represents humans studying fellow humans. This condition dictates the fate of sociology as a dicipine: An imperfectly perceiving object is examining objects that react. No matter how technically perfect methods become, variance in observations will always arise, because the sociological observer is a social animal subject to the same whims and fancies, the same pressures and ideologies, as those under study.

Given this, it is perhaps appropriate to ask once again the following hoary questions: Whose side are sociologists on when acting as sociologists? Whose values are influencing them? What ideologies do they hold? What are their personal preferences for one type of method as opposed to another?

If, as I have suggested, sociologists will always be criticized because they disclose a perspective or point of view that someone wished concealed, then they must recognize this as a potential contingency shaping their activities. If sociologists remain true to their discipline, this will always be the case. Some will say that the wrong group was studied, others may say that someone's methods were unethical, and still others may dislike the researcher's theory. Some critics may even say that sociologists are not involved enough in the "real world"—that they do not adequately concern themselves with the social consequences of their findings. To these persons, the researcher can only answer as Becker (1967a, p. 247) has:

> We take sides as our personal and political commitments dictate, use our theoretical and technical resources to avoid the distortions they might introduce into our work, limit our conclusions carefully, recognize the hierarchy of credibility for what it is, and field as best we can the accusations and doubts that will surely be our fate.

This book represents only one position among many on the current issues surrounding theory and method in sociology. The programmatic theme dominating my discussion has been deliberate. I believe that the sociologist can no longer treat theory and method as separate subdivisions within the discipline. They represent intertwined yet significantly different ways of acting on the symbolic environment. The two must be brought together in an integrated fashion, and my efforts represent a tentative and provisional attempt in this direction. It is my hope that the issues discussed in this book will be debated by others. Such is the nature of interaction in any context.

Glossary

Analytic induction: An analytic strategy that seeks universal explanations of the phenomenon in question, based on the analysis of negative cases and processual, interactive interpretations.

Biographical method: That combination of research approaches which draws upon life stories, life histories, case studies, oral histories, personal narratives, and self stories.

Capture: Securing naturalistic instances of a phenomenon being studied.

Causal proposition: A processual, interpretive statement that excludes rival interpretations, builds on negative cases, and establishes an invariant, recurring relationship between two or more processes. Analytic induction, multivariate analysis, and the experimental method are three major ways of developing causal, interpretive propositions.

Cause: (Two meanings) (1) *Scientific:* establishes covariance and time order, and excludes rival causal factors (internal and external validity); (2) *Everyday:* "because" and "in order to" explanations of how and why a given process occurs or did occur.

Contextualizing: Locating what is being studied in the biographies of interacting individuals.

Counterfactual reasoning: Reasoning based on events that did not occur.

Creative interviewing: Creative, attentive listening and sharing in the interview relationship. Involves trust and mutual respect.

Deconstruction: Critically examining prior theories and interpretations of a phenomenon.

First-order concept: The language of everyday life.

Gendered observations: All observations are doubly shaped by gender, gender politics, and the gender stratification system: (1) gender permeates social experience; (2) the gendered identity of the observer influences what is observed, how it is observed, and how it is interpreted.

Hermeneutics: Doing interpretation.

Interpretation: Clarifying the meaning of a phenomenon.

Interpretive theory: Interpretation based on thick description; does not generalize across cases, but treats each case as a universal singular.

Laboratory as provocative stage: Interactionist conception of the experimental laboratory as a stage where the dramas of social life are created and played out by all participants.

Naturalistic interactionism: The studied commitment to actively enter the worlds of interacting individuals and to render those worlds understandable from the point of view of those studied.

Participant observation: Participating in the lives of those studied while doing ethnography, or the writing of the world one studies. Involves triangulated research methods.

Positivism: Has five basic tenets: (1) seeks objectivity; (2) uses hypothetical-deductive theory; (3) attempts to build external lawlike statements; (4) uses formal, precise language; (5) separates facts from their meanings.

Postmodern ethnography (and theory):   Has the following characteristics: (1) is the discourse of the postmodern (post–World War II) world; (2) is poetic, interpretive, and fragmentary; (3) does not theorize societies as totalities, but sees societies and cultures as fragmentary, conflictual, and processual; (4) attempts to create texts that interpret and evoke the postmodern experience; (5) does away with the observer–observed paradigm of positivist science; (6) goes against the grain of deduction, induction, and synthesis.

Second-order concept: Terms and concepts taken from sociological theory, often placed on top of first-order concepts. These terms should be used with caution.

Sensitizing concept: A second-order concept built upon, or fitted to, first-order concepts (for example, Goffman's concept of stigma).

Sociologist as partisan: Taking sides in the research process.

Triangulation: Using multiple observers, methods, interpretive points of view, and levels and forms of empirical materials in the construction of interpretations.

Understanding: The process of fitting interpretations into an interpretive whole so that the meaning of an experience is comprehended and grounded in lived experience.

Universal singular: Each person universalizes his or her historical moment, but lives that universality in a unique way. Interpretive interactionism seeks to study universal singulars.

Visual sociology: A sociology that uses photography, audio-video film, and the analysis of film for the purposes of (1) revealing how society operates, (2) enhancing ethnographic studies and reports, and (3) recording social action produced in the laboratory context.

References

ADAMS, RICHARD N. AND JACK D. PREISS, eds. 1960. *Human Organization Research: Field Relations and Techniques.* Homewood, Ill.: Dorsey.

ADLER, PATRICIA A. AND PETER ADLER. 1987. *Membership Roles in Field Research.* Newbury Park, Calif.: Sage.

AGAR, MICHAEL H. 1986. *Speaking of Ethnography.* Beverly Hills, Calif.: Sage.

_____. 1980. "Stories, Background Knowledge, and Themes: Problems in the Analysis of Life History Narrative." *American Ethnologist,* 7:223–39.

ALEXANDER, C. NORMAN AND GORDON W. KNIGHT. 1971. "Situated Identities and Social Psychological Experimentation." *Sociometry,* 34(March):65–82.

_____ AND INGER SAGATUN. 1973. "An Attributional Analysis of Experimental Norms." *Sociometry,* 36: (June) 127–42.

ALEXANDER, JEFFREY, C. 1982. *Theoretical Logic in Sociology,* vol. 1. Berkeley: University of California Press.

ALLPORT, GORDON W. 1942. *The Use of Personal Documents in Psychological Research.* New York: Social Science Research Council.

ANASTASI, ANN. 1961. *Psychological Testing.* New York: Macmillan.

ANDREWS, DUDLEY. 1984. *Concepts in Film Theory.* New York: Oxford University Press.

ARIES, PHILIPPE. 1962. *Centuries of Childhood.* New York: Knopf.

ARMER, MICHAEL AND ALLEN GRIMSHAW, eds. 1973. *Comparative Social Research: Methodological Problems and Strategies.* New York: Wiley.

ARSENIAN, J.M. 1943. "Young Children in an Insecure Situation." *Journal of Abnormal and Social Psychology,* 38:225–49.

ASHER, STEVEN R. AND JOHN M. GOTTMAN, eds. 1981. *The Development of Children's Friendships.* Cambridge: Cambridge University Press.

BACK, KURT W. 1960. "The Well-Informed Informant." In Richard N. Adams and Jack D. Preiss, eds., *Human Organization Research: Field Relations and Techniques.* Homewood, Ill.: Dorsey, pp. 179–87.

BAIN, READ. 1936. "The Self–Other Words of a Child." *American Journal of Sociology,* 41:67–75.

BALL, DONALD W. 1968. "Toward a Sociology of Telephones and Telephoners." In Marcello Truzzi, ed., *Sociology and Everyday Life*. Englewood Cliffs, N.J.: Prentice-Hall, pp. 59–75.

———. 1967. "Conventional and Unconventional Conduct: Toward a Methodological Reorientation." Paper presented to the Pacific Sociological Association, March, at Long Beach, California.

BARKER, ROGER G. 1968. *Ecological Psychology*. Stanford, Calif.: Stanford University Press.

——— AND HERBERT WRIGHT. 1954. *Midwest and Its Children: The Psychological Ecology of an American Town*. Evanston, Ill.: Row, Peterson.

——— AND ———. 1951. *One Boy's Day*. New York: Harper & Row, Pub.

BARTHES, ROLAND. 1981. *Camera Lucida*. New York: Hill and Wang.

BARTON, ALLEN H. AND PAUL F. LAZARSFELD. 1955. "Some Functions of Qualitative Analysis in Social Research." *Frankfurter Beitrage zur Soziologie*, 1:321–61.

BATESON, GREGORY AND MARGARET MEAD. 1942. *Balinese Character: A Photographic Essay*. New York: New York Academy of Sciences.

BAUDRILLARD, JEAN. 1983. *Simulations*. New York: Semiotext (e), Foreign Agent Press.

BAZIN, ANDRE. 1971. *What Is Cinema?* Berkeley: University of California Press.

BECKER, HOWARD S. 1986. *Doing Things Together: Selected Papers*. Evanston, Ill.: Northwestern University Press.

———. 1985. *Writing for Social Scientists: How to Start and Finish Your Thesis, Book, or Article*. Chicago: University of Chicago Press.

———. 1982. *Art Worlds*. Berkeley: University of California Press.

———. 1981. *Exploring Society Photographically*. Evanston, Ill.: Mary and Leigh Block Gallery, Northwestern University Press.

———. 1970. *Sociological Work*. Chicago: Aldine.

———. 1967a. "Whose Side Are We On?" *Social Problems*, 14:239–48.

——— 1967b. "Introduction." Pp. 1–31 in Howard S. Becker (ed.). *Social Problems: A Modern Approach*. New York: John Wiley.

———. 1966. Introduction in Clifford Shaw, *The Jack-Roller*. Chicago: University of Chicago Press, pp. v–xvii.

———. 1965. Review of Philip E. Hammond, ed., *Sociologists at Work*. *American Sociological Review*, 30:602–3.

———. 1964. "Problems in the Publication of Field Studies." In Arthur J. Vidich, Joseph Bensman, and Maurice R. Stein, eds., *Reflections on Community Studies*. New York: John Wiley, pp. 267–84.

———. 1963. *Outsiders: Studies in the Sociology of Deviance*. New York: Free Press.

———. 1961. Postscript in Helen MacGill Hughes, ed., *The Fantastic Lodge: The Autobiography of a Girl Drug Addict*. Boston: Houghton Mifflin, pp. 203–6.

———. 1958. "Problems of Inference and Proof in Participant Observation." *American Sociological Review*, 23:652–59.

———. 1956. "Interviewing Medical Students." *American Journal of Sociology*, 62:199–201.

———. 1955. "Marihuana Use and Social Control." *Social Problems*, 3:35–44. Reprinted in Arnold M. Rose, ed., *Human Behavior and Social Processes*. Boston: Houghton Mifflin, 1962, pp. 589–607.

———. 1954. "Field Methods and Techniques: A Note on Interviewing Tactics." *Human Organization*, 12:31–32.

———. 1953. "Becoming a Marihuana User." *American Journal of Sociology*, 59:235–42.

——— AND BLANCHE GEER. 1960. "Participant Observation: The Analysis of Qualitative Field Data." In Richard Adams and Jack D. Preiss, eds., *Human Organization Research: Field Relations and Techniques*. Homewood, Ill.: Dorsey, pp. 267–89.

——— AND ———. 1957. "Participant Observation and Interviewing: A Comparison." *Human Organization*, 16:28–32.

_____ AND IRVING LOUIS HOROWITZ. 1986. "Radical Politics and Sociological Research: Observations on Methodology and Ideology." In Howard S. Becker, *Doing Things Together: Selected Papers.* Evanston, Ill.: Northwestern University Press, pp. 83–102. (Originally published in *American Journal of Sociology,* 1972, 78:48–66.)

_____, _____, EVERETT C. HUGHES, AND ANSELM L. STRAUSS. 1961. *Boys in White.* Chicago: University of Chicago Press.

BEECHER, HENRY E. 1966. "Documenting the Abuses." *Saturday Review,* 42:45–46.

BENNEY, MARK AND EVERETT C. HUGHES. 1956. "Of Sociology and the Interview: Editorial Preface." *American Journal of Sociology,* 62:137–42.

BERGER, JOSEPH, MORRIS ZELDITCH, JR., AND BO ANDERSON. 1966. *Sociological Theories in Progress.* Boston: Houghton Mifflin.

BERREMAN, GERALD D. 1962. *Behind Many Masks.* Ithaca, N.Y.: Cornell University, Society for Applied Anthropology.

BERTAUX, DANIEL. 1981a. Introduction in D. Bertaux, ed., *Biography and Society: The Life History Approach in the Social Sciences.* Beverly Hills: Sage, pp. 1–15.

_____, ed. 1981b. *Biography and Society: The Life History Approach in the Social Sciences.* Beverly Hills: Sage.

_____ AND MARTIN KOHLI. 1984. "The Life Story Approach: A Continental View." *Annual Review of Sociology,* 10:215–37.

BIERSTEDT, ROBERT. 1960. "Sociology and Humane Learning." *American Sociological Review,* 25:3–9.

_____. 1959. "Nominal and Real Definitions in Sociological Theory." In Llewellyn Gross, ed., *Symposium on Sociological Theory.* New York: Harper & Row Pub., pp. 121–44.

BIGUS, OTIS. 1972. "The Milkman and His Customer: A Cultivated Relationship." *Urban Life and Culture,* 2:131–65.

Biography and Society Newsletter. 1987. Vol. 8.

BIRDWHISTLE, RAY L. 1970. *Kinesics and Context.* Philadelphia: University of Pennsylvania Press.

BLACK, DONALD J. AND ALBERT J. REISS, JR., 1970. "Police Control of Juveniles." *American Sociological Review,* 35:63–67.

BLACK, JAMES AND DEAN CHAMPION. 1976. *Social Research.* New York: McGraw-Hill.

BLALOCK, HUBERT M., JR., ed. 1985. *Causal Models in the Social Sciences,* 2d ed. New York: Aldine.

_____. 1984. *Basic Dilemmas in the Social Sciences.* Beverly Hills: Sage.

_____. 1971. "Aggregation and Measurement Error." *Social Forces,* 50:151–65.

_____. 1967. "Causal Inferences in Natural Experiments: Some Complications in Matching Designs." *Sociometry,* 30:300–315.

_____. 1960. *Social Statistics.* New York: McGraw-Hill.

_____ AND ANN B. BLALOCK, eds. 1968. *Methodology in Social Research.* New York: McGraw-Hill.

BLAU, PETER M. 1964. "The Research Process in *The Dynamics of Bureaucracy.*" In Phillip E. Hammond, ed., *Sociologists at Work,* New York: Basic Books, pp. 16–49.

_____. 1963. *The Dynamics of Bureaucracy.* Chicago: University of Chicago Press.

BLUEBOND-LANGER, MYRA. 1975. "Awareness and Communication in Terminally Ill Children: Pattern, Process, and Pretense." Unpublished doctoral dissertation. Urbana, University of Illinois.

BLUMER, HERBERT. 1979. "Introduction to the *Transaction* Edition." *Critique of Research in the Social Sciences: An Appraisal of Thomas and Znaniecki's* The Polish Peasant in Europe and America. New Brunswick, New Jersey: Transaction Books.

_____. 1969a. "The Methodological Position of Symbolic Interactionism." In *Symbolic Interactionism.* Englewood Cliffs, N.J.: Prentice-Hall.

_____. 1969b. *Symbolic Interactionism.* Englewood Cliffs, N.J.: Prentice-Hall.

———. 1967. "Threats from Agency-Determined Research." In Irving Louis Horowitz, ed., *The Rise and Fall of Project Camelot*. Cambridge, Mass.: MIT Press, pp. 341–62.

———. 1966a. "Sociological Implications of the Thought of George Herbert Mead." *American Journal of Sociology*, 71:535–44.

———. 1966b. Foreword in Severyn T. Bruyn, *The Human Perspective in Sociology: The Methodology of Participant Observation*. Englewood Cliffs, N.J.: Prentice-Hall, pp. iii–vii.

———. 1964. "Comment." *Berkeley Journal of Sociology*, 9:118–22.

———. 1962. "Society as Symbolic Interaction." In Arnold M. Rose, ed., *Human Behavior and Social Processes*. Boston: Houghton Mifflin, pp. 179–92.

———. 1956. "Sociological Analysis and the Variable." *American Sociological Review*, 21:683–90.

———. 1955. "Attitudes and the Social Act." *Social Problems*. 3:59–65.

———. 1954. "What Is Wrong with Social Theory?" *American Sociological Review*, 19:3–10.

———. 1948. "Public Opinion and Public Opinion Polling." *American Sociological Review*, 13:542–54.

———. 1940. "The Problem of the Concept in Social Psychology." *American Journal of Sociology*, 45:707–19.

———. 1939. *Critique of Research in the Social Sciences I: An Appraisal of Thomas and Znaniecki's Polish Peasant*. New York: Social Science Research Council.

———. 1933. *Movies and Conduct*. New York: Macmillan.

———. 1931. "Science without Concepts." *American Journal of Sociology*, 36:515–33.

BOGDAN, ROBERT AND STEVEN J. TAYLOR. 1975. *Introduction to Qualitative Research Methods*. New York: John Wiley.

BONJEAN, CHARLES M., RICHARD J. HILL, AND S. DALE MCLEMORE. 1967. *Sociological Measurement: An Inventory of Scales and Indices*. San Francisco: Chandler.

BOOTH, CHARLES. 1967. In Harold W. Pfautz, ed., *On the City: Physical Pattern and Social Structure*. Chicago: University of Chicago Press. (Originally published 1903.)

BORGATTA, EDGAR F., AND GEORGE W. BOHRNSTEDT. 1981. "Level of Measurement: Once Over Again." In George W. Bohrnstedt and Edgar Borgatta, eds, *Social Measurement: Current Issues*. Beverly Hills: Sage, pp. 23–37.

BOSSARD, JAMES H.S. AND ELEANOR STOKER BOLL. 1960. *The Sociology of Child Development*. New York: Harper and Row, Pub.

BOTTOMORE, TOM. 1984. *The Frankfurt School*. London: Tavistock Publications.

BOUCHARD, THOMAS, JR. 1976. "Unobtrusive Methods: An Inventory of Uses." *Sociological Methods and Research*, 4:267–300.

BOYLE, RICHARD P. 1969. "Algebraic Systems for Normal and Hierarchical Sociograms." *Sociometry*, 32:99–119.

BRADLEY, J.V. 1968. *Distribution-Free Statistical Tests*. Englewood Cliffs, N.J.: Prentice-Hall.

BREDE, RICHARD. 1971. "The Policing of Juveniles in Chicago." Unpublished doctoral dissertation. Urbana: University of Illinois.

BROOKOVER, LINDA AND KURT W. BACK. 1966. "Time Sampling as a Field Technique." *Human Organization*, 25:64–70.

BRUNER, EDWARD M. 1986. "Experience and Its Expressions." In Victor W. Turner and Edward M. Bruner eds., *The Anthropology of Experience*. Urbana, Ill.: University of Illinois Press, pp. 3–30.

———. 1985. "Tourist Performance and the Ethnographic Pastoral: A Case Study from Kenya." Photographic slide essay presented to the Spring Colloquium Series of the Unit for Criticism and Interpretive Theory, February 25, Urbana, Illinois.

———, ed. 1984. *Text, Play, and Story: The Construction and Reconstruction of Self and Society*. Washington, D.C.: American Ethnographical Society.

BRUYN, SEVERYN. 1966. *The Human Perspective in Sociology: The Methodology of Participant Observation*. Englewood Cliffs, N.J.: Prentice-Hall.

BUCHER, RUE, CHARLES E. FRITZ, AND E.L. QUARANTELLI. 1956. "Tape Recorded Interviews in Social Research." *American Sociological Review*, 21:359–64.

BULMER, MARTIN, ed., 1982. *Social Research Ethics: An Examination of the Merits of Covert Participant Observation*. New York: Holmes & Meier.

BURGESS, ERNEST. 1966. "Discussion." In Clifford Shaw, *The Jack-Roller*. Chicago: University of Chicago Press, pp. 185–97.

BURKE, KENNETH. 1965. *Permanence and Change*. Indianapolis: Bobbs-Merrill.

CALKINS, CATHY CHARMEZ. 1970. "Time: Perspectives, Marking and Styles of Usage." *Social Problems*, 17:487–501.

CAMILLERI, SANTO F. 1962. "Theory, Probability, and Induction in Social Research." *American Sociological Review*, 27:170–78.

CAMPBELL, DONALD T. 1969. "Reforms as Experiments." *American Psychologist*, 24:409–29.

———. 1963a. "From Description to Experimentation: Interpreting Trends as Quasi-Experiments." In Chester W. Harris, ed., *Problems in Measuring Change*. Madison, Wis.: University of Wisconsin Press, pp. 212–42.

———. 1963b. "Social Attitudes and Other Acquired Behavioral Dispositions." In S. Koch, ed., *Psychology: A Study of a Science*, vol. 6, *Investigations of Man as Socius*. New York: McGraw-Hill.

———. 1957. "Factors Relevant to the Validity of Experiments in Social Settings." *Psychological Bulletin*, 54:297–312.

——— AND DONALD W. FISKE. 1959. "Convergent and Discriminant Validation by the Multitrait-Multimethod Matrix." *Psychological Bulletin*, 56:81–105.

——— AND JULIAN C. STANLEY. 1963. *Experimental and Quasi-Experimental Designs for Research*. Chicago: Rand McNally.

CAMUS, ALBERT. 1960. *The Myth of Sisyphus and Other Essays*. New York: Vintage Books.

CARTIER-BRESSON, HENRI. 1952. *The Decisive Moment*. New York: Simon & Schuster.

CAVAN, RUTH. 1928. *Suicide*. Chicago: University of Chicago Press.

———, PHILLIP M. HAUSER, AND SAMUEL A. STOUFFER. 1930. "Note on tyhe Statistical Treatment of Life History Material." *Social Forces*, 9(December):200–203.

CAVAN, SHERI. 1966. *Liquor License*. Chicago: Aldine.

CHALMERS, A.F. 1982. *What Is This Thing Called Science? An Assessment of the Nature and Status of Science and Its Methods*. Milton Keynes, England: Open University Press.

CHAMBLISS, WILLIAM J. 1975. *Box Man: A Professional Thief's Journal*. New York: Harper & Row, Pub.

CHURCHILL, LINDSEY 1971. "Ethnomethodology and Measurement." *Social Forces*, 50:182–91.

CICOUREL, AARON V. 1987. "The Interpenetration of Communicative Contexts: Examples from Medical Encounters." *Social Psychology Quarterly*, 50:217–26.

———. 1981. "The Role of Cognitive-Linguistic Concepts in Understanding Everyday Social Interaction." *Annual Review of Sociology*, 7:87–106.

———. 1974a. *Cognitive Sociology*. New York: Free Press.

———. 1974b. *Theory and Method in a Study of Argentine Fertility*. New York: John Wiley.

———. 1968. *The Social Organization of Juvenile Justice*. New York: John Wiley.

———. 1967. "Fertility, Family Planning and the Social Organization of Family Life: Some Methodological Issues." *Journal of Social Issues*, 20:57–81.

———. 1964. *Method and Measurement in Sociology*. New York: Free Press.

CLEAVER, ELDRIDGE. 1968. *Soul on Ice*. New York: McGraw-Hill.

CLIFFORD, JAMES. 1986a. "Introduction: Partial Truths." In James Clifford and George E. Marcus, eds., *Writing Culture: The Poetics and Politics of Ethnography*. Berkeley: University of California Press, pp. 1–26.

———. 1986b. "On Ethnographic Allegory." In James Clifford and George E. Marcus, eds., *Writing Culture: The Poetics and Politics of Ethnography*. Berkeley: University of California Press, pp. 98–121.

_____ AND GEORGE E. MARCUS, eds., 1986. *Writing Culture: The Poetics and Politics of Ethnography.* Berkeley: University of California Press.

COLEMAN, JAMES S. 1986. "Social Theory, Social Research and a Theory of Action." *American Journal of Sociology,* 91:1309–35.

_____. 1962. *The Adolescent Society.* New York: Free Press.

_____. 1958. "Relational Analysis: The Study of Social Organization with Survey Methods." *Human Organization,* 17:28–36.

COLLIER, JOHN, JR. AND MALCOLM COLLIER. 1986. *Visual Anthropology: Photography as a Research Method.* Albuquerque: University of New Mexico Press.

COLLINS, RANDALL. 1985. *Three Sociological Traditions.* New York: Oxford University Press.

_____. 1984. "Statistics Versus Words." In R. Collins, ed., *Sociological Theory 1984.* San Francisco: Jossey-Bass, pp. 329–62.

_____. 1975. *Conflict Sociology.* New York: Academic Press.

CONWELL, CHIC AND EDWIN H. SUTHERLAND. 1937. *The Professional Thief.* Chicago: University of Chicago Press.

COOK, JUDITH A. AND MARY MARGARET FONOW. 1986. "Knowledge and Women's Interests: Issues of Epistemology and Methodology in Feminist Sociological Research." *Sociological Inquiry,* 56:2–29.

COOK, THOMAS D. 1983. "Quasi-Experimentation: Its Ontology, Epistemology, and Methodology." In Gareth Morgan, ed., *Beyond Method: Strategies for Social Research.* Beverly Hills: Sage, pp. 74–94.

_____ AND DONALD T. CAMPBELL. 1979. *Quasi-Experimentation: Design and Analysis in Field Settings.* Chicago: Rand McNally.

COOLEY, CHARLES HORTON. 1922. *Human Nature and the Social Order.* New York: Scribner's.

_____. 1926. "The Roots of Social Knowledge." *American Journal of Sociology,* 32:59–79.

COSER, LEWIS. 1963. *The Sociology of Literature.* New York: Macmillan.

_____, ed. 1965. *Georg Simmel.* Englewood Cliffs, N.J.: Prentice-Hall.

COSTNER, HERBERT L. AND ROBERT K. LEIK. 1964. "Deductions from 'Axiomatic Theory.'" *American Sociological Review,* 20:819–35.

COUCH, CARL J. 1987a. *Researching Social Processes in the Laboratory.* Greenwich, Conn.: JAI Press.

_____. 1987b. "Objectivity: A Crutch and Club for Bureaucrats/Subjectivity: A Haven for Lost Souls." *Sociological Quarterly,* 28 (Spring):105–19.

_____. 1984. *Constructing Civilizations.* Greenwich, Conn.: JAI Press.

_____ STANLEY L. SAXTON AND MICHAEL A. KATOVICH, eds. 1986a and b. *Studies in Symbolic Interaction, Supplement 2: The Iowa School. Parts A and B.* Greenwich, Conn.: JAI Press.

COWIE, JAMES B. AND JULIAN B. ROEBUCK. 1975. *An Enthnography of a Chiropractic Clinic: Definitions of a Deviant Situation.* New York: Free Press.

COX, G.H., AND E. MARLEY. 1959. "The Estimation of Motility During Rest or Sleep." *Journal of Neurology, Neurosurgery and Psychiatry,* 22:57–60.

CRONBACH, LEE J. 1957. "Proposals Leading to Analytic Treatment of Social Perception Scores." In Renato Tagiuri and Luigi Petrullo, eds., *Person Perception and Interpersonal Behavior.* Stanford, Conn.: Stanford University Press, pp. 353–79.

_____. 1960. *Essentials of Psychological Testing,* 2d ed. New York: Harper & Row, Pub.

CULLER, JONATHAN. 1981. *The Pursuit of Signs: Semiotics, Literature, Deconstruction.* Ithaca, N.Y.: Cornell University Press.

Daedalus. 1969. "Ethical Aspects of Experimentation with Human Subjects." Spring (entire issue).

DALTON, MELVILLE. 1964. "Preconceptions and Methods in *Men Who Manage.*" In Phillip E. Hammond, ed., *Sociologists at Work.* New York: Basic Books, pp. 59–95.

DAVIS, ED. 1987. "Viewer's Interpretations of Alcoholism Films." Presented to the 1987 Annual Spring Symposium of the Society for the Study of Symbolic Interaction, Urbana, Ill.

DAVIS, JAMES. 1971. *Elementary Survey Analysis.* Englewood Cliffs, N.J.: Prentice-Hall.

_____. 1964. "Great Books and Small Groups: An Informal History of a National Survey." In Phillip Hammond, ed., *Sociologists at Work.* New York: Basic Books, pp. 212–34.

DAVIS, MORRIS AND SOL LEVINE. 1967. "Toward a Sociology of Public Transit." *Social Problems,* 15:84–91.

_____, ROBERT SEIBERT, AND WARREN BREED. 1966. "Interracial Seating Patterns on New Orleans Public Transit." *Social Problems,* 13:298–306.

DAVIS, MURRAY. 1973. *Intimate Relations.* New York: Free Press.

DE GRAZIA, SEBASTIAN. 1962. *Of Time, Work and Leisure.* Garden City, N.Y.: Doubleday.

DEMMING, W. EDWARDS. 1944. "On Errors in Surveys." *American Sociological Review,* 19:395–69.

DENZIN, NORMAN K. 1989. "Reading Tender Mercies: Two Interpretations." *Sociological Quarterly,* 30:1–19.

_____. 1988a. *Film and the American Alcoholic.* New York: Aldine de Gruyter.

_____. 1988b. *Interpretive Interactionism: Strategies of Qualitative Research.* Newbury Park, Calif.: Sage.

_____. 1987a. *The Alcoholic Self.* Newbury Park, Calif.: Sage.

_____. 1987b. *The Recovering Alcoholic.* Newbury Park, Calif.: Sage.

_____. 1987c. *Treating Alcoholism.* Newbury Park, Calif.: Sage.

_____. 1987d. "Under the Influence of Time: Reading the Interactional Text." *The Sociological Quarterly,* 28:327–42.

_____. 1987e. "On Semiotics and Symbolic Interaction." *Symbolic Interaction,* 10:1–20.

_____. 1987f. "The Death of Sociology in the 1980s." *American Journal of Sociology,* 93:175–80.

_____. 1986a. "Postmodern Social Theory." *Sociological Theory,* 4:194–204.

_____. 1986b. "Reflections on the Ethnographer's Camera." *Current Perspectives in Social Theory,* 7:105–23.

_____. 1986c. "Interpretive Interactionism and the Use of Life Stories." *Revista Internacional de Sociologia,* 44:321–39.

_____. 1986d. "Interpreting the Lives of Ordinary People: Sartre, Heidegger, Faulkner." *Life Stories/Recits de vie.* 2:6–19.

_____. 1986e. "On a Semiotic Approach to Mass Culture." *American Journal of Sociology,* 92:678–83.

_____. 1986f. "Reinterpreting *The Polish Peasant*." In Zygmunt Dulczewski, ed., *A Commemorative Book in Honor of Florian Znaniecki on the Centenary of His Birth.* Posnan, Poland: Uniwersytetus Im. A. Mickiewicza, pp. 61–74.

_____. 1985. "Reflections on the Social Psychologist's Camera." *Studies in Visual Communication,* 11:78–82.

_____. 1984a. "An Interpretation of Recent Feminist Theory: Review-Essay." *Sociology and Social Research,* 68:712–18.

_____. 1984b. *On Understanding Emotion.* San Francisco: Jossey-Bass.

_____. 1983. "Interpretive Interactionism." In Gareth Morgan, ed., *Beyond Method: Strategies for Social Research.* Beverly Hills: Sage.

_____. 1979. "On the Interactional Analysis of Social Organization." *Symbolic Interaction,* 2:59–72.

_____. 1978. *The Research Act,* 2d ed. New York: McGraw-Hill.

_____. 1977a. "Notes on the Criminogenic Hypothesis: A Case Study of the American Liquor Industry." *American Sociological Review,* 42:905–20.

_____. 1977b. *Childhood Socialization: Studies in the Development of Language, Social Behavior and Identity.* San Francisco: Jossey-Bass.

_____. 1975. "Play, Games and Interaction: The Contexts of Childhood Socialization." *Sociological Quarterly,* 16:458–78.

_____. 1974. "The Methodological Implications of Symbolic Interactionism for the Study of Deviance." *British Journal of Sociology*, 24:269–82.

_____. 1971. "The Logic of Naturalistic Inquiry." *Social Forces,* 50:166–82.

_____. 1970. *The Research Act: A Theoretical Introduction to Sociological Methods,* 1st ed. Chicago: Aldine.

_____. 1968. "On the Ethics of Disguised Observation." *Social Problems,* 15:502–4.

_____. 1966. "The Significant Others of a College Population." *Sociological Quarterly,* 7:298–310.

_____ AND CHARLES KELLER. 1981. "Frame Analysis Reconsidered." *Comtemporary Sociology,* 10:52–59.

DERRIDA, JACQUES. 1981. *Positions.* Chicago: University of Chicago Press.

DEUTSCHER, IRWIN. 1975. Foreword in Robert Bogdan and Steven J. Taylor, *Introduction to Qualitative Research Methods: A Phenomenological Approach to the Social Sciences.* New York: John Wiley.

_____. 1973. *What We Say: What We Do.* Glenville, Ill.: Scott, Foresman.

_____. 1969. "Looking Backward: Case Studies on the Progress of Methodology in Sociological Research." *American Sociologist,* 4:35–41.

DEXTER, LEWIS ANTHONY. 1970. *Elite and Specialized Interviewing.* Evanston, Ill.: Northwestern University Press.

DILTHEY, WILHELM L. 1976. *Selected Writings* (H. P. Rickman, ed. and trans.). Cambridge: Cambridge University Press. (Originally published 1900.)

DIXON, CAROL. 1972. "Guided Options as a Pattern of Control in a Headstart Program." *Urban Life and Culture,* 2:203–16.

DOLBY-STAHL, SANDRA K. 1985. "A Literary Folkloristic Methodology for the Study of Meaning in Personal Narrative." *Journal of Folklore Research,* 22:45–70.

DOLLARD, JOHN. 1935. *Criteria for the Life History.* New Haven, Conn.: Yale University Press.

DOUGLAS, JACK D. 1985. *Creative Interviewing.* Beverly Hills: Sage.

_____. 1976. *Investigative Social Research: Individual and Team Field Research.* Beverly Hills: Sage.

_____. 1967. *The Social Meanings of Suicide.* Princeton, N.J.: Princeton University Press.

DRABEK, THOMAS E. AND J. EUGENE HAAS. 1967. "Realism in Laboratory Simulation: Myth or Method?" *Social Forces,* 45:337–46.

DUNCAN, OTIS D. 1975. *Introduction to Structural Equation Models.* New York: Academic Press.

DURKHEIM, EMILE. 1964. *The Rules of Sociological Method,* ed. George E. G. Carlin, trans. Sarah A. Solovay and John H. Mueller. New York: Free Press. (originally published 1895)

DYCK, ARTHUR J. 1963. "The Social Contacts of Some Midwest Children with their Parents and Teachers." In Roger C. Barder, ed., *The Stream of Behavior: Explorations of Its Structure and Content.* New York: Appleton-Century-Crofts, pp. 78–98.

EDWARDS, ALLEN L. 1957a. *The Social Desirability Variable in Personality Assessment and Research.* New York: Dryden.

_____. 1957b. *Techniques of Attitude Scale Construction.* New York: Appleton-Century-Crofts.

EHRLICH, HOWARD J. 1963. "The Swastika Epidemic of 1959–1960: Anti-Semitism and Community Characteristics." *Social Problems,* 9:264–72.

ELDER, JOSEPH W. 1973. "Problems of Cross-Cultural Methodology: Instrumentation and Interviewing in India." In Michael Armer and Allen D. Grimshaw, eds., *Comparative Social Research: Methodological Problems and Strategies.* New York: John Wiley, pp. 119–44.

ELKIN, FREDERICK. 1947. "Specialists Interpret the Case of Harold Holzer." *Journal of Abnormal Social Psychology,* 42:99–111.

ERIKSON, KAI T. 1968. "A Reply to Denzin." *Social Problems,* 15:505–6.

_____. 1967. "A Comment on Disguised Observation in Sociology." *Social Problems,* 14:366–73.

ERSKINE, HAZEL G. 1967. "The Polls: More on Morality and Sex." *Public Opinion Quarterly*, 31:116–28.

FARGANIS, SONDRA. 1986. "Social Theory and Feminist Theory: The Need for Dialogue." *Sociological Inquiry*, 56:50–68.

FARIS, ROBERT E.L. 1967. *Chicago Sociology: 1920–1932*. San Francisco: Chandler.

FAULKNER, WILLIAM. 1967. "Address Upon Receiving the Nobel Prize for Literature." In Malcolm Cowley, ed., *The Portable Faulkner*. New York: Penguin, pp. 723-24.

FESTINGER, LEON. 1953. "Laboratory Experiments." In Leon Festinger and Daniel Katz, eds., *Research Methods in the Behavioral Sciences*. New York: Holt, Rinehart & Winston, pp. 136–72.

———, HENRY RIECKEN, AND STANLEY SCHACHTER. 1956. *When Prophecy Fails*. New York: Harper & Row, Pub.

FIEDLER, FRED E. 1967. *Theory of Leadership Effectiveness*. New York: McGraw-Hill.

FIELDING, NIGEL G. AND JANE L. FIELDING. 1986. *Linking Data*. Newbury Park, Calif.: Sage.

FOUCAULT, MICHEL. 1980. *Power/Knowledge: Selected Interviews and Other Writings, 1972-1977*. New York: Pantheon.

———. 1973. *The Order of Things: An Archaeology of the Human Sciences*. New York: Vintage.

FRANK, GELYA. 1979. "Finding the Common Denominator: A Phenomenological Critique of the Life History Method." *Ethos*, 7:68–94.

FREEDMAN, RONALD. 1950. "Incomplete Matching in Ex Post Facto Studies." *American Journal of Sociology*, 55:485–87.

FREEMAN, DEREK. 1983. *Margaret Mead and Samoa: The Making and Unmaking of an Anthropological Myth*. Cambridge, Mass.: Harvard University Press.

FRENCH, JOHN R.P., JR. 1953. "Experiments in Field Settings." In Leon Festinger and Daniel Katz, eds., *Research Methods in the Behavioral Sciences*. New York: Holt, Rinehart & Winston, pp. 98–135.

FRIEDLANDER, LEE. 1972. *Friends of Photography: Untitled 2 and 3*. Carmel: Friends of Photography.

FRIEDMAN, NEIL J. 1967. *The Social Nature of Psychological Research*. New York: Basic Books.

FURFEY, PAUL H. 1959. "Sociological Science and the Problem of Values." In Llewellyn Gross, ed., *Symposium on Sociological Theory*. New York: Harper & Row, Pub., pp. 509–30.

GADAMER, HANS G. 1975. *Truth and Method*. London: Sheed and Ward.

GARFINKEL, HAROLD. 1967. *Studies in Ethnomethodology*. Englewood Cliffs, N.J.: Prentice-Hall.

———, MICHAEL LYNCH, AND ERIC LIVINGSTON. 1981. "The Work of a Discovering Science Construed with Material from the Optically Discovered Pulsar." *Philosophy of the Social Sciences*, 11:131-58.

GEER, BLANCHE. 1964. "First Days in the Field." In Phillip E. Hammond, ed., *Sociologists at Work*. New York: Basic Books, pp. 322-44.

GEERTZ, CLIFFORD. 1983. *Local Knowledge: Further Essays in Interpretive Anthropology*. New York: Basic Books.

———. 1973. *The Interpretation of Cultures*. New York: Basic Books.

GERTH, HANS H., AND C. WRIGHT MILLS, trans. and eds. 1946. *From Max Weber: Essays in Sociology*. New York: Oxford University Press.

GIDDENS, ANTHONY. 1984. *The Constitution of Society*. Berkeley: University of California Press.

———. 1979. *Central Problems in Social Theory*. Berkeley: University of California Press.

GLASER, BARNEY G. AND ANSELM STRAUSS. 1968. *Time for Dying*. Chicago: Aldine.

——— AND———. 1967. *The Discovery of Grounded Theory*. Chicago: Aldine.

——— AND———. 1964. *Awareness of Dying*. Chicago. Aldine.

GLOCK, CHARLES Y. 1955. "Some Applications of the Panel Method to the Study of Change." In Paul Lazarsfeld and Morris Rosenberg, eds., *The Language of Social Research*. Glencoe, Ill.: Free Press, pp. 242–50.

GOFFMAN, ERVING. 1981. *Forms of Talk*. Philadelphia: University of Pennsylvania Press.

———. 1976. "Gender Advertisements." *Studies in Visual Communication*, 3:69–154.

———. 1974. *Frame Analysis*. New York: Harper & Row, Pub.

———. 1971: *Relations in Public*. New York: Basic Books.

———. 1967. *Interaction Ritual*. Chicago: Aldine.

———. 1963a. *Behavior in Public Places*. New York: Free Press.

———. 1963b. *Stigma: Notes on the Management of Spoiled Identity*. Englewood Cliffs, N.J.: Prentice-Hall.

———. 1961a. *Asylums*. Garden City, N.Y.: Doubleday.

———. 1961b. *Encounters*. Indianapolis: Bobbs-Merrill.

———. 1959. *The Presentation of Self in Everyday Life*. Garden City, N.Y.: Doubleday.

GOLD, RAYMOND L. 1958. "Roles in Sociological Field Observations." *Social Forces*, 36:217–23.

———. 1964. "In the Basement: The Apartment Building Janitor." In Peter L. Berger, ed., *The Human Shape of Work: Studies in the Sociology of Work*. New York: Macmillan, pp. 11–49.

GOLDE, PEGGY, ed. 1983a. *Women in the Field: Anthropological Experiences*, 2d ed. Berkeley: University of California Press.

———. 1983b. "Introduction," Pp. 1–15 in Peggy Golde (ed.). *Women in the Field: Anthropological Experiences*. Berkeley: University of California Press.

GOODE, WILLIAM J. 1965. *Women in Divorce*. New York: Free Press.

——— AND PAUL K. HATT. 1952. *Methods in Social Research*. New York: McGraw-Hill.

GOODENOUGH, WARD H. 1964. "Cultural Anthropology and Linguistics." In Dell Hymes, ed., *Language in Culture and Society: A Reader in Linguistics and Anthropology*. New York: Harper & Row, Pub., p. 36.

GORDEN, RAYMOND. L. 1969. *Interviewing: Strategy, Techniques and Tactics*. Homewood, Ill.: Dorsey.

GORDON, CHAD. 1968. "Self-Conceptions: Configurations of Content." In Chad Gordon and Kenneth J. Gergen, eds., *The Self in Interaction*, vol. 1. New York: John Wiley, pp. 115–36.

GOTTSCHALK, LOUIS, CLYDE KLUCKHOHN, AND ROBERT ANGELL. 1945. *The Use of Personal Documents in History, Anthropology, and Sociology*. New York: Social Science Research Council.

GOULDNER, ALVIN. 1970. *The Coming Crisis of Western Sociology*. New York: Basic Books.

———. 1968. "The Sociologist as Partisan: Sociology and the Welfare State." *American Sociologist*, 3:103–16.

———. 1962. "Anti-Minotaur: The Myth of a Value-Free Sociology." *Social Problems*, 9:199–213.

GRATHOFF, RICHARD H. 1970. *The Structure of Social Inconsistencies*. The Hague, Netherlands: Martinus Nijhoff.

GREEN, BERT F. 1954. "Attitude Measurement." In Gardner Lindzey, ed., *Handbook of Social Psychology*, vol. 1. Reading, Mass.: Addison-Wesley, pp. 335–69.

GREENWOOD, ERNEST. 1945. *Experimental Sociology*. Morningside, N.Y.: King's Crown Press.

GROSS, EDWARD AND GREGORY P. STONE. 1963. "Embarrassment and the Analysis of Role Requirements." *American Journal of Sociology*, 70:1–15.

GROVES, MARY ANN. 1974. "The Requesting Episode: Getting Children to Help One Another." Unpublished manuscript. Urbana, University of Illinois.

GUMP, P.V. AND P.H. SCHOGGEN. 1955. *Wally O'Neil at Camp*. Detroit. Wayne State University Library.

GUSFIELD, JOSEPH. 1981. *The Culture of Public Problems: Drinking-Driving and the Symbolic Order*: Chicago. University of Chicago Press.

GUTTMAN, L. 1950a. "The Problem of Attitude and Opinion Measurement." In S.A. Stouffer et al., *Measurement and Prediction*. Princeton, N.J.: Princeton University Press, pp. 49–59.

———. 1950b. "The Basis for Scalogram Analysis." In S.A. Stouffer et al., *Measurement and Prediction*. Princeton, N.J.: Princeton University Press, pp. 60–90.

_____. 1947. "The Cornell Technique of Scale and Intensity Analysis." *Education and Psychological Measurement*, 7:247–79.

_____. 1944. "A Basis for Scaling Qualitative Data." *American Sociological Review*, 9:139–50.

HABERMAS, JURGEN. 1984. *The Theory of Communicative Action*, vol. 1: *Reason and the Rationalization of Society*. Boston: Beacon Press. (Originally published 1981.)

_____. 1971. *Knowledge and Human Interests*. London: Heinemann.

HALL, EDWARD T. 1986. Foreword in John Collier, Jr., and Malcolm Collier, *Visual Anthropology: Photography as a Research Method*. Albuquerque: University of New Mexico Press, pp. xiii–xvii.

_____. 1966. *The Hidden Dimension*. New York: Doubleday.

_____. 1959. *The Silent Language*. Garden City, N.Y.: Doubleday.

HALL, JANE MASI. 1977. "Homer Spriggs: Chronicler of Brummetts Creek," *Journal of the Folklore Institute*, 14:31–50.

HALL, PETER M. 1987. "Presidential Address: Interactionism and Study of Social Organization." *Sociological Quarterly*, 28:1–22.

HALL, STUART. 1980. "Cultural Studies and the Centre: Some Problematics and Problems." In Stuart Hall, D. Hobson, A. Lowe, and Paul Willis, eds., *Culture, Media, and Language: Working Papers in Cultural Studies, 1972–1979*. London: Hutchinson, pp. 1–49.

HAMBLIN, ROBERT L. 1971. "Ratio Measurement in the Social Sciences." *Social Forces*, 50:191–206.

HAMMOND, PHILLIP E., ed. 1964. *Sociologists at Work*. New York: Basic Books.

HAYNER, NORMAN S. 1964. "Hotel Life: Proximity and Social Distance." In Ernest S. Burgess and Donald J. Bogue, eds., *Contributions to Urban Sociology*. Chicago: University of Chicago Press, pp. 314–23.

HEIDEGGER, MARTIN. 1962. *Being and Time*. New York: Harper & Row, Pub. (Originally published 1927.)

HEIDER, KARL. 1983. "Fieldwork with a Cinema." *Studies in Visual Communication*, 8:2–10.

_____. 1972. *The Dani of West Irian: An Ethnographic Companion to the Film* Dead Birds. Andover, Mass.: Module #2, Warner Modular Publications.

HEISE, DAVID R. 1969. "Problems in Path Analysis and Causal Inference." In Edgar F. Borgatta, ed., *Sociological Methodology: 1969*. San Francisco: Jossey-Bass, pp. 38–73.

HELLING, INGEBORG, K. 1987. "On 'The Bias of Method over Meaning or Interpretation in Biography and Society Investigations': A Discussion with Norman K. Denzin." *Biography & Society*, newsletter 8:71–78.

HENRY, JULES. 1963. *Culture Against Man*. New York: Random House.

HERON, JOHN. 1981. "Philosophical Basis for a New Paradigm." In Peter Reason and John Rowan, eds., *Human Inquiry: A Sourcebook of New Paradigm Research*. New York: John Wiley, pp. 20–39.

HEYL, BARBARA SHERMAN. 1979. *The Madame as Entrepreneur: Career Management in House Prostitution*. New Brunswick, N.J.: Transaction Books.

HICKMAN, C. ADDISON AND MANFORD H. KUHN. 1956. *Individuals, Groups and Economic Behavior*. New York: Dryden.

HILL, RICHARD J. 1969. "On the Relevance of Methodology." *Et Al.*, 2:26–29.

_____. 1953. "A Note on Inconsistency in Paired Comparison Techniques." *American Sociological Review*, 18:564–66.

HILMER, NORMAN A. 1968. "Anonymity, Confidentiality, and Invasions of Privacy: Responsibility of the Researcher." *American Journal of Public Health*, 58:324–30.

HIRSCHI, TRAVIS. 1969. *The Causes of Delinquency*. Berkeley: University of California Press.

_____ AND HANAN C. SELVIN. 1973. *Principles of Survey Analysis*. New York: Free Press.

_____ AND _____. 1967. *Deliquency Research: An Appraisal of Analytic Methods*. New York: Free Press.

HOMANS, GEORGE CASPER. 1950. *The Human Group.* New York: Harcourt Brace Jovanovich.

———. 1964. "Contemporary Theory in Sociology." In R.E.L. Ferris, ed., *Handbook of Modern Sociology.* Chicago: Rand McNally, pp. 951–77.

HOOD, THOMAS C. AND KURT W. BACK. 1971. "Self-Disclosure and the Volunteer: A Source of Bias in Laboratory Experiments." *Journal of Personality and Social Psychology,* 17(2):130–36.

HOROWITZ, IRVING LOUIS. 1965. "The Life and Death of Project Camelot." *Transaction,* 3:3–7, 44–47. Reprinted in *American Psychologist,* 2(1966):445–54.

HOVLAND, CARL AND MUZAFER SHERIF. 1952. "Judgmental Phenomena and Scales of Attitude Measurement." *Journal of Abnormal and Social Psychology,* 47:822–32.

HUGHES, EVERETT C. 1956. *Men and Their Work.* Glencoe, Ill.: Free Press.

——— AND HELEN MCGILL HUGHES. *Where Peoples Meet.* Glencoe, Ill.: Free Press.

HULETT, J.E., JR. 1964. "Communication and Social Order: The Search for a Theory." *Audio-Visual Communication Review,* 12:458–68.

HULIN, CHARLES L., FRITZ DRASGOW, AND CHARLES K. PARSONS. 1983. *Item Response Theory: Application to Psychological Measurement.* Homewood, Ill.: Dow Jones-Irwin.

HYMAN, HERBERT. 1955. *Survey Design and Analysis: Principles and Cases.* Glencoe, Ill.: Free Press.

———. 1954a. "The General Problem of Questionnaire Design." In Daniel Katz et al., eds., *Public Opinion and Propaganda.* New York: Holt, Rinehart & Winston, pp. 665–74.

———. 1954b. *Interviewing in Social Research.* Chicago: University of Chicago Press.

JACOBS, JERRY. 1967. "A Phenomenological Study of Suicide Notes." *Social Problems,* 15:60–72.

JANES, ROBERT W. 1961. "A Note on the Phases of the Community Role of the Participant Observer." *American Sociological Review,* 26:446–50.

JOHNSON, JOHN M. 1975. *Doing Field Research.* New York: Free Press.

KAHN, ROBERT L. AND CHARLES F. CANNELL. 1957. *The Dynamics of Interviewing: Theory, Technique, and Cases.* New York: John Wiley.

KATOVICH, MICHAEL A. 1984. "Symbolic Interactionism and Experimentation: The Laboratory as a Provocative Stage." *Studies in Symbolic Interaction,* 5:49–67.

KATZ, ELIHU AND PAUL F. LAZARSFELD. 1955. *Personal Influence.* Glencoe, Ill.: Free Press.

KENDALL, PATRICIA L. AND KATHERINE M. WOLF. 1955. "The Two Purposes of Deviant Case Analysis." In Paul F. Lazarsfeld and Morris Rosenberg, eds., *The Language of Social Research.* Glencoe, Ill.: Free Press, pp. 167–70.

KINCH, JOHN W. 1963. "A Formalized Theory of the Self-Concept." *American Journal of Sociology,* 68:481–86.

KISH, LESLIE. 1965. *Survey Sampling.* New York: John Wiley.

———. 1953. "Selection of the Sample." In Leon Festinger and Daniel Katz, eds., *Research Methods in the Behavioral Sciences.* New York: Holt, Rinehart & Winston, pp. 175–239.

KITSUSE, JOHN I. AND AARON V. CICOUREL. 1963. "A Note on the Uses of Official Statistics." *Social Problems,* 11:131–39.

KLOCKARS, CARL B. 1975. *The Professional Fence.* New York: Free Press.

KOHLI, MARTIN. 1986. "Biographical Research in the German Language Area." In Zygmunt Dulczewski, ed., *A Commemorative Book in Honor of Florian Znaniecki on the Centenary of His Birth.* Posnan, Poland: Uniwersytetus Im. A. Mickiewicza, pp. 91–110.

KNORR-CETINA, KAREN AND M.J. MULKAY, eds., 1982. *Science Observed.* Beverly Hills: Sage.

KRACAUER, SIEGFRIED. 1960. *Theory of Film: The Redemption of Physical Reality.* New York: Oxford University Press.

KRIEGER, SUSAN. 1983. *The Mirror Dance: Identity in a Women's Community.* Philadelphia: Temple University Press.

KUHN, MANFORD H. 1964a. "Major Trends in Symbolic Interaction Theory in the Past Twenty-five Years." *Sociological Quarterly,* 5:61–84.

_____. 1964b. "The Reference Group Reconsidered." *Sociological Quarterly*, 5:5–21.

_____. 1962. "The Interview and the Professional Relationship." In Arnold M. Rose, ed., *Human Behavior and Social Process*. Boston: Houghton Mifflin, pp. 193–206.

_____ AND THOMAS S. McPARTLAND. 1954. "An Empirical Investigation of Self Attitudes." *American Sociological Review*, 19:68–76.

KUHN, THOMAS. 1977. *The Essential Tension: Selected Studies in Scientific Tradition and Change*. Chicago: University of Chicago Press.

_____. 1962. *The Structure of Scientific Revolutions*. Chicago: University of Chicago Press.

LABOV, WILLIAM. 1972. *Language in the Inner City*. Philadelphia: University of Pennsylvania Press.

LAKATOS, I. AND A. MUSGRAVE. 1970. *Criticism and the Growth of Knowledge*. Cambridge: Cambridge University Press.

LAND, KENNETH C. 1969. "Principles of Path Analysis." In Edgar F. Borgatta, ed., *Sociological Methodolgy: 1969*. San Francisco: Jossey-Bass, pp. 3–37.

LANDESCO, JOHN. 1964. "Organized Crime in Chicago." In Ernest W. Burgess and Donald J. Bogue, eds., *Contributions to Urban Sociology*. Chicago: University of Chicago Press, pp. 559–76.

LANGNESS, L.L. 1965. *Life History in Anthropological Science*. New York: Holt, Rinehart & Winston.

LA PIERE, RICHARD T. 1969. "Comment on Irwin Deutscher's 'Looking Backward.'" *American Sociologist*, 4:41–42.

_____. 1934. "Attitudes vs. Actions." *Social Forces*, 13:230–37.

LATOUR, BRUNO AND STEVE WOOLGAR. 1979. *Laboratory Life: The Social Construction of Scientific Facts*. Beverly Hills: Sage.

LAZARSFELD, PAUL F. 1972. *Qualitative Analysis: Historical and Critical Essays*. Boston: Allyn & Bacon.

_____. 1958. "Evidence and Inference in Social Research." *Daedalus*, 87:99–130.

_____. 1955a. Foreword in Herbert Hyman, *Survey Design and Analysis*. Glencoe, Ill.: Free Press, pp. ix–xvii.

_____. 1955b. "Interpretation of Statistical Relations as a Research Operation." In Paul F. Lazarsfeld and Morris Rosenberg, eds., *The Language of Social Research*. Glencoe, Ill.: Free Press, pp. 115–25.

_____. 1954. "The Art of Asking Why: Three Principles Underlying the Formulation of Questionnaires." In Daniel Katz et al., eds., *Public Opinion and Propaganda*. New York: Holt, Rinehart & Winston, pp. 675–86.

_____, BERNARD BERELSON, AND HAZEL GAUDET. 1955. "The Process of Opinion and Attitude Formation." In Paul F. Lazarsfeld and Morris Rosenberg, eds., *The Language of Social Research*. Glencoe, Ill.: Free Press, pp. 231–42.

_____ AND HERBERT MENZEL. 1961. "On the Relation Between Individual and Collective Properties." In Amitai Etzioni, ed., *Complex Organization: A Sociological Reader*. New York: Holt, Rinehart & Winston, pp. 422–40.

_____ AND MORRIS ROSENBERG, eds. 1955. *The Language of Social Research*. Glencoe, Ill.: Free Press.

LAZERWITZ, BERNARD. 1968. "Sampling Theory and Procedures." In Hubert M. Blalock, Jr., and Ann B. Blalock, eds., *Methodology in Social Research*. New York: McGraw-Hill, pp. 278–328.

LEAR, JOHN. 1968. "Do We Need Rules for Experiments on People?" *Saturday Review*, 5:61–70.

LEE, ALFRED McCLUNG. 1972. *Toward a Humanist Sociology*. Englewood Cliffs, N.J.: Prentice-Hall.

LEIK, ROBERT K. 1965. "Irrelevant Aspects of Stooge Behavior: Implication for Leadership Studies and Experimental Methodolgoy." *Sociometry*, 28:259–71.

LEMERT, EDWIN A. 1967. *Human Deviance, Social Problems and Social Control*. Englewood Cliffs, N.J.: Prentice-Hall.

_____. 1958. "The Behavior of the Systematic Check Forger." *Social Problems*, 6:141–48.

_____. 1951. *Social Pathology*. New York: McGraw-Hill.

LEWIS, OSCAR. 1953. "Controls and Experiments in Field Work." In A.L. Kroeber, ed., *Anthropology Today*. Chicago: University of Chicago Press, pp. 452–75.

LIEBERSON, STANLEY. 1985. *Making It Count: The Improvement of Social Research and Theory*. Berkeley: University of California Press.

LIEBOW, ELLIOT. 1967. *Tally's Corner*. Boston: Litte, Brown.

LINCOLN, YVONNE S. AND EGON G. GUBA. 1985. *Naturalistic Inquiry*. Beverly Hills: Sage.

LINDESMITH, ALFRED. 1968. *Addiction and Opiates*. Chicago: Aldine.

_____. 1952. "Comment on W.S. Robinson's 'The Logical Structure of Analytic Induction.'" *American Sociological Review*, 17:492–93.

_____. 1947. *Opiate Addiction*. Bloomington, Ind.: Principia Press.

_____, ANSELM STRAUSS, AND NORMAN K. DENZIN. 1988. *Social Psychology*, 6th ed. Englewood Cliffs, N.J.: Prentice-Hall.

_____, _____, AND _____. 1978. *Social Psychology*, 5th ed. New York: Praeger.

LIPSET, SEYMOUR MARTIN. 1964. "The Biography of a Research Project: *Union Democracy*." In Phillip Hammond, ed., *Sociologists at Work*. New York: Basic Books, pp. 96–120.

_____, MARTIN TROW, AND JAMES COLEMAN. 1962. *Union Democracy*. Garden City, N.Y.: Anchor Books.

LOFLAND, JOHN. 1976. *Doing Social Life: The Qualitative Study of Human Interaction in Natural Settings*. New York: John Wiley.

_____. 1971. *Analyzing Social Settings*. Belmont, Calif.: Wadsworth.

_____. 1966. *Doomsday Cult*. Englewood Cliffs, N.J.: Prentice-Hall.

_____ AND LYN H. LOFLAND. 1984. *Analyzing Social Settings: A Guide to Qualitative Observation and Analysis*, 2d ed. Belmont, Calif.: Wadsworth.

LUNDBERG, GEORGE A. 1956. "Quantitative Methods in Sociology." *Social Forces*, 39:19–24.

_____. 1955. "The Natural Science Trend in Sociology." *American Journal of Sociology*, 61:191–202.

_____. 1926. "Case Work and the Statistical Method." *Social Forces*, 5:60–63.

LYMAN, STANFORD M. AND MARVIN B. SCOTT. 1967. "Territoriality: A Neglected Sociological Dimension." *Social Problems*, 15:236–49.

LYOTARD, JEAN-FRANÇOIS. 1984. *The Postmodern Condition: A Report on Knowledge*. Minneapolis: University of Minnesota Press. (originally published 1979)

MACCOBY, ELEANOR E. AND NATHAN MACCOBY. 1954. "The Interview: A Tool of Social Science." In Gardner Lindzey, ed., *Handbook of Social Psychology*, vol. 1. Reading, Mass.: Addison-Wesley, pp.449–87.

MACIVER, ROBERT M. 1931. "Is Sociology a Natural Science?" *American Journal of Sociology*, 25:25–35.

MAINES, DAVID R. 1987. "The Significance of Termporality for the Development of Sociological Theory." *Sociological Quarterly*, 28:303–12.

_____ AND MARI MOLSEED. 1986. "The Obsessive Discoverer's Complex and the Discovery of Growth in Sociological Theory." *American Journal of Sociology*, 92:158–64.

MALTIN, LEONARD. 1986. *TV Movies and Video Guide: 1987 Edition*. New York: NAL.

MANIS, JEROME AND BERNARD MELTZER, eds. 1972. *Symbolic Interaction: A Reader in Social Psychology*, 2d ed. Boston: Little, Brown.

MANNING, PETER K. 1987. *Semiotics and Fieldwork*. Newbury Park, Calif.: Sage.

_____. 1985. "Limits of the Semiotic Structuralist Perspective Upon Organizational Analysis." In Norman K. Denzin, ed., *Studies in Symbolic Interaction*. Greenwich, Conn.: JAI Press, pp. 79–111.

_____. 1982a. "Analytic Induction." In P.K. Manning and Robert B. Smith, eds., *A Handbook of Social Science Methods*, vol. 2. Cambridge, Mass.: Ballinger, pp. 273–302.

_____. 1982b. "Qualitative Methods." In P.K. Manning and Robert B. Smith, eds., *A Handbook of Social Science Methods*, vol. 2. Cambridge, Mass.: Ballinger, pp. 1–28.

_____. 1977. "Rules in Organizational Context: Narcotics Law Enforcement in Two Settings." *Sociological Quarterly*, 18:44–61.

_____. 1973. "Existential Sociology." *Sociological Quarterly*, 15:200–225.

_____. 1967. "Problems in Interpreting Interview Data." *Sociology and Social Research*, 15:302–16.

_____ AND HOROCIO FABREGA, JR. 1973. "The Experience of Self and Body: Health and Illness in the Chiapas Highlands." In George Psathas, ed., *Phenomenological Sociology: Issues and Implications*. New York: John Wiley, pp. 251–301.

_____ AND _____. 1976. "Fieldwork and the New Ethnography." *Man* (N.S.), 2:39–52.

MARCUS, GEORGE E. 1986. "Contemporary Problems of Ethnography in the Modern World System." In James Clifford and George E. Marcus, eds., *Writing Culture: The Poetics and Politics of Ethnography*. Berkeley: University of California Press, pp. 165–93.

MARSH, ROBERT. 1967. *Comparative Sociology*. New York: Harcourt Brace Jovanovich, Inc.

MARX, KARL. 1983. "From the Eighteenth Brumaire of Louis Bonaparte." In E. Kamenka, ed., *The Portable Karl Marx*. New York: Penguin, pp. 287–323.

MATZA, DAVID. 1969. *Becoming Deviant*. Englewood Cliffs, N.J.: Prentice-Hall.

MAYNARD, DOUGLAS, W. 1987. "Introduction: Language and Social Interaction." *Social Psychology Quarterly*, 50:v–vi.

MAYNE, ETHEL COLBURN, trans. 1964. *Letters of Fyodor Michailovitch Dostoevsky*. New York: McGraw-Hill.

McCALL, GEORGE J. AND J.L. SIMMONS, eds. 1969. *Issues in Participant Observation: A Text and Reader*. Reading, Mass.: Addison-Wesley.

McCALL, MICHAL. 1985. "Life History and Social Change." *Studies in Symbolic Interaction*, 6:169–82.

McGRATH, JOSEPH E. AND IRWIN ALTMAN. 1966. *Small Group Research: A Synthesis and Critique of the Field*. New York: Holt, Rinehart & Winston.

McGUIRE, WILLIAM J. 1969. "Theory-Oriented Research in Natural Settings: The Best of Both for Social Psychology." In Muzafer Sherif and Carolyn W. Sherif, eds., *Interdisciplinary Relationships in the Social Sciences*. Chicago: Aldine, pp. 21–51.

McPHAIL, CLARK AND RONALD T. WOHLSTEIN. 1986. "Collective Locomotion as Collective Behavior." *American Sociological Review*, 51:1–13.

_____ AND _____. 1982. "Using Film to Analyze Pedestrian Behavior." *Sociological Methods and Research*, 10:347–75.

MEAD, GEORGE HERBERT. 1934. *Mind, Self, and Society*. Chicago: University of Chicago Press.

_____. 1927. "The Objective Reality of Perspectives." In Edgar Sheffeld Brightman, ed., *Proceedings of the Sixth International Conference of Philosophy*. New York: Longmans, Green, pp. 75–85.

_____. 1917. "Scientific Method and Individual Thinker." In John Dewey, ed., *Creative Intelligence: Essays in the Pragmatic Attitude*. New York: Holt, Rinehart & Winston, pp. 176–227.

MEAD, MARGARET. 1923. *Coming of Age in Samoa*. New York: Morrow.

MEAD, MARGARET AND GREGORY BATESON. 1978. "Margaret Mead and Gregory Bateson on the Use of the Camera in Anthropology." *Studies in Visual Communication*, 4:78–80.

MERLEAU-PONTY, MAURICE. 1973. *The Prose of the World*. Evanston, Ill.: Northwestern University Press.

MERTON, ROBERT K. 1972. "Insiders and Outsiders: A Chapter in the Sociology of Knowledge." *American Journal of Sociology*, 78:9–47.

_____. 1967. *On Theoretical Sociology*. New York: Free Press.

_____. 1946. *Mass Persuasion*. New York: Harper & Row, Pub.

_____ AND PATRICIA L. KENDALL. 1946. "The Focused Interview." *American Journal of Sociology*, 51:541–57.

MICOSSI, ANITA L. 1971. "Conversion to Women's Lib." *Transaction*, 4:82–90.

MILLER, DELBERT C. 1964. *Handbook of Research Design and Social Measurement*. New York: D. McKay.

MILLER, STEPHEN M. 1952. "The Participant Observer and Over-rapport." *American Sociological Review*, 17:97–99.

MILLS, C. WRIGHT. 1959. *The Sociological Imagination*. New York: Oxford University Press.

MOLOTCH, HARVEY. 1970. "Oil in Santa Barbara and Power in America." *Sociological Inquiry*, 40:131–45.

_____ AND MARILYN LESTER. 1975. "Accidental News: The Great Oil Spill as Local Occurrence and National Event." *American Journal of Sociology*, 81:235–60.

_____ AND _____. 1974. "News as Purposive Behavior." *American Sociological Review*, 39:101–13.

MOLSEED, MARI. 1986. "Time and Form in Triadic Interaction." *Studies in Symbolic Interaction*, suppl. 2: The Iowa School (Part B). Greenwich, Conn.: JAI Press, pp. 255–67.

_____ AND DAVID R. MAINES. 1988. "Sources of Imprecision and Irrationality in Expectation States Theory." *Studies in Symbolic Interaction*, 8:181–217.

MORIN, EDGAR. 1984. *Sociologie*. Paris: Fayard.

MORRISON, DENTON AND RAMON HENKEL, eds. 1970. *The Significance Test Controversy*. Chicago: Aldine.

MUELLER, JOHN H. AND KARL F. SCHUESSLER. 1961. *Statistical Reasoning in Sociology*. Boston: Houghton Mifflin.

MULLINS, NICHOLAS C., WITH THE ASSISTANCE OF CAROLYN J. MULLINS. 1973. *Theory and Theory Groups in Contemporary American Sociology*. New York: Harper & Row.

MURPHY, G. AND LOIS MURPHY. 1950. *Social Psychology*. New York: Dryden Press.

_____ AND _____. 1962. "Soviet Life and Soviet Psychology." In Robert A. Bauer, ed., *Some Views on Soviet Psychology*. Washington, D.C.: American Psychological Association, pp. 253–76.

NAROLL, RAOUL. 1968. "Some Thoughts on Comparative Method in Cultural Anthropology." In Hubert M. Blalock, Jr. and Ann B. Blalock, eds., *Methodology in Social Research*. New York: McGraw-Hill, pp. 236–77.

NEBRASKA FEMINIST COLLECTIVE (MARY JO DEEGAN, BARBARA KEATING, JANE OLLENBURGER, SANDY KUENBOLD, AND SHERYL TILLSON). 1982. "The Sexist Dramas of Erving Goffman." Unpublished paper. University of Nebraska, Lincoln, Nebraska.

OELSEN, VIRGINIA L. AND ELVI WAIK WHITTAKER. 1967. "Role Making in Participant Observation: Processes in the Research-Actor Relationship." *Human Organization*, 26:273–81.

ORNE, MARTIN T. 1962. "On the Social Psychology of the Psychological Experiment: With Special Reference to Demand Characteristics and Their Implications." *American Psychologist*, 17:776–83.

ORWELL, GEORGE. 1934. *Burmese Days*. New York: Harcourt, Brace.

OSGOOD, C.E., G.J. SUCI, AND PERRY H. TANNENBAUM. 1957. *The Measurement of Meaning*. Urbana, Ill.: University of Illinois Press.

PARK, ROBERT E. 1952. "Human Communities." In Everett C. Hughes et al., eds., *The City and Human Ecology*. Glencoe, Ill.: Free Press, pp. 110–16.

_____. 1931. "The Sociological Methods of William Graham Summer, William I. Thomas and Florian Znaniecki." In Stewart A. Rice, ed., *Methods of Social Science: A Case Book*. Chicago: University of Chicago Press, pp. 154–75.

_____ AND ERNEST W. BURGESS. 1924. *Introduction to the Science of Sociology*, 2d ed. Chicago: University of Chicago Press.

PARSONS, TALCOTT. 1950. "The Prospects of Sociological Theory." *American Sociological Review*, 15:3–16.

————— AND EDWARD A. SHILS. 1959. *Toward a General Theory of Action.* Cambridge, Mass.: Harvard University Press.

PATTON, MICHAEL QUINN. 1980. *Qualitative Evaluation Methods.* Beverly Hills: Sage.

PAUL, BENJAMIN D. 1953. "Interview Techniques and Field Work." In A.L. Kroeber, ed., *Anthropology Today.* Chicago: University of Chicago Press, pp. 430–51.

PEIRCE, CHARLES SANDERS. 1965–1966. *Collected Papers of Charles Sanders Peirce,* vols. 1–6. In C. Hartshore and P. Weiss, eds.; vols. 7–8, A.W. Burks, ed. Cambridge, Mass.: Harvard University Press.

PETRAZYCHI, LEON. 1955. *Law and Morality: Leon Petrazychi,* Hugh W. Babb, trans. Cambridge, Mass.: Harvard University Press.

PHILLIPS, BERNARD. 1976. *Social Research: Strategy and Tactics,* 3d ed. New York: Macmillan.

PHILLIPS, DEREK L. 1973. *Knowledge from What? Abandoning Method.* San Francisco: Jossey-Bass.

—————. 1971. *Knowledge from What? Theories and Methods in Social Research.* Chicago: Rand McNally.

PHILLIPS, R.H. 1962. "Miami Goes Latin under Cuban Tide." *New York Times,* March 18:85.

PLUMMER, KEN. 1983. *Documents of Life: An Introduction to the Problems and Literature of a Humanistic Method.* London: George Allen & Unwin.

POLANYI, MICHAEL. 1958. *Personal Knowledge.* Chicago: University of Chicago Press.

POLSKY, NED. 1967. *Hustlers, Beats, and Others.* Chicago: Aldine.

POPPER, KARL R. 1968. *The Logic of Scientific Discovery.* London: Hutchinson.

POWER, MARTHA BAUMAN. 1985. "The Ritualization of Emotional Conduct in Early Childhood." *Studies in Symbolic Interaction,* 6:213–27.

PRATT, MARY LOUISE. 1986. "Fieldwork in Common Places." In James Clifford and George E. Marcus, eds., *Writing Culture: The Poetics and Politics of Ethnography.* Berkeley: University of California Press, pp. 27–50.

PSATHAS, GEORGE AND JAMES J. HENSLIN. 1967. "Dispatched Orders and the Cab Driver: A Study of Locating Activities." *Social Problems,* 14:424–43.

————— AND FRANCES C. WAKSLER. 1973. "Essential Features of Face-to-Face Interaction." In George Psathas, ed., *Phenomenological Sociology: Issues and Applications.* New York: John Wiley, pp. 159–83.

RABINOW, P. AND W.M. SULLIVAN, eds. 1979. *Interpretive Social Science: A Reader.* Berkeley: University of California Press.

READ, BILL. 1964. *The Days of Dylan Thomas.* New York: McGraw-Hill.

REBELSKY, FREDA AND CHERYL HANKS. 1971. "Fathers' Verbal Interactions with Infants in the First Three Months of Life." *Child Development,* 42:63–68.

RECORD, JANE CASSELS. 1967. "The Research Institute and the Pressure Group." In Gideon Sjoberg, ed., *Ethics, Politics, and Social Research.* Cambridge, Mass.: Schenkman, pp. 25–49.

REDFIELD, ROBERT. 1948. "The Art of Social Science." *American Journal of Sociology,* 55:181–90.

REISMAN, DAVID AND JEANNE WATSON. 1964. "The Sociability Project: A Chronicle of Frustration and Achievement." In Phillip E. Hammond, ed., *Sociologists at Work.* New York: Basic Books, pp. 235–321.

REISS, ALBERT J., JR. 1968. "Stuff and Nonsense about Social Surveys and Observation." In Howard S. Becker et al., eds., *Institutions and the Person: Papers Presented to Everett C. Hughes.* Chicago: Aldine, pp. 351–67.

—————. 1959. "Rural-Urban Differences in Interpersonal Contracts." *American Journal of Sociology,* 65:182–95.

RICHARDSON, STEPHAN A., BARBARA SNELL DOHRENWEND, AND DAVID KLEIN. 1965. *Interviewing: Its Forms and Functions.* New York: Basic Books.

RICOEUR, PAUL. 1985. *Time and Narrative,* vol. 2. Chicago: University of Chicago Press.

ROBERTS, H., ed. 1981. *Doing Feminist Research.* London: Routledge & Kegan Paul.

ROBINSON, W.S. 1951. "The Logical Structure of Analytic Induction." *American Sociological Review*, 16:812–18.

ROCK, PAUL. 1973. "Phenomenalism and Essentialism in the Sociology of Deviancy." *Sociology*, 7:17–29.

ROEBUCK, JULIAN B. AND WOLFGANG FRESE. 1975. *The Rendezvous: A Case Study of an After-Hours Club*. New York: Free Press.

ROSALDO, RENATO I. 1984. "Grief and a Headhunter's Rage: On the Cultural Force of Emotions." In Edward M. Bruner, ed., *Text, Play, and Story: The Construction and Reconstruction of Self and Society*. Washington, D.C.: The American Ethnological Society, pp. 178–95.

ROSE, ARNOLD, ed. 1962. *Human Behavior and Social Processes*. Boston: Houghton Mifflin.

ROSE, EDWARD. 1960. "The English Record of a Natural Sociology." *American Sociological Review*, 25:193–208.

ROSENTHAL, ROBERT. 1966. *Experimental Effects in Behavioral Research*. New York: Appleton-Century-Crofts.

ROSS, JOHN A. AND PERRY SMITH. 1965. "Experimental Designs of the Single-Stimulus, All-or-Nothing Type." *American Sociological Review*, 30:68–80.

ROTH, JULIUS A. 1966. "Hired Hand Research." *American Sociologist*, 1:190–96.

ROWE, JOHN HOWLAND. 1953. "Technical Aids in Anthropology: A Historical Survey." In A.L. Kroeber, ed., *Anthropology Today*. Chicago: University of Chicago Press, pp. 895–940.

ROY, DONALD. 1952. "Quota Restriction and Goldbricking in a Machine Shop." *American Journal of Sociology*, 57:427–42.

RYLE, GILBERT. 1968. "The Thinking of Thoughts." University of Saskatchewan University Lectures, no. 18. University of Saskatchewan, Regina.

———. 1971. *Collected Papers*, Volume 11. New York: Barnes & Noble.

SARBIN, THEODORE R. 1967. "On the Futility of the Proposition That Some People Are Labeled Mentally Ill." *Journal of Consulting Psychology*, 31:447–53.

SARTRE, JEAN-PAUL. 1987. *The Family Idiot: Gustave Flaubert, Vol. 2, 1821–1857*. Chicago: University of Chicago Press. (originally published 1971)

———. 1981. *The Family Idiot: Gustave Flaubert, Vol. 1, 1821–1857*. Chicago: University of Chicago Press. (originally published 1971)

———. 1976. *Critique of Dialectical Reason*. London: NLP.

———. 1963. *Search for a Method*. New York: Knopf.

SCHATZMAN, LEONARD AND ANSELM STRAUSS. 1973. *Field Research: Strategies for a Natural Society*. Englewood Cliffs, N.J.: Prentice-Hall.

SCHEFF, THOMAS J. 1966. *Being Mentally Ill*. Chicago: Aldine.

SHEGLOFF, EMANUEL A. 1987. "Analyzing Single Episodes of Interaction: An Exercise in Conversation Analysis." *Social Psychology Quarterly*, 50:101–14.

SCHRAG, CLARENCE. 1967. "Philosophical Issues in the Science of Sociology." *Sociology and Social Research*, 51:361–72.

SCHUTZ, ALFRED. 1963. "Common Sense and Scientific Interpretation of Human Action." In M. Natanson, ed., *Philosophy of the Social Sciences: A Reader*. New York: Random House, pp. 302–46.

———. 1962. *Collected Papers. Vol. 1: The Problems of Social Reality*, M. Natanson, ed. The Hague: Martinus Nijhoff.

SCHUTZE, FRITZ. 1983. "Biographieforschung und Narratives Interview." *Neue Praxis*, 3:283–93.

SCHWARTZ, MORRIS AND CHARLOTTE GREEN SCHWARTZ. 1955. "Problems in Participant Observation." *American Journal of Sociology*, 60:343–53.

——— AND J.H. SKOLNICK. 1962. "Two Studies of Legal Stigma." *Social Problems*, 10:133–38.

SEEMAN, MELVIN. 1967. "Powerlessness and Knowledge: A Comparative Study of Alienation and Learning." *Sociometry*, 30:105–23.

SELLTIZ, CLAIRE, MARIE JAHODA, MORTON DEUTSCH, AND STUART W. COOK. 1959. *Research Methods in Social Relations*, rev. ed., vol. 1. New York: Holt, Rinehart & Winston.

SHAW, CLIFFORD R. 1966. *The Jack-Roller*. Chicago: University of Chicago Press.

SHERMAN, SUSAN ROTH. 1967. "Demand Characteristics in an Experiment on Attitude Change." *Sociometry*, 30:246–61.

SHIBUTANI, TAMOTSU. 1966. *Improvised News: A Sociological Study of Rumor*. Indianapolis: Bobbs-Merrill.

———. 1961. *Society and Personality*. Englewood Cliffs, N.J.: Prentice-Hall.

SHILS, EDWARD A. 1959. "Social Inquiry and the Autonomy of the Individual." In Daniel Lerner, ed., *The Human Meaning of the Social Sciences*. Cleveland: Meridian, pp. 114–59.

SHIRER, WILLIAM. 1943. *Berlin Diary*. New York: W.W. Norton & Co., Inc.

SHORT, JAMES F., JR. 1963. Introduction in Frederic M. Thrasher, *The Gang*, abridged ed. Chicago: University of Chicago Press, pp. xv–liii.

SIEBER, SAM D. 1973. "The Integration of Fieldwork and Survey Methods." *American Journal of Sociology*, 78:1335–59.

SIEGEL, SIDNEY. 1956. *Nonparametric Statistics for the Behavioral Sciences*. New York: McGraw-Hill.

SILVERMAN, DAVID. 1985. *Qualitative Methodology and Sociology: Describing the Social World*. Brookfield, Vt: Gower.

———. 1973. "Interview Talk: Bringing Off a Research Instrument." *Sociology*, 7:31–48.

SIMMEL, GEORG. 1950. *The Sociology of Georg Simmel*, trans. Kurt Wolff. New York: Free Press.

———. 1908. "Sociology of the Senses: Visual Interaction." In Georg Simmel, *Soziologie*. Leipzig: Duncker and Humbolt, pp. 646–51. Also trans. and adapted by Robert E. Park and Ernest W. Burgess in *Introduction to the Science of Sociology*, 2d ed. Chicago: University of Chicago Press, pp. 356–61.

SIU, PAUL C.P. 1964. "The Isolation of Chinese Laundrymen." In Ernest W. Burgess and Donald J. Bogue, eds., *Contributions to Urban Sociology*. Chicago: University of Chicago Press, pp. 429–42.

SJOBERG, GIDEON, ed. 1967. *Ethics, Politics, and Social Research*. Cambridge, Mass.: Schenkman.

——— AND ROGER NETT. 1968. *A Methodology for Social Research*. New York: Harper & Row, Pub.

SKLAR, ROBERT. 1975. *Movie-Made America: A Social History of the Movies*. New York: Random House.

SMELSER, NEIL J. 1976. *Comparative Methods in the Social Sciences*. Englewood Cliffs, N.J.: Prentice-Hall.

———. 1968. *Essays in Sociological Explanation*. Englewood Cliffs, N.J.: Prentice-Hall.

SMITH, DOROTHY E. 1979. "A Sociology for Women." In Julia A. Sherman and Evelyn T. Beck, eds., *The Prism of Sex: Essays in the Sociology*. Madison: University of Wisconsin Press, pp. 135–87.

SMITH, HUBERT. 1983. *Living Maya*. New York: Holt, Rinehart & Winston.

SMITH, LAURENCE D. 1986. *Behaviorism and Logical Positivism: A Reassessment of the Alliance*. Stanford, Calif.: Stanford University Press.

SMITH, M. BREWSTER. 1974. *Humanizing Social Psychology*. San Francisco: Jossey-Bass, 1974.

SMITH, RICHARD L., CLARK MCPHAIL, AND ROBERT G. PICKENS. 1975. "Reactivity to Systematic Observation with Film: A Field Experiment," *Sociometry* 38:125–36.

SNODGRASS, JON. 1982. *The Jack-Roller at Seventy: A Fifty-Year Follow-Up*. Lexington, Mass.: Lexington Books.

Sociological Inquiry. 1986. Special Issue, "Gender Roles and Women's Issues," 56.

SOMMER, ROBERT J. 1968. *Personal Space*. Englewood Cliffs, N.J.: Prentice-Hall.

———. 1967. "Sociofugal Space." *American Journal of Sociology*. 72:654–60.

_____. 1962. "The Distance for Comfortable Conversation: A Further Study." *Sociometry*, 25:111–16.

_____. 1961. "Leadership and Group Geography." Sociometry, 24:99–110.

_____. 1959. "Studies in Personal Space." *Sociometry*, 22:247–60.

_____ AND NANCY JO FELIPE. 1966. "Invasions of Personal Space." *Social Problems*, 14:206–16.

SORENSON, RICHARD. 1976. *The Edge of the Forest: Land, Childhood and Change in a New Guinea Protoagricultural Society*. Washington, D.C.: Smithsonian Institution.

SOROKIN, PITIRIM A. AND CLARENCE Q. BERGER. 1938. *Time-Budgets of Human Behavior*. Cambridge, Mass.: Harvard University Press.

_____ AND ROBERT K. MERTON. 1937. "Social Time: A Methodological and Functional Analysis." *American Journal of Sociology*, 42:615–29.

_____ AND CARLE C. ZIMMERMAN. 1929. *Principles of Rural–Urban Sociology*. New York: Holt, Rinehart & Winston.

SPEIER, MATTHEW. 1970. "The Everyday World for the Child." In Jack D. Douglas, ed., *Understanding Everyday Life*. Chicago: Aldine, pp. 188–217.

SPITZER, STEPHEN P., JOHN R. STRATTON, JACK D. FITZGERALD, AND BRIGITTE MACH. 1966. "The Self Concept: Test Equivalence and Perceived Validity." *Sociological Quarterly*, 7:265–80.

SPRADLEY, JAMES. 1980. *Participant Observation*. New York: Holt, Rinehart & Winston.

_____. 1979. *The Ethnographic Interview*. New York: Holt, Rinehart & Winston.

SPYKMAN, NICHOLAS J. 1966. *The Social Theory of Georg Simmel*. New York: Atherton.

STAHL, SANDRA K.D. 1977. "The Personal Narrative as Folklore." *Journal of the Folklore Institute*, 14:9–30.

STAKE, ROBERT. 1987. *Quieting Reform: Social Science and Social Action in an Urban Youth Program*. Urbana: University of Illinois Press.

STEVENS, S.S. 1975. *Psychophysics: Introduction to Its Perceptual, Neural and Social Prospects*. New York: John Wiley.

_____. 1951. "Mathematics, Measurement, and Psychophysics." In S.S. Stevens, ed., *Handbook of Experimental Psychology*. New York: John Wiley, pp. 1–49.

STEWART, GEORGE LEE. 1972. "On First Being a John." *Urban Life and Culture*, 1:255–74.

STINCHCOMBE, ARTHUR L. 1968. *Constructing Social Theories*. New York: Harcourt Brace Jovanovich, Inc.

STONE, GREGORY P. 1962. "Appearance and the Self." In Arnold M. Rose, ed., *Human Behavior and Social Processes*. Boston: Houghton Mifflin, pp. 86–118.

_____. 1954. "City Shoppers and Urban Identification: Observations of the Social Psychology of City Life." *American Journal of Sociology*, 60:36–45.

_____ AND HARVEY A. FARBERMAN. 1967. "On the Edge of Rapprochement: Was Durkheim Moving Toward the Perspective of Symbolic Interaction?" *Sociological Quarterly*, 8:149–64.

_____ AND _____, eds. 1970. *Social Psychology from the Standpoint of Symbolic Interaction*. Boston: Blaisdale.

STOUFFER, SAMUEL A. 1950. "Some Observations on Study Design." *American Journal of Sociology*, 55:355–61.

_____. 1930. "Experimental Comparison of Statistical and Case History Methods in Attitude Research." Unpublished doctoral dissertation. Chicago: University of Chicago.

STRAUSS, ANSELM L. 1987. *Qualitative Analysis for Social Scientists*. New York: Cambridge University Press.

_____. 1968. "Strategies for Discovering Urban Theory." In Anselm L. Strauss, ed., *The American City: A Sourcebook for Urban Imagery*. Chicago: Aldine, pp. 515–30.

_____. 1959. *Mirrors and Masks*. Glencoe, Ill.: Free Press.

_____ AND LEONARD SCHATZMAN. 1955. "Cross-Class Interviewing: An Analysis of Interaction and Communicative Styles." *Human Organization*, 14:28–31.

_____, _____, RUE BUCHER, DANUTA EHRLICH, AND MELVIN SABSHIN. 1964. *Psychiatric Ideologies and Institutions.* New York: Free Press.

_____ AND BARNEY GLASER. 1970. *Anguish: A Case History of a Dying Trajectory.* Mill Valley, Calif.: The Sociology Press.

SUDMAN, SEYMOUR. 1976. "Sample Surveys." *Annual Review of Sociology,* 2:107–20.

_____ AND GRAHAM KALTON. 1986. "New Developments in the Sampling of Special Populations." *Annual Review of Sociology,* 12:401–29.

SUDNOW, DAVID. 1967. *Passing On: The Social Organization of Dying.* Englewood Cliffs, N.J.: Prentice-Hall.

SUTTLES, GERALD D. 1968. *The Social Order of the Slum.* Chicago: University of Chicago Press.

SVALASTOGA, KAARE. 1964. "Social Differentiation." In R.E.L. Faris, ed., *Handbook of Modern Sociology.* Chicago: Rand McNally, pp. 530–75.

TERKEL, STUDS. 1974. *Working.* New York: Random House.

THOMAS, WILLIAM I. AND DOROTHY SWAINE THOMAS. 1928. *The Child in America.* New York: Knopf.

_____ AND FLORIAN ZNANIECKI. 1927. *The Polish Peasant.* New York: Knopf.

THOMPSON, PAUL. 1978. *The Voice of the Past: Oral History.* Oxford: Oxford University Press.

THORNE, BARRIE, CHERIS KRAMARAE, AND NANCY HENLEY, eds. 1983. *Language, Gender and Society.* Rowley, Mass.: Newbury House.

THRASHER, FREDERICK M. 1963. *The Gang,* abridged ed. Chicago: University of Chicago Press.

THURSTONE LOUIS L. 1927. "Psychophysical Analysis." *American Journal of Psychology,* 38: 368–89.

_____ AND ERNEST J. CHAVE. 1929. *The Measurement of Attitude.* Chicago: University of Chicago Press.

TIBBETTS, PAUL. 1986. "The Strong Programme in Sociology: A Critique." Unpublished doctoral dissertation. University of Illinois, Urbana-Champaign.

Time. 1967. "Editorial Preface." July 7, p. 11.

TITON, JEFF TODD. 1980. "The Life Story." *Journal of American Folklore,* 93:276–92.

TORGERSON, W. S. 1958. *Theory and Methods of Scaling.* New York: John Wiley.

TREND, M.G. 1978. "On the Reconciliation of Qualitative and Quantitative Analyses: A Case Study. *Human Organization,* 37:345–54.

TROW, MARTIN. 1957. "Comment on Participant Observation and Interviewing: A Comparison." *Human Organization,* 16:33–35.

TURNER, CHARLES AND ELIZABETH MARTIN, eds. 1986. *Surveying Subjective Phenomena,* vols. 1 and 2. New York: Russell Sage Foundation.

TURNER, RALPH H. 1953. "The Quest for Universals in Sociological Research." *American Sociological Review,* 18:604–11.

TURNER, STEPHEN P. 1987. "Underdetermination and the Promise of Statistical Sociology." *Sociological Theory,* 5:172–84.

TURNER, VICTOR W. AND EDWARD M. BRUNER, eds. 1986. *The Anthropology of Experience.* Urbana: University of Illinois Press.

TYLER, STEPHEN A. 1986. "Post-Modern Ethnography: From Document of the Occult to Occult Document." In James Clifford and George E. Marcus, eds., *Writing Culture: The Poetics and Politics of Ethnography.* Berkeley: University of California Press, pp. 122–40.

ULIN, ROBERT C. 1984. *Understanding Cultures: Perspectives in Anthropology and Social Theory.* Austin: University of Texas Press.

UPSHAW, HARRY S. 1968. "Attitude Measurement." In Hubert M. Blalock, Jr., and Ann B. Blalock, eds., *Methodology in Social Research.* New York: McGraw-Hill, pp. 60–111.

VALENTINE, CHARLES A. 1968. *Culture and Poverty: Critique and Counter-Proposals.* Chicago: University of Chicago Press.

VALLIER, IVAN, ed. 1971. *Comparative Methods in Sociology: Essays on Trends and Applications.* Berkeley: University of California Press.

VAN MAANEN, JOHN. 1988. *Tales of the Field.* Chicago: University of Chicago Press.

Video Sociology Quarterly. 1982. vol. 1.

VIDICH, ARTHUR J. AND JOSEPH BENSMAN. 1964. "The Springdale Case: Academic Bureaucrats and Sensitive Townspeople." In Arthur J. Vidich, Joseph Bensman, and Maurice J. Sein, eds., *Reflections on Community Studies.* New York: John Wiley, pp. 313–49.

———— AND ————. 1958. *Small Town in Mass Society.* Princeton, N.J.: Princeton University Press.

————, ————, AND MAURICE R. STEIN, eds. 1964. *Reflections on Community Studies.* New York: John Wiley.

———— AND GILBERT SHAPIRO. 1955. "A Comparison of Participant Observation and Survey Data." *American Sociological Review,* 20:28–33.

WALLACE, SAMUEL E. 1965. *Skidrow as a Way of Life.* Totowa, N.J.: Bedminster.

WALLACE, WALTER L. 1983. *Principles of Scientific Sociology.* New York: Aldine de Gruyter.

WARREN, CAROL A.B. 1974. *Identity and Community in the Gay World.* New York: John Wiley.

WARREN, ROBERT PENN. 1946. *All the King's Men.* New York: Harper & Row, Pub.

WAX, ROSALIE HENKEY. 1971. *Doing Fieldwork.* Chicago: University of Chicago Press.

————. 1960. "Twelve Years Later: An Analysis of Field Experience." In Richard N. Adams and Jack J. Preiss, eds., *Human Organization Research: Field Relations and Techniques.* Homewood Ill.: Dorsey, pp. 166–78.

WEBB, EUGENE J. 1966. "Unconventionality, Triangulation and Inference." In *Proceedings of the 1966 Invitational Conference on Testing Problems.* Princeton, N.J.: Educational Testing Service, pp. 34–43.

————, DONALD T. CAMPBELL, RICHARD D. SCHWARTZ, AND LEE SECHREST. 1966. *Unobtrusive Measures: Nonreactive Research in the Social Sciences.* Chicago: Rand McNally.

————, DONALD T. CAMPBELL, RICHARD D. SCHWARTZ, LEE SECHREST, AND JANET BELEW GROVE. 1981. *Nonreactive Measures in the Social Sciences,* 2d ed. Boston: Houghton Mifflin.

WEBER, MAX. 1958. *From Max Weber: Essays in Sociology,* ed. and trans. H.H. Gerth and C. Wright Mills. New York: Oxford University Press.

WEINBERG, S. KIRSON. 1952. "Comment on W.S. Robinson's 'The Logical Structure of Analytic Induction.'" *American Sociological Review,* 17:493–94.

WEISS, ROBERT S. AND EUGENE JACOBSON. 1955. "A Method for the Analysis of the Structure of Complex Organizations." *American Sociological Review,* 20:661–68.

WEST, CANDACE AND DON H. ZIMMERMAN. 1983. "Small Insults: A Study of Interruptions in Cross-Sex Conversations." In Barrie Thorne, Cheris Kramarae, and Nancy Henley, eds. *Language, Gender and Society.* Rowley, Mass.: Newbury House, pp. 103–17.

WESTIE, FRANK R. 1957. "Toward Closer Relations Between Theory and Research: A Procedure and an Example." *American Sociological Review,* 22:149–54.

WHYTE, WILLIAM FOOTE. 1955. *Street Corner Society,* 2d ed. Chicago: University of Chicago Press.

WILEY, NORBERT. 1986. "Early American Sociology and *The Polish Peasant.*" *Sociological Theory,* 4:20–40.

————. 1985. "The Current Interregnum in American Sociology." *Social Research,* 52:179–207.

————. 1976. "Review Symposia: *Conflict and Sociology: Toward an Explanatory Science,* by Randall Collins." *Contemporary Sociology,* 5:235–39.

WILLIS, PAUL. 1981. *Learning to Labour: How Working Class Kids Get Working Class Jobs.* New York: Columbia University Press.

WINCH, PETER. 1958. *The Idea of a Social Science.* Boston: Routledge & Kegan Paul.

WOLFF, KURT H. 1960. "The Collection and Organization of Field Materials: A Research Report." In Richard N. Adams and Jack J. Preiss, eds., *Human Organization Research: Field Relations and Techniques.* Homewood, Ill.: Dorsey, pp. 250–54.

————, ed. 1959. *Georg Simmel, 1858–1918.* Columbus: Ohio State University Press.

_____, trans. 1950. *The Sociology of Georg Simmel*. Glencoe, Ill.: Free Press.

WOLFFE, DAEL. 1968. "The Use of Human Subjects." *Science,* 19.

WORDSWORTH, WILLIAM. 1948. *The Prelude, with a Selection from the Shorter Poems and the Sonnets and the 1800 Preface to Lyrical Ballads,* Carlos Baker, ed. New York: Holt, Rinehart & Winston.

WORTH, SOL. 1981. *Studying Visual Communication.* Philadelphia: University of Pennsylvania Press.

_____ AND JOHN ADAIR. 1972. *Through Navajo Eyes: An Exploration in Film Communication and Anthropology.* Bloomington: University of Indiana Press.

WRIGHT, HERBERT F. 1967. *Recording and Analyzing Child Behavior.* New York: Harper & Row., Pub.

_____. 1960. "Observational Child Study." In Paul H. Mussen, ed., *Handbook of Research Methods in Child Development.* New York: John Wiley, pp. 71–139.

WRIGHT, WILL. 1975. *Six Guns and Society: A Structural Study of the Western.* Berkeley-University of California Press.

WUEBBEN, PAUL L. 1968. "Experimental Design, Measurement, and Subjects: A Neglected Problem of Control." *Sociometry,* 31(March):89–101.

_____, BRUCE C. STRAITS AND GARY I. SCHULMAN. 1974. *The Experiment as a Social Occasion.* Berkeley, Calif.: Glendessary.

YOUNG, KIMBALL.1952. *Personality and Problems of Adjustment.* New York: Appleton-Century-Crofts.

YOUNG, PAULINE V. 1966. *Scientific Social Surveys and Research,* 4th ed. Englewood Cliffs, N.J.: Prentice-Hall.

ZELDITCH, MORRIS J. 1962. "Some Methodological Problems of Field Studies." *American Journal of Sociology,* 67:566–76.

ZETTERBERG, HANS. 1965. *On Theory and Verification in Sociology,* 2d ed. Totowa, N.J.: Bedminster.

_____. 1955. "On Axiomatic Theories." In Paul F. Lazarsfeld and Morris Rosenberg, eds., *The Language of Social Research.* Glencoe, Ill.: Free Press, pp. 533–40.

ZNANIECKI, FLORIAN. 1934. *The Method of Sociology.* New York: Farrar and Rinehart.

Index

Wilson, B., 187
Winch, P., 3
Within-method triangulation, 243–44
Wohlstein, R.T., 212, 224
Woolgar, S., 35, 65, 66
Wordsworth, William, 193
Work schedule, 63
Worth, S., 211, 214, 225, 232
Wright, H.F., 83, 86, 194
Wright, W., 223
Writing
    ethnographic, 177–80

narrative approach to, 45
    social science, 46–47, 48
Wuebben, P.L., 122, 128, 129

Young, K., 196

Zelditch, M., Jr., 50
Zetterberg, H., 51, 58, 60
Zimmerman, D.H., 86, 89